ROCKIES AND PLAINS 1978

COLORADO
IDAHO
MONTANA
NEBRASKA
NORTH DAKOTA
SOUTH DAKOTA
UTAH
WYOMING

COLORADO
IDAHO
MONTANA
NEBRASKA

NORTH DAKOTA
SOUTH DAKOTA
UTAH
WYOMING

FODOR'S MODERN GUIDES
FOUNDED BY EUGENE FODOR

Editorial Staff
ROBERT C. FISHER
editor
RICHARD MOORE
executive editor, London
LESLIE BROWN
managing editor
DOROTHY FOSTER
research director

Production Staff
C. R. BLOODGOOD
director
EILEEN ROLPH
managing director, London

Advertising Staff
E. W. NEWSOM
director
SANDRA LANG
assistant director

Rockies and Plains 1978:
Contributing Editors: ROGER COX, BRUCE HAMBY, BILL HOSOKAWA, LOWELL JOHNSON, RICHARD P. LEAVITT, LEAVITT F. MORRIS, BILL OWEN, ROY PECK, CARRIE RODGERS
Editorial Assistants: ROSEMARY BARRY, CASTLEWOOD, DAVID GREENFIELD
Illustrations: LYNN STURM
Symbols: LASZLO
City Plans: DYNO LOWENSTEIN
Maps: HAMMOND INC.

FODOR'S

ROCKIES AND PLAINS
1978

Created by Eugene Fodor

ROBERT C. FISHER
LESLIE BROWN
editors

STEWART UDALL
introduction

CURTIS W. CASEWIT
RALPH FRIEDMAN
HARRY E. FULLER, JR.
JOHN R. MILTON
MARY ROLL
area editors

DAVID McKAY COMPANY INC.—NEW YORK

© 1978 FODOR'S MODERN GUIDES, INC.
ISBN-0-679-00265-0 (cloth)
ISBN 0-679-00266-9 (Traveltex)

AREA GUIDES:
EUROPE
CANADA
CARIBBEAN, BAHAMAS
AND BERMUDA
INDIA
JAPAN AND KOREA

MEXICO
SCANDINAVIA
SOUTH AMERICA
SOUTHEAST ASIA
SOVIET UNION
U.S.A. (1 vol.)

COUNTRY GUIDES:
AUSTRIA
BELGIUM AND
LUXEMBOURG
CZECHOSLOVAKIA
EGYPT
FRANCE
GERMANY
GREAT BRITAIN
GREECE
HOLLAND
HUNGARY

IRAN
IRELAND
ISRAEL
ITALY
MOROCCO
PORTUGAL
SPAIN
SWITZERLAND
TUNISIA
TURKEY
YUGOSLAVIA

USA GUIDES:
NEW ENGLAND
NEW YORK AND
NEW JERSEY
MID-ATLANTIC
THE SOUTH
INDIAN AMERICA

THE MID-WEST
THE SOUTH-WEST
ROCKIES AND PLAINS
THE FAR WEST
HAWAII
OLD WEST

CITY GUIDES:
LONDON
VENICE

PARIS
VIENNA

PEKING

LANGUAGE GUIDE:
EUROPE TALKING

SPECIAL INTEREST GUIDES:
CRUISES EVERYWHERE
RAILWAYS OF THE WORLD

LATEST ADDITIONS TO THE SERIES:
AUSTRALIA, NEW ZEALAND
AND THE SOUTH PACIFIC
BRAZIL
EUROPE ON A BUDGET
JORDAN AND THE HOLY LAND

OLD SOUTH
ONLY-IN-AMERICA
VACATION GUIDE
OUTDOORS AMERICA
SEASIDE AMERICA

MANUFACTURED IN THE UNITED STATES OF AMERICA

CONTENTS

v

CONTENTS

HIGH ROCKIES, WIDE PLAINS

Backbone of the Continent

by

STEWART UDALL

Stewart L. Udall of Tucson, Arizona, was the 37th Secretary of the U.S. Department of the Interior. Under his guidance the department increased its emphasis on the science of conservation and expanded the National Park System. Since leaving the Cabinet, Mr. Udall has actively continued his forceful participation in ecological matters. He was born in St. Johns, Arizona—a town founded by his grandfather.

In every period of its development, America always has had more than its share of authentic heroes. The first Pilgrims who landed on a wintry day on the cold forbidding shores of Massachusetts were no less heroic than trailblazing Daniel Boone, or the Mountain Men whose raw courage took them across the great uncharted plains to the western states. These were the men who chose to hunt and trap in the distant mountains and in the lonely places, their survival dependent on their own cunning ways with nature. They took supplies, when they could get them, but the true Mountain Man soon learned to accommodate himself to the land, to know the berries and fruits he could eat, where the fishing and hunting were good. And he knew how to protect himself against wild animals and hostile Indians.

The Mountain Man didn't gallop about on a horse, swagger into saloons and engage in gun battles with bad guys who were sneaky, treacherous, mean and wore black hats. He was too busy fighting for survival in a never-ending battle with nature; essentially he was a loner. Perhaps that's why, in the public mind, the Mountain Man lacked the glamor and excitement we have attached to the personage of the cowboy. It's true the cowboy lived a hard life. He spent long hours in the saddle, slept on the ground, suffered the vagaries of hot and cold weather, and had little stimulating recreation. It's also true that the average cowboy was a terrible shot (most people killed during the Wild West days were done in by hired gun-slingers) and, as nursemaid to beef steers, hardly had a glamorous job.

Nonetheless, the cowboy persists as America's most popular hero in a continuing proliferation of movie and television "Westerns"; and the sale of Western fiction continues apace—Zane Grey's novels, for example, have sold more than 54,000,000 copies since his first horseman rode among the purple sage.

The old-time cowboy had a brief reign of two decades, 1865 to 1885. But in 1962, TV man David Brinkley pointed his television cameras at the modern cowboy. The program was filmed on a ranch in northern Wyoming and showed what Westerners already know; the work of a real cowboy is "violent, hard, dangerous, hot, and dirty," as true then as now. Today, the modern cowboy is more Western than his predecessor, who came from all parts of the United States and, in some instances, from Europe. Interestingly, the title "Champion Bronco Buster of the Plains" was won by an Englishman on July 4, 1869! His prize was a suit of clothes.

A President of the United States had a fling at being a cowboy during the summer of 1865. In the Badlands of North Dakota, Theodore Roosevelt hitched up a pair of cowboy pants, slipped into a buckskin shirt and strapped on a pearl-handled revolver. He then proceeded to make a lasting impression at his first roundup. One or two hardened cowboys nearly fell from their saddles as he rode along and called out to one of the men, "Hasten forward quickly there!" The incongruity of Harvard-educated Theodore Roosevelt in the Badlands is reflected by many of his biographers.

His somewhat precise tones still flavored by exposure to Harvard culture rang strangely in the ears of westerners. He did not smoke or drink. His worst profanity was an infrequent 'Damn!' and his usual expletive was 'By Godfrey!' ''

Not only in films and TV, but in literature, the cowpoke has captured the public imagination. At one time, it took sixty-one pages to list the articles and books about the West in a publication of the American Historical Association, *Writings on American History*. Now, the Western History Association, established in 1962, publishes its own journal, *The American West*.

Nation Tilts Westward

This tremendous interest in the West continues. Frank Lloyd Wright, the famous architect, noted that millions of people were still pouring into that third of the nation lying between the Rockies and the Pacific Ocean. He called it the "Great Westward Tilt."

When I write of the Rockies and the Plains, I am speaking of Colorado, Wyoming, Montana, Utah, North Dakota, South Dakota and Nebraska, as well as my home state of Arizona, and New Mexico. Actually, the eastern sections of Montana, Wyoming, Colorado, and New Mexico are considered in the Great Plains as well as in the Rocky Mountains—they overlap into two categories—geographically. The Great Plains have always had a proportionately larger rural and agricultural population than any other region in the nation, with the exception of the Great Basin in California. The Great Plains are a semi-arid land, which makes them strikingly different from the sub-humid and humid land to the east and the arid land to the west. In the United States, first homesteaders, like the earlier mountain-plainsmen and cattle-men, were enticed by the vast and open grasslands. These treeless plains promised rich crops and grass fodder without the backbreaking and tedious tasks of grubbing stumps, digging roots, and burning slash.

The Great Plains in the early period was a man's country—more so than any other portion of the frontier. The men loved the Plains—the women were distrustful of the Plains. "Why there isn't even a thing that one can hide behind!" was one woman's pathetic exclamation.

As Walter Prescott Webb pointed out in his classic *The Great Plains*: "The loneliness which women endured on the Great Plains must have been such as to crush the soul, provided one did not meet the isolation with an adventurous spirit. The woman who said that she could always tell by sunup whether she should have company during the day is an example. If in the early morning she could detect a cloud of dust, she knew the visitors were coming!"

Today, the Rocky Mountain and Plains country man or woman is com-pletely American, but also unique. Great distances separate the populated areas. In some towns the high point in the year is a visit, or two, to anything remotely resembling a city.

It is a big country—this Rocky Mountains and Plains. It offers every bit of the world's scenery, from the highest mountains to the desert; from lush river valleys to high grass plains; from glaciers to hot springs. Perhaps the most important thing of all in this big place is its informality. In many ways the people who live here are like mountain and plains men and women of four generations ago.

A poet of whom I'm quite fond, Robert Frost, once wrote: "What makes a nation in the beginning is a good piece of ground." Three-fourths of my years have been spent in and about the West where there are still good pieces of ground. By edict of nature, nearly all of the West was, and always will be, different from the rest of the country. Daniel Webster called it a "waste-land"; Francis Parkman, "the great American desert." From the first, the West was destined to write a special chapter in our history. The Plains Indians, the vast prairies, the mighty massif of the Rocky Mountains, the parched deserts were all formidable barriers to settlement and migration. Its searing winds and harsh climate, its uncertain rainfall and thin soils made living a continual struggle.

Today, the flow of westward-bound Americans makes the great migra-tions of the pioneer period seem almost insignificant. The crack of a bull-whacker's whip and the creaking sound of a prairie schooner in the 1850's are in sharp contrast to the hum of a powerful engine as it propels its passengers comfortably in the same direction today.

The West—Still the Last Frontier

However, there is a common theme—call it what you will: Great West-ward Tilt or Great Western Movement—the flow of American history has been westward in the pursuit of national and individual destiny. The last American frontier will always be the West. Generations were shaped by the forces which impelled them to shift the frontier farther West.

Americans who trek West, the pioneer or modern-day man, seek the same thing: economic opportunity, the climate, the spirit of adventure, or a desire to share in the bustle and vigor that have characterized western life. The major problems today are the same: the critical need for water, the sparse population in many areas, and the proper development of natural resources.

To some scholars the most distinctive feature of the American past was its three-century-long pioneering period. This pioneering experience seems to have endowed the American people with different characteristics and institutions from those of other peoples.

The frontier closed in 1890. A part of the American dream was over. Since then students of the West have been evaluating the days of the pioneers in relation to their own age. David Potter wrote that the moving frontier was one phase of the larger situation of opportunity and abundance which had marked the Americans as a "people of plenty." Self-reliance, courage, alertness, endurance, friendliness, informality are traits that emerged from the continuous cycles of land settlement.

"Americans are always moving on" was the opening line of Stephen Vincent Benet's unfinished heroic poem of the westward migrations, called "Western Star." Much of American literature has been dominated by this theme of restless movement on land or river or sea. Francis Parkman's *The Oregon Trail* was a stirring introduction to the West, along with other classics such as Walter Prescott Webb's *The Great Plains* and Bernard De Voto's *Across the Wide Missouri*.

To understand America you must see two aspects—that of restless mobility, and that of attachment to place, as emphasized by the regionalists and traditionalists. There is a double beat of migration and the sense of place. John Muir, the noted naturalist and wanderer in Yosemite, once wrote: "Climb the mountains and get their good tidings. Nature's peace will flow into you as sunshine flows into tree. The winds will glow their own freshness into you, and the storms their energy, while cares will drop off like autumn leaves."

The classical migration to the Western frontiers was perhaps the last spontaneous great migration in history. The explorers were followed by fur traders, followed by mountain men, ranchers, and miners, followed finally by farmers equipped with seed, cattle and implements. The later stages of this classical westward movement crossed the Great Plains and the mountain vastnesses of the Rockies and occupied the rich areas of the Pacific Northwest and California.

Not more than one out of twenty of those who took part in the Gold Rush to California found anything like success, yet we have forgotten the failures and remember only the big prizes.

By the 1850's the West was no longer quite the land of the unknown that it had been. Too many mountain men, too many settlers' parties, too many government survey teams had crossed the region to leave it a land of mystery. And yet, the West was so vast that there was always something new to be found. In 1858, Lt. Joseph Ives led the first party into the bottom of the Grand Canyon. The fascinating reports of such expeditions were a part of the magnet that continued to draw men West.

In 1902, Owen Wister's *The Virginian* was published. The famous line, "When you call me that, smile," from the hero to the outlaw, is from this book. This work caused many an Easterner to forsake his hearth and travel

West. Wister was Harvard-educated like his friend Theodore Roosevelt, to whom he dedicated his book. Wister's stories gave a true picture of a cowboy's life including the prototype of the brave cowboy who was soft-spoken with the women but a no-nonsense man with the outlaw.

After 1900, increasing numbers of Easterners ventured West to spend vacations. People have been venturing forth to the wild and woolly West ever since.

In 1908, President Theodore Roosevelt, who owned Elkhorn Ranch in the Badlands along the Little Missouri River in North Dakota, called a White House Conference to inquire into the state of the nation's natural resources. It was a landmark in the conservation history of the United States. It showed that the country knew little about its resources, and it excited public interest and action. Theodore Roosevelt set aside forest reserves, established five national parks, created bird and game preserves, promoted irrigation, and gave to the people their first real awareness of the need for conservation. T. R. gradually won the support of Western leaders, including lumber barons, for conservation.

Frederic Remington, the Western artist, was lamenting the passing of an era in 1905: "I knew the wild riders and the vacant land were about to vanish forever . . . I saw the living, breathing end of three American centuries of smoke and dust and sweat, and I now see quite another thing where it all took place, but it does not appeal to me." Remington in his paintings depicted the unfenced range, the stamina of cowboys, the courage of the people, and the dignity of free Indians.

The Idea for National Parks

It was another artist, George Catlin, who had the vision to understand the need to preserve this country's great natural treasures for the generations yet unborn. He had this realization in the 1830's "at a time when the plains seemed as unfathomable as the ocean, when pasture and grazing lands had no boundaries, and no one believed that the forests could be exhausted." In 1833, a prophetic passage of Catlin's was published in a New York Newspaper, after he had traveled up the Missouri River into the heart of the Indian country in 1832.

Catlin suggested that the "looks and customs of the vanishing races of the native man in America . . . might in future be seen [by some great protecting policy of government] preserved in their pristine beauty and wildness, in a magnificent park, where the world could see for ages to come the native Indian in his classic attire, galloping his wild horse . . . amid the fleeting herds of elks and buffaloes. What a beautiful and thrilling specimen for America to preserve and hold up to the view of her refined citizens and the world, in future ages."

Catlin's progressive idea was considered by the Congress in 1864, when the Yosemite grant was made to the State of California. Yosemite is now a national park.

Another lively artist of the Western scene was Alfred Miller. In 1837 he joined William Drummond Stewart, a British army captain who was starting a trip to Oregon for the American Fur Company. Miller's brilliant pictures, particularly of the country west of the North Platte River and in the Rocky Mountains, have given us much of the most accurate documentation ever made of the early West, picturing the life of the Indians and the rendezvous with fur traders. Many of Miller's sketches and paintings were reproduced in Bernard De Voto's *Across the Wide Missouri*. In 1951, the University of Oklahoma Press published *The West of Alfred Jacob Miller* by Marvin C. Ross.

In 1871, the paintings and photographs of the geysers, great canyon, and waterfalls of the upper Yellowstone River, made by Ferdinand V. Hayden, helped persuade Congress to set aside the area as the country's first National Park.

Who were the people who went West? There were artists, the government survey teams in the decade of the 1870's, the writers, the fur traders. Then there were the English—remember that cowboy in Colorado?—the Irish, the Germans, and other nationality groups. The West was the frontier to them, it was no man's land, but to the Indians it was their ancient homeland.

The greatest number of prehistoric Indian remains are in the Southwest. Many are in the area around the Four Corners where the lonely desertlands of Arizona, New Mexico, Colorado, and Utah meet—the only spot in the United States where the boundaries of four states come together. Here, some time between the years A.D. 1 and 1300, an unusual Indian civilization flourished for a time, then mysteriously disappeared. The Four Corners region is one of fantastic buttes and mesas, gullies, and deep canyons through which rivers bend in wide S-curves. Utah's most famous national monuments (Arches, Rainbow Bridge, Capitol Reef, and Natural Bridge) are in the almost roadless country of southeastern Utah near Four Corners.

Utahans, it has been said, have always had a way of doing things different. All the conventions of Western life in Utah went haywire.

The particular quality of life in Utah is almost wholly Mormon, although the total church membership numbers perhaps only three-fifths of the population. In popular terms the West has always been independent—and Utah especially so, perhaps, a consequence of the strong-minded New Englanders who founded the Mormon Church. Historically, Utah has been a detoured country: the Oregon Trail went north of it; other cross-country travel, south of it. Canyonlands, the newest national park in the United States, is in Utah wrapped in serenity, waiting for discovery and appreciation by visitors.

Home of Many Nationalities

The Mormons are also an important part of the social structure of Wyoming—along with the cowboy who is the dominant figure in Wyoming folklore. During the period of free land and migration, Wyoming became the home of many nationalities—Italians and Greeks in mining, Scandinavians in logging, Mexicans and Russian-Germans in the beet-raising centers, Basques in the north-central part of the state, Chinese along the Union Pacific Railroad, together with Hungarians, Czechs, Slovaks, Danes, Englishmen, Irishmen, Estonians, and Japanese. These groups helped settle and build up Wyoming, and have become an integral part of its life.

Several Old-World cultural traits are preserved in the melting pot environment of Wyoming. The Italians have their celebrations; the Chinese have their Chinese New Year; the Greeks have an impressive funeral rite; and Pioneer Day is observed in Mormon communities to retell the story of the Great Trek to Salt Lake Valley in 1847. Wyoming has Grand Teton National Park, which includes part of Jackson Hole, winter feeding ground of the largest elk herd in America. The Grand Tetons themselves are the most spectacular peaks in the chain that forms our continental backbone.

The people who migrated to Colorado are similar to those who settled in Wyoming: Italians, Hungarians, Slavs, Orientals, the Chinese in the mines, Japanese on the farms. German-Russians were lured from the Volga by the introduction of sugar-beet culture, which they knew well; later, Spanish-Americans flooded in from the southern valleys and from Mexico to work the beet fields. The story of Coloradans goes back even farther, of course, to the Indians of prehistoric times. Mesa Verde National Park is the most notable and best preserved prehistoric cliff dwelling in the United States. French voyageurs—hunters, trappers, and traders—also explored the northern streams of Colorado.

The magic cry "Gold!" was the signal for the great mass migrations of American history. Men of almost every nationality, occupation, and station in life swarmed into the Colorado mountains, and in their wake followed farmers, largely of European stock to settle in the fertile valleys. These are the Coloradoans.

The ethnic groups in Montana comprise descendants of the early French-Indian fur trappers; the English and Scotch who were usually the managers of the fur trade companies; the German and Irish who rushed to the Butte silver and copper ledges; and the Scandinavians who settled the dry-land sections after 1900. Today, persons of German extraction form the largest group, followed by the Norwegians and the English, Swedes, Irish, and Danes. Other nationalities include Poles, Czechoslovakians, Austrians, and Hungarians.

Germans were the first immigrants to arrive in any number in Nebraska and are now the largest group of foreign stock in the state. Many fled to America in 1848 following the political upheavals in Germany. They helped develop the sugar-beet industry. The Czechoslovak group, the next largest foreign stock group in Nebraska, has been understandingly interpreted in Willa Cather's books and hence made known to the country at large. Many of the early Slovak immigrants were of the "cottager" class and were first-rate farmers and hard-working people. They knew nothing of the isolated farmhouse, having lived in villages, so the frontier was a complete change for them and required great adaptability.

The Swedes and Danes came next to Nebraska and were well adapted not only to frontier life but to the climate as well. The Danes did much to advance progressive farming measures. The German-Russians were latecomers.

From territorial days until World War I a steady and evergrowing stream of immigrants poured into North Dakota from other states, Canada, and Europe. Although forty-two nations sent immigrants to the state, by far the greatest numbers came from northern Europe. Almost one-third arrived from Norway, while other countries, in the order of their contribution to the population, were Russia, Germany, Canada, Sweden, The Netherlands, Denmark, Hungary, Finland, Rumania, and Iceland.

The population of South Dakota remains preponderantly rural despite the steady but slow growth of urban centers. The bulk of the people are white, but there are many Indians living on or registered with eight reservations. The many nationalities represented among the people from the earliest days have produced a rural cosmopolitanism, with substantial contingents of

Norwegians, Germans, Swedes, Russian-Germans, Danes, Czechs, Dutch, Canadians, and English.

These are Westerners all: the industrious Mormons; the Chinese in the mines; the homesteaders on their Nebraska claims; the cowboy who calls the West his home; the lumber- and cattlemen; the Indians, the Spanish, the Anglo-Americans—even the Eastern dude who loves the West and possibly feels like an old plainsman when out in the wide-open spaces—the big country.

A stirring epic is the story of America's westward movement. At heart it is the story of the men and women of all races and different origins and beliefs who helped shape the character of a nation. It grows more and more fascinating as it grows more and more remote.

FACTS AT YOUR FINGERTIPS

WHEN TO GO. This region, running from the Canadian border in the north to the northern borders of New Mexico and Arizona in the south, naturally has a great variation in temperature, and at all seasons. Generally speaking, there is plenty of sunshine, and the humidity is low throughout the region. This latter condition tends to cut down on discomfort in all but the highest temperature periods. Desert degrees sometimes soar to the 110-115 mark, while some nearby mountain summits wear their stoles of ermine-white snow year round.

There are travelers who find the desert areas of Colorado and Utah too hot in summer, while many others revel in the region's clear, hot days—its cool, cool nights. Visitors may, of course, plan off-to-the-hills activities for the daytime hours, returning in the evening for a dip in that pool which is almost certain to be found at their hotel or motel.

From Thanksgiving to the middle of April there is some of the best skiing in the country at places like Aspen and Vail in Colorado and Alta and Snowbird near Salt Lake City. There is even year-round skiing on glaciers in Montana and Colorado.

Generally, average temperatures in winter are in the low 20's. Summer finds maximum temperatures in the mid-80's in the north to near 100 degrees in the south (in June, July, and August), with maximums in the 90's in surrounding months. But even in summer nights are cool, especially in the higher elevations.

Planning Your Trip. Once you have decided where you are going, and when, it's time to get down to the details of hotel reservations and, if you are not traveling by car, ticket reservations. If you don't want to bother with reservations on your own, a travel agent won't cost you a cent, except for specific charges like telegrams. He gets his fee from the hotel or carrier he books for you. A travel agent can also be of help for those who prefer to take their vacations on a ''package tour''—thus keeping planning to a minimum; and in explaining the details of the ''travel now, pay later'' vacation possibilities offered by the nation's carriers.

If you don't belong to an auto club, now is the time to join one. They can be very helpful about routings and offering emergency service on the road. If you plan the route yourself, make certain the map you get is dated for the current year (highways and thruways are appearing and being extended at an astonishingly rapid rate). Some of the major oil companies will send maps and mark preferred routes on them if you tell them what you have in mind. Try: *Exxon Touring Service*, P.O. Box 307, Florham Park, N.J. 07932; *ARCO Travel Service*, P.O. Box 93, Versailles, Kentucky 40383; *Texaco Travel Service*, 135 East 42 Street, New York, N.Y. 10017; or *Mobil Oil Corp. Touring Service*, 150 East 42 Street, New York, N.Y. 10017. In addition, most states have their own maps, which pinpoint attractions, list historical sites, parks, etc. Write the *Tourist Information Dept., State Capitol Bldg.*, in the state or states you plan to visit for current maps. City chambers of commerce and the convention and visitors bureaus are also good sources of information. Specific addresses are given under *Tourist Information* in the individual state chapters.

Plan to board your pets, discontinue paper and milk deliveries, and tell your local police and fire departments when you'll be leaving and when you expect to return. Ask a kindly neighbor to keep an eye on your house or apartment; fully protect your swimming pool against intruders. Have a neighbor keep your mail, or have it held at the post office. Consider having your telephone temporarily disconnected if you plan to be away more than a few weeks. Look into the purchase of trip insurance (including baggage), and make certain your auto, fire, and other insurance policies are up to date. Convert the greater portion of your trip money into travelers' checks. Arrange to have your lawn mowed at the usual times, and leave that kindly neighbor your itinerary (insofar as possible), car license number, and a key to your home (and tell police and firemen he has it).

PACKING. *What to take, what to wear*. Make a packing list for each member of the family. Then check off items as you pack them. It will save time, reduce confusion. Time-savers to carry along include extra photo film (plenty), suntan lotion, insect repellent, sufficient toothpaste, soap, etc. Always carry an extra pair of glasses, including sunglasses, particularly if they're prescription ones. A travel iron is always a good tote-along, as are some transparent plastic bags (small and large) for wet suits, socks, etc. They are also excellent for packing shoes, cosmetics, and other easily damaged items. If you fly remember that despite signs to the contrary airport security X-ray machines do in fact damage films in about 17 percent of the cases. Have them inspected separately or pack them in special protective bags. Fun extras to carry include binoculars, a compass, and a magnifying glass—useful in reading fine-print maps.

All members of the family should have sturdy shoes with nonslip soles. Keep them handy in the back of the car. You never know when you may want to stop and clamber along a rocky trail. Carry rain gear in a separate bag in the back of the car (so no one will have to get out and hunt for it in a downpour en route).

Women will probably want to stick to one or two basic colors for their wardrobes, so that they can manage with one set of accessories. If possible, include one knit or jersey dress or a pants suit. For dress-up evenings, take along a couple of "basic" dresses you can vary with a simple change of accessories. That way you can dress up or down to suit the occasion.

Be sure to check what temperatures will be like along the route. Traveling in mountains can mean cool evenings, even in summer—and so can traveling through the desert. An extra sweater is always a safe thing to pack, even if just to protect you from the air conditioning.

Men will probably want a jacket along for dining out, and a dress shirt and tie for formal occasions. Turtlenecks are now accepted almost everywhere and are a comfortable accessory. Don't forget extra slacks.

Planning a lot of sun time? Don't forget something to wear en route to the pool, beach, or lakefront, and for those first few days when you're getting reacquainted with sun on tender skin.

WHAT WILL IT COST? Two people can travel comfortably in this section of the U.S. for about $41.00 a day (not counting gasoline or other transportation costs), as you can see in the table below.

In some areas you can cut expenses by traveling off season, when hotel rates are usually lower. The budget-minded traveler can also find bargain accommodations at tourist homes or family-style YMCA's and YWCA's. Some state and federal parks also provide inexpensive lodging. And in this 7-state area 16 colleges offer dormitory accommodations to tourists during the summer vacations at single-room rates of $2-$10 per night with meals from $0.60 to $3.50. A directory of some 200 such bargains all over the U.S. is *Mort's Guide to Low-Cost Vacations and Lodgings on College Campuses, USA-Canada*, from CMG Publishing Co., P.O. Box 630, Princeton, N.J. 08540, $3.75 postpaid.

Another way to cut down on the cost of your trip is to look for out-of-the-way resorts. Travelers are frequently rewarded by discovering very attractive areas which haven't as yet begun to draw quantities of people.

Typical Expenses for Two People

Room at *moderate* hotel or motel	$17.00
Breakfast, including tip	3.00
Lunch at *inexpensive* restaurant, including tip	3.00
Dinner at *moderate* restaurant, including tip	8.50
Sightseeing bus tour	5.00
An evening drink	2.50
Admission to museum or historic site	2.00
	——
	$41.00

If you are budgeting your trip, don't forget to set aside a realistic amount for the possible rental of sports equipment (perhaps including a boat or canoe), entrance fees to amusement and historical sites, etc. Allow for tolls for bridges and superhighways (this can be a major item), extra film for cameras, and souvenirs.

After lodging, your next biggest expense will be food, and here you can make very substantial economies if you are willing to get along with only one meal a day (or less) in a restaurant. Plan to eat simply, and to picnic. It will save you time and money, and it will help you enjoy your trip more. That beautiful scenery does not have to whiz by at 55 miles per hour. Many states have picnic and rest areas, often well-equipped and in scenic spots, even on highways and thruways, so finding a pleasant place to stop is usually not difficult. Before you leave home put together a picnic kit.

Sturdy plastic plates and cups are cheaper in the long run than throw-away paper ones; and the same goes for permanent metal flatware rather than the throw-away plastic kind. Pack a small electric pot and two thermoses, one for water and one for milk, tea, or coffee. In other words, one hot, and one cold. If you go by car, take along a small cooler. Bread, milk, cold cereal, jam, tea or instant coffee, fruit, fresh vegetables that need no cooking (such as lettuce, cucumbers, carrots, tomatoes, and mushrooms), cold cuts, cheese, nuts, raisins, eggs (hard boil them in the electric pot in your room the night before)—with only things like these you can eat conveniently, cheaply, and well.

If you like a drink before dinner or bed, bring your own bottle. Most hotels and motels supply ice free or for very little, but the markup on alcoholic beverages in restaurants, bars, lounges and dining rooms is enormous, and in some states peculiar laws apply regarding alcohol consumption.

 HINTS TO THE MOTORIST. Probably the first precaution you will take is to have your car thoroughly checked by your regular dealer or service station to make sure that everything is in good shape. Secondly, you may find it wise to join an auto club that can provide you with trip planning information, insurance coverage, and emergency and repair service along the way. Thirdly, the *National Institute for Automotive Service Excellence*, which tests and certifies the competence of auto mechanics, publishes a directory of about 10,000 repair shops all over the U.S. which employ certified mechanics. It is available from *NIASE*, Suite 515, 1825 K Street N.W., Washington, D.C. 20005, for $1.95.

Shortly after you pass the ranger station a brief distance inside the comparatively new Canyonlands National Park in southern Utah, you encounter a sign, stuck in the sand. It reads: "Four-wheel drive vehicles only beyond this point." This is wild, rugged country, where you follow routes, not roads, through shifting sand, up trickling stream beds which can turn into raging torrents during a sudden storm, where the wheels of even four-wheel drive vehicles can sink hopelessly into the sand if they don't move along briskly, and where you climb a 27-degree face of sheer rock as part of getting over Elephant Hill. The Rockies and Plains area is the country of the Badlands of North and South Dakota, the mule-riding country of the Grand Canyon, the country of towering mountains interspersed with the broad flat spaces of the Plains—an area where, off the well-traveled, well-kept main roads, the motorist can have virtually any driving experience he cares to meet.

DESERT DRIVING

You will encounter long stretches of desert driving in the southern portions of this area. Better cars, better roads, and more service facilities make desert driving less a hazard than it once was. This desert here won't resemble the sands of the Sahara. It will have considerable vegetation and rock outcroppings. A principal point to check before crossing the hot desert is your tires. Put them at normal driving pressure or slightly below. Heat builds pressure. If your car seems to be bouncing too readily, stop to let your tires cool. If you have a good radiator, don't worry about extra water, but keep an eye on the water gauge. Be alert for sudden sandstorms and rainstorms. If you have a car radio, keep it tuned to local stations for information about unusual road conditions. In spite of its dryness, the desert, in a flash flood, can become a death trap. In sandstorms, pull off the road and wait it out.

MOUNTAIN DRIVING

Unless you venture onto exotic mountain roads, you should have little trouble with mountain driving. Today's mountain roads are engineered for the ordinary driver. They are normally wide, well graded, and safe. Be especially wary of exceeding the speed limits posted for curves. Keep to the right. If your normal driving is at low altitudes, have a garage mechanic check your carburetor. It may need adjusting for mountain driving. Use your motor for downhill runs, second or low gear to save your brakes. If your car stalls, and your temperature gauge is high, it could mean a vapor lock. Bathe the fuel pump with a damp cloth for a few minutes.

If you get stuck on any kind of road, pull off the highway onto the shoulder, raise the hood, attach something white (a handkerchief, scarf, or a piece of tissue) to the door handle on the driver's side, and sit inside and wait. This is especially effective on limited-access highways, usually patrolled vigilantly by state highway officers. A special warning to women stalled at night: Remain inside with the doors locked, and make sure the Good Samaritan is indeed what he seems. It is easier to find telephones along the major highways these days, since their locations are more frequently marked than they used to be. If you're a member of an automobile club, call the nearest garage listed in your emergency directory. Or ask the operator for help.

PULLING A TRAILER

If you plan to pull a trailer (boat or house) on your holiday trip, and have never done so before, don't just hook up and set out. You need a whole new set of driving skills—starting, stopping, cornering, passing, *being* passed, and, most tricky of all, backing. Reading about it will help a little, but not much. Try to practice in an open field or empty parking lot, but if this is not possible, take your maiden trip in light traffic. A few useful hints: In starting and stopping, do everything a little more slowly and gradually than is normal; in cornering, swing wider than usual, remembering the trailer won't follow exactly the rear wheels of the towing car. Too sharp a right turn will put your trailer wheels on the curb. In passing, remember you're longer than usual. Allow more safe distance ahead to pull back into the right lane. A slight bit of extra steering will help if you're *being* passed by a large truck or bus. In this situation, the trailer is inclined to sway from air currents. Don't worsen it by slowing down. It's better to speed up slightly. In backing, the basic technique is to turn the steering wheel opposite to the way you would want the car to go if you were driving it alone. From there on, it's practice, practice, practice. Most states have special safety regulations for trailers, and these change frequently. If you plan to operate your trailer in several states, check with your motor club, the police, or the state motor vehicle department about the rules. Also talk it over with the dealer from whom you buy or lease your trailer. Generally, speed limits for cars hauling trailers are lower, parking of trailers (and automobiles) is prohibited on expressways, and tunnels bar trailers equipped with cooking units which use propane gas.

PETS AND PACKING

Traveling by car with your pet dog or cat? More and more motels accept them but be sure to check before you register. Some turn them down, some want to look first, some offer special facilities. If it's a first-time trip for your pet, accustom it to car travel by short trips in your neighborhood. And when you're packing, include its favorite food, bowls, and toys. Discourage your dog from riding with its head out the window. Wind and dust particles can permanently damage its eyes. Dogs are especially susceptible to heat stroke. Don't leave your dog in a parked car on a hot day while you dawdle over lunch. Keep your dog's bowl handy for water during stops for gas; gasoline attendants are usually very cooperative about this.

One tip for frequent motel stops along the road is to pack two suitcases—one for the final destination, and the other with items for overnight stops: pajamas, shaving gear, cosmetics, toothbrushes, fresh shirt or dress. Put the overnight luggage into the trunk last, so it can be pulled out first on overnight stops. A safety hint: Don't string your suits and dresses on hangers along a chain or rod stretched across the back seat. This obstructs vision and can cause accidents.

 HOTELS AND MOTELS. *General Hints*. Don't be one of those who take potluck for lodgings. You'll waste a lot of time hunting for a place, and often won't be happy with the accommodations you finally find. If you are without reservations, by all means begin looking early in the afternoon. If you have reservations, but expect to arrive later than five or six p.m., advise the hotel or motel in advance. Some places will not, unless advised, hold reservations after six p.m.

If you are planning to stay in a popular resort region, at the height of the season, reserve well in advance. Include a deposit for all places except motels (and for motels if they request one). Many chain or associated motels and hotels will make advance reservations for you at affiliated hostelries along your route.

A number of hotels and motels have one-day laundry and dry-cleaning services, and many motels have coin laundries. Most motels, but not all, have telephones in the rooms. If you want to be sure of room service, however, better stay at a hotel. Many motels have swimming pools, and even beachfront hotels frequently have a pool. Even some motels in the heart of large cities have pools. An advantage at motels is the free parking. There's seldom a charge for parking at country and resort hotels.

Hotel and motel chains. In addition to the hundreds of excellent independent motels and hotels throughout the country, there are also many that belong to national or regional chains. A major advantage of the chains, to many travelers, is the ease of making reservations en route, or at one fell swoop in advance. If you are a guest at a member hotel or motel, the management will be delighted to secure you a sure booking at one of its affiliated hotels for the coming evening at no cost to you. Chains also usually have toll-free WATS (800) lines to assist you in making reservations on your own. This, of course, saves you time, worry, and money. In some chains, you have the added advantage of knowing what the standards are all the way. The insistence on uniform standards of comfort, cleanliness, and amenities is more common in motel than in hotel chains. (Easy to understand when you realize that most hotel chains are formed by buying up older, established hotels, while most motel chains have control of their units from start to finish.) This is not meant to denigrate the hotel chains; after all, individuality can be one of the great charms of a hotel. Some travelers, however, prefer independent motels and hotels because they are more likely to reflect the character of the surrounding area.

Since the single biggest expense of your whole trip is lodging, you may well be discouraged and angry at the prices of some hotel and motel rooms, particularly when you know you are paying for things you neither need nor want, such as a heated swimming pool, wall-to-wall carpeting, a huge color TV set, two huge double beds for only two people, meeting rooms, a cocktail lounge, maybe even a putting green. Nationwide, motel prices for two people now average $24-$30 a night; hotel prices run from $25 to $60, with the average around $35-$40. This explains the recent rapid spread of a number of budget motel chains.

The main national motel chains are Holiday Inn, Howard Johnson's; Quality Courts, Ramada Inns, Sheraton Motor Inns, and TraveLodge. Alongside the style that these places represent, however, are others, less luxurious and less costly. Here are the main ones: Days Inns of America, Inc., 2751 Buford Highway, Northeast, Atlanta 1, Georgia 30324 (various toll-free numbers); Downtowner Motor Inns, 202 Union Street, Memphis, Tenn., call 800) 238-5320; Family Inns of America, P.O. Box 2191, Knoxville, Tennessee 37901; Friendship Inns International, 739 South Fourth, West, Salt Lake City, Utah 84101, call 800) 323-9111; Motel 6, 1888 Century Park East, Suite 1900, Los Angeles, Cal. 90067; Penny Pincher Inns, 1125 Ellen Kay Drive, Marion, Ohio 43302, call 800) 447-4470; Scottish Inns of America, 104 Bridgewater Road, Knoxville, Tenn. 37919, call 800) 643-8960; Econo Travel Motor Hotel Corp., 20 Kroger Executive Center, P.O. Box 12188, Norfolk, Va. 23502, call 800) 466-6900.

HOTEL AND MOTEL CATEGORIES

Hotels and motels in all the Fodor guidebooks to the U.S.A. are divided into five categories, arranged primarily by price, but also taking into consideration the degree of comfort, the amount of service, and the atmosphere which will surround you in the establishment of your choice. Occasionally, an establishment with *deluxe* prices will offer only *expensive* service or atmosphere, and so we will list it as *expensive*. On the other hand, a hotel which charges only *moderate* prices may offer superior comfort and service, so we will list it as *expensive*. Our ratings are flexible and subject to change. We should also point out that many fine hotels and motels have to be omitted for lack of space.

Although the names of the various hotel and motel categories are standard throughout this series, the prices listed under each category may vary from area to area. This variance is meant to reflect local price standards, and take into account that what might be considered a *moderate* price in a large urban area might be quite *expensive* in a rural region. In every case, however, the dollar ranges for each category are clearly stated before each listing of establishments.

Super Deluxe: This category is reserved for only a few hotels. In addition to giving the visitor all the amenities discussed under the deluxe category (below), the super deluxe hotel has a special atmosphere of glamor, good taste, and dignity. Its history will inevitably be full of many anecdotes, and it will probably be a favored meeting spot of local society. In short, super deluxe means the tops.

Deluxe: The minimum facilities must include bath and shower in all rooms, valet and laundry service, suites available, a well-appointed restaurant and a bar (where local law permits), room service, TV and telephone in room, air conditioning and heat (unless locale makes one or the other unnecessary), pleasing decor, and an atmosphere of luxury, calm, and elegance. There should be ample and personalized service. In a deluxe *motel*, there may be less service rendered by employees and more by automatic machines (such as refrigerators and ice-making machines in your room), but there should be a minimum of do-it-yourself in a truly deluxe establishment.

Expensive: All rooms must have bath or shower, valet and laundry service, restaurant and bar (local law permitting), limited room service, TV and telephone in room, heat and air conditioning (locale not precluding), pleasing decor. Although decor may be as good as that in deluxe establishments, hotels and motels in this category are frequently designed for commercial travelers or for families in a hurry and are somewhat impersonal in terms of service. As for *motels* in this category, valet and laundry service will probably be lacking; the units will be outstanding primarily for their convenient location and functional character, not for their attractive or comfortable qualities.

(*Note:* We often list top-notch ultra-modern hotels in this category, in spite of the fact that they have rates as high as deluxe hotels and motels. We do this because certain elements are missing in these hotels—usually service. In spite of automated devices such as ice-cube-making machines and message-signaling buzzers, service in these hotels is not up to the standard by which we judge deluxe establishments. Room service is incredibly slow in some of these places, and the entire atmosphere is often one of expediency over comfort, economy of manpower and overhead taking precedence over attention to the desires of guests.)

Moderate: Each room should have an attached bath or shower, there should be a restaurant *or* coffee shop, TV available, telephone in room, heat and air conditioning (locale not precluding), relatively convenient location, clean and comfortable rooms, and public rooms. *Motels* in this category may not have attached bath or shower, may not have a restaurant or coffee shop (though one is usually nearby), and, of course, may have no public rooms to speak of.

Inexpensive: Nearby bath or shower, telephone available, clean rooms are the minimum.

Free parking is assumed at all motels and motor hotels; you must pay for parking at most city hotels, though certain establishments have free parking, frequently for occupants of higher-than-minimum-rate rooms. *Baby sitter* lists are always available in good hotels and motels, and *cribs* for the children are always on hand—sometimes at no cost, but more frequently at a cost of $1 or $2 per night. The cost of a *cot* in your room, to supplement the beds, is around $3 per night, but moving an *extra single bed* into a room costs around $7 in better hotels and motels.

Senior citizens may in some cases receive special discounts on lodgings. The Days Inn chain offers various discounts to anyone 55 or older. Holiday Inns give a 10% discount year-round to members of the NRTA (write to National Retired Teachers Association, Membership Division, 701 North Montgomery St., Ojai, California 93023) and the AARP (write to American Association of Retired Persons, Membership Division, 215 Long Beach Blvd., Long Beach, California 90802). Howard Johnson's Motor Lodges give 10% off to NRTA and AARP members (call 800-654-2000); and the ITT Sheraton chain gives 25% off (call 800-325-3535).

The closest thing America has to Europe's bed-and-breakfast is the private houses that go by the various names of tourist home, guest home, or guest house. These are often large, still fairly elegant old homes in quiet residential or semiresidential parts of larger towns or along secondary roads and the main streets of small towns and resorts. Styles and standards vary widely, of course; generally, private baths are less common and rates are pleasingly low. In many small towns such guest houses are excellent examples of the best a region has to offer of its own special atmosphere. Each one will be different, so that their advantage is precisely the opposite of that "no surprise" uniformity which motel chains pride themselves on. Few, if any, guests houses have heated pools, wall-to-wall carpeting, or exposed styrofoam-wooden beams in the bar.

Few if any even have bars. What you do get, in addition to economy, is the personal flavor of a family atmosphere in a private home. In popular tourist areas, state or local tourist information offices or chambers of commerce usually have lists of homes that let out spare rooms to paying guests, and such a listing usually means that the places on it have been inspected and meet some reliable standard of cleanliness, comfort, and reasonable pricing.

In larger towns and cities a good bet for clean, plain, reliable lodging is a YMCA or YWCA. These buildings are usually centrally located, and their rates tend to run to less than half of those of hotels. Nonmembers are welcome, but may pay slightly more than members. A few very large Ys may have accommodations for couples but usually sexes are segregated. Decor is spartan and the cafeteria fare plain and wholesome, but a definite advantage is the use of the building's pool, gym, reading room, information services, and other facilities. For a directory, write to National Council of the YMCA, 291 Broadway, New York, N.Y. 10007; and the National Board of the YWCA, 600 Lexington Avenue, New York, N.Y. 10022.

 DINING OUT. For evening dining, the best advice is to make reservations whenever possible. Most hotels and farm-vacation places have set dining hours. For motel stayers, life is simpler if the motel has a restaurant. If it hasn't, try to stay at one that is near a restaurant.

Some restaurants are fussy about customers' dress, particularly in the evening. For women, pants and pants suits are now almost universally acceptable. For men, tie and jacket remains the standard, but turtleneck sweaters are becoming more and more common. Shorts are almost always frowned on for both men and women. Standards of dress are becoming more relaxed, so a neatly dressed customer will usually experience no problem. If in doubt about accepted dress at a particular establishment, call ahead.

Roadside stands, turnpike restaurants, and cafeterias have no fixed standards of dress.

If you're traveling with children, you may want to find out if a restaurant has a children's menu and commensurate prices (many do).

When figuring the tip on your check, base it on the total charges for the meal, not on the grand total, if that total includes a sales tax. Don't tip on tax.

RESTAURANT CATEGORIES

The restaurants mentioned in this volume which are located in large metropolitan areas are categorized by type of cuisine: French, Chinese, Armenian, etc., with restaurants of a general nature listed as American-International. Restaurants in less populous areas are divided into price categories as follows: *super deluxe*, *deluxe*, *expensive*, *moderate*, and *inexpensive*. As a general rule, expect restaurants in metropolitan areas to be higher in price, but many restaurants that feature foreign cuisine are surprisingly inexpensive. We should also point out that limitations of space make it impossible to include every establishment. We have, therefore, listed those which we recommend as the best within each price range.

Although the names of the various restaurant categories are standard throughout this series, the prices listed under each category may vary from area to area. This variation is meant to reflect local price standards and take into account that what might be considered a *moderate* price in a large urban area might be quite *expensive* in a rural region. In every case, however, the dollar ranges for each category are clearly stated before each listing of establishments.

Super Deluxe: This category will probably be pertinent to only one or two metropolitan areas. It indicates an outstanding restaurant which is lavishly decorated, which may delight in the fear it inspires among the humble. Frequently over-priced and over-rated, it will charge the customer at least $12 for soup, entrée, and dessert. The average price for the same is apt to be closer to $16.00, although some will run much higher than this. As in all our other categories, this price range does not include cocktails, wines, cover or table charges, tip, or extravagant house specialties. The price range here indicates a typical roastbeef (prime ribs) dinner. The restaurant in this category must have a superb wine list, excellent service, immaculate kitchens, and a large, well-trained staff.

Deluxe: Many a fine restaurant around the country falls into this category. It will have its own well-deserved reputation for excellence, perhaps a house specialty or two for which it is famous, and an atmosphere of elegance or unique decor. It will have a good wine list where the law permits, and will be considered the best in town by the inhabitants. It will have a clean kitchen and attentive staff.

Expensive: In addition to the expected dishes, it will offer one or two house specialties, wine list, and cocktails (where law permits), air conditioning (unless locale makes it unnecessary), a general reputation for very good food and an adequte staff, an elegant decor, and appropriately dressed clientele.

Moderate: Cocktails and/or beer where law permits, air conditioning (when needed), clean kitchen, adequate staff, better-than-average service. General reputation for good, wholesome food.

Inexpensive: The bargain place in town, it is clean, even if plain. It will have air conditioning (when necessary), tables (not a counter), and clean kitchen and will attempt to provide adequate service.

BUSINESS HOURS AND LOCAL TIME. Time zones do not follow state lines throughout the Rockies and Plains states. All of Montana, Wyoming, and Colorado are on Mountain Time, as are the western halves of South Dakota and Nebraska. All of North Dakota and the eastern halves of South Dakota and Nebraska are on Central Time. In Utah, the western third is on Pacific Time and the rest on Mountain Time.

SUMMER SPORTS. *Swimming* is invigorating in many of the lakes and reservoirs and relaxing in the hot springs pools in Wyoming, Montana, Colorado, and South Dakota. The Great Salt Lake offers something quite different, salt water that is more buoyant than the oceans. Water skiing and sailing are popular on the larger lakes. Sailing is available on the lakes created by the many dams and on some reservoirs as well.

The many rivers and streams offer exciting possibilities for *canoeing*, *kayaking*, and *rafting*.

The Rocky Mountains offer ample opportunity for *hiking*, *backpacking*, and *mountain climbing* or *horseback riding*. Many areas are accessible only on foot or by horse.

Fishing in this area is very popular and the system of waterways quite extensive; whether your pleasure is fly fishing the rivers and streams for trout or fishing the lakes for the larger walleye, bass, and northern pike, you're certain of great sport and much excitement.

In light of this area's western frontier heritage, it's not surprising that *rodeo* is the most pervasive of the spectator sports throughout this region. In general the season runs from late spring into early fall; whether it takes place in Nebraska, where rodeo was born, in Wyoming, where Frontier Days attracts national champions, or at a small county fair, it's sure to be action-packed.

There are many fine *golf* courses throughout the area, such as the splendid layout at Jackson Hole in Wyoming. *Tennis* is also a popular sport, and courts are found at virtually every major resort or urban area.

WINTER SPORTS. *Skiing* is without a doubt the major winter sport of this area. New areas continue to be developed throughout the Rocky Mountains, especially Aspen and Vail in Colorado, and near Salt Lake City in Utah. Cross-country skiing, or *ski touring*, is becoming increasingly popular as both a means of escape from the cost of lift tickets and the ever-longer lift lines, and also as a means of enjoying the breathtaking scenery.

Each year, *snowmobiling* attracts more and more people who enjoy the thrill of speeding along snow-covered mountain trails or over open meadows. Many areas have organized rallies and races.

Ice skating on frozen lakes and ponds, or in year-round rinks, also has its share of enthusiasts.

Hunting for deer, antelope, elk, moose, and even bear brings hunters from all over into this area. There are also seasons for waterfowl, pheasant, quail, partridge, and grouse. In some cases, nonresidents are permitted to hunt the less populous of these species only with bow and arrows.

 ROUGHING IT. More, and improved, camping facilities are springing up each year across the country, in national parks, national forests, state parks, in private camping areas, and trailer parks, which by now have become national institutions. Farm vacations continue to gain adherents, especially among families with children. Some accommodations are quite deluxe, some extremely simple. Here and there a farm has a swimming pool, while others have facilities for trailers and camping. For a directory of farms which take vacationers (including details of rates, accommodations, dates, etc.), write to *Adventure Guides, Inc.*, 36 East 57 Street, New York, N.Y. 10022 for their 224-page book *Country Vacations U.S.A.* ($4.25 postpaid in the U.S.). Their other directory, *Adventure Travel U.S.A.*, gives details on guided wilderness trips, backpacking, canoeing, rock climbing, covered wagon treks, scuba diving, and more. Same size, price, and address.

Because of the great size of the United States and the distances involved, youth hostels have not developed in this country the way they have in Europe and Japan. In the entire 3½ million square miles of the U.S. there are upwards of 160 youth hostels, and because they are, in any case, designed primarily for people who are traveling under their own power, usually hiking or bicycling, rather than by car or commercial transportation, they tend to be away from towns and cities and in rural areas, near scenic spots. In the U.S. they are most frequent and practical in compact areas like New England. Although their members are mainly younger people, there is no age limit. You must be a member to use youth hostels; write to *American Youth Hostel Association, Inc.*, National Campus, Delaplane, Virginia 22025. A copy of the Hostel Guide and Handbook will be included in your membership. Accommodations are simple, dormitories are segregated by sex, common rooms and kitchen are shared, and everyone helps with the cleanup.

Useful Addresses: *National Parks Service*, U.S. Dept. of the Interior, Washington, D.C. 20025; *National Forest Service*, U.S. Dept. of Agriculture, Washington, D.C. 20025. For information on state parks, write *State Parks Dept., State Office Building* in the capitol of the state in which you are interested.

The National Campers & Hikers Assoc., Box 451, Orange, New Jersey 07051. Commercial camping organizations include *American Camping Assoc., Inc.*, Bradford Woods, Martinsville, Indiana 46151, and *Camping Council*, 17 East 48 Street, New York, N.Y. 10017.

 TIPPING. Tipping is supposed to be a personal thing, your way of expressing your appreciation of someone who has taken pleasure and pride in giving you attentive, efficient, and personal service. Because standards of personal service in the United States are highly uneven, you should, when you get genuinely good service, feel secure in rewarding it, and when you feel that the service you got was slovenly, indifferent, or surly, don't hesitate to show this by the size, or withholding, of your tip. Remember that in many places the help are paid very little and depend on tips for the better part of their income. This is supposed to give them incentive to serve you well. These days, the going rate for tipping on *restaurant* service is 15% on the amount *before* taxes. Tipping at counters is not universal, but many people leave $0.25 on anything up to $1, and 10% on anything over that. For *bellboys*, 25¢ per bag is usual. However, if you load him down with all manner of bags, hatboxes, cameras, coats, etc., you might consider giving an extra quarter or two. For one-night stays in most *hotels* and *motels*, you leave nothing. But if you stay longer, at the end of your stay leave the maid $1-$1.25 per day, or $5 per person per week for multiple occupancy. If you are staying at an *American Plan* hostelry (meals included), $1.50 per day per person for the waiter or waitress is considered sufficient, and is left at the end of your stay. If you have been surrounded by an army of servants (one bringing relishes, another rolls, etc.), add a few extra dollars and give the lump sum to the captain or *maître d'hôtel* when you leave, asking him to allocate it.

For the many other services you may encounter in a big hotel or resort, figure roughly as follows: doorman, 25¢ for taxi handling, 50¢ for help with baggage; bellhop, 25¢ per bag, more if you load him down with extras; parking attendant, 50¢; bartender, 15%; room service, 10-15% of that bill; laundry or valet service, 15%; pool attendant, 50¢ per day; snackbar waiter at pool, beach, or golf club, 50¢ per person for food and 15% of the beverage check; locker attendant, 50¢ per person per day, or $2.50 per week; golf caddies, $1-$2 per bag, or 15% of the greens fee for an 18-hole course, or $3 on a free course; barbers, 50¢; shoeshine attendants, 25¢; hairdressers, $1; manicurists, 50¢.

Transportation: Give 25¢ for any taxi fare under $1 and 15% for any above; however, drivers in New York, Las Vegas, and other major resorts *expect* 20%. Limousine service, 20%. Car rental agencies, nothing. Bus porters are tipped 25¢ per bag, drivers nothing. On charters and package tours, conductors and drivers usually get $5-$10 per day from the group as a whole, but be sure to ask whether this has already been figured into the package cost. On short local sightseeing runs, the driver-guide may get 25¢ per person, more if you think he has been especially helpful or personable. Airport bus drivers, nothing. Redcaps, in resort areas, 35¢ per suitcase, elsewhere, 25¢. Tipping at curbside check-in is unofficial, but same as above. On the plane, no tipping.

Railroads suggest you leave 10-15% per meal for dining car waiters, but the steward who seats you is not tipped. Sleeping-car porters get about $1 per person per night. The 25¢ or 35¢ you pay a railway station baggage porter is not a tip but the set fee that he must hand in at the end of the day along with the ticket stubs he has used. Therefore his tip is anything you give him above that, 25-50¢ per bag, depending on how heavy your luggage is.

HINTS TO HANDICAPPED TRAVELERS. Happily, more and more hotels and motels are becoming aware of those things which make traveling simpler for the handicapped. Two publications which give valuable information about motels, hotels, and restaurants (rating them, telling about steps, table heights, door widths, etc.) are *Where Turning Wheels Stop*, published by Paralyzed Veterans of America, 3636 16th St., N.W., Washington, D.C. 20010, and *The Wheelchair Traveler*, 22480 Cass Ave., Woodland Hills, Calif. 91364. Many of the nation's national parks have special facilities for the handicapped. These are described in *National Park Guide for the Handicapped*, available from the U.S. Government Printing Office, Washington, D.C. 20402. TWA publishes a free 12-page pamphlet entitled *Consumer Information about Air Travel for the Handicapped* to explain available special arrangements and how to get them. A central source of free information is the *Travel Information Center, Moss Rehabilitation Hospital*, 12th Street and Tabor Road, Philadelphia, Pa. 19141. And you may also get information from the *Easter Seal Society for Crippled Children and Adults*, Director of Education and Information Service, 2023 West Ogden Ave., Chicago, Illinois 60612.

COLORADO

Spacious Valleys, Towering Peaks

by

BILL HOSOKAWA, ROGER COX,

CARRIE RODGERS,

and CURTIS W. CASEWIT

As a member of The Denver Post *staff since 1946, Bill Hosokawa has traveled extensively throughout Colorado. He has also contributed to many national magazines.*

Roger Cox is a native of Grand Junction, Colorado, and is currently a freelance writer and editor in New York City.

Carrie Rodgers was once chosen as one of Glamour Magazine's *top ten college girls. She has lived in Colorado all her life.*

Curtis W. Casewit is the author of Colorado *(Viking Press),* The Mountain World *(Random House), and twenty other books.*

Struggling westward across the Great Plains more than a century ago, a now-forgotten pioneer at the head of a wagon train gazed at the Colorado Rockies in the far distance. The morning sun glanced off the frosted peaks, vivid in the parched air, beckoning with a promise of green forests, cool waters, and gold.

"The Shining Mountains," the pioneer muttered, half in awe at their beauty, half in exasperation at the massive granite stretched across the horizon.

Shining Mountains they have been ever since, dominating the Colorado scene. The Rockies are the source of much of Colorado's wealth. They are the magnet that attracted a substantial part of the population, the spine that splits it economically, the barrier that blocked development, and the resource that spurred it. Without the water stored during the winter in alpine snowbanks, the plains that make up half of Colorado would be little more than desert.

The state is a perfect rectangle, nearly four hundred miles east to west, almost three hundred miles north to south. The foothills poke out of the plains along a north-south line and then rise abruptly into mountains. Denver, altitude 5280 feet, is only about fifty highway miles from the Continental Divide at Berthoud Pass. Much of western Colorado is mountainous, broken by lush valleys and high plateaus. But from along the state's eastern fringe, where the rich Kansas and Nebraska prairie lifts imperceptibly into the dry High Plains, one need not drive far inside Colorado's borders to catch a view of the Rockies.

The highways span the Continental Divide through a number of high passes. But it is the airliner that provides the most compelling and meaningful sight of the Rockies—a tumbled, jumbled mass of forests, crags, and snowy peaks—stretching to the horizon. The great expanse of Colorado, eighth in size among the states, and the vastness of its wilderness (national forests cover one-fifth of the area), are impressively evident to the airline traveler. Fifty-four of Colorado's peaks measure 14,000 feet or higher; 1,500 are more than 10,000 feet tall.

Six major rivers rise in the Rockies. The Colorado and the Gunnison flow west, meeting at Grand Junction just before entering Utah; the Rio Grande flows southward; the Arkansas and South Platte wind eastward; the North Platte heads north into Wyoming. These rivers water nineteen states on their way to the sea, but before that they make life possible on the Colorado plains, supporting cities and irrigating vast acreages of farmland and pasture.

While contemporary Coloradans seek the mountains for recreation, solitude, or a livelihood, the first settlers stuck discreetly to the more hospitable low country. Folsom Man lived and hunted on the eastern plains 20,000 years ago. To mark his passing, he left well-fashioned stone arrowheads, spear points, and knives.

Four centuries before Columbus, cliff-dwelling Indians built and occupied multi-story apartment houses in the dry canyons of southwesternmost Colorado. No one is quite sure where they went, or why. The ruins of some of their homes are still preserved, most notably at Mesa Verde National Park, where visitors may stroll along ancient trails and ponder over this lost civilization.

Less than a half century after Columbus stumbled on the New World—in 1541 to be exact, the Spaniard Coronado led an exploratory party north from Mexico in search of fabled Quivera and the Seven Cities of Cibola, where the streets were allegedly paved with gold. Coronado found no gold and no streets. The exact route of his march is unclear, but it is likely he cut across what is now southeastern Colorado.

As early as 1700, French voyageurs pushed into the Rockies in search of furs, leaving behind such durable names as Cache la Poudre for the river on whose banks they hid their surplus gunpowder. And the same year that a doughty bunch of discontented colonists assembled in Philadelphia to declare their independence from England, Escalante and Dominguez, two Spanish friars in long robes, hiked from Santa Fe to the region of northwest Colorado before heading west.

Explorers, Then Trappers

Colorado was largely an uncharted and unknown wasteland when it became U.S. property under the Louisiana Purchase in 1803. Shortly thereafter President Jefferson ordered Lieutenant Zebulon M. Pike to investigate the area he had bought. Late in 1806 Pike reached the foot of the 14,110-foot peak named in his honor. An intrepid explorer but no mountain climber, Pike duly noted in his official report that it was unlikely the summit would ever be scaled. Each summer now, tens of thousands of visitors reach the peak in comfort via automobile or a cog railway. And members of the Ad Am An Club, which gets it name from the fact it takes in a member each year, hike up Pikes Peak each New Year's Eve to shoot off fireworks trucked up before snow closes the highway.

Pike's party missed quite a sight. In 1893 a Wellesley College English professor, Katherine Lee Bates, was enjoying the view from the peak when the words that became "America the Beautiful" began to take shape in her head. "Oh, beautiful for spacious skies, for amber waves of grain," she wrote. "For purple mountain majesties above the fruited plain."

The trek to the farmlands of the Northwest, the Mormon migration to Utah, and the 1849 California Gold Rush largely bypassed Colorado.

The land that had been ignored was to have its day. In 1858 Green Russell, a Georgia prospector married to a Cherokee Indian, found small amounts of placer gold on the banks of Cherry Creek where Denver now stands. With memories of the California gold rush still fresh, fortune-hunters scrambled west to stake the likeliest claims. Now it was "Pikes Peak or Bust," and many of the tenderfoot miners did go bust, for the sands were not nearly so rich as had been supposed. The hungry and disillusioned headed back to "the States," grumbling about the "Pikes Peak hoax." The hardy stuck it out and were rewarded in the spring of 1859 when John Gregory discovered rich gold deposits in a steep gulch forty miles west of the Cherry Greek settlements. This was to become the site of the twin towns of Central City and Blackhawk, called "the richest square mile on earth" until that title was wrested away thirty years later by another Colorado mining district, Cripple Creek.

Horace Greeley, then editor of the *New York Tribune*, was among the first easterners to reach Gregory's Gulch. He found some four thousand residents there, "including five white women and seven squaws living with white men." Half of the men had arrived within the week, with five hundred more coming in daily. Greeley reported everyone slept "in tents or under booths of pine boughs, cooking and eating in the open air." He wrote that there was gold to be found. Soon prospectors were pushing into the most isolated alpine valleys, washing the sands for gold, scarring the hillsides with painfully drilled holes.

Colorado's growth was swift and hectic. On Feb. 28, 1861, Congress approved a bill to establish Colorado Territory, and Colonel William Gilpin, a hero of the Mexican War, was appointed governor. The population at that time was established by a not altogether reliable census at 20,798 white males, 4,484 white females and 89 native to the territory—Cheyenne,

Arapaho, Comanche and Kiowa on the eastern plains, the Utes in the western mountains. When gold was discovered, more and more whites moved west, under the protection of Federal troops. As the Indians were displaced, there were armed disputes between various tribes and the Federal troops.

Young as it was, Colorado Territory had a key role in the Civil War. A motley volunteer army, quickly organized by Governor Gilpin, marched south to meet a Confederate cavalry force moving up from Texas under General Henry H. Sibley. They met at Glorieta Pass in northern New Mexico. The charging calvary proved to be no match for the miner-army, whose marksmanship had been sharpened in the mountains. Sibley's force was shattered and the gold fields preserved for the Union. Had the Confederacy seized Colorado gold, Jefferson Davis might have been able to shore up the South's economy.

Colorado derives its nickname, "The Centennial State," from the fact that it became a state one hundred years after the signing of the Declaration of Independence. It was the thirty-eighth state.

Even before that time Coloradans were forced to recognize how the Rockies could block the state's development and had occasion to demonstrate their mettle. Denver's hopes of a place on a transcontinental railroad were crushed when the Union Pacific decided to lay its tracks along a relatively flat route through southern Wyoming. Denver business leaders determined that if the railroad wouldn't come to them, they would go to the railroad. They organized the Denver Pacific to connect with the U.P. at Cheyenne.

Nowhere is the spirit of early Coloradans illustrated more dramatically than in the railroads they built—narrow-gauge lines that wound up and up over prohibitive grades into areas where the Iron Horse had no business. Reaching far above timberline, operators of these lines faced crushing winter maintenance problems. Still, thanks to these railroads, inaccessible areas were eventually opened for development, mining was made feasible, towns were supplied and the state stitched together. Some of these lines have been converted to standard gauge, but most, alas, have been abandoned as mining dwindled or trucks took over.

One of the last passenger-carrying, narrow-gauge runs is operated by the Denver & Rio Grande Railroad between Durango and the old mining town of Silverton, in some of the state's most spectacular scenery. At the peak of the summer tourist season two trains, drawn by ancient but powerful steam locomotives, make a daily round-trip. Another popular narrow gauge, the Cumbres & Toltec Scenic Railroad, runs a sixty-four-mile route between Antonito, Colorado, and Chama, New Mexico. The C&TS crests the summit of 10,015-foot Cumbres Pass, highest point reached in America by narrow-gauge rails.

In 1902, David H. Moffat, a Denver banker, organized a railroad to drive straight over the Rockies to the Pacific Coast. Corona Pass broke the railroad's back. The Continental Divide at this point is 11,680 feet above sea level. Winter storms made it impossible to maintain schedules. Finally, in 1922, the State Legislature passed a measure setting up the Moffat Tunnel Improvement District. Bonds were issued and work started on a tunnel under the Divide. The bore is six miles long, took five years to complete, and cost $18 million. Nonetheless, the tunnel finally gave Denver direct access to the sea. The old roadbed over Corona Pass is open in summer to adventurous motorists willing to brave chuckholes, sharp curves and dust. The views are magnificent.

Gold and silver spurred the state's growth in the decades after statehood. Great silver strikes in Leadville, Aspen, and Creede produced millions in new wealth. Between 1880 and 1890 Colorado's population doubled to 413,000. Then came the repeal of the Sherman Act in 1893, slashing the price of silver. Mines ceased operations, and towns died overnight.

During this black period only the Cripple Creek gold fields kept the state's economy afloat. Discovered in 1890, this area just southwest of Pikes Peak produced some $400 million worth of gold before the richest lodes were played out. Texas Guinan began her career as an entertainer in Cripple Creek. Lowell Thomas spent his boyhood there. Jack Dempsey worked in its mines and fought for a $50 purse. Only summer tourists keep Cripple Creek alive today, but the proposed reopening of the long-fallow mines may change the community's economy in the near future.

As mining dwindled, Coloradans realized their real wealth lay elsewhere. Farming—sugar beets, vegetable crops, melons, peaches, potatoes—was extended as irrigation projects made more water available. The plains yielded wheat and corn, and mountain pastures fattened growing herds of cattle and sheep. Manufacturing plants were established in some cities. At Pueblo, coal from Trinidad was used to smelt ores from Leadville, and the now giant C.F.&I. Steel Corporation took shape. Mining equipment firms, first established to meet local needs, began to ship their specialized machinery to South America, Europe, and Asia.

Meanwhile, the population grew steadily, even during the dust bowl years of the thirties when drought and wind devastated the southeastern corner of the state. Colorado's population topped one million for the first time in the 1930 census and boomed after World War II. Now 2½ million people live in the state.

Coloradans make their livings in many diverse ways. Oddly enough, manufacturing and construction top the list, producing $5.4 billion a year. Agriculture and stock-raising are next, averaging $1.8 billion annually. Travel and tourism (cool summers, scenery, dude ranches, fishing, skiing) account for another $772 million, spent by some nine million visitors. The one-time kingpin of Colorado's economy, mining, runs third with $941 million, about one half of which is produced by oil and gas.

The Soldiers Came Back

Three out of four Coloradans live in a string of cities stretched along the eastern foot of the Rockies, with Denver in the center. In fact, Grand Junction and Durango are the only communities west of the Divide to claim more than 10,000 residents. An estimated 1.4 million—more than half of all Coloradans—live in the Denver metropolitan complex.

The Denver of today is a far cry from the overgrown cow town of a generation ago. Thousands of servicemen who had trained during World War II at Lowry Air Base in Denver, Fort Carson near Colorado Springs, and Camp Hale for mountain troops near Leadville, had fallen in love with the West, vowed to come back, and did. City-jaded Easterners sought and found breathing space in Colorado. Wealthy Texans bought into Colorado real estate, not without some hard feelings among fishermen who found favorite trout streams posted. Other new blood was attracted by the expan-

ROCKIES & PLAINS

Vacation Guide

& Road Atlas

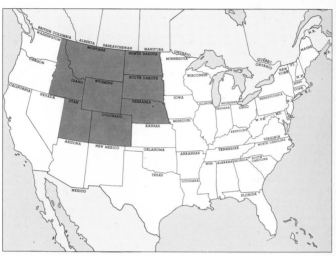

SYMBOLS USED IN THIS ATLAS

Limited Access Highways	
National Parkways	
Toll Roads and Interchanges	(TOLL)
Major Highways	
Other Important Roads	
Mileage Between Dots	17
Ferries	FT.
U.S. Interstate Route Numbers	

Routes with odd numbers run north and south, the even-numbered routes east and west. Numbers progress lowest to highest from west to east and from south to north. Major routes have one- or two-digit numbers and the long, evenly spaced routes have numbers ending in 0 or 5.

Connecting full or partial circumferential routes around or in urban areas carry a three-digit number, using the main route number with an **even** number prefix. Radial and spur routes are also three-digits, using the main route number with an **odd** number prefix. For example: an auxiliary route to I—80 might be classified as I—180 or I—280.

Federal Route Numbers	35 35
State and Other Route Numbers	17 17
Trans-Canada Highway	
Points of Interest, Recreation Areas	▪ ▢
Major Commercial Airports	✈
National Capitals	⊛
State and Provincial Capitals	⊛

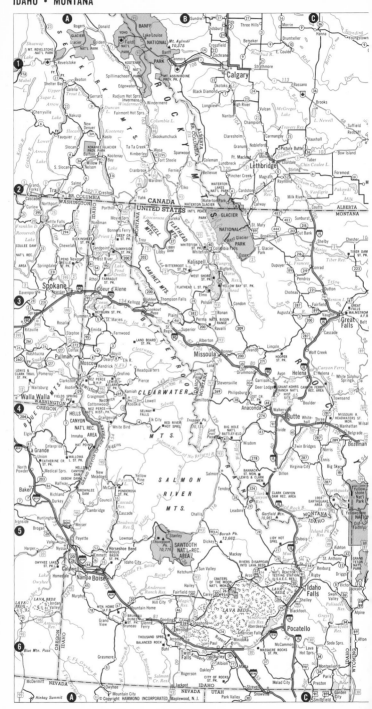

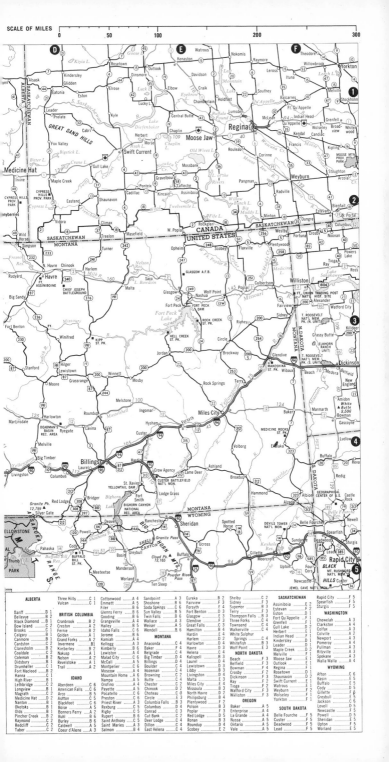

WYOMING · UTAH · COLORADO

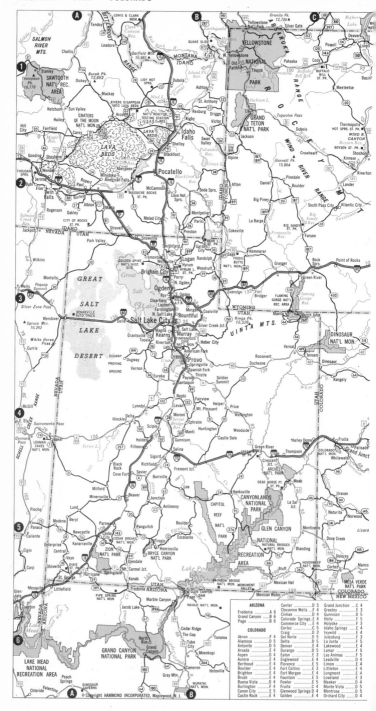

© Copyright HAMMOND INCORPORATED, Maplewood, N. J.

ARIZONA		
Fredonia	A	6
Grand Canyon	B	6
Page	B	6

COLORADO		
Akron	F	4
Alamosa	D	5
Antonito	D	5
Arboles	C	5
Arvada	D	4
Aspen	D	4
Aurora	D	4
Berthoud	D	4
Boulder	E	4
Brighton	E	4
Brush	F	4
Buena Vista	D	4
Burlington	F	4
Canon City	D	5
Castle Rock	E	4

Center	D	5
Cheyenne Wells	F	4
Climax	D	4
Colorado Springs	E	4
Commerce City	D	4
Cortez	C	5
Craig	C	3
Del Norte	D	5
Delta	C	4
Denver	D	4
Durango	C	5
Eaton	E	3
Englewood	D	4
Florence	D	5
Fort Collins	E	3
Fort Morgan	F	4
Fowler	E	5
Fruita	C	4

Glenwood Springs	D	4
Golden	E	4
Grand Junction	C	4
Greeley	E	3
Gunnison	D	5
Holly	F	5
Holyoke	F	3
Idaho Springs	D	4
Ivywild	E	4
Julesburg	F	3
La Junta	E	5
Lakewood	D	4
Lamar	F	5
Las Animas	F	5
Leadville	D	4
Limon	E	4
Littleton	D	4
Longmont	E	3
Loveland	E	3
Meeker	C	3
Monte Vista	D	5
Montrose	C	4
Orchard City	C	4

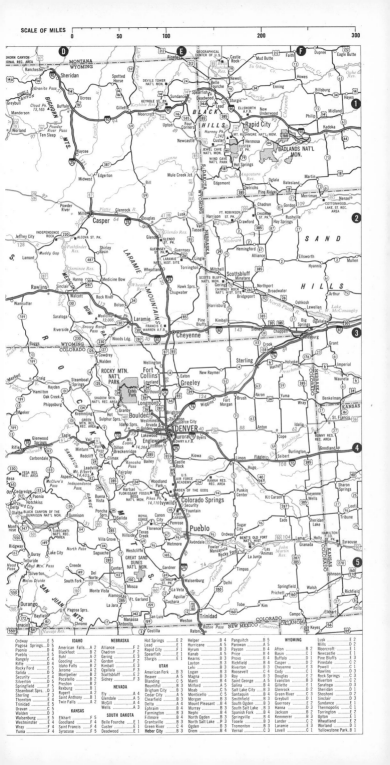

Ordway	E 5	**IDAHO**		**NEBRASKA**		Hot Springs	E 2
Pagosa Springs	D 5	American Falls	A 2	Alliance	E 2	Hurricane	A 5
Paonia	E 4	Blackfoot	A 2	Chadron	E 1	Hyrum	B 3
Pueblo	E 5	Buhl	A 2	Gering	E 3	Kanab	B 3
Rangely	D 4	Gooding	A 2	Gordon	E 2	Kearns	B 3
Rifle	D 4	Idaho Falls	B 2	Kimball	E 3	Layton	B 3
Rocky Ford	E 5	Jerome	A 2	Ogallala	F 3	Lehi	B 3
Salida	D 5	Montpelier	B 2	Scottsbluff	E 2	Logan	B 3
Security	E 4	Pocatello	B 2	Sidney	E 3	Magna	B 3
Silverton	D 5	Preston	B 2			Manti	B 3
Springfield	F 5	Rexburg	B 2	**NEVADA**		Milford	A 4
Steamboat Springs	D 3	Rupert	A 2	Ely	A 4	Moab	C 4
Sterling	F 3	Saint Anthony	B 1	Glendale	A 5	Monticello	C 5
Thornton	E 4	Twin Falls	A 2	McGill	A 4	Morgan	B 3
Trinidad	E 5			Wells	A 3	Mount Pleasant	B 4
Uravan	D 4	**KANSAS**				Murray	B 3
Walden	D 3	Elkhart	F 5	**SOUTH DAKOTA**		Nephi	B 4
Walsenburg	E 5	Goodland	F 4	Belle Fourche	E 1	North Ogden	B 3
Westminster	E 4	Saint Francis	F 4	Deadwood	E 1	North Salt Lake	B 3
Wray	F 4	Syracuse	F 5			Ogden	B 3
Yuma	F 4					Orem	B 4

UTAH		Helper	B 4	Panguitch	B 5	**WYOMING**		Lusk	E 2
American Fork	B 3	Hurricane	A 5	Parowan	A 5	Afton	B 2	Mills	D 2
Beaver	A 4	Hyrum	B 3	Payson	B 4	Basin	C 1	Moorcroft	D 1
Blanding	C 5	Kanab	B 3	Price	B 4	Buffalo	C 1	Newcastle	E 1
Bountiful	B 3	Kearns	B 3	Provo	B 3	Casper	D 2	Pine Bluffs	E 3
Brigham City	B 3	Layton	B 3	Richfield	B 4	Cheyenne	E 3	Pinedale	B 2
Cedar City	A 5	Lehi	B 3	Riverton	B 3	Cody	C 1	Powell	C 1
Clearfield	B 3	Logan	B 3	Roosevelt	C 4	Douglas	D 2	Rawlins	C 3
Delta	A 4	Magna	B 3	Roy	B 3	Evanston	B 3	Rock Springs	C 3
Farmington	B 3	Manti	B 3	Saint George	A 5	Gillette	D 1	Riverton	C 2
Fillmore	A 4	Milford	A 4	Salina	B 4	Glenrock	D 2	Saratoga	D 3
Grantsville	B 3	Moab	C 4	Salt Lake City	B 3	Green River	B 3	Sheridan	D 1
Green River	C 4	Monticello	C 5	Santaquin	B 4	Greybull	C 1	Shoshoni	C 2
Heber City	B 3	Morgan	B 3	Smithfield	B 3	Guernsey	E 2	Sinclair	C 3
		Mount Pleasant	B 4	South Ogden	B 3	Hanna	C 3	Sundance	E 1
		Murray	B 3	South Salt Lake	B 3	Jackson	B 2	Thermopolis	C 2
		Nephi	B 4	Spanish Fork	B 4	Kemmerer	B 3	Torrington	E 2
		North Ogden	B 3	Springville	B 4	Lander	C 2	Upton	E 1
		North Salt Lake	B 3	Tooele	B 3	Laramie	D 3	Wheatland	D 2
		Ogden	B 3	Tremonton	B 3	Lovell	C 1	Worland	D 1
		Orem	B 4	Vernal	C 3			Yellowstone Nat'l Park	B 1

NORTH DAKOTA • SOUTH DAKOTA

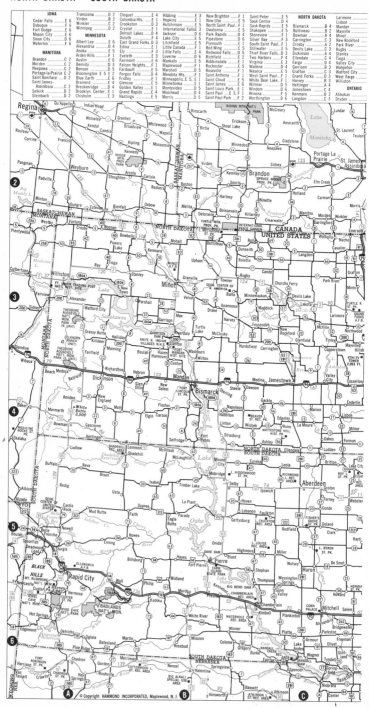

IOWA

Cedar Falls	E 6
Dubuque	F 6
Fort Dodge	E 6
Mason City	E 6
Sioux City	D 6
Waterloo	E 6

MANITOBA

Brandon	C 2
Morden	D 2
Neepawa	C 2
Portage-la-Prairie	C 2
Saint Boniface	D 2
Saint James	
Assiniboia	D 2
Selkirk	D 2
Steinbach	D 2

MINNESOTA

Albert Lea	E 6
Alexandria	E 6
Anoka	E 1
Arden Hills	F 1
Austin	E 6
Bemidji	D 3
Benson	E 6
Bloomington	E 5 E 2
Blue Earth	E 6
Brainerd	E 4
Breckenridge	D 4
Brooklyn Center	E 1
Chisholm	E 3

Transcona	D 2
Virden	B 2
Winkler	D 2
Winnipeg	D 2

Cloquet	E 4
Columbia Hts.	E 1
Crookston	D 3
Crystal	E 1
Detroit Lakes	D 4
Duluth	E 4
East Grand Forks	D 3
Edina	E 1
Ely	F 3
Eveleth	E 3
Fairmont	E 6
Falcon Heights	F 1
Faribault	E 6
Fergus Falls	E 4
Glencoe	E 5
Golden Valley	E 1
Grand Rapids	E 3
Hastings	E 5

Hibbing	E 3
Hopkins	E 1
Hutchinson	E 5
International Falls	E 3
Jackson	D 6
Lake City	E 5
Litchfield	E 5
Little Canada	F 1
Little Falls	E 4
Luverne	D 6
Mankato	E 6
Maplewood	F 1
Marshall	D 5
Mendota Hts.	F 1
Minneapolis	E 5, E 1
Minnetonka	E 1
Montevideo	D 5
Moorhead	D 4
Morris	D 5

New Brighton	F 1
New Ulm	E 5
North Saint Paul	F 1
Owatonna	E 6
Park Rapids	D 4
Pipestone	D 6
Plymouth	E 1
Red Wing	E 5
Redwood Falls	D 5
Richfield	E 1
Robbinsdale	E 1
Rochester	E 5
Roseville	F 1
Saint Anthony	F 1
Saint Cloud	E 5
Saint James	E 6
Saint Louis Park	E 1
Saint Paul	E 5, F 1
Saint Paul Park	F 2

Saint Peter	E 5
Sauk Centre	E 5
Sauk Rapids	E 5
Shakopee	E 5
Shoreview	F 1
Silver Bay	F 3
South Saint Paul	F 1
Stillwater	E 5
Thief River Falls	D 3
Two Harbors	E 4
Virginia	E 3
Wadena	E 4
Waseca	E 5
West Saint Paul	F 1
White Bear Lake	F 1
Willmar	D 5
Windom	D 6
Winona	E 5
Worthington	D 6

NORTH DAKOTA

Bismarck	B 4
Bottineau	B 2
Bowman	A 4
Carrington	C 3
Crosby	A 2
Devils Lake	C 3
Dickinson	A 4
Ellendale	C 4
Fargo	D 4
Garrison	B 3
Grafton	C 2
Grand Forks	D 3
Harvey	B 3
Hettinger	A 4
Jamestown	C 4
Kenmare	B 2
Langdon	C 2

Larimore	D 3
Lisbon	D 4
Mandan	B 4
Mayville	D 3
Minot	B 2
New Rockford	C 3
Park River	D 3
Rugby	B 2
Stanley	B 2
Tioga	B 2
Valley City	C 4
Wahpeton	D 4
Watford City	A 3
West Fargo	D 4
Williston	A 3

ONTARIO

Atikokan	C 3
Dryden	C 3

© Copyright HAMMOND INCORPORATED, Maplewood, N. J.

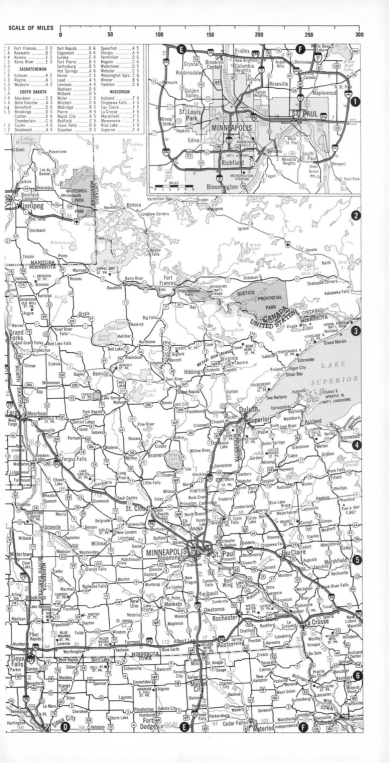

NEBRASKA

SCALE OF MILES

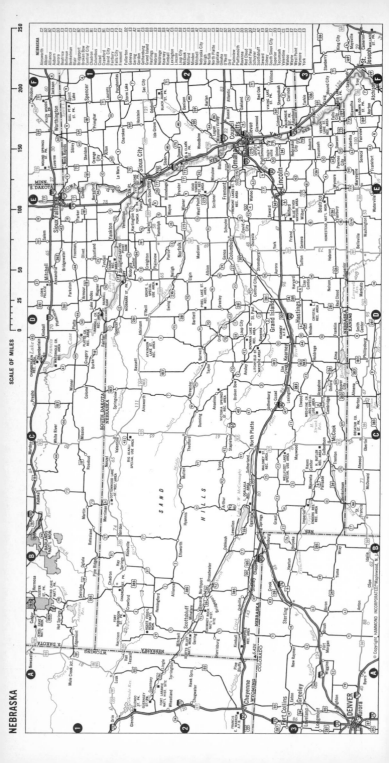

sion of oil, research, and aerospace-oriented industries. These newcomers were responsible for profound changes in the state's intellectual climate and outlook.

The arrival of Palmer Hoyt from Portland, Ore., coincided with the population influx. As editor and publisher of *The Denver Post*, the state's largest newspaper, Hoyt was as responsible as any one man for jolting Colorado out of its traditional provincialism. Perhaps it is significant that Denver's airfield soon became an international airport, and that it has two sister cities, Brest, France, and Takayama, Japan.

Although Stetsons and cowboy boots can be seen on any downtown street, Denver's attitudes are as urbane and cosmopolitan as those of any metropolis. The big difference is the pace, which visitors quickly recognize as less frenetic than that of the high-tension East. Denver is also a young city, concerned with youthful activities.

Seventeenth Street, Denver's banking, investments, insurance, and transportation center, probably displays almost as many Ivy League suits per capita as Madison Avenue. But at the end of the day a Denver executive, instead of belting down a quick Martini before running for a train, hops into his car, drives to the suburbs in twenty or thirty minutes, and sips his drink on the patio of his ranch-type home. For a night out, there's a choice of dining at any of several dozen excellent restaurants serving everything from authentic French and German cuisine to enchiladas, almond duck, sukiyaki, and genuine Thai fare. True to Western tradition, however, many Denverites seem to prefer Colorado cornfed steaks or prime ribs and tossed green salad.

In a great many instances it was the outdoors that lured the newcomers to the West, and if anything, this interest seems to intensify rather than diminish after they arrive. The skiing season often lasts six months, and there is fishing year-round; in summer there is camping, boating, hiking, riding, driving, golfing, and just plain mountain-admiring; in fall there is good hunting for both upland birds and big game. More and more city-dwelling Coloradans are buying mountain cabins, boats, and campers.

Like the tourists who demand hot showers, white linen, and innerspring mattresses after a day of roughing it, Coloradans demand and enjoy the amenities of a sophisticated civilization. The Symphony, the Junior League Benefit, the Debutante Ball, the first night at Bonfils Civic Theatre are important events for ladies in furs and jewels and some of their escorts in dinner jackets. Yet these same individuals support with equal enthusiasm the National Western Stock Show and Rodeo, where fat cattle and fearless cowboys vie for attention.

Not many years ago it could be charged with reasonable accuracy that Coloradans were a bit self-conscious about their isolation and inclined to be apologetic about their supposed lack of culture and horny-handed past. Not so today. Jet planes fly in less than two hours to the West Coast, three hours to the East. The Interstate system is rapidly shortening highway distances. Coloradans have made their pilgrimages to New York and San Francisco, to Paris and London and Rome, to Hong Kong and Tokyo and Bangkok, and their collective verdict has been that travel is great but it's hard to beat Colorado. The state's adopted sons and daughters sing its praise loudest. Anyone who's lived in Colorado more than a year considers himself virtually a native—and talks as though he invented it.

EXPLORING DENVER

If you've had a long trip to Denver there's nothing more appropriate than a leisurely walking tour for getting the kinks out of your legs and to acclimate yourself to the mile-high air. The altitude doesn't bother most persons, but you may find yourself just a bit short of breath for a few days, so take it easy at first.

Best place to start is the Colorado Visitors' Bureau, at 225 West Colfax Avenue, just off the main business section and at the edge of the Civic Center complex. This tourist information center is housed in an attractive red sandstone and glass building immediately across the street from city hall (distinguishable by the clock tower and chimes), which Denverites call the City and County Building.

At 225 West Colfax you'll be welcomed by a pleasant young woman who can supply you with detailed maps, weather and road reports, the latest ski readings in winter, and a list of local rodeos and other celebrations in summer. She can also tell you about accommodations, restaurant facilities, trailer camps, fish and game regulations, and a lot of other data to make your Colorado visit more enjoyable. Browse among the racks filled with pamphlets.

Now you're ready to begin your tour. Cross West Colfax toward the City and County Building, and be careful of the traffic. Many downtown Denver intersections have "Walk" and "Don't Walk" lights. When the "Walk" sign goes on, pedestrians are permitted to move in any direction, even catty-corner, while automobiles wait. (Traffic Engineer Henry Barnes initiated the system in the late 1940s, and it worked so well he was rewarded eventually with the opportunity to solve New York City's traffic problems.)

Turn right, or west, toward the mountains. Adjoining the City and County Building, behind a wrought iron fence, is the United States Mint, where automatic machinery produces pennies, nickels, dimes, quarters, and half dollars. Tour hours vary. Mint tours begin at the Cherokee Street entrance. No advance reservations are needed, although at the height of the summer tourist season, waits of an hour or more are not uncommon.

You'll hear the chatter of stamping machinery and the clatter of coins through the open windows as you move on into the City and County Building. Denver's municipal affairs are conducted in this imposing, four-story, white granite structure faced with Doric columns. The mayor's office and city council chambers are here, as well as courtrooms and various city bureaus. Shortly before Thanksgiving each year, work starts on the lighting and decorating of Civic Center, a municipally financed project that has become a Denver tradition. In the week preceding and following Christmas, the streets are thronged each evening by those who have come to admire the display.

From the front steps of the City and County Building, take time to look out across the grassy mall, dotted with shade trees, that stretches eastward to the gold-domed Colorado State Capitol. The Capitol, constructed of Colorado gray granite, is a miniaturized version of the U.S. Capitol in Washington, D.C., and the mall is likewise a smaller version of the Washington mall. Fountains, a Greek Theater for public gatherings, and monuments to Denver and Colorado pioneers grace the area, which is carefully tended and brightened in summer by extensive flower beds. To the left, in a classic colon-

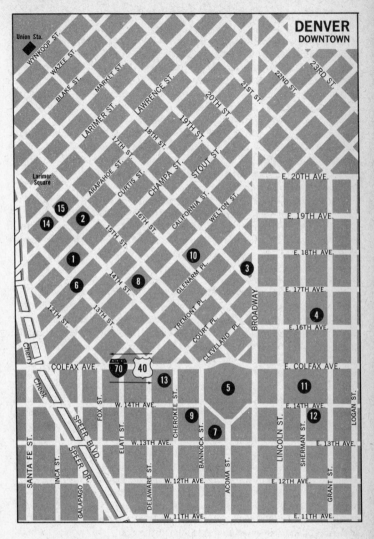

.Points of Interest

1) Auditorium Arena & Theater
2) Brooks Tower
3) Brown Palace Hotel
4) Capitol Life Center
5) Civic Center
6) Convention Center, Currigan Hall
7) Denver Art Museum
8) Denver Post Building
9) Denver University Law Center
10) Masonic Temple Building
11) State Capitol
12) State Historical Museum
13) U.S. Mint
14) University of Colorado

naded building, is the municipal body that holds Denver's life in its hands—
the Board of Water Commissioners, charged with providing the city with a
reliable supply of pure water from the vast mountain basins.

Now, turn south along Bannock Street a half block to West 14th Avenue.
Here on the corner is the University of Denver College of Law, part of the
downtown campus of the privately endowed school.

Now the route of our stroll turns east along 14th. On the other side of
Bannock Street is the Denver Art Museum, noted for both its contemporary
and traditional American and European exhibits. This six-story building on
the south side of the Civic Center is composed of more than one million
specially designed, faceted-glass tiles. It also has an interesting Oriental art
collection, but perhaps it is best known for the encouragement it has given
local painters, sculptors, and ceramicists with regional shows and sales. Try
the Art Museum for lunch!

Next to the museum complex, fronting on Broadway, is the $3 million
Denver Public Library. Paintings and records, as well as books, are loaned
out. The Western History Department is considered one of the nation's best
in this field. Priceless photo collections, Colorado newspaper files dating
back to 1859, and rare volumes are available to the serious researcher.

Panorama of the Rockies

Proceed two blocks eastward along 14th, which now has become East
14th Avenue. On the right, at the two corners of Sherman Street, are the
State Capitol Annex and the State Historical Museum. On the left is the
massive, neo-classic Capitol. The museum, open daily, offers an insight
into Colorado history with mementos of the bonanza mining years, dioramas
of early-day Denver, artifacts of the Pueblo Indian culture, and even several
mummified remains of Cliff-Dwellers.

The Capitol, completed in 1896, is typical of the porticoed and domed
public buildings of that period; however, the dome, gilded with Colorado
gold leaf at a cost of $23,000, is noteworthy as a tribute to the mining
industry. The State Capitol is floodlighted at night.

The thirteenth step of the western entrance is exactly one mile above sea
level. A bronze plaque used to be mounted there, but it and its replacements
kept disappearing, and Colorado now frugally notes the elevation with a
message chiseled into the stone. On a clear day (Denver also has a smog
problem) a vast panorama of the Rockies is visible from the top of the stairs.
Heroic murals by Allen True depicting state history cover the main-floor
wall. Portraits of leading historical figures appear in the stained-glass
windows of the Senate chamber and under the dome.

"Capitol Hill," once the site of the luxurious homes of mining tycoons, is
largely an apartment-house area now. However, a dwindling number of
mansions can be seen, and one of them, Molly Brown's House, is nationally
known. This Victorian marvel, at 1320 Pennsylvania Street, was the home
of Molly and her husband, James J. Brown, a wealthy mine owner. Molly
became known for her flamboyant tastes and for the great heroism she
displayed in the Titanic disaster. She became a famous folk heroine with the
musical "The Unsinkable Molly Brown." The home is closed on Monday.
The mansion tour is worthwhile for history buffs.

Three short blocks east of Logan Street is the Episcopal Cathedral of St.
John's, at E. 14th Avenue and Washington Street. Built in the massive

fifteenth-century Gothic style, the cathedral has some fine examples of English stained glass and German carved wooden figures. (This church's first home: a log cabin, built shortly after Denver was founded.)

Now it is time to turn around and head back toward downtown Denver. Instead of retracing your steps, walk north one block to Colfax Avenue, then turn left. At the corner of Colfax and Logan is the Roman Catholic Cathedral of the Immaculate Conception, a massive French Gothic structure with two lofty spires. A white Carrara marble altar, thirty feet high, and twenty-two stained-glass windows designed at the Royal Bavarian Institute, grace the interior.

Time to think about lunch? You are now within a block or two of some of Denver's finest restaurants. At Colfax and Grant, only one block from the Cathedral and across the street from the Capitol, is the Quorum Restaurant, operated by Pierre Wolfe, a Swiss-trained Alsatian (continental cuisine). Nearby, at 16th and Broadway, Leo's has a reputation for Oriental food.

Or perhaps you'd prefer to stroll north on Sherman to 17th Avenue and turn left again, past the University Club to the Denver-United States National Bank Center, on Broadway. Designed by the famous architect I. M. Pei, this was the first of Denver's beautiful postwar buildings. A promenade, fountains and trout pools give a feeling of spaciousness.

Adjoining the Bank Center is the Cosmopolitan Hotel, with its Gun Room, noted for roast baron of beef, and Trader Vic's, a Polynesian restaurant.

The Brown Palace

Across from the Bank Center you'll find Denver's most famous hotel, the Brown Palace. The triangular brownstone structure is built around a lobby whose ceiling extends up the full eight stories of the hotel. This dramatic lobby is well worth a stop. Here are the swank Palace Arms restaurant, and the Ship Tavern, which gets extra busy from noon to 2 P.M.

From the Brown, walk one block, stopping at Kohlberg's, dealer in genuine Indian merchandise since 1888.

If you turn left on Glenarm and walk a half block you'll reach the thirty-story Security Life Building, whose Top of the Rockies restaurant on the top floor provides cocktails, lunches, dinners, and an amazing view, although this one is from behind glass. Security Life also has an outside elevator. It's an exciting experience to watch Denver fall swiftly away as you shoot up the side of the building.

Whichever building you choose, the tour leads back to 16th Street, Denver's main shopping avenue. Turn left, toward Broadway. At the corner of Tremont Place, only a half block from the Security Life Building and on the same cross street as the Brown Palace, is Denver's largest department store, the May-D&F. It's an odd name, but a legitimate one. The "May" portion indicates it is part of the May Company chain, founded in the silver camp of Leadville by the pioneer merchant David May. The "D&F" stands for Daniels and Fisher, a respected old Denver store that was absorbed by the May Company. Stroll through the store, then take the second-floor overpass directly into the lobby of the Denver Hilton Hotel. En route, in the passageway, you'll find Michelle's, an unusual coffee, pastry, and ice cream shop patterned after a Mediterranean sidewalk cafe.

The Hilton is notable for its block-long lobby, a magnificent investment in space (as befits its role as a leading Colorado hostelry) in a time when architects and builders begrudge every square foot of non-revenue-producing area. An escalator takes you from the lobby to the ground-floor arcade. Now your walking tour is ended. The Visitor's Bureau is only a block away. But you haven't exhausted Denver's sightseeing opportunities by a long shot, and many of those remaining are "must-see's," such as Larimer Square, between 14th and 15th streets on Larimer. This restored historical area, nine blocks west of the Hilton, has some of downtown Denver's most sophisticated shops and restaurants. Don't miss it.

Outside the Downtown Area

For more sightseeing in east Denver, there is the Denver Museum of Natural History in one corner of 640-acre City Park. Fossilized bones of prehistoric animals found in the Rocky Mountain region furnish several outstanding displays. Other exhibits show Rocky Mountain, Arctic, and South American animals and birds mounted in extremely lifelike natural-habitat displays. The Denver Museum of Natural History also houses a planetarium that has programs going on all year. City Park itself has a large zoo, including a children's ranch zoo. In summer there are boating, plenty of tennis, free band concerts at night, and an electric fountain. Also in east Denver, adjoining Cheesman Park (where you have an exceptional view of the mountains), are the Denver Botanic Gardens, featuring a million-dollar conservatory for tropical flowers and plants.

In northeast Denver is the Mile High Kennel Club, where greyhounds race during the summer season. Even if you aren't interested in either wagering or greyhounds, you'll find the track is a cheerful, colorful, meticulously operated "people place," visited by nearly ten thousand persons every evening.

In southwest Denver, just outside suburban Littleton, is the Centennial Turf Club, offering a summer schedule of thoroughbred horse racing and an opportunity to try the pari-mutuel system while supporting efforts to improve the breed. Many of the horses that race here, incidentally, are Colorado bred.

To the northwest are two fine summer amusement parks, Elitch Gardens and Lakeside. Elitch's is famous for its formal floral gardens and the nation's oldest summer stock theater (with big-name Broadway talent). Lakeside offers speedboat rides, stock car races, and a toy train that chuffs its way completely around Lake Rhoda. Farther west, at 17555 West 44th Avenue, is the Colorado Railroad Museum, calculated to please a rail buff. Steam locomotives of various sizes and vintages, railroad cars, narrow-gauge equipment, and many other displays of railroadiana have been assembled here by the Colorado Railroad Club.

PRACTICAL INFORMATION FOR THE DENVER AREA

HOW TO GET AROUND. *By bus:* the Denver R.T.D. (Regional Transportation District) operates the city's buses. Buses run not only within Denver proper, but also out into the suburbs. Route and schedule information is available by calling 778-6000.

By taxi: cabs in Denver may be hailed or requested by phone. Taxis are usually plentiful in the city. Yellow Cab, 892-1212, is one of the major operators.

From the airport: taxi service to and from the airport is expensive. Airport limousine service, which stops at the major hotels, costs $2.

TOURIST INFORMATION. For information and brochures about Denver contact the Hospitality Center, Denver Convention and Colorado Visitors' Bureau, 225 W. Colfax Ave., Denver 80202.

 SEASONAL EVENTS. *January: National Western Stock Show and Rodeo* takes place for nine days in mid-month. The *Western Annual Exhibition* at the Denver Art Museum opens and runs into *March.*

February: Garden and Home Show.

March: Denver Symphony has a series of free concerts. *St. Patrick's Day Parade* downtown.

April: Easter Sunrise services at Red Rocks. *Denver Bears* baseball season opens.

May: Lakeside Amusement Park, and *Elitch Gardens, Theatre and Bands* open to run throughout the summer. Thoroughbred and *quarter-horse racing* at Centennial Race Track begins, with pari-mutuel betting through mid-Nov.

June: Greyhound racing at Mile High Kennel Club throughout the summer, with pari-mutuel betting.

July: The *All Colorado Art Show* at the Denver Art Museum, mid-month through Sept. Free *band concerts* through Aug. take place in City Park.

September: Denver Broncos professional football season opens.

October: Early in the month is the *Larimer Square Oktoberfest.* The *Denver Symphony* and *Bonfils Memorial Theater* begin eight- and nine-month seasons.

December: Lights are turned on for the *Denver Civic Center Christmas Display.*

 MUSEUMS AND GALLERIES. The *Denver Museum of Natural History* at City Park is one of the outstanding museums in the West. The ''inhabitants'' of this unique museum are shown in natural surroundings, whether they lived in prehistoric times or wander the world today. Open daily. The *Colorado State Historical Museum,* 14th and Sherman, covers Colorado from prehistoric times to today. The *Denver Art Museum,* 100 W. 14th Ave., includes a permanent collection of European, Egyptian, Greek, and English works in the south wing; the *Schleier Gallery,* with its American collection; *Oriental Galleries,* with permanent collections on Asia; the *Living Arts Center,* with modern arts and designs, all at Civic Center.

 HISTORIC SITES. Denver has demolished some of her historic sites (the Mining Exchange Building, the Old Customs House, the Tabor Opera House, the Windsor Hotel) to make way for parking lots, but there are still a few to be visited. The ''Unsinkable Molly Brown's'' house is at 340 Pennsylvania St. Not far away, at 770 Pennsylvania, there stands the Grand Humphrey Mansion, which can also be visited. The *Governor's Mansion,* at 400 E. 8th Ave., a gift to the state from the Boettcher Foundation, is a 27-room Colonial structure with beautifully landscaped grounds. Tours are available on Tues. each year, starting in May.

 FAMOUS LIBRARIES. The *Denver Public Library,* at 1357 Broadway and twenty branch locations, is the largest in the Rocky Mountain region. The Western History section is renowned. Many programs and exhibits are presented for the public.

TOURS. *AA Sightseeing Tours, Continental Sightseeing Lines,* and *Grey Line Tours* offer daily excursions around the city, as well as to the Denver Mountain Parks System, Estes Park, Pikes Peak, Mt. Evans, Central City—and the Air Force Academy, in the summer.

INDUSTRIAL TOURS. *Denver Wholesale Florists,* 48th and Dahlia (399-0970), specializes in carnations. *Sunstrand Aviation,* maker of aerospace power systems, has a fascinating tour for space-minded people, at 2480 W. 70th Ave. The *Packaging Corporation of America,* 5501 Brighton Blvd., manufacturers of corrugated containers, has an interesting tour. The *Denver Post,* 650 15th St., conducts hourly tours showing how a metropolitan newspaper is published. *Rio Grande Railway Shops,* Burnham Shops, 8th Ave. at Osage St., have tours every thirty minutes, and special tours for children.

SPECIAL INTEREST TOURS. *The Denver Mint,* at Colfax and Delaware Sts., has tours during the summer both a.m. and p.m., Mon. through Fri. Children must be accompanied by an adult.

GARDENS. The *Denver Botanic Gardens* beckon with many exotic trees and tropical plants, all housed in an intriguing greenhouse. The garden also offers mountain views. Library and Garden House open on weekdays.

MUSIC. Denver offers a variety of musical entertainment throughout the year. During the summer months outdoor band concerts are given nightly in City Park, with a background of changing fountain displays. *Red Rocks' Music Festival* during July and August, at Denver's outstanding mountain park, features nationally known talent. Throughout the year, various musical events are staged at the Denver Auditorium; and the *Denver Symphony,* under the baton of Brian Priestman, gives concerts twice a week in the winter to near sellout crowds, plus special youth concerts. A *businessmen's orchestra* performs regularly. Nightclubs around town bring in nationally known talent on a fairly regular basis.

STAGE AND REVUES. *Elitch Gardens,* a large amusement park at 38th and Tennyson St., is the home of America's oldest summer theater. A new production is mounted each week with nationally known stars. The *Denver Civic Ballet,* an amateur group, performs throughout the year, with a major Christmas performance annually. Denver's respected *Bonfils Theater* presents several productions throughout the year. The drama department at the *University of Denver* presents an excellent selection of plays throughout the year, with interesting and unusual settings. The new *Denver Center for The Performing Arts* plays host to a number of national companies of Broadway productions. Another "live" theater is the *Changing Scene;* also study the Sunday paper for the *Gaslight Theatre* offerings.

NIGHTCLUBS. Denver offers a wide variety of nighttime entertainment. *Taylor's Supper Club,* at 7000 W. Colfax Ave., has been home for the Taylors for some fifteen years. The entertainment is good.

During the summer months *Elitch's* brings in theater productions and popular entertainers.

Ebbets Field, at 15th and Curtis streets, imports popular musical groups and nightclub entertainers, as does *Marvelous Marv's* in Larimer Square.

• Rock and other youth-oriented concerts generally take place in the *Denver Coliseum*.

BARS. The better bars in Denver are primarily either the hotel bars or the quiet bar-and-grill type. The city also abounds with entertainment bars and neighborhood taverns. *Trader Vic's* in the Cosmopolitan Hotel and *Shaner's* at 610 17th St., do booming downtown luncheon trades with the local executives and are excellent places for good food and good drinks, rapidly served. Both are dimly lit, and one is not rushed in either establishment. The *Ship's Tavern* at the *Brown Palace Hotel* is a favorite with the newspaper world as well as the general public. The drinks are good, and the prime ribs cannot be beat. This is one bar where an unescorted woman may relax. It is a policy here that no male may join a woman or group of women once they are seated; a woman must meet her escort outside the tavern and be seated with him.

SUMMER SPORTS. Denver has eighteen public *golf courses* and a number of excellent private clubs. The city parks have *tennis courts* and *swimming pools*. There are several *archery, trap,* and *rifle* ranges. *Boating* is possible on Sloans Lake, W. 26th Ave. at Sheridan Blvd., and at Cherry Creek Reservoir, ten miles southeast on State 83. Both have facilities for sail and power boats, and for water-skiing.

WINTER SPORTS. *Skiing:* the closest major ski area is just forty-four miles away, others are a bit farther but still readily accessible. Thanks to the Eisenhower Tunnel, many additional ski areas are within an easy drive of Denver. *Ice skating:* year-round skating is available at Denver University, or, in season, Court Place Plaza, downtown at 16th St. and Court Pl., and on the numerous lakes and ponds of the city's parks.

SPECTATOR SPORTS. *Automobile racing:* Englewood and Lakeside speedways offer drag and sports car racing throughout the summer, and the Continental Divide Raceways is only a twenty-minute drive south. *Baseball:* The *Denver Bears* oppose American Association foes at the Denver Mile High Stadium during the summer. *Basketball:* the *Denver Rockets* of the American Basketball Association and the University of Denver basketball team. *Football:* the *Denver Broncos* of the National Football League. *Golf:* Denver hosts numerous golf tournaments during the summer months. *Hockey:* the *Denver Spurs* of the World Hockey League are popular, as is the team from the University of Denver. *Horse and dog racing:* horseracing takes place at the Centennial Turf Club and greyhound races at the Mile High Kennel Club. *Rodeo:* the National Western Stock Show and Rodeo is held in January at the Stockyards and the Coliseum.

SHOPPING. At the hub of the Rocky Mountain region, Denver has much to offer in the way of interesting and unusual shops. Some of particular interest to the traveler include *Kohberg's* at 1720 Champa, with its own Indian silversmith; it sells valuable Indian artifacts and is a fascinating browsing shop. Jewelry of distinctive design may be seen at *Donald Pick's*, 550 East 12th. Mr. Pick is an authority on star sapphires. *Miller's Stockman Supply*, at 1350 Stout St., is one of the world's largest suppliers of gear and clothing for the cowboy and cattleman. In the *Cherry Creek Shopping Center* and the surrounding area are a number of notable shops, among them *Poco Imports*, 2617 East Third Ave. This is a charming, informal shop of Mexican imports. For the fashion-conscious male in the party, *Homer Reed, Ltd.*, 17th and Glenarm St., and *Robert Wilson's* at 1712 E. 6th Ave., are both interesting. The ladies will enjoy *Montaldo's*, 1632 California St., or *Cates First Avenue*, 105 Fillmore Street. Not far away, in the Cherry Creek Center, the *Tattered Cover* bookstore stocks practically every Western, travel, outdoors, and sports title. Skiers and sports enthusiasts will enjoy *Bob Kidders Ski Shop*, 1035 Cherokee St., and the *Ski Market*, 1156 Broadway, which offers an enormous selection of goods. At the Hilton Inn is *Joliffe's Oriental Art Shop. Harry Hoffman's*, at 18th and Glenarm Sts., one of the West's supermarket-style liquor emporiums, will interest many. *Cinderella City*, a super-large shopping complex in Englewood, the southern part of Denver, has a variety of types and sizes of shops, from the larger department stores to the smallest boutiques. *Larimer Square*, around 1400 and 1500 Larimer St., houses some of the newest and most unique shops in Denver, from *Poor Richards Leather Shoppe* (with fine hand-crafted leathers) to bike shops, import shops from around the world, candle corners, and more.

 WHAT TO DO WITH THE CHILDREN. A full day may easily be spent in *City Park*, with its zoo, children's zoo, and playgrounds. The *Denver Museum of Natural History and Planetarium* are in the park and should not be missed. Band concerts are given nightly in the summer months. *Congress Park* has a large outdoor swimming pool, and *Cherry Creek Reservoir* offers boating, swimming, and water-skiing. *Elitch Gardens* has a delightful kiddieland, as well as the usual amusement-park attractions and beautiful flower gardens. *Lakeside Amusement Park*, with stock-car races, speedboating, and amusement rides, has long been a favorite with the young. *Celebrity Sports Center*, 888 S. Colorado Boulevard, features game arcades, bowling, indoor Olympic size pool. *Mile High Stadium*, home of the Denver Bears baseball team and the Denver Broncos football team, offers an evening of spectator sport whenever the teams are playing at home. The *Denver Public Library* and *Phipps Auditorium* often have films or lectures of interest to children. Young ladies will delight in the *Goodwill Industries Doll Museum*, and both boys and girls will enjoy the *Wax Museum*. *Miniature golf* in the summer will keep youngsters busy at *Zeckendorf Plaza* at May-D&F. The *Colorado Railroad Museum*, in a depot-style building, houses many early Colorado railroad items. A trip to *The Fort*, an authentic reproduction of Bent's Fort, may be of interest—your children may try a piece of buffalo meat and browse in the trading post.

 HOTELS AND MOTELS in Denver range from the old, established, world-famous Brown Palace through its sister lodgings in the deluxe and expensive categories, then on to the many fine hotels scattered along the metropolitan area's highways and side streets. Many of the latter are connected to national chain operations. Cost figures are generally for the minimum or moderate priced rooms, unless a range is indicated. Listings are in order of price category.

The price categories in this section, for double occupancy, will average as follows: *Deluxe* $30, *Expensive* $25, *Moderate* $18, and *Inexpensive* $14. For a more complete description of these categories, see the *Hotels & Motels* part of THE ROCKIES & PLAINS *Facts at Your Fingertips* at the front of this volume.

DENVER

The Brown Palace. *Deluxe*. Tremont and 17th Sts. Truly one of the world's fine hotels, with superb service, western hospitality, and tasteful decoration. Elegant dining in the *Palace Arms* or the *San Marco Room*, relaxed dining in the *Ship Tavern*, where prime rib reigns. Beauty and barber shops, drugstore.

Cosmopolitan Hotel. *Deluxe*. Broadway and 18th Ave. In the heart of the entertainment and financial district, this large hotel provides TV, beauty shop, restaurant, cocktail lounge, entertainment.

Denver Hilton. *Deluxe*. 1550 Court Pl. A large establishment catering to Colorado's major conventions. The block-long second-floor lobby is unusual. Five dining areas and handsome cocktail lounge. Heated pool, saunas, color TV; barber and beauty shops, drugstore, airport bus available. In-building parking.

Executive Tower. *Deluxe*. 1405 Curtis St. A downtown skyscraper hotel, popular with convention guests. Health club.

Radisson Denver Hotel. *Deluxe*. 1790 Grant St. This enlarged hotel is located a short distance from the downtown area and features a sun deck and roof garden. Heated rooftop pool. Dining room, coffee shop, cocktail lounge, barber and beauty shops, drugstore, free parking. *Playboy Club* on top floor.

Regency Inn. *Deluxe*. 3900 Elati St. at W. 38th Ave. A large hotel in north Denver, popular with conventions. Two pools, saunas, exercise rooms, barber and beauty shops, gourmet restaurant and cocktail lounge. Free airport bus.

Writers' Manor. *Deluxe*. 1730 S. Colorado Blvd. A large, spacious motel with two heated pools, sauna. *Henrici's* serves excellent food and beverages.

Cherry Creek Inn. *Expensive*. 600 S. Colorado Blvd., 1 mi. north of Colorado Blvd. I-25 exit. This large motel offers a quiet, relaxed stay in southeast Denver. Heated pool, playground, barber and beauty shops. The *Red Slipper Room* is best known for its Sunday brunches.

Marriott Hotel. *Expensive*. I-25 at Hampden. Excellent location en route to Colorado Springs. All the modern facilities/amenities. Quality rooms. Indoor-outdoor pool. Recommended.

Ramada Inn Foothills. *Expensive*. 6th Ave. & Simms, on the way to ski areas. Pool and sauna. Attractive establishment.

Sheraton Inn-Airport. *Expensive*. 3535 Quebec St. at Stapleton Airport. This modern hotel offers indoor heated pool, sauna, health club, restaurant and cocktail lounge. Free airport bus.

Stouffer's Denver Inn. *Expensive*. 3203 Quebec. At airport. A well-run super motel with large indoor pool, sauna, and outstanding dining facilities.

Broadway Plaza. *Moderate*. Broadway at 11th Ave., 4 blks. south of State Capitol. In addition to attractive rooms, there are rooftop sundeck, free coffee. 24-hour cafe nearby.

Colburn Hotel. *Moderate*. 980 Grant Street, close to downtown area. All rooms with baths. Some kitchenettes and facilities for permanent guests.

Continental Denver Motor Hotel. *Moderate*. Valley Hwy, at N. Speer Blvd. This large, easily accessible motel offers guests a large heated pool, barber, free coffee, good dining room, coffee shop, cocktail lounge, dancing.

Denver TraveLodge. *Moderate*. Valley Hwy. at Speer Blvd. Small motel offers free coffee, sundeck. 24-hour coffee shop nearby.

Kipling Inn. *Moderate*. 715 Kipling St., 9½ mi. southwest just off US 6 in Lakewood. This west Denver motel offers heated pool, playground, restaurant, and cocktail lounge. Some units with kitchens.

Quality Inn-Central. *Moderate*. 1840 Sherman St. A large motel within walking distance of downtown, away from the traffic, offering heated pool, restaurant, and cocktail lounge. Covered parking.

American Family Lodge. *Inexpensive*. 5888 N. Broadway, 4 mi. north at I-25 exit 110. A good family motel with large, attractive rooms, heated pool, playground.

American Family Lodge-West. *Inexpensive*. 4735 Kipling St., 8 mi. west on I-70 in Wheatridge. Large motel with heated pool. 24-hour cafe opposite.

Anchor. *Inexpensive*. 2323 S. Broadway, 4 mi. south on State 87. Small motel, free coffee, pets, sundeck. 24-hour cafe nearby.

 DINING OUT. Denver is an eating-out town and offers much in the way of interesting and unusual fare. While there are many excellent restaurants serving international cuisine, those serving steak and lobster are particularly prevalent and popular. Most good restaurants prefer that reservations be made for dinner. Prices are for the medium-priced meals unless a range is indicated. For other worthwhile restaurants, check hotel listings. Restaurants are in order of price category.

Restaurant categories are as follows: *Deluxe* $11 and up, *Expensive* $6-$11, *Moderate* $4-$6, and *Inexpensive* $2-$4.50. These prices are for hors d'oeuvres or soup, *entrée*.

EDITORS' CHOICES

Rating restaurants is, at best, a subjective business, and obviously a matter of personal taste. It is, therefore, difficult to call a restaurant "the best" and hope to get unanimous agreement. The restaurants listed below are our choices of the best eating places in Denver, and the places we would choose if we were visiting the city.

TANTE LOUISE   Continental Cuisine
A delight of a European-style restaurant, from the fresh flowers on each table to the steak au poivre, the marinated hare, the veal medallions, and the lamb shanks. Superb appetizers, desserts, house wines. Intimate setting. About $30 for two, all inclusive. Easy to reach on 4900 East Colfax Ave.

PALACE ARMS   American Cuisine
This is the choice of most of Denver's social lions, and a favorite with Presidents. The decor is evocative of France, with posh props. The food is carefully prepared, and the service is in the grand manner. Native steaks are a specialty. Average price for dinner (per person): $15. 17th St. at Tremont Place (Brown Palace Hotel). If the Palace Arms is full, ask for the San Marco Room. Elegant atmosphere.

THE BROKER   American
The privacy-affording booths of this former bank vault make for a special experience. Dine on classic beef Wellington, or try the Broker's 15-oz. steak. Extensive wine list. Quiet, romantic. $30 for two. Dressy. 821 17th Street.

LAFFITE   Continental Cuisine
Located in Larimer Square, the restored district that housed the first businesses ever built in Denver. Italian specialties are complemented by excellent seafood and some Creole dishes. Special shrimp bar in the basement. Average price for dinner (per person): $13.50. 14th & Larimer Streets.

KYOTO Japanese Food

Four chefs from Japan hold forth in the Japanese center. Tatami rooms for those who care for authentic seating on the grass-matted floors, and also hibachi tables at which you eat where food is cooked. 1905 Lawrence Streets (Sakura Square).

Other recommended restaurants:

CONTINENTAL

Quorum. *Expensive.* 233 E. Colfax Ave. A favorite with the Capitol set across the street. Denver's award-winning restaurant features Neptune *mousseline*, *veal oscar*, *entrecote au poivre*, *tournedos*, and flaming desserts. Excellent cuisine and wine cellar. Open for lunch.

Top of the Rockies. *Expensive.* 1616 Glenarm Pl. in the Security Life Building. Following the breath-taking ride in a glass-enclosed elevator, the quiet decor of a French alpine village greets you. The view of the city and mountains from the thirtieth floor adds beauty to the charm of the restaurant. Specialties are Chateaubriand, flaming dishes. Dancing, entertainment.

AMERICAN/INTERNATIONAL

Cherry Creek Inn. *Expensive.* International/American dinners in Gay Nineties Old West setting. Well-known for Sunday brunches. 600 South Colorado Blvd.

Continental Broker. *Expensive.* Massive, international menu. Courtyard lunching, dining. Under Swiss management. Fine wines. 235 Fillmore.

The Fort. *Expensive.* 17 mi. southwest, just off US 285 near Morrison. Modeled after an early-day Colorado fur trading fort, this charming restaurant is set in the foothills overlooking Denver. Buffalo, elk, and beef steaks are charcoal-broiled Indian and trapper style.

Jake's. *Expensive.* 3900 Elati St. at W. 38th Ave. in the Regency Inn Hotel. Elegant, candlelit dining. House specialties are beef Wellington, prime rib, Chateaubriand, lobster thermidor, house pastries. High prices.

The Apple Tree Shanty. *Moderate.* Takes no reservations but usually enough room for families. The formula, "simple food blessed with love," works out. Pit-prepared ribs a house specialty. Sizable dessert menu. Dutch-style waitresses in sugar-candy setting. 8710 East Colfax.

Hungry Farmer. *Moderate.* 6925 W. Alameda, 1 mi. south of US 6 in Lakewood. Hearty farm food is served in a large barn. Prime rib, steak, barbecued ribs, chicken are only part of Granny's selection.

Drumstick. *Inexpensive.* 6501 W. Colfax Ave. This family restaurant serves chicken, shrimp, deluxe hamburgers. Daily specials including all-you-can-eat chicken 'n dumplings. Good value.

OLD ENGLISH

Henrici's Tudor Crown. *Expensive.* Merry Olde England in Denver, complete with oak beams, stained-glass windows, Windsor chairs, Simpson-on-the-Strand prime rib, Dover sole, and other English dishes. Cocktails. 1730 S. Colorado Blvd., in the Writer's Manor Motel.

Oak Room. *Expensive.* Warm English manor atmosphere, with many appetizers and excellent entrees. Menu tucked inside an English encyclopedia and other Olde Worlde touches. Good service. 3203 Quebec at Stouffer's Denver Inn.

WESTERN AMERICAN

El Rancho Colorado. *Expensive*. 18 mi. west at I-70 exit 55A in Golden. In addition to steak and prime rib, they serve fresh, boned rainbow trout. The rustic atmosphere includes a terrace cocktail lounge with a fireplace called "The Forge." A charming restaurant in the heart of the mountains.

North Woods Inn. *Moderate*. 6115 S. Santa Fe Dr., 12 mi. southwest on US 85 in Littleton. This locally popular restaurant serves steak, lobster, and logging-camp food with their own sourdough bread. The decor is north woods. Extra-large portions.

SEAFOOD

Boston Half Shell. *Expensive*. 1020 15th at Arapahoe in Brooks Towers. In a New England harborside decor, fresh seafood flown in daily. Live Maine lobster is a specialty. Nightly music in the piano bar.

Fisherman's Cove. *Expensive*. 1512 Curtis St. Fresh- and salt-water seafood, flown in fresh daily, is served in an atmosphere that recaptures the 18th-century New England fishing village. Decor includes authentic antiques and artifacts of that era. Waterfall fills live lobster tank.

ORIENTAL

Leo's Place. *Expensive*. A Victorian, antique-filled downtown favorite. Overbooked at lunch, reservations for superb Oriental (and American) suppers. Specialty: rack of lamb. Outstanding quality. 16th & Broadway.

Trader Vic's. *Expensive*. Broadway and 18th Ave. in the Cosmopolitan Hotel. Polynesian, Cantonese, and Continental dishes are served in a South Seas decor. Exotic drinks are available from the bar.

The Chiling Restaurant. *Moderate*. Mandarin specialties include unique Mongolian barbeque. Six meats and many sauces, buffet-style. Seconds allowed. Interesting Oriental liquor. 2980 South Colorado Blvd.

The Lotus Room. *Inexpensive*. A busy Chinese family restaurant, frequented by many Denverites. Excellent chop suey, Chinese duck, and countless other dishes. Good value. Informal. West 9th & Speer.

MEXICAN

Casa Bonita. *Inexpensive*. West Colfax at JCRS Center. Authentic Mexican food in a multi-tiered restaurant decorated with murals that tell the history of Mexico. *Albondigas*, Mexican meatballs, are an unusual specialty. Cafeteria style at lunch, table service in the evening.

GERMAN

The Ridgeview Inn. *Moderate*. Genuine German offerings for a hungry clientele. Sauerbraten, schnitzel, Kassler, Rindsrouladen—the real article, not *ersatz*. Peter Hellerman, proprietor, hails from Germany. Imported beers. West 44th at Garrison, in Wheatridge.

Heidelberg. *Inexpensive*. Modest, family-run place, popular with budgeters and students. German pot roast, veal cutlets, smoked pork, plus American steaks. 1175 East Colfax.

ITALIAN

Josephinas. *Expensive*. Roaring Twenties ambiance on Larimer Square. Excellent Italian lasagna, spaghetti, pizza, chicken. Bar. 1433 Larimer.

Mario's. *Expensive.* 1747 Tremont Pl. While you enjoy fine Italian-American cuisine, "Mario's Singers" serenade you with their renditions of grand opera, light opera, and popular Broadway musical hits. A unique restaurant with an Italian cafe atmosphere.

FRENCH

The Brasserie. *Expensive.* French cooking with a flair. Dinners include lamb, veal, rabbit, fine chicken in wine. Open for lunch. 158 Fillmore, in the Cherry Creek Shopping Center.

Mon Petit. *Expensive.* A dining adventure that might be called "Mon Grand." Palatial villa supping. One of the area's most elaborate menus and wine lists. Classy decor. 7000 West 38th Ave., Wheatridge.

EXPLORING COLORADO

Colorado is such a large state, with so many interesting attractions, that a visitor could spend two weeks exploring it and still not cover every area, or all its important features. It takes more than a day just to drive through it: Julesburg in the northeastern corner (named for Jules Beni, the Overland Stage station agent whose ears were cut off by badman Jake Slade) is all of 591 highway miles across plains and over peaks from Cortez in the southwestern corner (Ute and Navajo country).

To see the essentials, plan three one-day trips from Denver, plus one more ambitious circular trip around the state.

Only two major sections of the state are missed in these tours. The first is the eastern plains, notably the agriculturally rich South Platte and Arkansas river valleys, with warm-water fishing, harvest festivals, and pheasant hunting. The other is the sparsely populated northwest (trout fishing in the upper Yampa River and its tributaries, skiing at Steamboat Springs, deer and elk hunting, and Dinosaur National Park where one can watch paleontologists working to uncover dinosaur fossils).

A First Tour

Take the Valley Highway I-25) north out of Denver. Turn off on the Denver-Boulder Turnpike, which is plainly marked, 3.5 miles north of the Denver limits.

Approaching Boulder, the towering, tilted, slablike peaks on the left are the Flatirons. At their base, standing out like a medieval castle, is the home of the National Center for Atmospheric Research. Nearby are the National Bureau of Standards Laboratories, which study, among other things, radio waves, and cryogenics, the science of extremely cold temperatures. Boulder is the home of the University of Colorado, whose parklike campus and distinctive red sandstone buildings at the foot of the Flatirons make it one of the nation's most beautiful schools. Folsom Field, where Big Eight Conference football games are played, seats 50,000. A spectacular side trip is a drive up Flagstaff Mountain for picnics and a view of Boulder and the plains. Time your mountaintop arrival for dinner at Flagstaff House, a restaurant with a veiw.

Now you have several choices. You can continue north through Boulder fifteen miles along State 7 to Lyons. The road leads along the foothills with a broad panorama to the right of an agricultural plain dotted with irrigation reservoirs. Lyons, where much Colorado sandstone is quarried for use in patios and building, is also the entrance to the North St. Vrain Canyon, leading to Estes Park. This is a pleasant twenty-mile climb up relatively gentle slopes, much of it within Roosevelt National Forest.

Or, for a view of more unusual country, turn west in Boulder on State 119 for a sixteen-mile drive up Boulder Canyon to the rugged mountain town of Nederland. The last two miles wind along the edge of Barker Reservoir, deep, cold, and fair for fishing when full. Turn right at Nederland onto State 172, the Peak to Peak Highway. It winds through lodgepole pine and aspen forests, with startling views of the Continental Divide's rocky ridges. From Nederland it is forty-five easy miles to Estes Park by way of the tiny communities of Ward, Raymond, and Allenspark. Spur roads on each side of 172 lead to alpine lakes with picnic areas and hiking trails, and to slumbering old mining camps long abandoned to wind, weather, and pack-rats. Don't be in a hurry to cover this stretch. Excursions along these side roads will prove rewarding. Of particular interest is Arapaho Glacier, which supplies a portion of Boulder's municipal water; it can be reached by a hike that requires a full morning.

Rocky Mountain National Park

Only a tenderfoot looks for a park at Estes Park. "Park" is an old western term for a mountain valley, and this was Joel Estes' domain in 1860. When two other families moved in to share this huge, rugged hollow in the Rockies, Estes moved out, complaining of "too many" people. Estes Park is the gateway to Rocky Mountain National Park, a 405-square-mile reserve of towering peaks and untouched forests set aside for the public in 1915. The town of Estes Park has a year-round population of only about 1,500, but in summer tens of thousands of tourists flock to the resort hotels, dude ranches, motels, and campgrounds in the area. An aerial tramway to the top of 8,896-foot Prospect Mountain offers a good view of the peaks and valleys. Boating and fishing on Lake Estes, scores of miles of riding and hiking trails, and hundreds of miles of trout streams are other attractions in this area. The summit of Longs Peak (14,256 feet) can be scaled via trail by most persons in reasonably good health, but its sheer East Face—known as the "Diamond"—is one of the nation's most challenging climbs.

The wilds of Rocky Mountain National Park may be explored afoot at leisure, or one can drive through the Park over the nation's renowned Trail Ridge Road, skirting chasms a thousand feet deep, and winding over the windswept tundra above the timberline. Summer comes late to the high country, but brings with it a profusion of exquisite, tiny wildflowers. Near the top of Milner Pass, elevation 10,758 feet (where you cross the Continental Divide), is a museum of tundra ecology where the wonderfully diverse flora and fauna of this climatically inhospitable land are displayed. Trail Ridge Road is usually closed by snow in late October or early November and not reopened until Memorial Day, sometimes only after strenuous work by road crews, while young athletes celebrate the event by skiing on the snow at the top and on the icy water of Grand Lake at the western foot of the road. In midsummer, however, the country above timberline is delightfully cool after the heat of the plains. Grand Lake (8,380 feet) is considered one of North America's loftiest yacht anchorages.

It is sixty-two miles from Estes Park to the town of Granby, on the western side of the Divide. Allow yourself three hours for a leisurely drive, more if you can afford it. Three sizable lakes—Grand Lake, Shadow Mountain and Granby Reservoir—make the Granby area a recreation center. Dude ranches abound. The Colorado River and its tributaries provide trout fishing. The lakes have been planted with kokanee salmon, among other species, and they provide fair angling as well as a unique sport—snagging with treble hooks—during the early winter spawning season. Since the kokanee die, anyway, after they spawn, snagging is permitted to avoid wasting a food resource. Granby is also in the center of the Middle Park area, noted for its dude and cattle ranches, and lumbering.

Turn east at Granby on US 40. It is an eighty-nine-mile drive back to Denver. The highway runs through vast hay meadows, past Fraser (where President Eisenhower liked to fish), the Winter Park ski development at the western mouth of the Moffat Tunnel, and up over 11,314-foot Berthoud Pass. At the summit a chair lift carries hardy tourists higher in summer for some impressive vistas from atop the Continental Divide.

Once you've crossed Berthoud, it's only an hour's drive, all downhill, to Denver, by way of the old mining town of Idaho Springs.

Here's the second circle tour:

Drive west out of Denver on Alameda Avenue, past expanding housing developments and sprawling Denver Federal Center, headquarters for major government agencies. The Bureau of Reclamation Laboratories tests dam designs and trains hydraulic engineers from all parts of the Free World. Alameda Avenue eventually swings over the rock outcroppings known as the Hogbacks and opens up on Red Rocks Park. There is a 10,000-seat amphitheater between two towering red sandstone promontories. One, shaped like the prow of a giant liner, is called "Shiprock." The other is "Creation Rock." Silt deposits under a prehistoric sea formed the layers that went into these rocks; a cataclysmic upheaval forced the sea to retreat, shattering the rock formations and thrusting them upward. Erosion by wind and rain carved the red stone into the fanciful shapes visible today. Many visitors find it well worth their time to park their cars and climb into the amphitheater for a view of Denver in the distance. Easter Sunrise services are held here, and concerts are scheduled during the summer. The stage is one hundred feet wide, and the acoustics are said to be ideal for musical productions.

First Territorial Capital

From Red Rocks Park, backtrack to the Hogback Road (State 26) and drive north a mile to US 40. State 26 turns into US 40 at I-70. Bear right, downhill, on US 40, which takes you back toward Denver. Stay on the highway about a mile, then take the turnoff to the left toward Golden on County 93. The turnoff is plainly marked. Another mile takes you to four-lane US 6, and Golden is just a mile farther on. Here is the site of the first territorial capital, the Colorado School of Mines (where tomorrow's civil, mining, and petroleum engineers get a first-rate education), and the Coors Brewery, which is open for tours.

From Golden, return to US 6 for a thirteen-mile drive up winding Clear Creek Canyon. The highway crosses and recrosses a brawling mountain stream that, despite its name, is rarely clear. The road bores through some tunnels and clings to the creek bank at the foot of beetling cliffs. It is difficult to believe that the route follows the bed of a long-abandoned railroad.

The Old Opera House

At the fork reading "Central City," turn right onto State 119. Seven more miles of gentle climbing brings you to Blackhawk, which looks like a set from a Western movie. Turn left here on State 279. Central City is only a mile up this steep, twisting road, but it is a memorable ride. The earth on each side is cruelly gashed by the remains of gold mines. Victorian homes, many restored and used as summer residences, cling precariously to the hillsides. Once 15,000 persons lived in these two communities. Now the permanent residents number scarcely more than 350. But summer is a lively time. The Central City Opera House on Eureka Street, built in 1878 with granite walls four feet thick, is the home of an opera and play season. Artists from the Metropolitan and other leading opera companies fly out to vacation and sing. The operas are followed by a Broadway hit play, often staged with the original cast. The Opera House, the Teller House Hotel completed in 1872 (President Grant slept here), and other historic buildings are well preserved. Along with Victorian furnishings, diamond dust mirrors and the like, the Teller House boasts the fabled *Face on Barroom Floor*, painted on the floor of the Gold Nugget Bar in 1936 by the late Herndon Davis. The face, of a dark and brooding beauty, is protected by plate glass.

The pavement ends at Central City (8,560 feet and cool even in midsummer), but the adventure is just starting. Continue up the Quartz Hill Road, usually kept in good shape, to Russell Gulch. Now begins a looping, twisting, seven-mile descent to Idaho Springs. It's not dangerous if you're careful, but it's a long way straight down if you should slip! The scenery, especially in fall when the distant hillsides blaze with golden aspen, is well worth the hairpin curves.

Idaho Springs, named for the hot springs known to the Indians and still used today, is the center of a once-rich mining district that has readjusted its sights to the tourist trade. Take the overpass that crosses US 6-40 and follow State 103 along Chicago Creek. Summer homes dot the area. The road climbs steadily through stands of lodgepole pine and aspen for fourteen miles, and suddenly there's gemlike Echo Lake, 10,600 feet above sea level. Camping and picnic facilities are available. Echo Lake is among the mountain parks maintained by the city of Denver, and trails lead to scenic vantage points looking both north and south along the Rockies.

America's Highest Road

Echo Lake is only part-way up to the top of 14,260-ft Mount Evans. The highway twists and climbs another fourteen miles, past icy Summit Lake (where sometimes a herd of mountain sheep frolics and distracts trout fishermen) to the very peak of Mount Evans. This is the nation's highest automobile road. Despite the elevation, the trip is not difficult for experienced drivers. Refreshments and souvenirs are available at Crest House, while atop a rock pile a few feet away you'll see the laboratories where cosmic ray and other high-altitude experiments are carried on. One of the thrills of a drive to the top is watching a summer thunderstorm taking shape to swirl and boil over the forests far below. The altitude is not harmful to the average person in good health, although exertion is difficult in the oxygen-thin air.

Cars likewise will perform at less than usual efficiency. The road above Echo Lake is closed in winter by snow.

Those who prefer to view their mountains from a distance can skip the Mount Evans trip and continue on paved State 103. It climbs briefly, drops to cross 9,807-foot Squaw Pass, then descends in long, easy grades, each turn opening up new mountain vistas. The end of the trail here is Bergen Park, another unit in the 20,000-acre Denver mountain parks system. A tiny community has grown up at this crossroads. One of the attractions is Clock Manor, a museum devoted to timepieces of all kinds.

Another three miles of driving returns you to US 40 (I-70), which leads past Genesee, another of Denver's mountain parks. If you see a cluster of out-of-state automobiles parked at the edge of the highway, it probably means the buffalo have come out of the timber and are grazing close by.

Don't be in too great a hurry now. The best is yet to come. Two miles farther, take a left turn onto State 68 to 7,500-foot Lookout Mountain, only two miles away. Buffalo Bill's tomb is located here, along with a museum containing Cody's guns, clothing, and mementoes of his career. If at all possible, plan to reach Lookout Mountain just before dusk. Watch Metropolitan Denver's lights wink on as darkness creeps across the plains—hundreds of thousands of lights stretching in every direction, criss-crossing a half mile below in a latticework of brilliance. The air will be cool and scented with pine, and Denver will offer you an unforgettable sight from this mountain lookout.

Although it is possible to return to US 40, the more interesting descent is down the seven-mile Lariat Trail, so named because the road twists like a rope. Each turn provides a view of Denver's lights from a different angle. At the foot of the mountain is Golden once again, and from here it's a twenty-minute trip back to Denver via US 6.

The third circle tour from Denver southbound on I-25 leads to Pikes Peak, and the city of Colorado Springs. I-25 first swings past the University of Denver stadium and the comfortable upper-middle-class southeast Denver residential area. After several miles of apartment complexes the road gives way to rolling wheatfields and pastureland.

Thirty miles south of Denver is Castle Rock, seat of Douglas County, and a town that takes its name from a distinctive castle-shaped rock rearing behind the community. A rough road winds to the summit, where, on a clear day (and it's usually clear), one can see nearly two hundred miles in every direction. Indians and early explorers used it as a landmark.

The terrain rises almost imperceptibly over the next nine miles until the highway crosses the Palmer Lake divide south of Larkspur.

Air Force Academy

Pikes Peak is closer now, and so is the Air Force Academy, youngest and flashiest of the service schools. The entrance is plainly marked. Stop at the sentry box to pick up a map, then drive directly to the overlook for a general view of the main Academy buildings across the expansive intramural athletic fields. The academic area is not open to the public, but various other areas are. Everyday except Sunday and during the brief summer vacations when the cadets are visiting Air Force bases, the cadet corps assembles at 11:30 A.M. to march in formation to lunch at the dining hall. This is a solemn, stirring parade to martial music and a sight worth seeing. Also open to the public is the many-spired glass and aluminum chapel, variously described as an accordion-like collection of wigwams and an inspiring contemporary cathedral. The roads through the 17,900-acre Academy grounds are open during daylight hours, and it is possible to drive through the reservation and join I-25 just north of Colorado Springs.

Colorado Springs

Colorado Springs is the state's second largest city, long famous as a watering place and summer resort. It was founded in 1871 by General William Jackson Palmer, promoter of the Denver and Rio Grande Railroad. General Palmer, who made or unmade towns depending on where he built his railroads, was also prominent in the planning of Colorado Springs, which he determined would have a gracious and cultured atmosphere not unlike his home town of London. Thus its nickname "Little Lun'on," also attributable to its popularity with British visitors. Pikes Peak looms over the city. In fact, the mountain seems to rise right at the end of Pikes Peak Avenue in downtown Colorado Springs. (There are many places in Colorado with the name "Springs"—Pagosa Springs, Poncha Springs, Steamboat Springs— but only Colorado Springs is referred to as "The Springs.") Vacationers can spend days visiting the various attractions in this area. A few of the more notable ones are described in this chapter.

Garden of the Gods is an area of odd and unusual formations of bright sandstone hues. In summer, the Junior Chamber of Commerce sponsors chuckwagon dinners here three times a week. (Reservations necessary.)

In Colorado Springs proper is the Fine Arts Center, with its permanent collection of southwestern Indian, religious, and folk art, as well as contemporary American works. The Pioneer Museum archives contain locally important historical mementos. The Van Briggle Pottery works offers tours of its plant, where art and garden pottery is created with locally mined clays.

Just south of Colorado Springs is the five-star *Broadmoor Hotel* complex founded by Spencer Penrose. This is a complete resort community in itself, with a luxury hotel, seven dining rooms, convention hall, 36-hole golf course, an outdoor pool, year-round ice-skating rink, rodeo grounds, miniature railway, skiing slope in winter (with a snowmaking machine), carriage museum, and zoo. The zoo is on Cheyenne Mountain and features a number of rare animals. Particularly outstanding is the primate house. High above the zoo, reached by a toll road, is the Shrine of the Sun memorial to Will Rogers. A granite tower, one hundred feet high, houses carillons. The interior walls are decorated with frescoes by the late Randall Davey. An observation balcony provides a sweeping view of Colorado's eastern plains.

Adjoining Colorado Springs on the west, along US 24, is Manitou Springs, a thriving tourist center. The mineral springs from which the community gets its name are still active. Tourist attractions, most of which charge fees, abound. Manitou Springs is also the terminal for the long trip by cog railway to the summit of Pikes Peak and the cable car system to the top of Mount Manitou.

Driving up Pikes Peak

Four miles beyond Manitou Springs, up steep and historic Ute Pass, is Cascade, the cutoff point for the automobile highway up Pikes Peak. The climbing season usually starts in early June and lasts until the first weekend in October, although this toll road may be open longer. The highway climbs 7,309 feet in nineteen miles to the summit. The Pikes Peak Hill Climb automobile races are held each July 4.

US 24 continues gently uphill to Woodland Park, center of a dude ranch and recreation area. Seven miles farther is Divide, where the road forks. US 24 goes on into South Park. State 67, turning left, offers a leisurely eighteen-mile drive through hay meadows and pine groves on the "back" side of Pikes Peak until, at the crest of Tenderfoot Hill, the once fabulously rich Cripple Creek-Victor Gold Fields stretch before you. In summer Cripple Creek bustles with tourists, but when they are gone the basin is peopled by only a handful of residents, many of whom are natives of the area who hope that one day gold mining will become profitable again. The hillsides are dotted with the tailings dumps of abandoned mines and weather-scarred wooden buildings that seem to lean more precariously after every winter. Oldtime residents maintain a free museum, where one can get an accurate idea of what the area was like when twenty thousand persons worked, brawled, reared families, got drunk, became rich, or went broke in Cripple Creek and its satellite communities. (Cripple Creek and its sister ghost town, Victor, can also be reached from Colorado Springs by the Gold Camp road, a gravel route that winds, twists, and tunnels for thirty-six miles through wild, spectacular country over the abandoned roadbed of the Cripple Creek Short Line Railroad.)

Cripple Creek's liveliest attraction is the Imperial Hotel, refurbished by Wayne and Dorothy Mackin, where in summer a professional cast stages oldtime Western melodramas. (Reservations are advisable.)

US 85 is an alternate route into Denver from the south, generally following the course of the South Platte. West of the highway, across Plum Creek, almost hidden in the bottom growth, is Louviers, where Du Pont Powder Plant manufactures the dynamite used in mines and mountain construction work.

Fourth Tour—Circling Colorado

This 1,250-mile circular tour of Colorado, beginning and ending in Denver, is designed to take a minimum of four days and hit most of the state's interesting areas not covered in the three previous tours. The trip can be extended to five, six, or more days simply by lingering at places that appeal to the visitor and exploring nearby attractions.

From Denver, this tour immediately heads southwest on US 285, past Morrison (which is a stone's throw from Red Rocks Park; see *Second Tour*) and up the gash slashed by Turkey Creek into the dark granite foothills of the Rockies. Although the ridges tower high above the road, the highway is wide and the grade gentle. Generally, the route follows the old Denver-Leadville stagecoach route, on which travelers braved rutted trails, primitive accommodations, and desperadoes to reach the silver diggings in the two-mile-high Leadville area. Later, the Colorado, South Park & Pacific Railroad traveled much the same course in an ambitious if foolhardy effort to reach the coast via Leadville. (The dreams of these men were greater than their knowledge of railroad economics. To meet expenses, it was necessary to charge more to transport freight from Denver to Leadville than from New York to San Francisco by way of Cape Horn.) Only a few crumbling ties and rusting spikes, covered by underbrush, remain.

At Bailey, US 285 winds along the banks of the South Platte River. Near Grant, high on a hill to the right, there appears the fifty-two-foot-tall glazed white statue of *Christ of the Rockies*. It stands guard over the highway and picnic grounds which are illuminated at night. Also near Grant, the 23.3-mile-long Roberts Tunnel under the Continental Divide discharges water collected on the Western Slope into the South Platte for eventual delivery to Denver homes and industries.

Favorite Mountain Scene

Sixty-five miles from Denver rises 10,000-foot Kenosha Pass, one of the state's lowest. The highway curves to open a magnificent panorama of South Park, a lofty valley stretching forty miles to the south and west, rimmed by darkly wooded hills and snowcapped peaks. (This view of South Park is the favorite mountain scene of many Coloradans.) Several tributaries of the South Platte twist and loop over the park's broad hay meadows (the growing season is too short for other agricultural pursuits), and sleek Herefords and Black Angus cattle graze placidly on land that once heard the thunder of buffalo hooves.

Fairplay, eighty-five miles from Denver, is the valley's largest community, with a permanent population of a little more than four hundred. The town was named by men who settled the area in 1859 after having been chased out of the nearby Tarryall placer beds by competitive miners. Near the center of Fairplay is a stone monument to "Prunes," a burro that mooched a living from the townsfolk for years after having labored several decades for a variety of prospectors. Local residents have also recreated an oldtime mining town called South Park City, where a visitor can see what frontier life was like more than a century ago.

The tourist may continue down South Park and over Trout Creek Pass thirty-four miles to Buena Vista, on the Arkansas River. The State Reformatory is at Buena Vista, at the base of the Collegiate Range, a string of 14,000-foot peaks with such names as Princeton, Yale, Harvard, and Oxford.

Our circular tour, however, turns north (right) at Fairplay on State 9 toward 11,541-foot Hoosier Pass. Five miles beyond Fairplay is what remains of Alma, once a busy mining and placer site and one of the state's first gold camps. It was here that a dance hall girl, known only as Silver Heels, remained to nurse miners stricken in a smallpox epidemic when others fled. Eventually she too contracted smallpox. She survived, but her beauty was destroyed, and one night she slipped away. According to legend a heavily veiled woman, presumably Silver Heels, returned several times to visit the graves of miners who died in the epidemic. A mountain to the northwest of this community is named in her honor. A rough dirt road leads from Alma over 13,185-foot Mosquito Pass to Leadville, but this is not recommended for the average tourist.

Hoosier Pass over the Continental Divide cuts through the 14,000-foot peaks of the Park Range. A few miles north of the pass is Breckenridge, another former mining camp, which became an extensive ski and summer home development. In 1936, it was discovered that a strip of land surrounding Breckenridge had never been taken into the United States. Somehow, the various purchases and annexations had not included the area. The late governor Ed C. Johnson issued a proclamation to make the land a part of the United States and Colorado.

Highway 9 follows the Blue River to Frisco and the Dillon Reservoir, an enormous lake filled for the first time in the summer of 1965. The water stored here is diverted from the Colorado River watershed to the state's eastern slope, flowing under the Continental Divide via the Roberts Tunnel to Grant, on the way to Denver's mains. The reservoir covered the site of the original town of Dillon, which was moved to a wooded hillside on the northern edge of the lake. Dillon Reservoir has become a center for boating and fishing, with extensive jeep and riding trails in the mountains surrounding it. There are many condominiums and deluxe motor hotels, such as the Silverthorne Ramada, to accommodate the four-season tourists.

Our route turns left at Frisco onto US 6, along the rippling waters of Tenmile Creek. The seven-mile-long drive to Wheeler Junction is unusual— the massive rock walls that rise almost straight up in a sheer cliff are unlike most Colorado canyons, whose walls taper up in a sharp V.

The left fork of the highway at Wheeler Junction (State 91) leads to Leadville, a community of more than 4,300, two miles above sea level. During the late nineteenth century, when it was one of the world's richest silver producers, it had a population of some 30,000. The glory that was is preserved in places like the Hotel Vendome, Healy House Museum, and the Tabor Opera House. The greatest of the silver kings was H. A. W. Tabor, who built a multi-million-dollar fortune on a $17 grubstake, then died virtually destitute. The Tabor story is the basis for the American opera *The Ballad of Baby Doe*, which was the name of Tabor's blond second wife. His divorce from his prim and proper first spouse, Augusta, to marry Baby Doe, was a scandal that rocked both Colorado and Washington, where Tabor had gone as an interim senator. Tabor's last words of advice to Baby Doe were, "hold on to the Matchless," the mine which had made him as much as $100,000 a month. The unfortunate Baby Doe lived her last days as a recluse in a cabin at the Matchless, and she was found frozen to death there in 1935. The mine is preserved as a museum. Many residents of Leadville work at Climax, twelve miles away, where a mountain is systematically being cut down to produce most of the free world's molybdenum, a steel-hardening alloy.

In the interest of conserving time, however, the tour turns right at Wheeler Junction, remaining on US 6. It leads over Vail Pass and down along Gore Creek to Vail Village, where an alpine ski town has sprouted along with condominium apartments, and luxury homes. Fortunate is the visitor whose arrival coincides with the turning of the aspen, usually in mid-September. The lower reaches of the entire Gore Range seem to be orange and gold. The lift ride to mid-Vail and the spacious sundecks there provide an unforgettable vista, particularly if an early snow has frosted the high peaks.

Highway 6 (also I-70) continues westward past Eagle, the answer to a sportsman's dreams, with trout in the Eagle river, and elk or deer in the nearby hills. West of Eagle, the mountains give way to a high plateau. The Colorado and Eagle rivers meet at Dotsero, where two branches of the Denver & Rio Grande Railway come together for the run down spectacular Glenwood Canyon. Here the Colorado River has cut a 1,000-foot chasm between slate-colored cliffs. North of the Colorado lies the White River wilderness area, heavily wooded and virtually unscarred by roads. More than 900,000 acres are set aside in this preserve. Some of the state's best fishing—rainbow, German brown, and brook trout which weigh uniformly more than two pounds each—is to be found in lonely lakes and rushing streams at the end of a fifteen-mile horseback trek. So isolated is the White River country that many longtime Coloradans have never set foot in it. Experienced packers are available as guides.

At the lower end of Glenwood Canyon is Glenwood Springs, principal supply point of a vast recreation area. Within Glenwood is a 600-foot-long swimming pool, open the year-round, fed by hot and cold sulphur springs. Presidents Teddy Roosevelt and Taft vacationed here. The Roaring Fork, one of the outstanding fishing streams in a state of outstanding streams, enters the Colorado here.

Aspen Fun and Culture

Forty-two miles south of Glenwood Springs, via State 82, is famed Aspen, Colorado's top ski center and a former silver-mining town that was transformed into a mountain cultural mecca by the money and vision of the late Chicago industrialist, Walter P. Paepcke. The summer Aspen Music Festival and Music School, and the Aspen Institute for Humanistic Studies, which sponsors lectures and seminars on a variety of significant subjects, are now widely known. Within a twenty-mile radius of Aspen are some twenty-five trout lakes and a thousand miles of trout streams, plus countless miles of hiking and riding trails. Mountains to challenge expert climbers are numerous, while winter explorers can ride sleds behind the Huskies of Toklat Kennels at Ashcroft or photograph ghostly ruins abandoned to the elements when the silver petered out. Not far from Aspen, up the Crystal River Valley, is Marble, where stone for the Lincoln Memorial and the Tomb of the Unknown Soldier was quarried. Four huge ski developments—Aspen Mountain, Aspen Highlands, Snowmass, and Buttermilk Mountain—offer hundreds of miles of ski runs of varying difficulty, and some of the lifts run in summer to take tourists to scenic lookouts. For the more adventurous driver, State 82 continues over 12,095-foot Independence Pass, graveled but rough, to Leadville. The Pass is closed in winter.

The tour route, however, backtracks down to Glenwood Springs, and then, via US 6, it proceeds twenty-six miles to Rifle. Rifle is at the edge of what may be the world's greatest deposit of oil shale. Mineral beds two thousand and more feet thick lie in mahogany-colored cliffs to the north and west of Rifle, extending into Utah and Wyoming. These deposits hold more oil than all the petroleum man has used since the beginning of time. Colorado's shale reserves alone are estimated at one trillion, four hundred billion barrels of oil. Scientists employed by both the government and private industry have been researching economical methods of extracting the oil from the rock.

Grand Junction—Uranium Capital

From Rifle, US 6 runs parallel to the Colorado River sixty-two miles to Grand Junction, largest city in western Colorado, with a population of approximately twenty-five thousand.

Grand Junction, which gets its name from the joining of the Colorado and Gunnison rivers, is a thriving transportation and shipping center. In the mid-fifties it boomed as the capital of the uranium rush. The boom has tapered off, but Grand Junction remains important as the location of the Atomic Energy Commission's raw materials (uranium) procurement office. A few years ago downtown Grand Junction merchants, in an effort to keep business from fleeing to suburban shopping centers, approved a mall-type shopping park along the main street. The experiment not only resulted in beautification of the downtown area, but was an economic success.

Ten miles west of Grand Junction is Colorado National Monument, twenty-eight square miles of dramatically eroded stone spires, canyons, and fossil beds. Two to three hours spent in a circle drive along the dark canyon rims is time well invested.

Make sure your gas tank is full before taking US 50 southeast out of Grand Junction. Nine miles up the highway is the tiny crossing called Whitewater. Turn right here onto State 141, and prepare to enter some of Colorado's wildest, loneliest canyon country, an area largely overlooked by many tourists. The highway, paved and well-maintained, stretches through sage-brush flats and dry washes for forty-four miles to Gateway, where it crosses the muddy, shallow Dolores River. For the next thirty-seven miles to Uravan, the road borders first the Dolores, and then the San Miguel (pronounced San M'gill) rivers, leading past towering red sandstone cliffs, polished by wind and sand into monolithic slabs, and often into the shapes of ships and pyramids.

Back in 1881, gold-seekers found a soft yellow-orange ore near what is now Uravan. Its main use was for coloring pottery. In 1898, several tons of this ore were shipped to France, and Mme. Marie Curie used it in experiments that resulted in the extraction of radium. For the next thirty years, this region produced about half the world's radium supply. A mill was built at Uravan to process vanadium, a steel-hardener, from the same ores. During World War II, in the crash program to develop a nuclear bomb, the waste rock in the tailings piles at the Uravan mill was reprocessed to extract the suddenly precious uranium which had been thrown away. The mill, now operated by Union Carbide, extracts uranium from local mines, and vanadium has become just a by-product.

Nineteen miles past Uravan, take the right fork to State 141 for the fifty-seven-mile drive to Dove Creek. This apparent wasteland has a strange, lonely beauty of its own, but you'll be glad to reach civilization once more at Dove Creek, center of a prosperous pinto bean-growing area. Total distance from Grand Junction to Dove is 169 miles. Dove Creek was little more than a raw frontier until farmers from the dust bowl in eastern Colorado came in to conquer the arid flats. Zane Grey, the western author, lived here for some years.

You are back in the mainstream again. US 666 is a fast, smooth road to Cortez, thirty-seven miles southeast, trading center for sheep herders, cow-men, miners, prospectors, oilfield hands, and residents of the Ute Mountain Indian Reservation. Cortez is the jumping-off place to Shiprock and the Navajo Indian country of New Mexico and to Monument Valley, Flagstaff, and the Grand Canyon in Arizona, by way of the new highway through the Four Corners. This is where Utah, Arizona, New Mexico, and Colorado meet, the only place where four states come precisely together. With a population of close to six thousand, Cortez is also the closest city to Mesa Verde National Park, only ten miles to the east.

There is no other national park quite like Mesa Verde, which means "green table" in Spanish. The table is a plateau rising fifteen hundred feet above the surrounding valleys. In canyons hewn into the plateau, an early tribe of Indians grew corn with water brought in by primitive irrigation systems, and built apartment-like dwellings under overhanging cliffs. One settlement, called Cliff House, has two hundred rooms on eight levels. A study of tree rings indicates the area suffered a severe drought in the thirteenth century, and the Indians wandered away circa 1276. Thanks to the dry air and the protection of the caves, many well-preserved dwellings and artifacts were found by the first white men. The National Park Service has restored many of the ruins and conducts tours among them, with lectures about the people who lived in them seven hundred years ago. Visitors would be wise to visit the museum at park headquarters before joining the tours. The tours are free and start at frequent intervals during the summer season. Limited accommodations are available in the park.

Spectacular Mountains

Thirty-six miles east of the park entrance is Durango, metropolis of southwestern Colorado, with a population of more than 11,000. Once a wide-open frontier town, Durango is a prosperous trading, tourist, and college center. It is the home of Fort Lewis College, whose campus is atop a steep hill overlooking the city. The houses hug the base of the San Juan mountains, which many Coloradans consider the most spectacular in the state. Fishing, hunting, and skiing are available within a few miles of downtown.

The best-known summer attraction here is the Rio Grande's narrow-gauge train to Silverton, a forty-five-mile trip up the gorge of Rio de las Animas Perdidas (River of Lost Souls), shortened by natives to the Animas River. Belching smoke and cinders, an ancient steam engine puffs through thick forests and along steep cliffsides for an unforgettable ride into yesterday.

The time in Silverton is just long enough to lunch, stroll around the streets and peer into abandoned buildings, and browse among the curio shops. If you don't find any agates on the Animas River's gravel bars, numerous youngsters are anxious to sell you specimens of iron pyrite, azurite, malachite, or quartz crystals for twenty-five to fifty cents. Although it once boasted 10,000 residents, Silverton now has considerably fewer than a thousand. It is the seat of San Juan County, which has the distinction of being so high and rugged that it has not one acre of farmland in it.

To save time, some visitors prefer to ride up on the train and be met at Silverton by a member of the party who has driven the fifty miles via US 550, continuing north without returning to Durango. (Those who make the round trip by train report the descent is just as interesting as the ascent.)

Highway 550 rises quickly from Silverton to 11,018-foot Red Mountain Pass (named for the reddish hue of the soil), strikingly beautiful in summer but impassable in winter. This is the "Million Dollar Highway," which follows a toll road route laid out by Otto Mears in the 1880s. The origin of the name is obscure. Some say it was so named because of the cost, while others contend it is because gold-bearing gravel was used before its value was discovered.

Beyond the pass is Ouray (prounced U-ray), built in a mountain pocket a mile and a half above sea level. This is the heart of the "Switzerland of the

Rockies.'' Within a fifteen-mile radius of Ouray are seventy-one peaks, seven of which exceed the height of 14,000 feet, and seventeen others that are more than 12,000 feet high. Nearby is the Camp Bird Mine where Thomas F. Walsh, father of Evelyn Walsh McLean, made his fortune. At one time it produced as much as four million dollars a year in gold. Ouray has piped water from hot springs into a public swimming pool, and maintains a picnic area in Box Canyon where Canyon Creek plunges down a dark, misty gorge. If you can spare the time, by all means take a jeep trip into the high country along trails calculated to frighten even a mountain goat. The paved highways are spectacular enough, but the high trails which only a jeep can navigate offer something totally different to appreciate in this area of rugged vistas.

From Ouray the highway descends gradually to Montrose, thirty-seven miles away, center of a farming, mining, and stock-raising area. Fourteen miles outside Montrose is Black Canyon of the Gunnison National Monument.

From Montrose, turn east again on US 50. The road winds through the Gunnison Valley, a rich ranching area. A series of three dams, part of the Curecanti Project to harness the Gunnison, will drown out much of that river's famous trout fishing, but more than five hundred miles of other streams remain in the area. The town of Gunnison, home of Western State College, lies fifty-nine miles east of Montrose. Twenty-eight miles north of Gunnison is Crested Butte, once a dying mining town, now the location of a winter sports center.

The tour continues sixty miles eastward of Gunnison along US 50 over magnificent, sweeping Monarch Pass (11,312 feet), where skiers find some of the state's deepest snows, to the crossroads of Poncha Springs, where dozens of hot springs bubble with water containing salts similar to those at Hot Springs, Arkansas.

You have a choice here. US 285 heads north to Buena Vista, South Park, and Denver. US 50 continues east to Canon City and Pueblo. (Canon City is the location of the state prison and the Royal Gorge, where the world's highest suspension bridge crosses the 1,000-foot-deep gorge of the Arkansas River.)

Let's go south, for in that direction lie some little-known facets of Colorado, and a culture whose roots reach back to the earliest settlers. Just south of gentle Poncha Pass begins the San Luis Valley, in the Rio Grande National Forest, once the bed of an inland sea. As much as forty-five miles wide, the valley is more than one hundred miles long and extends across the border into New Mexico. On the east it is bounded by the stark Sangre de Cristo (Blood of Christ) range, so named because of the ruddy sunset glow, and on the west by the western portion of the Rio Grande National Forest.

Shortly after entering the valley, US 285 curves west to Saguache (an Indian name, pronounced *Sa-watch*), remembered in Colorado history as the place where Alferd Packer was imprisoned while awaiting trial. Packer was found guilty of eating five companions to keep himself alive when trapped by deep snow in the mountains near Lake City.

The road, straight as a gun barrel, heads south to Monte Vista through countryside dotted with artesian wells and richly productive of potatoes, alfalfa, wheat, and malting barley.

Alamosa, seventeen miles beyond Monte Vista, is the valley's largest city, with 3,900 residents. It is a rail and shipping hub for lettuce, spinach, peas, and other crops grown in the cool, high atmosphere. Some twenty-four miles south of Alamosa is the village of Manassa, immortalized by sportswriters of a generation ago as the birthplace of Jack Dempsey, the "Manassa Mauler."

Thirteen miles north of Alamosa, tiny Mosco becomes the turning-off point for State 150, to Great Sand Dunes National Monument. Here, a thousand miles from any ocean, nature in a whimsical mood piled up restless sand dunes extending for some ten miles along the foot of the Sangre de Cristo mountains. The crests of the dunes rise to as much as six hundred feet above the valley floor.

The circle tour turns east at Alamosa onto US 160, skirting 14,317-foot Blanca Peak before reaching Fort Garland, twenty-six miles away. Fort Garland was manned by federal troops from 1858 to 1883, and Kit Carson was its commanding officer for a time. Some of the fort buildings have been restored, and a state museum displays mementoes of Indian-fighting days.

I-25, a four-lane highway that runs virtually all the way from Cheyenne, Wyoming, on the north, to the New Mexico border, skirts Walsenburg's eastern fringes.

The tour swings north from Walsenburg, forty-eight miles on I-25, to Pueblo. This is Colorado's third largest city, with a metropolitan population of more than 103,500. In underindustrialized Colorado, Pueblo is the center of the state's heavy industry. The Colorado Fuel and Iron plant produces steel ingots, sheet, rails, and wire for the West's many needs, and many satellite industries have grown up alongside the steel mill. The demand for mill labor brought in people of many ethnic backgrounds. Pueblo is also the site of the state mental hospital, and is a trading center for the rich farm towns of the Arkansas Valley which strings out eastward to the Kansas border. Lakes, streams, and guest ranches in the San Isabel National Forest are within a few miles of Pueblo. A large section of the flat, dry land between Pueblo and Colorado Springs, about 40 miles to the north, is within the Fort Carson military reservation, used as an Army training site. I-25 provides fast, smooth access from Pueblo to Colorado Springs and to the start and terminus of the tour, Denver, 112 miles to the north.

PRACTICAL INFORMATION FOR COLORADO

FACTS AND FIGURES. Colorado gets its name from the Spanish for "red" or "muddy," referring to the Colorado River. Colorado's nicknames are *Centennial State* (because it entered the Union on August 1, 1876) and *Silver State*. The state flower is the Rocky Mountain columbine; state tree, the Colorado blue spruce; the state bird, the lark bunting; state animal, the Rocky Mountain bighorn sheep; the state motto is *Nil sine Numine* ("Nothing without Providence"); the state song is "Where the Columbines Grow." Colorado is in the mountain time zone. Its area is 104,247 sq. mi.; altitude, 3,350-14,431 ft. The state population (1976 estimate) is 2,534,000. Denver, Colorado's largest city, is the state capital.

The Continental Divide and the Rocky Mountains cut a north-south path down the center of Colorado, forming the headwaters of six great rivers and dividing the state into the flat eastern region of the Great Plains and the high plateaus and deep gorges of the west. The mountainous western area contains some of the highest peaks in the country as well as some of America's finest resort areas. Cattle- and sheep-raising play a major role and, although the great days of gold and silver are over, mining remains important. The state is a leading source of molybdenum and uranium. Both agriculture and industry are hampered by lack of water—Colorado's biggest problem.

The climate is marked by sunny, pleasantly dry summers and cold winters, with little rainfall.

HOW TO GET THERE. *By air:* Colorado is served by United, Trans World, Continental, Braniff, Frontier, Texas International, Western, North Central, and Aspen Airways on regular schedules into Denver's Stapleton International Airport. Colorado Springs, Pueblo, and Grand Junction also have major service.

By train: Amtrak has passenger service into Denver originating in Chicago or San Francisco. Connecting service into Grand Junction is available from the Denver & Rio Grande Western Railway.

By car: main highways into the state are I-25 from Wyoming in the north and New Mexico in the south; I-70 from Utah in the west and Kansas in the east; and I-80S from Nebraska in he northeast.

By bus: Greyhound and Continental Trailways both serve Colorado.

HOW TO GET AROUND. *By air:* in addition to the major service into Denver, Frontier, Aspen Airways, Rocky Mountain, and United provide air transportation within the state. Steamboat Springs-Hayden-Craig, Grand Junction. Aspen, Delta-Montrose, Gunnison, Cortez, Durango, Alamosa, Lamar, Pueblo, Eagle/Vail and Colorado Springs are all served by one or more of these airlines.

By train: Denver & Rio Grande Western operates passenger service between Denver and Grand Junction.

By bus: R.T.D., Continental Trailways, Denver-Boulder R.T.D. Bus Company, and Greyhound serve Colorado communities.

By car: the major east-west route is I-70; from north to south on the Eastern slope take I-25, also known as the Valley Highway. US 50 and 550 serve the southwest corner and US 40 the northwest.

TOURIST INFORMATION. For specific information and descriptive brochures contact the Denver Convention and Colorado Visitors' Bureau, 225 W. Colfax Ave., Denver 80202.

SEASONAL COLORADO EVENTS. In *January*, there is the *Winter Skol Carnival* in Aspen and *ski races* throughout the state. Steamboat Springs, Leadville, and Crested Butte host *winter carnivals* in *February*, the *Roch Cup Races*, downhill and slalom, take place in Aspen, the Gunnison *Webster Players, Ltd.* give performances, and Georgetown celebrates *Fasching*, nine days of German festivities at mid-month.

March brings *cutter races* to Steamboat Springs, *ski races* to various areas, and the *U.S. National Men's Curling Championships* to the Broadmoor World Arena in Colorado Springs.

The *Estes Park Hobby Show* and *Boulder Symphony Spring Concerts* open in *April*. *Easter Sunrise Services* take place at the Garden of the Gods near Colorado Springs, as well as in the Red Rocks Park near Morrison.

May events include *rodeos, horse racing, golf tournaments*, Canon City's *Blossom Festival*, the *opening of Trail Ridge Road*, Basin's *May Day Slalom*, the Alamosa Rail Fan Club's annual *narrow-gauge railroad trip*, and *horse shows* throughout the state.

Melodramas open in *June* in Cripple Creek, Durango, and various other towns; there are Colorado *Philharmonic Concerts* in Evergreen, *June Week and Graduation* ceremonies at the United States Air Force Academy in Colorado Springs, Grand

Lake's *Sunrise Slalom*, Central City's *Opera and Drama Festival, water-skiing* tournaments, and the *Arkansas River International White Water Boat Race* at Salida (these are exciting kayak races while the river is at flood stage).

July means *stockcar races, rodeos,* and *horse shows* including the *National Arabian Horse Show* at Estes Park. Fourth of July activities abound, among them: the *Pikes Peak Hill Climb and auto race*; the *Koshare Indians* hold summer ceremonials at La Junta; Grand Lake has a *buffalo barbecue*; the *Aspen Music Festival* begins and runs through August; Boulder's *Shakespeare Festival* opens in Mary Rippon Theater; the "world's highest, longest, roughest, and toughest" race, the *Pack Burro Championship Race* over Hoosier Pass, takes place between Fairplay and Breckenridge; and the *Broadmoor International Theatre* at the Broadmoor Hotel in Colorado Springs imports name entertainers through August.

In *August*, Grand Junction has *Intermountain Market Days*; Alamosa stages a *Kit Carson Riders Futurity Race and Derby*; Grand Lake has the *Shadow Mountain Sailboat Regatta*; Littleton holds the *National Little Britches Rodeo Finals*; the *Colorado State Fair* takes place at Pueblo; the *Pikes Peak or Bust Rodeo* is at Colorado Springs; and the *Navajo Trail Festival* in Durango includes a rodeo, square dancing, parade, and horse racing.

The University of Colorado's *Big 8 football* season begins in *September*. Glenwood Springs has its annual *Art Festival*, and *Aspencades*, trips into the mountains to see the colorful changes autumn brings to the aspens; *rodeos* and *harvest festivals* are also common.

October: Potato Day in Glenwood Springs, the *Stone Age Fair* in Loveland, and the opening of the *big-game hunting* season.

Most of the state's thirty-four *ski areas open* in *November. Goose hunting* season opens.

Hockey season begins at the World Arena in Colorado Springs in *December*. Georgetown, the mountain town, has an old-fashioned market then; La Junta has the *Koshare Indians' Winter Night Ceremonial*; On New Year's Eve is the Ad Am An *fireworks display* on Pikes Peak.

 NATIONAL PARKS. The Black Canyon of the *Gunnison National Monument* is probably the deepest, darkest, wildest, and rockiest piece of real estate you will ever see. The Gunnison River has cut a narrow gorge, at times only forty feet wide, through nearly solid granite, to depths ranging from 1,730 feet to 2,425 feet. From the higher elevations it is possible to see the frothing white water below against a background of sunlight reflected from pink mica in the otherwise black walls. Legend has it that the canyon is so dark and narrow at the bottom that it is possible in broad daylight to see the stars by looking straight up. Well-organized boat trips down the river and descents on Indian trails may be taken, but only experienced climbers should attempt any other route down the canyon. Some of the best fishing in Colorado is to be found on the Gunnison. The North Rim of the canyon is reached by a gravel road east of Crawford on State 92. The South Rim is reached by US 50 to Montrose and then State 347 six mi. east. Park rangers have nightly programs during the summer. Campsites and picnic areas are available. Closed in winter by snow.

State 340 west from Grand Junction or US 70 from Fruita will lead into Rim Rock Drive of *Colorado National Monument*, 1,000 to 2,000 feet above the Grand Valley. Five-hundred-foot-high *Independence Rock, Window Rock,* the *coke ovens* and *Red Canyon* may be seen from lookouts along the 22-mile drive. Meadows of wildflowers and forests of juniper and pine surround the mountains. Wildlife, protected by the National Park Service, roam the area. Dinosaur beds are still being excavated here. Nearby, the largest flat-topped peak in the United States, *Grand Mesa*, sprinkled with lakes and two miles high, may be reached on State 64. The Visitors' Centers at park headquarters will assist the traveler in the area. Nightly programs by rangers during the summer. Campsites with excellent facilities and picnic areas are available. Well-marked trails beckon to hikers.

Dinosaur National Monument, in the northwestern corner of Colorado, is reached from US 40 at Dinosaur, park headquarters. Much of the scenic beauty is a result of erosion by the Yampa and Green rivers. *Steamboat Rock*, carved out of layers of sandstone by the confluence of the Yampa and Green is now seven hundred feet above the river surface which once flowed over it. Its broad slab sides act as a sounding board for nearby *Echo Park*. Pictographs estimated to be 1,000 years old may be seen. Archeologists removed the delicate bones of dinosaurs from their sedimentary storehouses. More than twenty skeletons have been reconstructed here dating back some 100,000 years ago. The skeletons are housed in a museum reached through Jenson, Utah, twenty miles west of Dinosaur on US 40. Roads into the monument may be closed in winter due to snow. Campsites and raft trips are available in the region.

The only place in America where four states meet at one point is the junction of Arizona, New Mexico, Utah, and Colorado. The area is locally called "The Four Corners." *Hovenweep National Monument* is reached by a gravel park road west of Pleasant View, off State 666. The monument is a series of long-abandoned Pueblo settlements which punctuate the barren land and extend into southern Utah. The prehistoric buildings, evidently built by a people similar to those who built Mesa Verde, are open for inspection. A ranger is on duty at Square Tower. Campsites and picnic areas are available. In rainy or snowy weather check in Cortez before attempting the dirt road.

Mesa Verde National Park will doubtlessly impress the traveler. Just as fossils tell us how plants and animals lived long ago, the ruins of these cliff dwellings tell us of a prehistoric civilization from nearly a thousand years before the American Revolution.

It is believed that about eight hundred years ago a severe drought forced the tribes which built Mesa Verde to leave their plateau for an area more favorable to agriculture. No one knows for certain who they were or to where these Indian tribes disappeared. *Mesa Verde* ("Green Tabletop") describes the general topography of the surface of the park, not the caves and canyons below. There are three general types of ruins open for inspection: pithouses, pueblos, and cliff dwellings. The *pithouses* are shallow holes in the ground, usually covered with straw or grass roofs, which were inhabited by one family. The *pueblo*, developed later, is a compound of several houses adjoining an open court. The pueblos form a village around the *kiva*, which was used for religious ceremonies. The *cliff dwellings* were built much later and offered excellent protection to their inhabitants. The *Cliff Palace* was built two hundred feet off the canyon floor and contains some two hundred rooms. The *Spruce Tree House* is relatively easy to enter and remains one of the best preserved. It has 114 rooms and eight *kivas* and is not unlike today's apartment houses. No one may enter the fragile cliff dwellings unless accompanied by a park ranger.

The museum at Park Headquarters will add to the visitor's understanding of Mesa Verde and her people of long ago. The Park may be reached by car on US 160, thirty-eight miles west of Durango. There are twenty-one miles of park roads from the park entrance. Bus service from Spruce Tree Lodge is available for those who do not wish to drive their cars into the park; *Continental Trailways* has daily buses to Spruce Tree Lodge from Durango. *Frontier Airlines* serves Durango and Cortez ten miles west of Mesa Verde. A limited number of overnight accommodations are available at the park entrance, as are improved facilities for house trailers. A restaurant, service station, AAA road service, and tire agency exist. Evening campfire talks are given by park rangers and archeologists, and visiting Navajos from the neighboring reservation frequently demonstrate tribal dances and chants. Horseback trips through the area can be arranged at headquarters.

Rocky Mountain National Park, with headquarters at Estes Park, is scenically stunning. *Trail Ridge Road* (US 34), the highway which runs through part of the

Park, has been called "breathtaking." The highest paved highway in the U.S., its fifteen miles of road above timberline, some at altitudes of 12,000 feet, look down on great sloping meadows of wildflowers. Slowly melting glaciers provide the water supply for a host of waterfalls, streams, and deep mountain lakes. On *Long's Peak* (14,255 feet), snowballs can be made in the middle of July. At the western end of Trail Ridge Road is *Grand Lake*, which covers an area of 515 acres, and at 8,400 feet is the home of what may be the highest yacht club in the world. Water sports are popular here, but be prepared for the icy waters of a lake whose depths have never been completely sounded.

Great Sand Dunes National Monument, located on State 150, thirty-six miles northeast of Alamosa, contains the highest naturally formed sand piles in the United States, some exceeding a height of eight hundred feet above the valley floor. The constant pressure of the wind sculpts the finely pulverized sand into a wonderland of hills, valleys, and plains. During the day the dunes can be visible for seventy miles, radiating a rosy warmth of sun on hot sand. The color and mood shift with the angle of the sun, as lengthening shadows change the dunes to violet and mauve. The dunes also produce some of the greatest lightning displays in America. The combination of wind and heat rising from the 55 square miles of sand creates titanic thunderstorms accompanied by extraordinary lightning bolts. The Visitors' Center contains history and information on the area; campsites and picnic grounds are available, and a nature trail is marked for hikers.

Florissant Fossil Beds National Monument, one-half mile south of Florissant on County 1, is a 6,000-acre site once covered by a prehistoric lake. Thirty-five million years ago, erupting volcanoes filled the lake with ash and lava. Today perfectly detailed fossils of the insects, seeds, and leaves of that period can be found in this area, along with standing petrified Sequoia stumps.

 HOT SPRINGS. Colorado has a number of hot springs, among them *Glenwood Springs, Idaho Springs, Pagosa Springs, Hot Sulphur Springs,* and *Steamboat Springs*, most with facilities for enjoying the waters. Of these, Glenwood Springs is the most extensive, with two outdoor pools, one of them two blocks long. Open all year, these are fed by natural warm mineral waters. *Hot mineral baths* are available at the Vapor Cave Baths and Health Spa.

 CAMPING OUT. Campers in Colorado will discover fully developed campsites in the state's national forests, national monuments, and national parks, in addition to scores of state and local areas. Most are equipped for tents, trailers, and campers. Water, sanitary facilities, and garbage disposal are available and some sites have swimming, boating, and fishing.

A Colorado Parks Pass, good for driver and passengers, is required for the state recreation areas. These are available from some parks, and from most sporting-goods stores. In addition, some parks may require a campground fee.

Further information can be obtained from the Division of Game, Fish and Parks, 6060 Broadway, Denver 80216.

 TRAILER TIPS. In Grand Junction, one-half mile south of I-70 on exit 8 at 3238 F Rd., a KOA site has heated pool, sewer, and electric hookups. North of Durango is the Ponderosa site off US 550. Sewer, air-conditioning, and electric heater hookups are also available at extra cost. In Estes Park, just across the road from Lake Estes on US 34, is a park offering water, electricity and sewer hookups. Seven miles north of Pueblo at I-25 exit 47 is the Buffalo Springs site with free dump station, electrical hookups, sewer, playground, country store, game room. Scenic view of Pikes Peak.

FARM VACATIONS AND GUEST RANCHES. For the vacationer who likes to enjoy the great outdoors but still demands his creature comforts, Colorado has much to offer in the way of dude-ranch vacations. Reservations should be made well in advance.

The *C Lazy U Ranch*, seven miles northwest of Granby on State 125 and US 40, is a well-known working guest ranch. Activities run from supervised programs for youngsters 5 to 12, to shuffleboard, skeet shooting, tennis, square dancing, lake and stream fishing, and barbecues, as well as the usual ranch activities. The heated pool has a flagstone terrace adjoining a cocktail lounge with a panoramic view of the ranch. During some weeks in winter, the ranch hosts appreciative skiers.

There are two important dude ranches in Winter Park. Both offer excellent accommodations and fine programs. The Idlewild Dude and Guest Ranch has some tennis, while the Sitzmark Ranch, not far away, is known for its outstanding food and the personal attention of its owner. Also located in the mountains, the Peaceful Valley Ranch, Lyons, made a name for itself as a riding center.

In south-central Colorado, on State 96 west of Pueblo, the *Don K Ranch* boasts its own ghost town. With the San Isabel Forest and the Sangre de Cristo Range to prowl, good food, heated pool, cocktail lounge, children's counselors, this may be the place for your Colorado vacation.

Two Bar Seven Ranch on the Colorado-Wyoming line, US 287, while small, has a host of various and unusual activities for guests. Probably the most popular and unusual is the annual trek from the ranch to Cheyenne via horseback and wagon for the annual *Cheyenne Frontier Days* celebration, held the last full week in July.

These are only a few of the dozens of good dude ranches in Colorado that welcome visitors. For more information, write: Colorado Dude & Guest Ranch Association, Box 6440, Cherry Creek Station, Denver 80206.

MUSEUMS AND GALLERIES. The *University of Colorado Museum and Art Gallery* in Boulder is open to the public Mon. through Sat. The *Denver Museum of Natural History* is quite extensive. (Location: City Park).

Central City's Opera House should be seen. The H. A. W. Tabor Collection is housed in the *Gold Mine Museum*. Open daily.

The *Colorado Springs Fine Arts Center* and *Taylor Museum* offer an unusual collection of southwestern United States primitive folk art and American Indian art. The building itself is an unusual piece of architecture. The *National Carvers Museum* has permanent and changing exhibits of the work of nationally and internationally known carvers.

Hagans Clock Manor Museum in Evergreen features a collection of clocks and music boxes. Guided tours, lectures, films, and programs.

The *Hotel De Paris* and the *Hamill House*, both in Georgetown, contain Victorian furnishings and architecture. Some of the best representatives of Victorian architecture in America are in this sleepy little mountain community. Both these museums are open daily in the summer, and both charge a small admission fee.

Children are welcome in the *Buffalo Bill Museum* on *Lookout Mountain*, which contains items dealing with Cody's life and associates. Open daily.

The *Colorado School of Mines* in Golden operates a geology museum which should be seen by anyone interested in minerals, fossils, rock, or ores. The *Colorado Railroad Museum*, the largest railroad display in the Rockies, is housed in an 1880-style railroad station in Golden.

La Junta is the home of the *Koshare Indian Dancers* and their museum, located at *Otero Junior College*. This *Kiva* contains Indian art, handicrafts, and lore. Open all year.

H. A. W. Tabor left his mark on Colorado's culture. Leadville preserved and restored his last mine and the opera house he built for the town. Both the *Matchless Mine* and the *Tabor Opera House* are worth seeing. Tabor also built the opera house in Central City, used in summer as a theater and opera house.

The *El Pueblo Museum* in Pueblo features a full-size re-creation of El Pueblo Fort, built in 1842, as well as history of the local steel industry.

Trinidad offers the *Baca House* and the *Bloom Mansion* for public visits. The Baca House is an 1869 adobe residence; the Bloom Mansion is the 1882 baroque Victorian residence of a local cattle baron.

Numerous towns in Colorado have a museum of some sort. The state historical society maintains a number of forts, monuments, residences, and sites throughout the state.

HISTORIC SITES. *Old Fort Garland*, on US 160, forty-seven miles west of Walsenburg, is a restored Army post that was once commanded by Kit Carson. On US 85 south of Platteville is a reproduction of *Fort Vasquez*, a fur-trading post of the 1830s. *Pike's Stockade*, a moated log structure built in 1807 by Zebulon Pike, is on US 285 east of La Jara. Buffalo Bill Cody's grave is atop Lookout Mountain, west of Denver on US 40.

Mining played an important part in Colorado's history, and more than three hundred *ghost towns* still survive today as remnants of the state's legendary past. The Central City-Black Hawk area was once known as the "richest square mile on earth," and the ghost towns of Nevadaville and Apex, and *Teller House* and *1878 Opera House* are reminders of the mining that came and went. The "world's greatest gold camp" was at Cripple Creek-Victor, where several excellent ghost towns survive. At the edge of Fairplay, one of Colorado's oldest cities, the 100-year-old town of South Park City has been reconstructed.

FAMOUS LIBRARIES. All the colleges and universities in the state have good libraries, open to the public, and the *Mineralogy Library* at the *Colorado School of Mines* in Golden is outstanding.

TOURS. *AA Sightseeing Tours* and *Continental Sightseeing Lines* in Denver and *Grey Line Tours* in Denver and Colorado Springs offer sightseeing tours around Colorado as well as locally. The *Burlington* and the *Denver & Rio Grande Western* railroads have tours, as do the *Greyhound Bus Company*, *Continental Trailways Bus Company* and *R.T.D.* Many of the smaller cities and towns have *taxi companies* that will gladly take the tourist on a sightseeing trip in the local area. In the fall a number of *"Aspencades"* depart from various towns to view the spectacular colors of the changing leaves. Check with local chambers of commerce for exact dates and times. *Jeep tours* are popular in various parts of the state as a way to enjoy the mountains and get into little-traveled areas in a manner more comfortable than on the back of a horse or by foot. Again, local chambers of commerce can help in arrangements.

INDUSTRIAL TOURS. While in Climax be sure to see the *Climax Molybdenum Company's* mining operations. In Golden, the *Coors Brewery* has a tour. Loveland's *Great Western Sugar Company* offers tours through its plant, where locally grown sugar beets are processed. *Colorado Fuel and Iron Company* in Pueblo conducts tours of its steel-making operation.

SPECIAL INTEREST TOURS. The Durango to Silverton narrow-gauge railroad passes through spectacular Rocky Mountain scenery. First built in 1882 principally to carry precious metals out of the area, this rail line still uses steam locomotives. The train leaves Durango every summer morning and arrives at Silverton at noon. The return trip leaves Silverton in the afternoon and reaches Durango before supper. Trains run daily from late May to early Oct.

ENTERTAINMENT. The Broadmoor Hotel in Colorado Springs brings in "name" entertainment, particularly to their *Broadmoor International Theatre*. During the ski season, both Vail and Aspen feature some night club activity.

BARS. Colorado's best bars are interesting in their own right. *The Golden Bee*, at the Broadmoor Hotel in Colorado Springs, is an authentic replica of a 19th-century English pub. Central City boasts a wide variety of Old West drinking places. The famous "Face on the Barroom Floor" is in the bar at *Teller House*. The *Red Ram* in Georgetown, and its Rathskeller, are well liked.

DRINKING LAWS. Colorado Law requires that anyone purchasing hard liquor, wine, or "6%" beer must be *21 years of age*. Persons over 18 may purchase so-called "3.2" beer. Drinks must be off the table at closing hour. Package goods are not sold in the bar, but may be obtained in package stores, open until midnight, Mon. through Sat. Children may sit at a table if they are accompanied by an adult.

MUSIC. Tops among the many musical activities outside of Denver is the *Aspen Music Festival*, held each summer with nationally known artists. Likewise, there are classical concerts in Vail; moreover, the Denver Symphony Orchestra travels to other resorts and towns. Many large Colorado cities and towns have local orchestras and bands which perform throughout the year, and the many colleges and universities in the state all feature musical events throughout the school term. Central City features two major operas each summer in the Opera House—these are performed by top-ranking singers.

STAGE AND REVUES. Central City's *annual summer festival* generally includes the presentation of a major play with a Broadway cast. Boulder has a summer *Shakespeare Festival*, backed by the *University Theater* group. Other colleges and universities throughout the state have student theaters and often bring in outside talent to perform. Various towns throughout the state have melodramas which are presented Wild West style, with much hissing at the villains and cheering of the heroes. Among the state's best known are the melodramas at the Imperial Hotel (Cripple Creek), and at Heritage Square, above Golden. The *Dark Horse Players*, of Estes Park, offer performances throughout the summer months. At Steamboat Springs, the world-known *Perry Mansfield Camp* presents a dance and drama festival in July and August. The *Troupe of American College Players* in Grand Lake presents a different show every night (theater in the round).

SUMMER SPORTS. *Fishing*: 7,100 miles of unposted fishing streams and 2,200 cold-water lakes and reservoirs provide ample opportunity to catch the fabled Rocky Mountain trout. Rainbow, brook, native, and brown trout are all famous for their fight, and while the fishing season lasts year-round, the best months are July and Aug. A 5-day nonresident fishing license is $10. They are readily available at sporting-goods stores.

Hunting: more than 41,000 deer, 23,000 elk, and other wild game are taken each year in Colorado. Antelope too are hunted.

There are seasons on pheasant, grouse, quail, ducks, Canadian geese, and ptarmigan, this last hunted above timberline. License fees and information about seasons can be obtained from the Department of Natural Resources, Division of Wildlife, 6060 Broadway, Denver 80216.

Water-skiing, *swimming*, *boating*, *rafting*, and *scuba diving* are popular, with numerous lakes and reservoirs open for use. *Tennis, golf, mountain climbing, rock hunting, hiking, horseback riding*, and even *panning for gold* are also possible.

WINTER SPORTS. Colorado has long been famous for its *skiing* facilities, and new improvements are made each season. High elevations, low humidity, and well-planned slopes make for good skiing from November through May, with summer skiing on *St. Mary's Glacier*, above Idaho Springs, accessible via I-70.

Basin, sixty-six miles from Denver on I-70, *Loveland Basin* and *Loveland Valley*, fifty-six miles west of Denver, on I-70, *Copper Mountain* and *Keystone*, also west of Denver, offer open slopes, chair lifts, and a variety of terrain. *Aspen, Buttermilk, Snowmass*, and *Aspen Highlands* make up one of the largest ski complexes in the country—a full-blown resort town with accommodations running from luxurious to economical and food from hot dogs to gourmet dinners. The town is devoted to skiing and skiers, and its facilities are in demand (reserve early). *Winterskol*, in January of each year, turns the old mining town into one giant carnival. The *Broadmoor Hotel* has its own ski run, with snow-making in case nature fails to cooperate. *Crested Butte, Breckenridge*, and *Steamboat* are all areas with deluxe facilities for families. *Winter Park*, owned and operated by the City of Denver as part of its park system, grows yearly. The Denver & Rio Grande Western Railroad runs a ski train to *Winter Park*; the *High Country Inn* at the foot of the mountain is so charming that many people who do not ski take the train up to stay at the lodge enjoying the view, food, and drink. Another good Winter Park Lodge is *The Sitzmark*.

There is an ever-growing number of smaller, weekend areas ideally suited for the skiing family, and, while their facilities won't match those of Vail or Aspen, they are adequate. Colorado ski areas are accessible by automobile, with the state highway crews doing an excellent job on the roads; bus service is available to the large areas; and the D&RGW train serves Winter Park on weekends. All areas have ski schools in operation, and the cost of the lesson will be money well spent. Most areas have ski shops for the sale and rental of equipment.

Opportunity for *ice skating* exists in Colorado. The *Broadmoor* has a large indoor rink. Several towns around the state have municipal ice rinks, and skates may generally be rented for a small charge.

SPECTATOR SPORTS. *Auto racing:* the famous Pikes Peak Hill Climb takes place July 4th outside Colorado Springs and, at the Continental Divide Raceways in Castle Rock, there is stock and sports car racing from May to Sept. *Greyhound racing:* from late Mar. to early June at Cloverleaf in Loveland, from early June to mid-Aug. at Pueblo Kennel Association in Pueblo, and during Sept. and Oct. at Rocky Mountain Kennel Club. *Horse racing:* at the Centennial Race Track in Littleton (March through September). *Rodeo:* although many communities have rodeos, some of the best known are the "Pikes Peak or Bust Rodeo" in Colorado Springs during the second week in Aug., and the Colorado State Fair and Rodeo in Pueblo beginning late Aug. Others take place at Craig, Montrose, Estes Park, Salida, Gunnison, Loveland, Canon City, Steamboat Springs, Boulder, Monte Vista, and Glenwood Springs.

SHOPPING. Colorado has more than its share of ordinary curio shops and souvenir counters, but it also provides some different and interesting shops. Aspen's *Sports Shop Lindner* has a good collection of unusual sportswear, as does the House of Ireland. The Arrow Shop, Aspen, is an adventure in Western folklore, with

Indian and Eskimo arts and crafts. *Terese David of Aspen* advertises "crazy clothes for matching people" and also has items for the "little people." Colorado Springs' *Broadmoor Hotel* has a branch of *Abercrombie and Fitch*, known by sportsmen the world over. *Gerry's Mountain Shop*, 821 Pearl Street in Boulder, supplies many expeditions in the mountain-climbing world. The *Pottery Parlor*, 534 Main Avenue, Durango, has pottery in all manner of shapes, sizes, and colors.

WHAT TO DO WITH THE CHILDREN. Children in Colorado can find activities of all kinds and types to keep them busy. The *Cheyenne Mountain Zoo* in Colorado Springs will delight them. The *North Pole*, northwest of Colorado Springs, is the home of Santa's Workshop. A Wild West stagecoach, miniature train, Santa's car, and a magic-mine ride, plus doll-makers, puppeteers, magicians, glassblowers, gnomes, elves, and story book characters all make for enjoyment. *Ghost Town*, in Colorado Springs, caters to the imaginations of adults and children alike. Parks and museums throughout the state cater to children and attempt to make their visits both fun and educational. The national forests and monuments are made to order for children who love the outdoors, but it would be well to warn them about wandering off alone. The old mining towns, especially Central City and Leadville, will offer dozens of places for browsing, looking, and learning. Abandoned mines should not be entered, since the timbers are dry and could collapse; but many old mines have been safety-checked and may be entered with a guide, usually for a small fee. The *Garden of the Gods* and *Cave of the Winds*, both near Colorado Springs, offer unusual sights. Both wonderful for a day's excursion are the narrow-gauge railroad from Durango to Silverton and the *Cumbres & Toltec Scenic Railroad* from Antonito, Colorado, to Chama, New Mexico.

INDIANS. Colorado's history is inextricably bound to Indian culture and lore. Today the state has two reservations, the *Ute Mountain* and *The Southern Ute Reservations*, in southwestern Colorado. Nearly 1,000 Mountain Utes live on the reservations, which, while clinging to many ancestral traditions, have modern conveniences. Each summer the Utes stage their traditional *Sun Dance*. Visitors are welcome, but cameras are not allowed. The visitors are expected to view the dances with attention and respect. The Southern Utes hold their *Bear Dance* near Ignacio in May.

PHOTOGRAPHY. In the high altitude and low humidity of Colorado, the air is clear and thin and there is an abundance of ultra-violet light which, though invisible, is picked up as a blue haze by colorfilm. The use of a skylight filter cuts out these rays, and your pictures will appear normal. The light at these high altitudes is very bright, and pictures of sunlit scenes require 1/2 to 1 full stop less exposure than you would ordinarily use. If you can afford the extra cost in film of exposing 1/2 stop over and under in addition to what seems to be the correct exposure, you are nearly certain of getting a perfectly exposed photograph. Professional photographers often use this technique.

If your camera has interchangeable lenses, a wide-angle lens can capture not only the broad panoramic shots from the high peaks, but also insure that both the river and sky will appear in photos of the deep canyons.

RECOMMENDED READING. Robert Brown's *Colorado Ghost Towns* will give insight into some of the ways of the Old West; *Timberline*, by Gene Fowler, is a delightful peek into the Denver of not-so-very-long-ago; Marshall Sprague's *Colorado* examines the history of the state; *The Colorado Studio Book*, characterizing the essentials of modern Colorado, is a large, beautiful book by photographer Jim

Katzel and Curtis Casewit; *Stampede to Timberline*, by Muriel Sibell Wolle, tells of ghost towns and mining camps; and *Skiing Colorado* (*Colorado Ski Country*) looks into the ski areas and resorts.

 HOTELS AND MOTELS. Accommodations in the non-ski resort areas of Colorado tend to be friendly and warm toward the motoring family. These operations depend heavily on summer revenue and will make every effort to make travelers comfortable. The ski area accommodations tend to be somewhat more expensive, and their bounty of powdery snow puts these hotels and motels in a "sellers' market"— especially during winter holidays.

The price categories in this section, for double occupancy, will average as follows: *Deluxe* $35, *Expensive* $30, *Moderate* $18, and *Inexpensive* $14. For a more complete description of these categories, see the *Hotels & Motels* section of THE ROCKIES & PLAINS *Facts at Your Fingertips* at the front of this volume.

ALAMOSA
Alamosa Inn. *Moderate*. On US 160 at 285. Heated pool, saunas, dining room and cocktail lounge.

ASPEN
Aspen Inn. *Deluxe*. A motel in downtown Aspen. Sitter list, heated pool, lawn games, skiing, health club, restaurant, bar, entertainment.

Aspen Meadows. *Deluxe*. West edge of town. This large complex offers chalet accommodations with central building containing all hotel services, plus health center, saunas, steam baths, tennis courts, swimming pool, cocktail lounge.

Pomegranate Inn. *Deluxe*. 2 miles west on State 82. Rooms with fireplaces, suites, heated pool and therapy pool, ice cream parlor, billiard room. Restaurant.

The Applejack Inn. *Expensive*. With small indoor heated pool, balconies, sun deck. Free continental breakfasts.

Maroon Creek Lodge. *Expensive*. 2½ mi. southwest on Maroon Creek Rd. Car advisable. Early American decor in units containing living room, kitchenette, bath, and one or two bedrooms. Heated pool, sauna. Spectacular view.

The Prospector. *Expensive*. E. Hyman at S. Monarch. A small, long-established, informal place. Breakfast is included in daily rates. Heated pool.

The Smuggler. *Moderate*. 101 W. Main St. Attractive units, larger ones have living areas. Lounge with fireplace and coffee bar. Heated pool.

The Villa of Aspen. *Moderate*. On State 82. A friendly lodge with stone fireplace, complimentary continental breakfast, heated pool, children's play area, outdoor barbecue, courtesy car. Baby sitters available.

BOULDER
Golden Buff Motor Loege. *Expensive*. 1725 28th St. Established motel convenient to University of Colorado campus. Large, well-decorated rooms, heated pool, putting green.

Hilton-House Motor Hotel. *Expensive*. 1345 28th St. A large, modern high-rise motel with landscaped grounds, dining facilities, cocktail lounge, swimming pool, tennis courts. Free parking.

Holiday Inn of Boulder. *Expensive*. 800 28th St. Large national-chain motel. Pool, dining room.

Royal Inn of Boulder. *Expensive*. 770 28th St. Across from University of Colorado. Restaurant, bar, pools, attractively furnished rooms, private patios.

University Inn. *Moderate*. 1632 Broadway. Small, pleasant motel. Heated pool. Near downtown Boulder.

BRECKENRIDGE
Breckenridge Inn. *Expensive*. 600 S. Ridge St. In the heart of the Breckenridge ski area, this lodge offers excellent dining room, cocktail lounge, bowling, heated pool, tennis courts. Summer activities.

BRUSH
Empire Motel. *Inexpensive*. 1408 Edison. Small motel with heated pool, large shaded lawns. Miniature golf next door.

BUENA VISTA
Sumac Lodge. *Moderate*. On State 24. Pond, mountain view, shaded lawn, coin laundry.

Topaz Lodge. *Moderate*. On State 24. Small, friendly lodge.

BURLINGTON
Chaparrel Motor Inn. *Moderate*. 1/2mi. north on State 385. Heated pool, playground, pets limited.

Western Motor Inn. *Moderate*. Off US 25. Pets, restaurant, and coffee shop.

CANON CITY
Royal Gorge. *Expensive*. 1925 Fremont Dr. Heated pool, pets, cafe, bar. Attractive rooms.

El Camino. *Inexpensive*. 2980 E. Main St. Attractive motel with mini-golf, playground, cafe 1/2 mi.

COLORADO SPRINGS
Antlers Plaza. *Deluxe*. Pikes Peak Ave. at Chase Stone Center. Located in the heart of downtown Colorado Springs. A modern, luxury, 15-story complex complete with lounge, coffee shop, and specialty dining room. Modest rooftop heated pool, bar, dancing, entertainment. Barber and beauty shops.

Broadmoor Resort. *Deluxe*. 5 mi. south on US 85, 87, then west on State 122. This distinctive, world-famous resort is set on 5,000 acres. A center for large convention groups, facilities include large heated outdoor pool, saunas, many dining rooms, barber, beauty and other shops. Recreational facilities include elaborate golf, tennis, riding, skiing, ice rinks, boats, squash, handball, skeet, scuba. Entertainment, dancing, movies.

Dravo Manor Motor Hotel. *Expensive*. 1703 S. Nevada. A small, well-kept motel with heated pool, restaurant, bar.

Holiday Inn-Central. *Expensive*. 8th and Cimarron Sts. Good location. Large motel with heated pool, restaurant, bar, dancing, entertainment.

Palmer House. *Expensive.* I-25 at Fillmore St. exit. Large, beautifully planned Best Western establishment with spacious rooms, heated pool, restaurant, cocktail lounge, dancing, entertainment.

Imperial "400." *Moderate.* 1231 S. Nevada. Modern, small chain motel with heated pool, basic necessities, cafe nearby.

Imperial 400. *Moderate.* 714 N. Nevada. Centrally located. Some kitchens.

Ponderosa Motel. *Moderate.* 5700 N. Nevada. Large, modern motel with heated pool, playground; cafe not far. Free coffee.

CORTEZ
Sands of Cortez. *Moderate.* 1100 E. Main St. Heated indoor pool, playground, pets, restaurant and lounge.

Turquoise. *Moderate.* 535 E. Main St. Heated pool, restaurant and cocktail lounge. Free airport bus.

CRAIG
Cosgriff. *Moderate.* 110 E. Victory Way. Pleasant rooms, dining room and cocktail lounge. Close to City Park.

CRESTED BUTTE
Crested Butte Lodge. *Deluxe.* 2 1/2 mi. north off State 135. Heated pool, sauna, playground, pets limited in this luxurious modern lodge. Summer activities as well as skiing in winter.

Matterhorn Inn. *Deluxe.* 3 1/4 mi. off State 135. Pleasant rooms off central halls. Restaurant and cocktail lounge. Closed Apr. to June.

CRIPPLE CREEK
The Imperial Hotel. *Inexpensive.* 123 N. 3rd St. A relic of the 1891 Gold Rush—beautifully restored. The Imperial Players present an authentic melodrama in the *Gold Bar Room Theater.* Open June to Sept. The dining room is excellent. Cocktail lounge.

DILLON
Lake Dillon Condotel. *Expensive.* Lodge Pole Rd., on Dillon Reservoir. Free coffee, limited pets, therapy pool, pool table. Cafe nearby. Some units with kitchenettes (priced higher).

Ramada-Silverthorne. *Expensive.* Well-run motor hotel; ideal location close to major ski areas, and summer recreation. Some super-large units. Large indoor pool. Sauna. Good restaurant & bar. Discotheque.

DURANGO
Tamarron. *Deluxe.* 18 mi. north of Durango. Magnificent resort accommodations in one of the nation's more outstanding resorts. Many sports facilities. High-class dining.

Strater Hotel. *Expensive.* 669 Main Ave. Small, modern, nice rooms. All public rooms are in Gay '90s decor. Delightful cocktail lounge, good dining room. *Diamond Belle Bar*, melodramas in the *Diamond Circle Theater* during summer.

General Palmer House. *Moderate.* 567 Main Ave. A Gay '90s relic, restored, modernized, and a delight to stay in. Small pets, cafe, bar. D & RGW narrow-gauge railroad depot adjacent.

Silver Spruce. *Inexpensive*. 2929 N. Main Ave. Pets, cafe 2 blks. Small, comfortable motel.

EMPIRE

Hotel Splendide. *Moderate*. A successful restoration of an 1870 mining-town hotel. Very small but with an unusually good dining room and intriguing bar.

ESTES PARK

Stanley Hotel. Deluxe. A stylish old resort hotel with Victorian rooms. Fine ambiance. Large outdoor pool. Tennis court. Children's playground. Three restaurants.

Lake Estes Motor Inn. *Expensive*. 1650 Big Thompson Hwy. Medium-sized, with three heated pools, playground, horses available, pleasant rooms. Closed in winter.

Swiss Village Resort. *Expensive*. Charming chalets and lodge accommodations. Riverside dining. Horses. Restful, isolated. Summer only.

Trail Ridge. *Moderate*. 1701 Moraine Ave. 1½ mi. southwest on State 66. Comfortable motel with pool, restaurant, and cocktail lounge. Some efficiencies.

FORT COLLINS

Holiday Inn. *Expensive*. 3 mi. east on State 14. Chain member with heated pool, restaurant, cocktail lounge, entertainment, beauty shop. Free airport bus.

University Motor Inn. *Moderate*, 914 S. College Ave. Opposite Colorado State University, wIth heated pool, cafe.

FORT MORGAN

Park Terrace Motor Hotel. *Moderate*. Small, with cute rooms, heated pool, coffee shop.

GEORGETOWN

Georgetown Motor Inn. *Moderate*. On east edge of town, I-70 exit 43. Alpine inn in a scenic, historic location. Restaurant, cocktail lounge.

GLENWOOD SPRINGS

Holiday Inn. *Expensive*. 2 mi. west at I-70 exit. Chain member, with heated pool, saunas. Restaurant, bar, entertainment, dancing. Car needed.

Glenwood Hot Springs Lodge. *Moderate*. Center on I-70. Large motel with comfortable rooms. 2-block-long hot-spring pool, terrace dining, playground, sportswear shop, cocktail lounge.

Hotel Denver. *Inexpensive*. 7th and Cooper Sts. Popular with businessmen. Pets, restaurant, cocktail lounge.

GRANBY

El Monte Lodge. *Moderate*. 1/2mi. west on US 40. TV, heated pool, playground, pets limited. Restaurant and cocktail lounge.

GRAND JUNCTION

Bar-X Motel. *Moderate*. 1600 North Ave., ½ mi. northeast on US 6, 24. Modern, with spacious grounds; across street from golf course. Heated pool, restaurant, bar, free airport bus.

El Palomino. *Moderate.* 2400 North Ave., 1½ mi. northeast on US 6, 24. Opposite shopping center; heated pool, playground, free coffee, shuffleboard, picnic area. Pleasant rooms.

American Family Lodge. *Inexpensive.* 721 Horizon Dr., 3 1/2mi. north at I-70 airport exit. Attractive rooms, heated pool, playground, pets. Cafe opposite.

Holiday. *Inexpensive.* 1460 North Ave., on US 6. Limited pets, free coffee. Cafe adjacent.

GRAND LAKE

Daven Haven Lodge. *Expensive.* ¼ mi. south of Main St. Small summer resort on the shores of Grand Lake. Boats, water-skiing, mini-golf, shuffleboard, badminton, heated pool. Cocktail lounge and two dining rooms.

Riggs AA. *Inexpensive.* 2 blks. west on State 278. Playground, pets, free coffee, cafe nearby. Closed Nov. to Apr.

GREELEY

Inn Towne Motel. *Moderate.* 1803 9th St. Comfortable motel. Free coffee, some kitchen units available. Cafe 3 blocks.

Sundown. *Inexpensive.* 2131 8th Ave., 1 mi. south on US 85. Two blocks from University of Northern Colorado. Free coffee. Cafe opposite.

IDAHO SPRINGS

Peoriana Motel. *Inexpensive.* 1 mi. east on US 6, 40. Small, a favorite of skiers, has large, well-furnished rooms, cafe nearby.

KEYSTONE

Keystone Lodge. *Deluxe.* Magnificent European-style, low-slung hotel with many luxury touches. Skiing at doorstep. Indoor-outdoor pool for year-round use. French restaurant. Cafe. Shops in village.

LAMAR

El Mar Motel. *Inexpensive.* 1210 S. Main St. Small, modern, heated pool, cocktail lounge and restaurant.

LEADVILLE

Silver King Motor Inn. *Expensive.* Sauna, pets, restaurant and cocktail lounge.

LONGMONT

Lamplighter. *Moderate.* 1642 N. Main St. Comfortable motel with indoor heated pool, TV, free coffee.

Bar-C. *Inexpensive.* 1524 N. Main St. Small motel, limited pets, free coffee, cafe nearby.

LOVELAND

King's Court. *Moderate.* 928 Lincoln St. Small motel with heated pool, free coffee, nicely landscaped grounds. Cafe 3 blocks.

MESA VERDE NATIONAL PARK

Far View Motel. *Expensive.* At Navajo Hill, 15 mi. from park entrance. Private balconies provide a view of the canyon. Camping sites and trailer facilities available. Cafeteria. Summer reservations advisable.

MONTROSE

Red Arrow. *Expensive.* 1 mi. east on US 50. Attractive rooms in this motel with heated pool, playground, free coffee, sundeck. Cafe nearby.

Black Canyon Motel. *Moderate.* 1 mi. east on US 50. Small, with well-furnished rooms, heated pool, playground, pets, restaurant next door. Free airport bus.

Lazy I G Motel. *Moderate.* 1 mi. east on US 50. Very small, has deluxe rooms, heated pool, free coffee, playground.

OURAY

Box Canyon. *Moderate.* At the mouth of the canyon, with a spectacular view. Playground, pets, free coffee. Horses available. Cafe nearby.

Ouray Chalet. *Inexpensive.* On US 550, State 789. Small motel with sundeck, free coffee. Cafe nearby.

PAGOSA SPRINGS

Spring Inn. *Moderate.* 2 blks. south on US 160. Very small inn with mineral-water baths, delightful rooms, cocktail lounge and restaurant, pets.

PUEBLO

Holiday Inn. *Expensive.* 4001 N. Elizabeth. A large chain member. Heated pool, restaurant and cocktail lounge.

Pueblo West Inn. *Expensive.* 201 McCulloch Blvd. Very attractive motel with heated pool, restaurant and cocktail lounge. 18-hole golf course, tennis courts, heliport.

Ramada Inn. *Expensive.* 2001 N. Hudson Ave. Motor hotel with heated pool, good dining room, cocktail lounge, playground, beauty shop, free airport bus.

Rambler. *Moderate.* 4400 N. Elizabeth St. Heated pool, 24-hour cafe nearby.

Town House. *Moderate.* 8th St. at Santa Fe Ave. Medium-sized with heated pool, dining room, coffee shop, cocktail lounge.

SILVERTON

Grand Imperial Hotel. *Moderate.* 1219 Main St. A Victorian hotel, recently restored, features restaurant, beauty shop, movies; jeeps available. Closed Oct. to May.

STEAMBOAT SPRINGS

Holiday Inn. *Expensive.* 3 mi. east on US 40. Two stories, very attractive, with some balconies. Heated pool, kennel, sauna, restaurant and cocktail lounge.

Ptarmigan Inn. *Expensive.* 2 mi. east on US 40. This very attractive motel is located directly under Mt. Werner. Heated pool, sauna, restaurant and cocktail lounge.

Western Lodge. *Moderate.* Downtown opposite the park. Heated pool, free coffee. Cafe nearby.

Harbor Hotel. *Inexpensive.* Old, restored, downtown hotel, with modest restaurant, Western bar. Bus stops here.

STERLING

Holiday Inn-Sterling. *Expensive*. All the expected amenities.

Sterling Motor Lodge. *Inexpensive*. 731 N. 3rd St. Playground, pets limited, free coffee, 24-hour cafe nearby.

TRINIDAD

Country Club Motor Inn. *Deluxe*. Nice rooms with oversize beds, heated pool, playground, beauty and barber shops, restaurant.

Ramada Inn. *Expensive*. Pleasant, small chain member, delightful rooms, heated pool, cocktail lounge, dining room, coffee shop, weekend entertainment.

VAIL

Christiania-at-Vail. *Deluxe*. On Hanson Ranch Rd. Large, friendly, informal lodge at the foot of the mountain. Heated pool, sauna, limited pets, free coffee. Some condominiums. Restaurant nearby.

Hilton Inn. *Deluxe*. Large hotel with all the comforts. Pool. Restaurant. Free parking.

The Lodge at Vail. *Deluxe*. Splendid alpine lodge, cafeteria, sauna, cocktail lounge, large heated pool, sauna.

Vail Village Inn. *Deluxe*. 1 block north of I-70. Large motor inn with unique architecture, Olympic outdoor pool, dining room, coffee shop, cocktail lounge, fireplace lounge, sundecks, good location.

WALSENBURG

Country Host. *Moderate*. 1¼ mi. north at jct. State 69. Playground, limited pets, free coffee, trailer park available. Cafe adjacent.

WINTER PARK

Sitzmark Lodge and Guest Ranch. *Expensive*. Well-run establishment with clean rooms, good food, friendly atmosphere. Rathskeller Bar. Close to two ski areas, with free shuttles. Horses in summer.

High Country Inn. *Expensive*. Leading Best Western Lodge with bubble-protected all-year pool, sauna, game rooms, bar, quality food. Summer hiking/climbing programs. Skiing close by.

 YOUTH HOSTELS. Denver has both a *YWCA* and a *YMCA* with resident and transient facilities. At several major *ski* areas in the state a number of dormitory-type accommodations are available at an inexpensive rate. *Hotels and motels* throughout the state, and particularly in college towns, offer lower rates to groups. *Fraternity and sorority houses* on most college campuses are open in summer months, and members from other schools may be able to stay in them if they're not filled with summer-school students.

 DINING OUT. Dining out in Colorado towns can be great fun for the traveling family. Many of the smaller towns have different or unusual restaurants featuring local specialties, such as fine Mexican food. Prices are for the medium-priced items on the menu. For other worthwhile restaurants, check the hotel listings. Restaurants are in order of price category.

Restaurant categories are as follows: *Deluxe*: $12 and up, *Expensive*: $6-$12,

Moderate: $4-$6, and *Inexpensive:* under $4. These prices are for *hors d'oeuvres* or soup, *entrée*, and dessert. Not included are drinks, tax, or tips. For a more complete explanation of restaurant categories, refer to THE ROCKIES & PLAINS *Facts at Your Fingertips* at the front of this volume.

ASPEN

Copper Kettle. *Deluxe.* Each night authentic dishes from a different nation or area are featured. This establishment should not be missed by anyone who truly enjoys quiet dining and above-average service. Cocktail lounge. Reservations. *Prix fixe.*

The Crystal Palace. *Deluxe.* Victorian decor. The *prix fixe* dinners accompanied by Broadway shows are good. Cocktail lounge. Reservations essential. Difficult to get into during peak ski season.

Golden Horn. *Expensive.* Austrian cuisine. Efficient, unobtrusive service, warm decor, sparkling crystal, and a Caesar salad are a few of the attractions. Cocktail lounge, entertainment. Reservations.

Guido's Swiss Inn. *Expensive.* A Swiss chalet under Ajax Mountain with much to offer. If you are a cheese fondue fan, by all means order it here. Cocktail lounge.

The Red Onion. *Expensive.* A mining-day saloon, in fact the only one in town still operating at its original location. The saloon remains as it was in 1892, but the dining room is contemporary. Gourmet dinners and charcoal-broiled steaks are specialties. Cocktail lounge, entertainment. An old Aspen tradition.

Skiers Chalet. *Moderate.* Aspen St. at #1 lift. Good for families, this candlelit restaurant overlooks the town and mountain. Charcoal-broiled steaks.

BOULDER

Flagstaff House. *Expensive.* On Flagstaff Mountain, offering fine views. Varied Continental/American menu including filet à la Wellington, Alaska king crab. Prime rib a specialty. Cocktail patio. Overlooks city, mountains. A treat in summer.

Greenbriar. *Expensive.* Jamestown Star Rte., 8 mi. north on US 36 at jct. Lefthand Canyon Rd. Continental and American menu features veal Oscar, beef Wellington, shrimp Provençale, live Maine lobster, San Francisco French bread. Own desserts. Old World atmosphere. Chef-owned. Cocktail lounge.

Red Lion Inn. *Expensive.* Boulder Canyon Rd., 4 mi. west on State 119. Continental and American menu includes prime rib, elk, antelope, duck à l'orange. Cocktail lounge.

Tico's. *Inexpensive.* 1101 Walnut St. Mexican and American menu. Cocktail lounge.

BRECKENRIDGE

Briar Rose. *Expensive.* Victorian 1890s decor on the site of an old mining boarding house. Specialty is steak. Own saloon.

The Parlour Steak House. *Expensive.* Charming, century-old house; intimate candlelit setting. Excellent food. Specialties include steak, artichokes. Reservations required.

CANON CITY

Merlino's Belvedere. *Moderate.* Locally popular Italian restaurant with bar.

CENTRAL CITY

Black Forest Inn. *Expensive*. 1/4mi. east on State 279 in Black Hawk. A well-managed Bavarian restaurant. Authentic German dishes expertly prepared. Elk, venison, pheasant, and other native game featured in the fall. Open noon to 10 p.m. Closed Jan to Feb. One of Colorado's more outstanding ethnic restaurants. Chef-owned and run.

Teller House Eureka Room. *Expensive*. Laden with romance and history, the Teller House has been restored to its former splendor. Cocktail lounge. Teller Bar with "Face on the Bar Room Floor."

Johnson's Smorgasbord. *Moderate*. 121 Main St. on State 279. Buffet, plus cocktails, or enjoy your choice of sandwiches or full-course dinners. Open year-round.

COLORADO SPRINGS

Broadmoor Hotel Dining Rooms. *Deluxe* to *Moderate*. In the Broadmoor Hotel. There are a number of fine restaurants in this complex: the *Broadmoor Tavern*, the *Tropical Garden Room*, the *Main Dining Room*, the elegant *Charles Court*, the *Penrose Dining Room* with a splendid view of Cheyenne Mountain, and the *Golden Bee*, an English pub of the 19th century that was brought over and rebuilt. The *Penrose Room* and the *Charles Court* received many awards and boast sophisticated gourmet menus.

Red Cloud Inn. *Expensive*. . 10 mi. west at US 24 Topeka Ave. exit in Cascade. Chateaubriand, king crab legs. Own pies.

Flying W Ranch. *Moderate*. 6100 Wilson Rd. A truly Western supper, served on tin plates by lantern light on picnic tables. Children's plates. Western entertainment follows dinner. This is a working cattle and horse ranch. Reservations required.

Stagecoach Inn. *Moderate*. 702 Manitou Ave., 4 mi. west on US 24 Business in Manitou Springs. In an early American decor, chicken, prime rib, rainbow trout are specialties. Own baking.

The Village Inn. *Moderate*. 217 E. Pikes Peak Ave. Located in a beautiful old church, this restaurant serves consistently good food, from a versatile menu. Cocktail lounge.

Mission Bell Inn. *Inexpensive*. 178 Crystal Park Rd. in Manitou Springs. Locally popular Mexican restaurant in a Spanish decor.

DILLON

La France Restaurant. *Expensive*. Chef-owned, authentic French country cooking. Limited menu. *Prix fixe*. Good wines. French atmosphere. Attracts many skiers and summer vacationers.

DURANGO

The Canyon Restaurant-Tamarron. *Deluxe*. 18 mi. from Durango. International cuisine in the grand manner. Long wine list.

Grand Palace. *Moderate*. 557 Main St. Located in 19th-century surroundings in Rio Grandeland, the Rio Grande Railroad's recreation of an early-day frontier town. Cocktail lounge.

ESTES PARK

La Chaumiere. *Expensive.* At Pinewood Springs near Estes. Well-known French country restaurant. Good wines.

Stanley Dinner Theatre. *Expensive.* Carefully cooked international food. Varied entertainment. Lovely hilltop surroundings. Cocktails.

Old Plantation. *Moderate.* On Main St. Yankee pot roast, baked chicken, rainbow trout are specialties. Own pastries. Summer and fall only.

FORT COLLINS

Safari. *Moderate.* Dine amid African decor on steak, chicken. Bar. Entertainment.

Silver Queen. *Expensive.* American menu whose specialties include steak and chicken. Remarkable salad bar. Victorian decor. High prices.

Red Ram. *Moderate.* An old Georgetown tradition. German food prepared by an American chef. Stone-walled *Rathskeller* is candlelit and a favorite with skiers and the college crowds.

GLENWOOD SPRINGS

Buffalo Valley Inn. *Moderate.* 3½ mi. southeast on State 82. In a rustic, early Western setting. Steaks and ribs are prepared over an old-time applewood cooking pit. Children's menu available; small bar.

GRAND JUNCTION

Cork & Embers. *Expensive.* Candlelit steak restaurant. Nice salad bar. Cocktails.

Cafe Caravan. *Moderate.* Features general menu and buffet.

GREELEY

Garden Kitchen. *Inexpensive.* Chinese dinners. Own rolls and pastries.

LOUISVILLE

Colacci's. *Inexpensive.* 810 Main St. While this restaurant makes its own pasta and sauces, it's also known for steaks and shrimp. Cocktail lounge. Frequented by people from Boulder and Denver.

LYONS

Black Bear Inn. *Expensive.* This German menu features sauerbraten, schnitzel, own cheesecake, apple strudel, chocolate cake. Charming candlelit decor, has entertainment on weekends.

MONTROSE

Country Diner. *Moderate.* 1 blk. north of Ute Museum on Chipeta Ave. This restaurant does its own baking and specializes in steak. A good place to take the family.

OURAY

1876 Gourmet. *Expensive.* An interesting menu that changes daily, plus steaks. Own baking. Beams and paneling from a 100-year-old mine and period lamps make up the charming decor. Cocktails. Closed in winter.

PUEBLO

Top o' the Town. *Expensive.* 4201 Elizabeth St. Specialties are prime rib, steak, seafood. This locally busy restaurant is open all year.

SALIDA

The Spa. *Moderate*. A restful, quiet dining room with a glorious view of the surrounding mountains. Specialties are steak and trout with children's plates. Own baking. Open 6 a.m. to 10 p.m., winter to 8 p.m.

SILVERTON

Grand Imperial. *Moderate*. Pleasant hotel dining room with varied menu. Salad bar, own baking. Cocktail lounge.

STEAMBOAT SPRINGS

The Gallery. *Expensive*. Atop Storm Meadow Athletic Club. This Continental and American menu is served amidst beam ceilings and paintings. Specialties include broiled steak, beef Wellington, shrimp Donatello. Reservations essential during peak of ski season. An established restaurant with much repeat business.

VAIL

Gasthof Gramshammer. *Deluxe*. Austrian menu. Children's plates are available. Tyrolean atmosphere. *Antlers Room* features rack of venison, elk steak.

Left Bank. *Expensive*. Genuine French cuisine which includes a first-class coq au vin. Excellent house wines. Popular.

Lord Gore. *Expensive*. In an elegant atmosphere, beef, veal, and wild game are featured. Cocktail lounge.

WINTER PARK

The Chalet Restaurant. *Moderate*. Ambitious German fare, with some American items. Chef-owned. Good open wines.

Sitzmark. *Moderate*. A simple supper menu, but quality is stressed. Outstanding breakfasts at this skiers' restaurant. Wines.

IDAHO

Outdoor Life—Mountain Style

by

RALPH FRIEDMAN

Ralph Friedman is a freelance writer and teacher living in Portland, Oregon. He is the author of several regional books, a newspaper columnist, and a contributor to many publications. Mr. Friedman teaches freelance writing and Oregon folklore for Portland Community College.

The early history of Idaho (Indian, "gem of the mountains") is bound up with that of the states of Oregon and Washington. Idaho formed a part of Washington Territory until 1863, when it became the Territory of Idaho, with Lewiston as its capital. At that time it included Montana and Wyoming (separated in 1864 and 1868). These final changes reduced the limits of Idaho to a total area of about 85,000 square miles, described in the act of admission to statehood in 1890.

It seems unlikely that a Territory should have wanted to divest itself of acreage—especially when so much emphasis was, and still is, placed on bigness—yet this is what happened in the Pacific Northwest.

Washington Territory had "won independence" from Oregon Territory in 1853, and this new political area included all of what is now Idaho.

Then in 1860 gold was discovered on the Clearwater River, and armies without banners hastened to the strike. Other rich strikes followed: the Salmon River area, Boise Basin, Owyhee district, and elsewhere. Mining towns mushroomed, with populations in the thousands. In July 1861 this mining country cast the largest vote in the Washington territorial elections.

But the people of Washington feared that their destiny would lie in the callous hands of crude sluice-panners squatting by far-off streams. The solution: amputation. A movement was started to organize Idaho Territory and thus separate the miners from Washington.

The Idaho Territory

Idaho Territory was organized in 1863, much to the confusion of many of its people. By the time it was admitted to the Union in 1890—as an "anti-Mormon" state, of all things—a river of strangeness had run under a bridge of bewilderment.

First, although it had been "understood" in Washington, D.C., that Idaho would vote Republican, the state chose instead a Populist candidate in its first presidential election, in 1892.

Second, despite the religious feeling in 1890, today more than half of the active church members in the state are Mormons, i.e., belonging to the Church of Jesus Christ of Latter-Day Saints.

When Idaho Territory was organized it was bigger than Texas, containing as it did the areas of the present states of Idaho, Montana, and Wyoming. But little more than 14 months later, Montana Territory came into being, with its present dimensions, and in 1868 Wyoming Territory was created. This reduced Idaho to its present irregular shape, with its elongated, mountainous panhandle sandwiched between Washington and Montana and with the sprawling Snake River Plain and the desolate Owyhee plateaus.

The surface of the state is rough and mountainous, diversified by fertile river valleys, upland meadows, rolling prairies, broad plateaus, arid deserts with many rugged canyons, picturesque lakes, and deep gulches. The altitude is generally high, the extremes being 738 feet at Lewiston and 12,662 feet at Mt. Borah. Prominent in the midst of the Snake River Plain are the detached peaks Three Buttes, famous landmarks for travelers and tourists for many years. Big Butte is a volcanic cone rising to a height of 7,659 feet above sea level, and nearly 2,500 feet above the plain.

Take away the mountains from Idaho and all that is left are the Snake River Plain, the Owyhee desert, and a few small panhandle vales. Yet there are high places even in the desolate Owyhee Desert, where ranches are listed on some maps as though either to fill in the barren spaces or to bring hope to wayward adventurers who have braved the lonely traces, paths that seem to be as long-ago traveled as the ruts of the Oregon Trail that are still found elsewhere in the state. Such places are high at least in comparison with those of a great many other states. Five thousand feet above sea level would be reaching for the sky in New Jersey or Illinois, but there are ghost buttes on the Owyhee Desert more than 6,000 feet high, and nobody thinks of giving them a special look, if there is anybody around to do the looking.

The early gold miners didn't raise a fuss about living in 6,179-foot-high Silver City, just north of the desert. The elevation was—and is—simply one of those topographical facts that every generation of Idahoans has shrugged away.

Thrown up in 1863 as a ramshackle camp and then really worked at to make it a first-class settlement, including mansions that would have been deemed estimable by far older and more urban communities, Silver City is now as complete a ghost town as can be found anywhere in the country. No paved roads lead to it, and for common-sense reasons the best time to visit is from June through September.

The seat of Owyhee County, in which Silver City is located, is Murphy, where a paved state road runs out. The population of Murphy is about 75, making it one of the smallest county seats in the nation. The 1970 census showed Owyhee County to have about 6,500 people, most of whom live in the fertile northwestern part of the county, but the county seat remains at Murphy, away from the populated valley, though Marsing has 600 people and Homedale about 1,500.

Maybe the people of Owyhee County keep Murphy as the county seat simply because it's there, no matter how inconvenient it may be to the vast majority, or perhaps because Murphy symbolizes for them the romance of their past and the ruggedness of their land. Population per square mile is fewer than one. Much of the land is not only unsettled, it is unexplored; one of the recent sheriffs remarked that, "There are plenty of miles of county where no man has ever set foot or rode horse, either."

Within the state are 52 peaks over 10,000 feet high, including 14 peaks higher than 11,000 feet, and six peaks over 12,000 feet. In addition there are 65 named peaks 9,000 to 10,000 feet; 30 peaks 8,000 to 9,000 feet; and hundreds of peaks and summits below 8,000 feet.

The mountains so dominate Idaho that few roads cross the state east to west—and two of these, set close together, are in the very narrow panhandle. In one area there is not a single east-west paved road across the state for more than 200 miles. The center of the state is traversed north to south, between the Nevada and Montana borders, by US 93. To reach some parts of Idaho from some other parts it is quicker and easier to motor through Montana than to stay entirely within the confines of Idaho.

The lack of roads is sometimes a headache to Idahoans, but it also serves to illustrate the vast stretches of terrain that man has kept free from his own spoiling drives. Still, keeping Idaho beautiful and unpolluted has not been without a struggle—a seesaw, often-compromising battle fought out between conservationists and those who want the land for profit or (in the same vein) for their own discretionary use.

Preserving Idaho's Purity

Conservationists have waged intense campaigns to retain the purity of the magnificent White Cloud Peaks and the Salmon River—the "River of No Return"—and, in general, to keep the mountains, woods, and rivers from being spoiled by single-goal mining, lumber, and other industrial interests, as well as persons who want to establish homes on streams, thus diluting the wilderness character of the environs and the clearness of the waters. There are today stretches on the Salmon that look like rivulets compared with what was there (or ceased to be there) as recently as 1965.

Several strong measures have been taken in recent years to reclaim the land from rural blight and other unattractive man-made accretions. In 1973 the U.S. Forest Service practically dismantled a town, including a post office, because the hamlet marred the beauty of a recreational area.

There are today in Idaho few issues so heated or so transpolitical as the single issue of land and water use.

The collapse of the Teton Dam early in June, 1976, was only another round in the struggle between the mercantile concept of growth at any price and the ecological values of the environmentalists. The undaunted growth partisans took the disaster in stride, as their grandfathers had continued on after other kinds of adversities. But the day of playing pioneer in the old way seems outmoded by the harsher realities of pure survival.

"Sportsman's Paradise" on Government Property

There are tens of thousands of acres unmarked by roads or towns. Travel is by packhorse, or boat, or aircraft. Indeed, Idaho has established campsites that are reachable only by light plane.

More than 75 percent of Idaho's timber is owned by the federal government. These include forests of Douglas fir, ponderosa pine, true firs, Idaho white pine, Engelmann spruce, western larch, lodgepole pine, western red cedar, and western hemlock—the leading trees, in the order named. (Almost one-third the board feet of timber is Douglas fir.)

When Idahoans speak of their state as a sportsman's paradise, it is with the conviction that they are reciting unassailable verity.

There are two famous fishing grounds in two lake regions: one, in the panhandle, includes Pend Oreille, Coeur d'Alene, and Priest Lakes; the other includes Henry and Bear Lakes. These lake regions are among the finest fishing grounds in the United States.

The forest reserves of Idaho cover about 21 million acres. (The sawmill at Potlatch is said to be the largest producer in the world.) Among the wild animals in the forests are the grizzly bear, brown bear, black bear, raccoon, badger, wolf, fox, and coyote. Fur-bearing animals are represented by the lynx, mink, and beaver. The bison, once common, is now seldom seen—except perhaps at a zoo. Bighorn sheep and Rocky Mountain goats are occasionally observed. Deer, elk, and antelope are still numerous—a real "sportsman's paradise."

Only the journalist with the mind and soul of a petty-cash bookkeeper would list every lake and stream and forest. Suffice it to say that there are at least 2,000 lakes—and that many of them lie beyond the range of the roads. Not even planes and boats will get you everywhere. You go in by horse or by foot or not at all.

Most of Idaho's rivers empty into the Snake, which merges with the Columbia. The great provisioning depot for the mines was Walla Walla, Washington, near both great streams, and the routes to the early mines passed the confluence of the Snake and Clearwater rivers. It was here that Lewiston arose, a dusty (or muddy) fling of odd-assorted shacks, looking like the demoniac constructions of a drunken wood-butcher hellbent to run through his spree before being caught.

How It All Started

It was in Lewiston, the trading outpost of Walla Walla, that the first and second sessions of the Territorial legislature were held, starting in December of 1863 and November of 1864. But by the time the legislators could get around to seriously debating where the Territorial capital would be located, the issue had been resolved for them. A delegation—you can guess from where—stole the seal and legislative records and galloped off with them to Boise City (now Boise), where an otherwise innocent frame building was designated as the seat of Idaho Territory. And in Boise the capitol has remained.

There were a few gasps, of course, but nothing drastic happened. The impatient were hurrying on too swiftly toward the future to be irritated by small matters. Those with wisdom and perspective philosophized that anything odd was simply to be added to the area's strange and often turbulent history.

Even the name of the Territory had confusion in its origin. Granted that Idaho (first used in 1859, in the naming of Idaho Springs, Colorado) was a contraction of Shoshone words *Eee-da-how*. But was the generally accepted translation, "gem of the mountains," correct? Some thought *Ee-da-how* simply meant an exclamatory announcement that another sunrise, or morning, had arrived, meaning it was time to arise and get on with life.

But then came the Idaho Historical Society, with another version of how Idaho got its name. Let the Society's case be presented:

"When a name was needed early in 1860 for a new Territory in the Pike's Peak mining country, a lobbyist for the miners thought up the word 'Idaho.' He explained that the name meant 'gem of the mountains.' Congress was persuaded to designate the proposed territory 'Idaho,' and one of the mining towns there was named 'Idaho Springs.' Then, just before final consideration of the matter, the United States Senate changed the territorial name to 'Colorado,' because 'Idaho' was not an Indian word.

"In the meantime, use of the name 'Idaho' had spread from Washington, D.C., to the Pacific Northwest. A Columbia River steamboat, named the *Idaho* by Joseph S. Ruckel, a friend of the Colorado lobbyists, was launched June 9, 1860, for service between the Cascades and The Dalles (in Oregon). Later that year gold was found in the Nez Percé country. By 1862 the new Clearwater and Salmon River discoveries were known as the Idaho mines, after the steamboat used in the gold rush up the Lower Columbia. 'Idaho' had the advantage of being an excellent name, and that is why it gained popularity.

"Only two years after completing action on Colorado, Congress had to create a new Territory for the Idaho mines. The Idaho and Colorado name confusion forgotten, Congress chose 'Idaho' as the name for the new Territory established March 4, 1863. Strangely enough, Senator Henry Wilson of Massachusetts sponsored the final choice of name in both cases; he got the 1861 Territory redesignated 'Colorado' instead of 'Idaho' because 'Idaho' was not an Indian word. Two years later, he prevailed upon the Senate to use the name 'Idaho' after all."

Well, you can take your choice. But anyone with a curious mind will ask: Where, then, did the lobbyist get the name of "Idaho"? How did he know that it meant "gem of the mountains"? Was he inventing a word, which seems unlikely, or had he heard it from the Indians—in which case "Idaho" becomes once more an Indian word.

Lewis and Clark were the first white men here, Pacific-bound in 1805 and homeward-bound in 1806. They saw more mountains and less sunshine than they liked, and they also saw something that was to turn Idaho into a frontier war zone.

There were so many fur-bearing animals, they reported, that they were getting in each other's way. This was the signal for a rush of fur companies, old and new, to the streams of Idaho.

First to arrive was the remarkable David Thompson, probably the greatest land explorer and cartographer the continent has ever known. Sent out by the North-West Co., he established in 1809 on the eastern banks of Lake Pend

Oreille the trading post of Kullyspell House, the first white-man's building in the state.

A rare man in an industry of buccaneers, chauvinists, and cheats, Thompson sold no whiskey to the Indians and permitted none on the post. He treated the Indians (his wife was of the Metis tribe) as brothers and sisters, and no man in the annals of North American fur trading was more loved by them.

In his old age, and nearly blind, he was forced to sell his precious surveying instruments and even his overcoat to purchase bread for his wife and himself. He died at the age of 87 and was buried in Mt. Royal Cemetery, Montreal, without even a stone to mark his lonely grave. The Indians would have done better by David Thompson than did the fur barons, who reaped fortunes from his toils.

The Furious Fur Trade

A year after Kullyspell House, Major Andrew Henry of the Missouri Fur Co. built a trading post on the Snake River, near present Rexburg, the first establishment of a U.S. citizen built west of the Continental Divide.

The Mountain Men flocked to Idaho, some operating as free agents, some as employees of fur companies. These fur trappers, living and working in a primitive country, seldom lasted long enough to grow old. Major Henry lost 27 men on his first trip into the mountain country; Nathaniel Wyeth, another early entrepreneur, started with 200 men and at the end of three years had only 40. Some died from disease, some from starvation, many others at the hands of the Indians.

The fur business was big business. As many as 80,000 beaver pelts were taken from the Snake River drainage in a single season by trappers of the largest companies. The companies employed every maneuver imaginable to outwit and outmuscle each other for gains of the slaughter, and when means short of murder did not suffice, murder did. Large companies, usually owned by cosmopolitan men of means who had enormous finances at their command, swallowed small companies, usually owned by trappers who had sought to leave the ranks of piece-wage workers and set themselves up in the business they knew, with only their strength, know-how, and shoestring capital.

Before the covered wagons rolled through the Snake plain, the Rev. Henry Harmon Spalding arrived from the East with Marcus Whitman. The same year, 1836, that Whitman established Waiilatpu Mission, near presentday Walla Walla, Spalding opened Lapwai Mission, near where Lewiston now stands.

Six years later Fathers Jean de Smet and Nicholas LaPointe arrived in the panhandle to direct the Catholic Church's work among the Coeur d'Alene Indians.

Neither the Presbyterian nor the Catholic missions had a significant effect upon the history of Idaho, and relations between them were often strained, marked by jealousies and rumor-mongering.

In 1855 the first Mormon mission entered Idaho, and five years later a band of Mormon home-seekers, under the impression they had not ventured outside of Utah, established at Franklin, just north of Idaho's southern boundary, the first permanent agricultural settlement in the Territory. With the Mormons came the introduction of irrigation.

It was in this year of 1860 that gold was discovered in the Clearwater country. The covered wagons were still trudging on to Oregon and California, and the emigrants did not pause here. It was fortune-seekers from Oregon, Washington, Nevada, and California who flocked here, and Idaho became the first state to be settled from the West, rather than from the East.

The first Territorial governors appointed, however, were from the East. Most of them failed to show up, or showed up and left immediately, took office and disappeared, or like several secretaries of state, who "ran the store" while waiting for a governor, they made embezzling their main business.

The Blessings of the Soil

E. D. Pierce, who made the initial gold discovery, felt he knew almost exactly where the yellow metal was to be found. But prospector Noah Kellogg, up in the Coeur d'Alenes in 1884, had his runaway jackass to thank. On the spot where he caught up with his pesky critter he discovered sparkling galena ore, and soon a stampede was on. The quartz discovered was to make this one of the richest silver-lead regions in the world.

Fabulous as the early finds were, one-half the mineral wealth (gold, silver, copper, lead, and zinc) of Idaho found to date has come from its earth since World War II.

With silver-lead mining came corporations eager for profits, and the organization of miners into militant unions. There were many clashes between the representatives of the owners and the miners, climaxed by a fierce legal struggle revolving around the dynamite-bomb assassination of Governor Steunenberg in 1906. The courtroom trial saw the great Clarence Darrow, for the defense, pitted against William E. Borah, who was later to be elected six times to the United States Senate. Darrow won.

In addition to Borah, the state has placed in public office a number of unusual persons, including the strong-willed reformer Moses Alexander as governor, the only Jew ever to hold high public office in the state; and as U.S. Senator, Glen Taylor, who risked—and lost—his political future on his decision to run as vice-presidential candidate on the Progressive Party ticket of 1948, headed by Henry A. Wallace.

Following his election as president, Jimmy Carter named Idaho's popular governor, Cecil Andrus, to be Secretary of the Interior.

After the gold flurry of the 1860s, most of Idaho developed along agricultural lines. The larger part of the agricultural land is to be found on the plateau along the Snake River. Excellent crops are produced by the aid of extensive irrigation projects, most of them in the Snake River valley, which has a moderate and equable temperature. At first cattle and sheep were dominant. Then, with irrigation, the farmer invaded the open range. As Emerson Hough wrote in *The Story of the Cowboy*, "The house dog sits on the hills where yesterday the coyote sang. The fences are short and small and within them grow green things instead of gray."

Today, although Idaho has only a single city, Boise, with a population of 100,000 people, it is swiftly becoming industrialized. With a diversified economy, including a boom in tourism, Idaho is deep into the twentieth century, with the problems arising from such progress not too far behind.

Still, when Idahoans do dream of bigness, they also like to turn aside and think of the many dirt-road hamlets with a stack of hay and a rail fence across the street from the drowsy general store, and in the background the pleasing foothills of mighty ranges.

If Idahoans didn't like their neighbors so much, they would think that the real Idaho is where the people aren't—up there where you can't get to, unless you want to go as the mountain men did.

EXPLORING IDAHO

Boise is the capital and largest city of Idaho. A flourishing agricultural, horticultural, and stock-raising region lies about the city, and rich mines occur in the surrounding mountains. It is also one of the most important trade centers for wool in the United States. Though it lies in the southwest section of the state, it is the hub of tourism and will be our starting and finishing point for tours around Idaho.

Standing on the Boise River, at the upper end of the green Boise Valley, this capital is basically a residential city of homes and trees. It was named by French-Canadian voyagers who, after plodding for weeks through gritty, dust-choked wastelands, cried out, upon seeing trees: *"Les Bois!"* Boise is pronounced either *Boy-see* or *Boy-zee*; local ears hear both so often they cannot distinguish the difference.

The city boasts a new four-year college; a regionally famous philharmonic orchestra, with a resident conductor; a virile Little Theater; the Boise Art Gallery, whose traveling exhibitions bring paintings to a hundred towns and hamlets; and Basque folk-dance groups.

Basque dancing is a feature here because, although there has been of recent decades a heavy emigration of the Basques (especially to the Argentine Republic, Cuba, and Mexico), the state of Idaho still has more of these people than any place other than their homeland in the French and Spanish Pyrenees. The Basques first came here as shepherds, but open-range sheepherding has greatly declined, and most of them have become so Americanized that dance groups have been formed to help preserve, through the stirring rhythms of the traditional *Auresku*, *La Jota*, and *Purrusalda*, some spirit of the fading Basque culture.

And there are other points of interest within Boise. The State Capitol, monumental and classical in aspect, with Corinthian columns supporting a Corinthian pediment, is faced with sandstone from nearby Table Rock.

Ft. Boise, established July 4, 1863, as a U.S. military post to protect Oregon Trail emigrants and the new gold-mining population of the Boise Basin from Indians, has largely given way to a Veterans Administration Hospital, but several early buildings belonging to the fort still stand near the hospital. In the same area is O'Farrell Cabin, one of Boise's original dwellings and the first to shelter women and children.

The Old U.S. Assay Office, 210 Main St., was built in 1871 and operated until the mid-1930s. During those years, the Assay Office received more than $75 million in gold and silver bullion from the mines of southern Idaho and eastern Oregon.

Julia Davis Park, by the Boise River, contains the Idaho Historical Museum; Boise Art Gallery; State Library; Pioneer Village, with its 1863-built Pearce and Coston cabins (the latter fashioned of driftwood and put together with pegs); early stagecoaches, fire engines, and other vehicles;

"Big Mike," a powerful steam locomotive; zoo; rose garden; boating lagoon; recreation fields; amusement park; and free picnic grounds.

One of the more appealing buildings to visit is, of all places, the Union Pacific Passenger Station on Capitol Boulevard. Rising above the Boise River, this imposing building of brick and stucco is especially impressive at night, when the tall bell tower is accented from below by large floodlights. Man-made "natural" beauty also attracts visitors to the nearby Howard V. Platt Gardens displays of plants and waterfalls.

West of Boise

Now, from Boise, begins the western tour. Take Idaho 44, out State St., 8 miles. Turn onto Idaho 55, and drive 20 miles to Horseshoe Bend, a trading post of about 500. (West of Horseshoe Bend, along Idaho 52, rolls a pleasant fruit valley. Emmett, 20 miles west, is Idaho-famous for its cherries.)

Continuing north on Idaho 55, follow the North Fork of the Payette River 79 miles to McCall, at the edge of Payette Lake and the Payette Lakes Recreational Area. From here planes fly into the primitive areas; several back-packers' headquarters are in this town of 1,800. There are excellent tourist accommodations, fishing, boating, swimming, and camping. The U.S. Forest Service "Smokejumper" Center at McCall welcomes visitors.

From McCall, roads lead deep into the wilds of the Payette National Forest. One, mostly graded, picks its way 31 miles north to Burgdorf Hot Springs, where there are a swimming pool, campsites, cabins, and, of course, thermal springs.

Another road, graded, cuts a swath through the woods 52 miles to Yellow Pine, on the East Fork of the South Fork of the Salmon, where there is a typical dude ranch. Guides are available for fishing and hunting trips. Hunters go after mountain sheep or goats, or, on a deluxe expedition, elk, deer, and bear.

Beyond McCall, Idaho 55 jaunts through a round meadowed valley 12 miles to New Meadows, where the road runs out. To the south are dairy farms, gentle plateaus, and forests of yellow pines; to the north are the barren mountains and the shadowy canyons of the Little Salmon River. There is only one road north at this point—US 95. Riggins, 35 miles above New Meadows, lies in a T-shaped canyon at the confluence of the Little Salmon and Salmon rivers. To the west, 15 miles as the crow flies, is Hells Canyon, deepest gorge on the continent. Between Riggins and the gorge rise the Seven Devils, snow-capped most of the year. High on the slopes and in the saddles are glinting blue lakes encircled by evergreen pine, fir, spruce, and tamarack clusters.

Where Indians Feared to Tread

The Salmon River is the mythical "River of No Return," so named by the Indians, whose bravest of the brave were turned back by the steep canyon walls and rapids. But though the myth persists, the boats of the white man now travel upriver as well as downstream. Each year an increasing number of boats do try the Salmon, enjoying the adventure of riding the turbulent rapids. A few hermits live along it, in a mode more common to the nineteenth than the twentieth century.

A dirt road runs 20 miles up the Salmon from Riggins. The terrain is wild, scary, and photogenic. Nine miles up this trace from US 95 is a hot springs, with swimming pool, cabins, and picnic area.

Now, beyond Riggins, the highway swings alongside the lusty Salmon River. The deep, steep canyon cut by the stream is sometimes, near noon, sprinkled with sunshine, but more often it is carpeted by the cool shadows of twilight, though twilight may be hours away above the canyon walls.

Emerging from the chasm, the road is accosted by steep mountains, on whose lower slopes cling tiny farms. These massifs give way to mountains where beetling rocks crop through the brown parchment of the vegetation, while below, the Salmon bubbles along as it hurries to join the Snake. At White Bird, 29 miles above Riggins, it veers westward, to keep its ancient rendezvous.

It was in White Bird Canyon, north of this hamlet, that the first battle in the Nez Percé War was fought, in 1877, when the people of Chief Joseph repulsed the efforts of soldiers to stomp them into the ground.

Beyond White Bird village the historic road climbs almost 3,000 feet. At the summit there are panoramas of the Seven Devils, blue-misted canyons, and ranges to the east lost in purple obscurity. The descent is down slopes of gay and fragrant wildflowers and onto a sweeping plateau of amber grain-fields, whose center is Grangeville, 21 miles north of White Bird.

Today Grangeville is the marketplace of the lovely Camas Prairie, a realm of gold minted by seed and sun. But in the 1860s the town was the jumping-off point to a dozen gold camps. Some of these, far back, are touched by saddle trips through the Selway-Bitterroot Primitive Area. For up-to-date particulars, write Nez Percé National Forest Service Headquarters or Chamber of Commerce, both at Grangeville.

A dirt road south ends in 4 miles at Mt. Idaho, where the first Republican convention in Idaho Territory was held. Today it is another ghost town.

A more ambitious drive is up the Clearwater River to Elk City, 61 miles east of Grangeville via Idaho 14. This is an area of densely wooded canyon walls hovering above the tumultuous river, of glistening evergreens and ferns, and of wildflowers, miles of them, that launch wave after wave of almost suffocating fragrance.

Elk City, near the lip of Salmon River Breaks and Idaho Primitive Areas, is at the end of the paved road. The settlement actually numbers 450 persons, a veritable metropolis in these parts, where a collection of 20 souls constitutes a social center. Yet Elk City held 20,000 when it was a roaring gold camp. Nearby, as distance in these parts is measured, is the resort of Red River Hot Springs.

Razor Edge Ridges

Another route from Grangeville might be to follow Idaho 13 to Kooskia, 26 miles to the northeast. Now you are in Lewis and Clark country. The explorers staggered out of the mountains here in the autumn of 1805, half-starved and half-frozen after a frightful crossing over the icy and snow-covered razor-edge ridges.

Early in the 1960s, US 12, which parallels this Lolo Indian trail, was finally completed as a direct route between Lewiston and Missoula. In the 100 miles between Kooskia and the Montana border there is only one hamlet. Lowell (population 30), 23 miles east of Kooskia. But there are numerous campsites along the Lochsa River, the mountains roll away in all directions, and just above, and sometimes at roadside, is the treacherous path followed by Lewis and Clark. This is history close up.

North of Kooskia, follow US 12 for 7 miles to Kamiah, where the oldest Protestant church in Idaho stands. The front, mounted on two columns, looks like one birdhouse built on top of another. Near Kamiah is the East Kamiah Site of the Nez Percé National Park.

Continue along the Clearwater for 15 miles to the junction with Idaho 11. This road jogs 30 miles through immense stands of yellow pine, white pine, and fir to Pierce, where gold was first discovered in Idaho, in 1860. For decades the town looked like a Western movie-set; but now it is changing, and the population has soared from 500 to 1200—about what it held as a rough mining camp in 1861. (It was to get a lot bigger before the placer gold ran out and the miners departed.)

From Pierce backtrack on Idaho 11 for 12 miles to Weippe, near where the Lewis and Clark party first encountered the Nez Percé, and then another 16 miles to Greer, a tiny hamlet at the junction of US 12. Eight miles north, up US 12, stands gold rush Orofino, which had 12,000 people in 1861, with all their belongings and necessities for building a town brought in by pack train, which was for two years the only form of transportation. Orofino today has 4,000 population and is built on industry, agriculture, and tourism. A few miles below Orofino is the Lewis and Clark Canoe Camp, where the Nez Percé taught the elkskin-clad trailblazers how to make canoes by burning out fallen trees. It was in these canoes that the explorers made their way to the Pacific.

From Orofino, US 12 follows the Clearwater downstream about 40 miles to Lewiston, one of Idaho's most historic and interesting cities. At the confluence of the Snake and Clearwater, and walled in by mountains, it is as much a trading center today for the rich grainlands and fruit orchards which slope high above it in three directions as it was a frenetic supply and transportation hub for the upstream gold rush town of the 1860s. For many years practically all the stores in this city of 30,000 were on one long street, but in recent years shopping centers have been built on the nearby plateaus.

Idaho's only seaport (some ocean-going vessels come up the Columbia and Snake to dock here), Lewiston is at the lowest elevation in the state, only 738 feet. It is also one of the warmest places in the state and has been called Idaho's "Banana Belt."

From Lewiston Hill, there are panoramas of rivers, forests, waves of wheatland, and the city itself below.

Potlatch Forest offers free tours of its giant sawmill complex. Luna House Museum, in a pioneer residence, displays native art from early American civilizations. One of the most famous rodeos in the West, the Lewiston Roundup, is held in the second week of September.

River Boat Trips

One of the outstanding river boat trips in the West begins and ends here. A mail-supply boat, which plies up the Snake River almost to the gates of Hells Canyon, carries passengers and is also used solely for excursions. (For up-to-date fares and schedules, write: Chamber of Commerce, Lewiston, ID 83501.)

Nez Percé National Historic Park, at Spalding, site of Old Lapwai Mission, founded in 1836, is 10 miles from Lewiston. An old museum is worth the trip. Here, too, is the Spalding Area of the park. Three miles on is Lapwai, headquarters of the Nez Percé Indian Reservation. Visitors welcome.

Back at Lewiston, cross the Clearwater and take Idaho 3 to Genesee, Juliaetta, Kendrick, Deary, Santa, and on to St. Maries, a combined distance of about 100 miles. The road travels over, through, and past undulating prairie lands, long hills that seem in the distance like a succession of ocean swells, benchlands, and deep gorges. Juliaetta, with a population of about 400, is the home of the fine Arrow Museum, a collection of Indian artifacts.

St. Maries, a rustic county seat stretched out on softish hills, is the southern terminus of freight and passenger boats plying the St. Joe River, said to be the highest navigable stream in the world. It is called "shadowy St. Joe" by residents, because of the brooding, shifting reflections cast on the still surface of the stream by lovely foliage.

From St. Maries, boats go to Heyburn State Park (12 miles via Idaho 5), and some boats cruise into Coeur d'Alene Lake and up to its northern shore. Many shaded campgrounds are along the river and the lake.

Idaho 3 travels west of St. Maries for 11 miles and then northeast 22 miles, to Cataldo Mission, the oldest building in the state. You are now on I-90. Turn east and drive 12 miles to Kellogg, in the Coeur d'Alene mining district. A cornucopia of lead, silver, gold, and zinc (and an occasional scene of tragedy), it is neat and bustling, totally unlike the typical slag-ugly mining town. Those interested in touring mine facilities are advised to contact the Bunker Hill Smelter Plant in Kellogg and the Lucky Friday Mine in Mullan, 17 miles east of Kellogg on I-90.

Wallace, 10 miles east of Kellogg and 7 miles west of Mullan, and Burke, 7 miles north of Wallace, are on the axis of a large silver and lead mining area. Burke, with a population of 80, is the most colorful of the mining towns. Its one street is pressed against the side of a deep gulch.

Backtrack to the junction of Idaho 3 and US 95 Alt., and follow the latter road 56 miles north up the east shore of Coeur d'Alene Lake to the town of Coeur d'Alene.

Coeur d'Alene's Lovely Lake

This drive ought to be made slowly and with frequent pauses at the turnoffs, for there is enchantment every yard of the winding overlook. The lake is lovely to the point of disbelief. At times it appears to be a cloud floating off into space, one moment it may look like a field of windblown poppies, and the next like acres of glittering diamonds, within a 5-mile stretch it can be violet-tinted, rose-hued, and orange-blossomed. No lake in the Northwest evokes such imagery, has such a color range, or seems so ethereal.

Coeur d'Alene is the largest city in the Idaho panhandle, with tourist accommodations ranging from the elegant to the simple. No one ought to come here without taking the excursion boat ride to Heyburn State Park.

Follow US 95 north 18 miles, through crisp woods, vales, and lakes, to Bayview turnoff. Eight miles east, at Bayview, is the southern extremity of Lake Pend Oreille (pronounced *pon-duh-ray*), the largest lake in Idaho. Fabled for its fishing, it is the home of the Kamloops trout, biggest in the world. Four mountain ranges press against the lake, and the waters are broken by numerous isles. Bayview has cottages, apartments, campsites, trailer parks, stores, restaurants, rental boats, and a beach.

Return to US 95 and motor 28 miles, through woods brightened by small lakes, to Sandpoint, a cedar-shipping center on Pend Oreille Lake.

However, the lake is seen best by paved road from Idaho 200 (which skirts it for 25 miles) to Clark Fork, on the eastern side of the lake. Just west of here is the site of the first trading post (1809) in the Oregon Country.

From Sandpoint follow US 2 along the Pend Oreille River to Priest River—a delightful half-hour-or-so drive—and turn north on Idaho 57 to Coolin turnoff, 21 miles. Go east 4 miles to Priest Lake and up 4 miles to the Priest Lake Recreational Area. Priest is a "primitive" lake. The only settlement close to it is Nordman, 15 miles above the Coolin junction on Idaho 57; it has only 50 people. Even unpaved roads to the lake are few, and Upper Priest Lake is reachable only by boat.

The thrust of the Selkirk Mountains is shrouded by forests, hemming Priest in with lofty stands of virgin fir, pine, and spruce; ferns, shrubs, and wilderness weave intricate patterns between the trees. The forest contains bear, deer, elk, and wildcat. The recreational area has campsites, and there are resorts near Coolin.

Return to Priest River and take US 2 seven miles west to Albini Falls Dam, always impressive. Turn south on Idaho 41 and breeze through more lake country to Coeur d'Alene, 47 miles.

Now ride US 95 for 68 miles through the golden wheatlands of the western Palouse Hills to Moscow. Here on a slope is the University of Idaho campus, a landscaping masterpiece.

The road continues south to the summit of Lewiston Hill, where it spins down to Lewiston, 35 miles below Moscow.

Continuing south, US 95 lances pastoral hillsides and tablelands, where every farm is a sylvan setting and wildflowers lie in ambush among the pastures, springing up where least expected. So the road goes to Grangeville, 72 miles. Then it winds down White Bird Hill, through the shadows of Salmon River Canyon, past the meadowlands of the Little Salmon, and on into New Meadows, 87 miles.

At Council, 26 miles south, a gravel road meanders 41 miles to Cuprum, gateway for awesome views of Hells Canyon. Accommodations there. At Cambridge, 23 miles farther south, a paved road of 29 miles reaches a Hells Canyon dam.

Now US 95, leaving the blue haze of mountains, enters grain and dairy and then orchard country, reaching Weiser in 32 miles.

About 125 years ago the site was known to Oregon Trailers as a fording point on the Snake River. Today Weiser is the center of rich fruitland and has earned a regional reputation for its nearby water recreation spots, the closest being only half-a-mile west of town, at the Idaho Power Co. boat dock.

From Weiser, follow US 95 and then I-80N, south and east through numerous fruit, dairy, and industrial villages and towns, to Nampa, 56 miles, where the colorful Snake River Stampede is staged each mid-July. Lake Lowell, 6 miles southwest, harbors millions of migratory birds. There is boating, swimming, fishing, and picnicking.

From Nampa, it is 20 miles to Boise via I-80N.

Eastern Tour

Back again at Boise, the futuristic freeway Interstate 80N strides boldly eastward across prairie terrain, as we reverse the path taken by the covered wagons on the Oregon Trail. In 42 miles the road reaches Mountain Home, once a bleak clump of shacks scrounging for life on a sagebrush flat (an Air Force base was built nearby, and now the modern town has a population of 7,000).

Eighteen miles from Mountain Home the highway meets the Snake River, and 9 miles farther, at Glenns Ferry, is Three Island Ford, an historic crossing on the Oregon Trail. Twenty miles on, at Bliss, a hamlet of about 100 souls, the road forks. I-80N has been carrying three other national roads: US 20, 26, and 30. Now, at Bliss, US 20 and 26, combined, shoot straight east, while I-80N cuts southeast and US 30 plows straight south. Gooding, 11 miles east of Bliss on US 20-26, is the gateway to Mammoth Cave, Shoshone Ice Caves, Sun Valley, and Craters of the Moon.

From Bliss, US 30 travels 19 miles to Thousand Springs, cascading down the glistening banks above the road. The sprays and gushes are believed to be the outlet of Lost River, or of several buried rivers.

Ten miles more—and Buhl. Lying under the breaks of a deep canyon eroded by the Snake is the world's largest trout hatchery, which produces annually more than 1.5 million pounds of Rocky Mountain Rainbows. Visitors are cordially welcomed.

On a further side trip, take the county road due south 11 miles to Castleford. Follow directions 5½ miles to Balanced Rock, awesome among even the fantastically shaped pillars and colonnades in Devils Creek Gorge. The 40-foot tower resting on a tiny block of stone looks as though a feather would knock it over—but it has stood this way for eons.

Twin Falls, 15 miles east of Buhl, is southcentral Idaho's largest city, with a population of some 22,000. Idaho's most beautiful bridge, a cantilever span 1,350 feet long and 476 feet high, and part of US 93 just north of town, affords a striking view of the Snake River canyon.

Shoshone Falls, about 4 miles northeast of Twin Falls, is spectacular in the spring, when the Snake at full water takes a sheer 212-foot drop over the basaltic horseshoe rim nearly 1,000 feet wide. During the summer, when water is diverted for irrigation, the river trickles rather than plunges, but the naked rimrock is not without its own stark beauty.

From Twin Falls, US 30 furrows the Snake River plain, a basin of prosperous farms. Burley, 40 miles east, is a potato-products center, with large processing plants.

Now turn south on Idaho 27 to Oakley, 22 miles. This town has fewer than 700 persons, but its Pioneer Days Rodeo, in late July, was long one of the state's liveliest. From Oakley follow a gravel road southeast 22 miles to the Cassia City of Rocks, a 25-square-mile area of eroded stones resembling a scattered village. There is immense historical significance here, too, for this silent "city" was the junction of two famous trails—the Sublette Cutoff (to Oregon) and the California Trail. Here the wagons divided and many an adieu was said at the foot of the eroded cathedrals, towers, and shattered walls. Upon the walls are recorded thousands of names and dates, as well as messages left for those not yet arrived. Below the "city" is Almo, whose 40 persons are blessed by an abundance of gorgeous scenery. A paved road leads 16 miles to Idaho 77. Albion, 11 miles onward, is a tiny former college town whose charm lies in its decaying buildings, repositories of pioneer lore.

Continue north 12 miles to I-80N again. Turn east, at a point 9 miles east and 2 miles north of Burley. Forty-eight miles farther on, past a turnoff to Minidoka Dam and past Massacre Rocks, lies American Falls, settled during the days of the Oregon Trail. In 1900, the area from American Falls to 170 miles west of it supported little more than sagebrush, coyotes, cheat grass, and lizards. Today it is all one huge irrigated garden. Within a few minutes' drive of the city is the mile-wide American Falls Dam and its 36-mile-long reservoir. The reservoir recreation area offers boating, swimming, fishing, and picnicking.

The indoor pool at Indian Springs, 4 miles south on Idaho 37, is one of Idaho's finest. Pocatello, 24 miles east of American Falls, is eastern Idaho's largest city (with a population on its way toward 50,000) and the seat of Idaho State University. Along the Portneuf River, which flows through the west side of the city, beaver-workings are still observable. In Ross Park there is evidence of Indian art work carved into stone cliffs.

Thirty-three miles southeast of Pocatello, on US 30, is Lava Hot Springs, one of Idaho's many wonders. Mineral waters boiling out of lava rocks— each spring with a different mineral content—form the basis for a state-owned resort consisting of mineral plunges and natatoriums. Accommodations are nearby. Up the cold Portneuf River, within easy hiking distance of the village, are 50 small waterfalls and the smoke holes of old volcanoes.

Return to Pocatello, turn north on US 91, and drive 11 miles to Ft. Hall, agency headquarters for the Shoshone and Bannock tribes on the Ft. Hall Indian Reservation. In July the famed Sun Dances, religious observances followed by buffalo feasts, are held at Ross Fork and Bannock Creek. In early August the reservation stages the exciting 4-day Shoshone-Bannock Indian Festival, complete with historical pageant, war and social dancing, Indian games, parade, all-Indian rodeo, displays, buffalo feast, and crowning of Miss Shoshone-Bannock.

Fur Traders and Pioneers

This area is also the site of the old trading post Ft. Hall, built over 100 years ago. It became a wayside inn for wagon trains and the only inhabited place between Ft. Bridger in Wyoming and Ft. Boise on the Oregon border, until it was demolished by floods in 1863. An estimated 250,000 people came through here on their way to Oregon and California. Here Jason Lee, on his way to missionary fame in Oregon, preached the first Protestant sermon west of the Rockies. Within an hour a Mountain Man was killed in the carousing that followed Lee's stern message. Undaunted, Lee thereupon performed the first Protestant funeral service in Idaho.

Blackfoot, 12 miles onward, is a potato, dairy, and cattle center. The Eastern Idaho State Fair, held in early September, is a colorful grassroots show. Taking I-15 north, within 20 miles the road passes The Lavas, a bizarre conglomeration of volcanic effects. Within 10 more miles, Idaho Falls is reached, the state's third largest city, with a population edging toward 40,000.

Idaho Falls is a lovely city, its beauty enhanced by a low but turbulent 1,500-foot-wide waterfall in the Snake River, which hums through the city. A landscaped picnic area drapes the river banks. A significant fraction of the trout stocking in the state comes from Sportsman's Park on the Snake River, where half a million fish are raised annually. Tautphaus Park features a campground and rodeo area.

Although the Mormon Temple, a superb piece of architecture, is not open to the public, the visitors' center offers slides and guided tours of the area. Idaho Falls reflects the agricultural wealth of the upper Snake River Valley in its many products: seed-pea, potato, beet, honey, dairy, flour. Its stockyards are Idaho's largest. To the northwest is located the central control of the Atomic Energy Commission's National Reactor Testing Center.

East of Idaho Falls, US 26 runs through pleasant vales and woods, and in 72 miles the road reaches the Wyoming border. The last 30 miles run first along the Snake River trench; then past earth-filled Palisades Dam, 270 feet high and 2,100 feet long; then past the dam's reservoir, a camping and boating area. At Alpine, on the border, follow US 89 to Jackson, Wyoming (29 miles), gateway to the Tetons and Yellowstone. Turning west at Jackson on Wyoming 22, cross 8,429-foot Teton Pass, and 24 miles from Jackson reach Victor, Idaho, where old-fashioned melodramas are presented at Pierre's Summer Playhouse.

Where Mountain Men Met

From Victor turn north on Idaho 33. Six miles up the road is Teton Basin, known in early days as Pierre's Hole. This idyllic vale, facing the grandeur of the Tetons, was one of the most celebrated and infamous rendezvous areas during the fur-trapping years.

Here took place an annual conclave of fur-company traders and suppliers from the East and Mountain Men from the back country. The stated objective was the exchange of commodities, but the Mountain Men, traveling alone or in small bands, and always in peril the rest of the year, used the rendezvous to gamble, horserace, drink themselves near blind, fight (with fists or other weapons), and buy or seize the "love" of Indian women. Each year before the camp broke and its occupants scattered, the traders and suppliers were wealthier, the Mountain Men were usually as poor as before, and several men lay buried, their knife and bullet holes still fresh. Men also died with heads broken by a fall from a racehorse. If the horse was a good-looking animal, there might be a fight for it—and perhaps another death.

Two miles on, sitting astride the largest bed of coal in the state, is Driggs, hub of the Grand Targhee Recreation Area. Tetonia, 8 miles farther, stares straight east at the Grand Tetons. The villagers, fewer than 200, have all the fresh air, elbow room, and scenery they want.

Continue on Idaho 33 for 32 miles to US 20, 6 miles above Rexburg, or take Idaho 32 north for 21 miles to Ashton. If you take Idaho 33 you will pass the site of Teton Dam, whose collapse in 1977 wrought great tragedy to farmsteads and villages of Newdale, Sugar City, and Teton, and to the city of Rexburg. If you drive Idaho 32 you will follow the granite peaks of the Grand Tetons, worth crossing a continent to view. Ashton, a pleasant settlement of some 1,200, 26 miles above Rexburg, reaches out to open aspen glades, emerald meadows, and cold, clear streams.

At Ashton veer off again, this time on lilting Idaho 47, 9 miles to the tourist resort of Warm River, and, within the next 25 miles, to Upper and Lower Mesa Falls. Upper Mesa has a drop of 114 feet, while Lower Mesa plunges 65 feet, but the distance is meaningless compared with the boil of the water, the cascading pools at the bottom (campgrounds close by), the richness of the forests above the canyon walls, and the magic green of the escarpments, deep-dyed and wrinkled.

Back at Ashton, continue north on US 20 (which is also US 191 here). Twenty miles up begins one of the most unusual "cities" in the United States—Island Park Village (population: 136), whose main streest is 21 miles long. (It was 33 miles long about a decade ago.) Lodge and resort owners incorporated their area into the "village." Entirely inside the Targhee National Forest, Island Park contains two lakes and 75 miles of streams. It also encloses—5 miles off the national highway, via Idaho 84—Big Springs, the source of the South Fork of the Snake River. Gushing from the base of a mountain, within 100 feet of its birthplace, the South Fork is almost a full-grown river.

Fourteen miles above the turnoff to Big Springs, Idaho 87 makes its appearance. It is in Idaho for only a few miles but in that distance it touches Henry's Lake, so prominent in Mountain Man lore. (It is also renowned for fishing.) At the Idaho 87 junction, US 20-191 bends east and in 10 miles comes to West Yellowstone, the Idaho entrance to Yellowstone National Park.

Return south on US 20 to Ashton—but first you may want to have another taste of Henry's Lake, Idaho's most legendary trout fishing and game area. The 5-mile-long lake, fed by a multitude of rivulets squirming out of the lofty mountains that envelop the basin, is more than 6,000 feet in elevation. Tourist accommodations are plentiful.

From Ashton, continue south 14 miles to St. Anthony. A dirt road west of town crawls north through a flatland to the Scenic Sand Dunes (or St. Anthony Sand Dunes), about a mile wide and 30 miles long, south to north. At sunset the colors of the dunes are dazzling, red and gold and lemon streaked with pink.

A monument to Ft. Henry, built in 1810, stands at St. Anthony, though the actual location was 6 miles northwest. The fort was the first in the Snake River system.

Twelve miles south of St. Anthony is Rexburg, a growing agricultural center and the seat of pleasant Madison County.

At Rexburg, take Idaho 88 west, through a broad, flat valley, for 20 miles to I-15 (also US 91 here). The national highway plows through bleak landscapes for 52 miles to the Montana border. (The road is bound for Butte.)

Continue west on Idaho 88 from the I-15 (and US 91) junction for 14 miles to Mud Lake. The large body of water here harbors thousands of migratory ducks and geese. Here take Idaho 28 northwest to the crossing of Idaho 22, 16 miles. You can also reach this point by taking Interstate 15 (also US 91) to Dubois, 24 miles, and traveling west on Idaho 22 for 30 miles.

From the junction of Idaho 22 and Idaho 28, the latter road needles between steep mountain ranges for 106 miles, to Salmon. There is not a lonelier paved road in the state. The only points of roadside habitation are the country-store, gas-pump map dots of Blue Dome and Gilmore, the 100-or-so-persons hamlet of Leadore, a cluster of 50 persons at Tendoy, and Baker, with a population of 100. (Somehow, each mile on this sparsely traveled road seems like three miles on other roads.)

Tendoy was named for a Shoshone chief, and when you come to Tendoy you are deep in old Shoshone country. Ten miles east, on what is now a gravel road, Lewis and Clark crossed the Continental Divide at 7,373-foot Lemhi Pass.

A Celebrated Indian Maiden

Four miles onward is a monument to Sacajawea, the Shoshone woman who acted as guide for the Lewis and Clark party and who supposedly was born in these hills.

Those interested in nature trips use the town of Salmon as a base of operations, and the normal population of about 3,000 is greatly increased by the summer visitors. Being the largest town in the vicinity, it is also the headquarters of the Salmon National Forest. Some of its importance is due to vast cattle and mining industries surrounding the town.

The valley in which Salmon was built is as pretty as a subalpine wildflower, and the town itself occupies an attractive spot at the confluence of the Salmon and Lemhi Rivers. Island Park, a timbered area of five acres on the river, is a popular campground.

Some boat trips down the stormy Salmon River are organized here, and are guided by white-water men who make their living taking hunting, fishing, and sightseeing parties down the stream.

However, most floats down the Salmon begin at North Fork, 21 miles above Salmon. North Fork boasts several modern motels, restaurants, grocery stores, and bars—"all the needs of the sportsman or recreationist."

At North Fork, after flowing for 100 miles almost straight toward the Continental Divide, at the Montana border the Salmon River dramatically turns west and for 200 miles churns through great Primitive regions to join the Snake below Hells Canyon. In its hectic journey it gurgles and grinds its way through a gorge a thousand feet deeper than the Grand Canyon of the Colorado. It is the longest stream lying wholly within any one of the coterminous forty-eight states.

A gravel road clings to the river westward for 49 miles, traveling at river grade through a precipitous narrow canyon. At 41 miles the Middle Fork enters the main stream. On this gravel road few habitations are seen, and those that are observed dip many years back in time. The only settlement is Shoup, a collection of shacks and a population of ten, 19 miles from North Fork. Wildlife, including the regal mountain sheep, are spotted occasionally. Beyond North Fork, the road—US 93—travels only 26 miles before crossing into Montana at 6,995-foot Lost Trail Pass. (Missoula lies 105 miles away.)

Our eastern Idaho tour now turns south. Below Salmon US 93 soon enters the upper gorge of the Salmon River, which the road follows for better than 100 miles.

The gorge is not simply a corridor of cliffs evenly spaced from the stream. Sometimes the canyon is a steep, narrow defile, and sometimes it seems to fall away, sloping into hills. Just when one becomes accustomed to looking at ridges, solitary crags break the skyline. Rounded bluffs give way to sudden thrusts of towers; a burly monument stands facing an exquisitely sculptured castle. The colorings are as varied as the formations.

Fifty-eight miles below Salmon lies Challis, a town even more captivating in its setting than Salmon. The mountains of the Lemhi Range, northeast, are a mass of luscious colors, particularly at sunset under drifting clouds; sunrise also gorgeously tints the bluffs above the river.

Challis is reached from Salmon via US 93, but at Challis there is a change in road designation. From Challis down through Stanley, Ketchum, Hailey, and into Shoshone, the road is now Idaho 75, also known as the Sawtooth Scenic Highway.

Challis is the gateway to strange rivers, an antelope valley, mountains that seem to rise from sky platforms, thick stands of Douglas fir and lodgepole pine, and little lakes that dimple and freckle the wilderness. All are in the far-flung Challis National Forest. Dirt roads and trails lead to many improved campgrounds, and pack trips are made up here for expeditions into areas where no tenderfoot should venture without the hand of experience as a guide.

Two miles below Challis, Idaho 75 meets US 93, formerly US 93 Alt. To reach here from where we took off for Salmon, at the junction of Idaho 22 and 28, follow Idaho 22 and US 26 southwest 46 miles to Arco and go north 78 miles on US 93. The road, US 93, passes Mt. Borah, also known as Borah Peak, at 12,662 feet Idaho's tallest mountain.

US 93 also passes, on the stretch from Arco to Challis, Mackay Dam and Reservoir and the Grand Canyon in miniature—so there's quite a bit to see on this road.

Idaho 75, continuing south and then running west, follows the Salmon River upstream through rugged masses of cloud-shattering peaks for 55 miles, to Stanley, entrance to the Stanley Basin Recreational Area in the Sawtooth Mountains. In this basin, stretching for 25 miles between craggy mountains, the Salmon is born, nurtured by cold streams and lakes fed by mountain snows.

South of Stanley, in the Sawtooth National Recreational Area and Wilderness, is a multitude of lakes cupped under the jagged Sawtooth peaks. Gravel roads lead to the edges of a few, others can only be reached by trail. Campsites are to be found on the banks of most lakes, and on the most accessible lakes there are lodges and other tourist accommodations.

A World-Famous Resort

The highway south of Stanley passes roads to several lakes, including the well-known Redfish and Alturas, before climbing 8,701-foot Galena Summit. From this "top of the world" drive the Sawtooths seem close enough to touch. Sixty miles from Stanley, Idaho 75 comes to Sun Valley.

Long recognized as one of the world's famous winter resorts, Sun Valley has for some years also been popular as a summer playground. Sun Valley is a village unto itself, with even its own hospital. In addition to the usual ice skating, swimming, riding, tennis, and fishing, there are mind-shattering trips into the wilderness.

A mile below Sun Valley is Ketchum, the last home of Ernest Hemingway, who wrote some sections of *For Whom the Bell Tolls*—"The part with all the snow in it," as he recalled years later—in Room 205 of the Sun Valley Lodge. He lived in a house on the Wood River, supped at the Christiana Inn the night before his death, and his body now lies in the town's rustic cemetery.

Twelve miles south along the Wood River is Hailey, site of the fine Blaine County Historical Museum. Four miles below Hailey is Bellevue, a sweet rustic village of 600 folks, give or take a few, and 10 miles below Bellevue is a junction with Idaho 68. To reach this junction from Arco, on US 93, travel 44 miles southwest to Carey, a hamlet of 300, and then 20 miles west on Idaho 68 to Idaho 75. US 93 passes through a corner of the Craters of the Moon National Monument. This utterly desolate 83-square-mile area is a fantastic, grotesque Dante's inferno of basaltic features. A 7-mile loop drive passes by some of the volcanic landscapes, while a variety of trails lead to others. The loop drive, its side roads, and several short walks can all be made in about one hour—if you're in a hurry. Visitors are often surprised to see a few trees and hosts of wildflowers in this universe of death. They are even more surprised to learn that quite a few animals make their home here.

South of the Idaho 68 junction, Idaho 75 leaves behind the shadows of the Sawtooths and rolls into the Snake River Plain. At 10 miles, a turnoff leads one mile to Shoshone Ice Caves, lying in the hollow core of a once molten river of lava. Above-ground you might be sweating—this is hot summer country—but in the caves a few feet below you will need a warm sweater.

Idaho 75 leads south 17 miles to Shoshone, market center of a large sheep-raising area. (Along the way, the road passes a turnoff to Mammoth Cave, a mile from the road. Some people consider Mammoth a more awesome and remarkable cavern than Shoshone.) As can be guessed, not everyone pronounces Shoshone the same way; evidently both *Sho-shone* and *Sho-sho-nee* are acceptable. The name is an Americanization of the Indian *Shoshoni*, meaning "Great Spirit."

At Shoshone, Idaho 75 has its southern terminus. US 93 comes into Shoshone from Arco and Carey, and south of Shoshone the road is US 93.

Turn west on US 26 at Shoshone and drive 16 miles to Gooding, the center of the bountiful Big Wood and Little Wood River Valleys, prairies th at remind Midwesterners of home.

More famous than the city itself is the nearby City of Rocks, a 6-square-mile area of colored shale and sandstone formations. As is peculiar to such rock configurations, there is resemblance to ancient ruins: battered pillars and jagged columns, tumbled castles, sagging towers, shattered cathedrals, fallen spires, sagging balconies, and stairways broken in two.

From Gooding it is 11 miles via US 26 to Bliss and then an easy 90-minute (or less) drive on I-80N to Boise, where our exploration of Idaho began.

PRACTICAL INFORMATION FOR IDAHO

FACTS & FIGURES. Idaho has two nicknames: "Gem State" and "Spud State" (the former for its wide variety and abundance of minerals and the second for its big, tasty potatoes). The state flower is the syringa; the state tree, the white pine; the state bird, the mountain bluebird. *Esto Perpetua* ("May It Last Forever") is the state motto. "Here We Have Idaho" is the state song. Boise, the state's biggest city (population: about 100,000), is also the capital. The 1975 interim census showed Idaho to have 828,040 people, a hefty percentile gain over the 1970 figure of 711,910. Projected population for 1980 is 970,000; for 1985, 1,119,320; for 1990, 1,256,200; and for 2000, 1,467,270.

HOW TO GET THERE. *By air: United* and *Hughes Air-west* serve Boise out of Los Angeles, Portland, Salt Lake City, and Seattle. In addition, *United* flies direct from Chicago, Denver, San Francisco, and New York. *Hughes Airwest* reaches Boise out of Calgary, Edmonton, Stockton, Burbank, Las Vegas,

Pasco, Phoenix, San Diego, and Santa Ana. Pocatello is served by *Western* out of Salt Lake City, Phoenix, Denver, Butte, Reno, Helena, Great Falls, Billings, Las Vegas, Los Angeles, and San Francisco. Twin Falls and Pocatello can be reached by *Hughes Airwest* out of Seattle, Portland, Salt Lake City, San Francisco, Los Angeles, Santa Ana, Ontario, Burbank, Palm Springs, Yuma, Phoenix, Tucson, Pasco, Yakima, Sacramento, Monterey, and Stockton. *Hughes Airwest* flies to Lewiston out of Los Angeles, Palm Springs, Las Vegas, Santa Ana, Phoenix, Reno, Medford, Burbank, Calgary, Edmonton, and San Diego. *Cascade* flies to Lewiston from Spokane and *Sun Valley Key* flies out of Salt Lake City to Sun Valley.

By train: Amtrak stops at Sandpoint on the way to Seattle and at Pocatello and Boise on the way to Portland.

By car: From Utah: Interstate 80N to Rupert and Burley; Interstate 15 to Pocatello. From Nevada: US 93 to Twin Falls. From Oregon: US 95 to Caldwell; Interstate 80N to Caldwell, Nampa, and Boise. From Washington: Interstate 90 to Coeur d'Alene; US 2 to Sandpoint; US 12 and US 195 to Lewiston; Wash. 270 to Moscow. From Montana: US 2 to Bonners Ferry; Interstate 15 to Idaho Falls; US 12 to Kamiah; US 93 to Salmon; Interstate 90 to Wallace and Kellogg. From Wyoming: US 20-US 191 to St. Anthony; US 26 to Idaho Falls. From Canada: Canada Route 21 from Creston to border and Idaho 1 to Bonners Ferry; Canada Route 3 to border and US 95 to Eastport and Bonners Ferry.

By bus: Greyhound reaches all major cities: Trailways' route is across Interstate 80N, the heartland of Idaho.

 HOW TO GET AROUND. Transportation in a state that has a geography as varied as Idaho's poses a great challenge. From the days when the Nez Percé Indians brought in the now-famed Appaloosa horse, through the development of commercial airlines, Idahoans have used virtually every mode of travel.

By air: Hughes Airwest serves Boise, Lewiston, Pocatello, Idaho Falls, and Twin Falls.

By car: One of early America's most important thoroughfares, the Oregon Trail, traversed the broad southern part of Idaho, and today interstate highways follow the Oregon Trail closely, as well as the Mullan Road, in the Idaho Panhandle, at the top of the state. Improved transportation is a factor in bringing together this state that has for so many years been divided geographically, commercially, and even politically. The slow spiral routes on US 95 have been straightened, many highways have been widened, new roads have been built—all in the past 15 years. Interstate 90 is superseding US 10 across the panhandle; Interstate 80N and Interstate 15 have replaced US 30 and US 91 along much of the Oregon Trail route; Interstate 15 is succeeding US 91 in eastern Idaho. The route followed by Lewis and Clark across north-central Idaho is paralleled by US 12 and that, too, is relatively new, as roads go. Before it was built there was only wilderness. Even today there is no vehicle service available on this road for about 75 miles. US 93 from Shoshone to Stanley and on to Challis has been redesignated Idaho 75, and has been named the Sawtooth Scenic Highway. In addition, US 93A from north of Shoshone via Arco to a junction south of Challis has been redesignated US 93. Magnificent scenery, from 8701-foot Galena Summit to Sawtooth Mountain valleys and along the Salmon River, make renamed Idaho 75 a popular tourist run. US 95, cutting along the western part of the state, from Canada to Oregon, is the longest road and touches the most varied scenery.

Car rental: Avis and Hertz have car rental offices in Boise, Idaho Falls, Pocatello, Sun Valley, and Twin Falls. Hertz has additional offices in Caldwell, Hailey, Lewiston, and Soda Springs.

By bus: A dozen bus lines operate in this far-flung state. Connecting bus or limousine service is available at points served by airlines.

By train: The daily *Empire Builder* and the triweekly North Coast *Hiawatha* stop at Sandpoint on the Seattle-Chicago run. The *Pioneer*, on the Portland-Salt Lake City run, stops daily at Boise and Pocatello.

Access to the vast primitive areas of the state is principally by pack horse and charter plane. Guides are widely utilized by big-game hunters. There are also many wilderness trails that have known only the tread of moccasin or boot.

TOURIST INFORMATION SERVICES. Best all-round source of information is *Idaho Department of Commerce and Development*, Room 108, Capitol Building, Boise 83720 (tel. 208/384-2470.) The local chambers of commerce are good sources on individual communities (in Boise, tel. 344-5515). A number of roadside information booths are staffed in summer.

Information about the Hells Canyon-Seven Devils Scenic Area, Salmon River Primitive Breaks Area, and Selway-Bitterroot Wilderness can be obtained from the United States Forest Service, Nez Perce National Forest, 319 E. Main, Grangeville, ID 83530; on the Idaho Primitive Area from USFS, Challis National Forest, Challis, ID 83226; on Birds of Prey Natural Area from Bureau of Land Management, Boise District, 230 Collins Rd., Boise, ID 83702; on Middle Fork of the Salmon Wild River from USFS, Salmon National Forest, Forest Service Building, Salmon, ID 83467; on Middle Fork of the Clearwater Wild River from USFS, Clearwater National Forest, Orofino, ID 83544.

For information on Idaho's national forests, write: Kaniksu National Forest, Sandpoint, ID 83864; Kootenai National Forest, 418 Mineral Ave., Libby, MT 59923; Coeur d'Alene National Forest, Coeur d'Alene, ID 83814; St. Joe National Forest, St. Maries, ID 83861; Clearwater National Forest, Federal Building, Orofino, ID 83544; Nez Percé National Forest, Grangeville, ID 83530; Bitterroot National Forest, 316 North 3rd St., Hamilton, MT 59840; Payette National Forest, McCall, ID 83638; Salmon National Forest, Forest Service Building, Salmon, ID 83467; Challis National Forest, Challis, ID 83226; Boise National Forest, 210 Main St., Boise, ID 83701; Sawtooth National Forest, 1525 Addison E., Twin Falls, ID 83301; Targhee National Forest, 420 N. Bridge St., St. Anthony, ID 83445; Caribou National Forest, 427 N. 6th Ave., Pocatello, ID 83201; Cache National Forest, Federal Building, Logan, UT 84321.

For information on state parks, write: State Parks & Recreation, 6621 Warm Springs Ave., Boise, ID 83706; on education and recreational aspects of dams— Regional Director, Bureau of Reclamation, P.O. Box 043, Federal Building, 550 West Fort St., Boise, ID 83702; on hunting and fishing—Idaho Fish & Game Dept., P.O. Box 25, Boise, ID 83707; on guide service in the mountains and on the rivers— Idaho Outfitters and Guides Association, P.O. Box 95, Boise, ID 83701.

SEASONAL EVENTS. Idaho's seasonal attractions are strongly tied to the heritage of the land, the people being more interested in celebrating themselves than in crowing for tourists. This indigenous folk spirit makes the events more charming to outsiders. Special festivals and celebrations generally begin in May and extend thru mid-September. For up-to-date information on specific dates (which sometimes change from year to year), write: Idaho Division of Tourism and Industrial Development, Room 108, Capitol Building, Boise, ID 83720.

May: *Boise*, Music Week, citywide music program in schools, churches, colleges; *Sandpoint*, Kamloops & Kokanee Week, fishing derby; *Riggins*, Salmon River Rodeo; *Fruitland*, Fruitland Food Fair; *Payette*, Apple Blossom Festival & Boomerang Days; *Lewiston*, Orchards Blossom Festival.

June: *Deary*, Strawberry Festival; *Worley*, Whaa-Laa Days, Coeur d'Alene Indian games and war dances; *Kamiah*, Kamiah Rodeo; *Weiser*, Experimental Aircraft Association Fly-In; *Rigby*, Jefferson County Stampede; *Blackfoot*, Blackfoot Annual Rodeo; *Weiser*, National Old-Time Fiddlers Contest & Festival; *Meridian*, Pancake Feed & Meridian Dairy Show; *Emmett*, Cherry Festival & Squaw Butte Rock-hounds Show; *Craigmont*, June Picnic, featuring noon buffalo barbecue; *Smelter-ville*, Frontier Days, including rodeo; *Craigmont*, Talmaks Annual Camp Meeting, religious revival for Nez Percés of region.

July: *Nordman*, Frontier Days, including buffalo barbecue; *Grangeville*, Border Days, including amateur rodeo; *Rupert*, Rupert Night Rodeo; *Hailey*, Days of the Old West, including rodeo and lamb barbecue; *Paris*, Bear Lake Ranger Rodeo; *Salmon*, Salmon River Days; *Buhl*, Sagebrush Days, including free barbecue; *Teton Valley*, Pierre's Hole Rendezvous, old-fashioned melodrama accompanied by buf-falo barbecue, parade of Indians, fiddling, Indian exhibition dancing, and rodeo; *Winchester*, Winchester Days, including fiddlers' contest; *McCall*, Square & Round Dance Funstitute; *Craigmont*, Talmaks Annual Camp Meeting, religious revival for Nez Percés of region; *Pocatello*, Frontier Days Rodeo; *Fort Hall*, Sun Dances, Shoshone-Bannock religious observance and buffalo feast; *Blackfoot*, Snake River Valley Horse Show; *Sun Valley*, Trail Creek Cabin Basque Benefit, including Oinkari Dancers; *Priest River*, Priest River Loggers Celebration; *Nampa*, Snake River Stampede; *Bonners Ferry*, Kootenai River Days, including old-time fiddlers' contest and rodeo; *Coeur d'Alene*, Scottish Highland Festival & Tatoo; *Silver City*, Annual Meeting of the Owyhee Cattlemen's Association in famous ghost town, includes barbecue and all-night dancing; *Harrison*, Oldtimer's Celebration, includes Theatre revue and barbecue; *Coeur d'Alene*, Outdoor Arts & Crafts Festival; *Koos-kia*, Kooskia Day, includes fiddlers' jamboree; *Moscow*, Idaho State Square & Round Dance Festival; *Plummer*, Indian Days & Plummer Festival.

August: *Hayden Lake*, Barbecue Day; *Caldwell*, Caldwell Night Rodeo; *Pierce*, 1860 Days, includes longhorn barbecue; *Fort Hall*, All-Indian Festival of Shoshone-Bannock tribes, includes historical pageant, Indian dances and games, all-Indian rodeo, buffalo feast; *McCall*, Annual Water Carnival & Regatta; *Island Park*, Island Park Rodeo; *Burley*, Country-Western Jamboree; *Lapwai*, Pi-nee-Waus Days, Nez Percé soul music, war dancing, salmon bake, Indian games; *Cataldo*, yearly pilgrim-age to old Cataldo Mission and Catholic Mass held by Coeur d'Alene Indians in ancient tongue; *Craigmont* or *Winchester*, Mud Springs Camp, Nez Percé games and feasting; *Boise*, Western Idaho State Fair.

September: *Blackfoot*, Eastern Idaho State Fair; *Twin Falls*, Twin Falls County Fair & Rodeo; *Garden Valley*, Payette River Cattlemen's Annual Barbecue, includ-ing amateur rodeo; *Riggins*, Raft Race & Barbecue; *Kamiah*, Barbecue Day; *St. Maries*, Paul Bunyan Days, including lumberjack competition; *Ketchum*, Wood River Valley Four-Wheel Drive Rodeo; *Lewiston*, Lewiston Round-Up; *Boise*, Arts & Crafts Festival.

 NATIONAL FORESTS. Visitors to Idaho are amazed at how much of the state is still unspoiled, though environmen-talists are constantly battling to prevent ruination every-where. Eight national forests lie entirely within the boun-daries of Idaho and seven others partly within the boundaries, giving the state about 21 million acres of National Forest lands. (In addition, there is a National Grasslands of approximately 50,000 acres.) Within the national forests are the *Selway-Bitterroot Wilderness Area*, with almost 1 million acres; the Sawtooth National Recreation and Wilderness Area, with more than 750,000 acres; the *Idaho Primitive Area*, with more than 1,230,000 acres; adjoining the Idaho Primitive Area, the *Salmon River Breaks Primitive Area*, with almost 220,000 acres; the *Hells Canyon-Seven Devils Scenic Area*, with 130,000 acres; the *Middle Fork of the Salmon Wild River*; and the *Middle Fork of the Clearwater Wild River*. Within the national forests of Idaho are about 20,000 miles of trails and more than 400 campgrounds, with a total of about 5,000 campsites. The recreational opportunities are as sophisticated as water-skiing at well-developed lakes and as primitive as backpacking in the wilderness area.

Major forests include: *Boise*, the largest in Idaho, with almost 3 million acres.

Highways reaching the forest are US 20, US 95, Interstate 80N, and Idaho 21 and 55. Nearby towns are Boise, Cascade, Emmett, Idaho City, and Mountain Home. Attractions include the Sawtooth Wilderness Area and other rugged backcountry; abandoned mines and ghost towns; virgin stands of ponderosa pine; scenes of early Indian camps and red-white battles; Arrowrock, Anderson Ranch, Cascade, Deadwood, and Lucky Peak Reservoirs, and scores of lakes; the headwaters of the Boise and Payette Rivers; scenic drives in Payette and Boise River canyons, along the Boise Ridge and edge of Sawtooth Wilderness Area; lake and stream fishing for trout and salmon. The forest has more than one-fourth the campgrounds in the national forests of Idaho, a cluster of picnic grounds, and contains resorts, motels, dude ranches, and the Bogus Basin Winter Sports Area.

Caribou: Practically all of it is in Idaho, about 1 million acres in the state. Highways reaching it are US 191, 26, 30, and Idaho 34 and 36. Nearby towns are Idaho Falls, Montpelier, Pocatello, Malad City, Soda Springs, and Franklin. Attractions include towering mountain ranges divided by lovely valleys, historic markers and trails, natural soda springs, rushing streams and waterfalls, and many scenic drives, including the Snake River-McCoy Road along the south bank of the South Fork of the Snake River. The forest has more than 20 campgrounds, about 10 picnic grounds, a winter sports area, and contains resorts and motels.

Challis: The second largest national forest in Idaho, with about 2.5 million acres. Highways reaching the forest are US 20 and 93, and Idaho 75. Nearby towns are Challis, Salmon, and Stanley. Attractions are so numerous and so awesome as to stupefy the researcher. Outstanding are White Cloud Peaks; Lost River Range, with Mt. Borah, at 12,662 feet the highest peak in Idaho; Salmon River and White Knob Mountain Ranges; Sawtooth National Recreation Area; riding and hiking trails, and wilderness boating and packing trips. The forest has more than 50 campgrounds and a sprinkling of picnic grounds, and contains resorts, hotels, cabins, and dude ranches, with commercial packers and guides available.

Clearwater: Large stands of white pine are scattered through the more than 1.5 million acres. Reached by US 12 and Idaho 8 and 11. Nearest towns are Kooskia, Kamiah, Orofino, and Lewiston. Attractions include the historic Lolo Trail, over which the Lewis and Clark party struggled in blizzards; Selway-Bitterroot Wilderness; scenic drives on the North Fork of the Clearwater River and US 12; trout and salmon fishing. The forest has more than 25 camp and picnic grounds and several for picnic only, and contains motels and cabins. Pack-trip outfitters available.

Coeur d'Alene (about 725,000 acres), in the northern part of the state, is reached by US 95, Interstate 90, and Idaho 3. Nearby towns are Coeur d'Alene, Kellogg, Spirit Lake, and Wallace. Attractions include the 1846-built Cataldo Mission and 30-mile long (104 miles of shoreline) Coeur d'Alene Lake. The forest has more than 10 camp and picnic grounds, several for picnic only, and Lookout Pass Winter Sports Area, and resort hotels and cabins.

Kaniksu, the northernmost of the forests, reaches to the Canadian border, with about 900,000 acres. It is accessible by US 2 and 95, Interstate 90, and Idaho 57. Nearby towns are Bonners Ferry, Priest River, and Sandpoint. Attractions include two magnificent lakes, Pend Oreille and Priest; the 107-mile Pend Oreille Loop Drive; Selkirk Mountain Range; historic Kullyspell House; Roosevelt Ancient Grove of Cedars; Chimney Rock; Cabinet Mountain Wilderness; lake and stream fishing; and a lot of rugged backcountry. The forest has about 30 camp and picnic grounds, about a dozen for picnic only, and three swimming sites. It also contains the Schweitzer Basin Winter Ski Area, resorts, hotels, lodges, and cabins.

Nez Percé, in the western part of the state, has more than 2 million acres. Reaching it are US 95 and 12, and Idaho 13 and 14. Nearby towns are Grangeville, Kooskia, and Riggins. Attractions include the Selway-Bitterroot Wilderness; Salmon River Breaks Primitive Area; Seven Devils Range, between the Salmon and Snake Rivers; Red River Hot Springs; historic Elk City; lake and stream fishing; hiking and horse trails; wilderness pack trips, and scenic drives along the Lochsa, Salmon, and Selway

Rivers. The forest has about 40 camp and picnic grounds and several for picnic only. It also contains resorts, hotels, and cabins. Pack-trip outfitters are available.

Payette, just south of the Nez Percé National Forest, has about 2.4 million acres and is reached by US 95, and Idaho 71 and 55. Nearby towns are Cascade, Council, McCall, New Meadows, and Weiser. Attractions include Hells Canyon-Seven Devils Scenic Area (Hells Canyon is deepest gorge on the continent), Payette Lakes Recreational Area, more than 150 fishing lakes, more than 1,500 miles of fishing streams, trout and salmon fishing, scenic drives, and wilderness trips. The forest has about 30 campgrounds and includes the Payette Lakes Winter Sports Area and dude ranches.

Salmon, in the sparsely settled eastern part of the state, has more than 1.7 million acres. It can be reached by US 93 and Idaho 28. Nearby towns are Salmon and Leadore. Attractions include the Idaho Primitive Area, Big Horn Crags, historic Lewis and Clark Trail, Salmon River Canyon, Salmon River and Panther Creek forest trails, and boat trips on the "River of No Return." The forest has about 20 campgrounds and contains dude ranches. Pack-trip guides and outfitters available.

St. Joe National Forest, just below the panhandle, with about 900,000 acres, is reached by US 95, Interstate 90, and Idaho 3 and 8. Nearby towns are Moscow, Potlatch, and St. Maries. Attractions include the wild Bitterroot Range of the Idaho-Montana divide, St. Maries River Valley, canyon area of the Little North Fork of the Clearwater River, the Clearwater-St. Joe River divide, the Palouse River area, virgin stands of white pine, large timber operations, scenic drives along the St. Joe River from source to mouth in Coeur d'Alene Lake, and lake and stream fishing. The forest has more than 20 camp and picnic grounds, several grounds for picnic only, a swimming site, and the North-South Winter Sports Area. Dude ranches are nearby, and there are cabins on the St. Joe River.

Sawtooth, in the southcentral part of the state, has about 1,730,000 acres in Idaho and may be reached by Interstate 80N, Interstate 15W, US 30 and 93, and Idaho 27, 37, 68, 77, and 81. Nearby towns are Burley, Gooding, Ketchum, and Twin Falls. Attractions include Sun Valley, Sawtooth Wilderness Area, panoramic views of the Snake River Valley, the incredibly eroded "Silent City of Rocks" (famous as a dividing point of the Oregon and California Trails); hot springs, multicolored mountains, charming lakes, fishing, scenic drives, and saddle and pack trips. The forest has about 70 campgrounds and more than 15 grounds for picnic only, one swimming site, and eight winter sports areas, including Magic Mountain, Mt. Harrison, Soldier Creek, and Sun Valley, and contains many dude ranches, camps, and motels.

Targhee, pressed against Wyoming (and close to Grand Teton National Park), has more than 1.3 million acres. It is reached by US 20 and 26, Interstate 15, and Idaho 31, 32, 33, 47, and 87. Nearby towns are Ashton, Driggs, Dubois, Idaho Falls, Rexburg, St. Anthony, and Victor. Attractions include Island Park Reservoir, Grand Canyon of the Snake River, Cave Falls, Falls River, Palisades Dam, scenic drives, lake and stream fishing, and riding and hiking trails into the untrammeled mountains. The forest includes about 30 campgrounds and several grounds for picnic only, and contains three winter sports areas (Bear Gulch, Moose Creek, and Pine Basin), as well as resorts, motels, dude ranches, fishing camps, and boating facilities. Pack outfits for hunting parties are available.

For detailed information on each national forest, see *Tourist Information Services*.

STATE PARKS. The Idaho State Department of Parks and Recreation maintains some 20 parks, waysides, and recreation areas totaling more than 24,800 acres. Located in all sections of the state, these areas provide more than 650 picnic sites and about one thousand campsites and a wide variety of outdoor recreation activities. (The Idaho State Highway Department maintains about 60 safety rest areas for the convenience and comfort of the motoring public. Located on the major highways throughout the state, most rest areas provide rest stations, drinking water, and picnic tables under shade trees or sun shelters.)

Included in the state parks are: *Indian Creek*, 35 miles north of the town of Priest River, at road end, and in thick woods on the shore of dreamy Priest Lake. Fishing, boating, swimming, water skiing; has 51 tent, 22 trailer sites. *Dickinsheet*, near Priest Lake, is close to fine fishing in Priest Lake and Priest River; 10 tent sites. *Farragut*, near the shore of fish-famous Pend Oreille Lake, has 100 tent and 54 picnic sites. *Round Lake*, 8 miles south of Sandpoint and 2 miles west of US 95, near Pend Oreille Lake, has 53 tent sites. *Heyburn*, on Idaho 5 between Plummer and St. Maries, and near the entry of the St. Joe River into Coeur d'Alene Lake, has over 7,800 acres and contains 114 tent, 22 trailer, and 68 picnic sites. *Ponderosa*, at McCall, on the northern tip of Payette Lake, has 170 trailer and 45 picnic sites, and is in the center of a vast forest and water recreationland. *Packer John's Cabin*, near New Meadows, has 20 tent, 20 trailer, and 20 picnic sites. *Mann Creek*, 13 miles north of Weiser, on US 95, has a beach and a fine fishing and boating reputation. *Black Canyon*, a short drive northeast of Emmett, on Idaho 52, offers swimming off a beach, fishing, boating, and picnicking. *Lucky Peak*, on a reservoir 8 miles east of Boise on Idaho 21, has 200 picnic sites, boating, fishing, swimming. *Henry's Lake*, 17 miles southwest of West Yellowstone, Montana, is on a famous Mountain Man lake; swimming, 32 trailer sites. *Bruneau Dunes*, 7 miles northeast of Bruneau on Idaho 51, is in spectacular sand three-deep canyon area; 32 tent, 16 trailer, 20 picnic sites. *Three Island*, at Glenns Ferry, off US 30, is at famous Oregon Trail fording; boating, swimming; 5 trailer, 35 picnic sites. *Massacre Rocks*, 20 miles southwest of American Falls, on US 30, has historic trails; 52 trailer, 26 picnic sites. *Indian Rocks*, near McCammon Interchange off Interstate 15 in the southeastern part of the state, contains historical interests; has 51 tent sites. *Lava Hot Springs*, on US 30, and a short drive from Indian Rocks, has a pool, bath house, hot springs, golfing, swimming, fishing; is near ski area and river resort. *Bear Lake*, 2 miles east of Idaho 89 at Bear Lake, near the Utah border, offers swimming, fishing, boating.

For detailed information on state parks, write: State Parks & Recreation, 6621 Warm Springs Ave., Boise, ID 83706.

CAMPING OUT. Idaho has campgrounds throughout the state. In the national forests alone there are more than 400 campgrounds, with a total of about 5,000 tent and trailer sites. (For specific forests, see section on *National Forests*.)

The state parks of Idaho provide about one thousand campsites in all parts of the state. (For specific parks, see section above, *State Parks*.)

The Bureau of Land Management has 125 campsites and 76 picnic units on its 13 recreation sites. (For specific information write to Bureau of Land Management, address given in *Tourist Information Services*.)

The Corps of Engineers has 130 sites for trailers in 3 campgrounds near Priest River and one near Sandpoint. (For specific information, write: U.S. Corps of Engineers, Building 602, City-County Airport, Walla Walla, WA 99362.

Over 250 public recreation sites have been provided by private companies in Idaho. These parks offer over 8,320 campsites as well as the usual range of outdoor recreation activities. Examples: Potlatch Forests, Inc. has camping on Campbell's Pond, 9 miles northwest of Pierce, and at E. C. Rettig Forest, 15 miles north of Pierce. Idaho Power Co. has 4 campgrounds on the Snake River in the Hells Canyon area: Brownlee Reservoir, Hells Canyon Reservoir, Copperfield Park, and McCormick Park, all with trailer hookups. Idaho Power Co. also has trailer sites at its Salmon Dam grounds, 2 miles west of Rogerson, US 93. (No charge for use of campgrounds on corporate property.)

Craters of the Moon National Monument has more than 50 trailer units.

Cascade Reservoir, near Cascade (Idaho 55), has 2 campgrounds, Donnelly Park and Cascade Park, with a total of 70 trailer sites.

A number of communities in the state offer overnight camping in their parks. These include Lewiston, whose Kiwanis Park has trailer stalls; Old Fort Boise Park in

Parma, also with trailer facilities; and Shoshone Falls Park in Twin Falls, with units for tents and trailers.

KOA Kampgrounds are so many that you can, touring around the state, stay at one every night if you properly arrange your schedule. Included are Blackfoot, Boise, Bonners Ferry, Burley, Caldwell, Coeur d'Alene, Hayden Lake, Idaho Falls, Island Park, Jerome-Twin Falls, Lava Hot Springs, Lewiston, Mountain Home, Pocatello, Salmon, Sandpoint, Sun Valley, Victor, and Weiser.

For more detailed information on city parks and KOA campgrounds, write: Idaho Division of Tourism and Industrial Development. (See section *Tourist Information Services.*)

 TRAILER TIPS. There are, literally, hundreds of places to park trailers, RVs, and campers. There are many sites in national forests, state parks, Bureau of Land Management facilities, corporation-owned areas, parks in some municipalities, and KOA Kampgrounds. (See section on *Camping Out.*) In addition, there are these places, most of them in or near towns, which welcome overnighters: American Falls, *Ee-Dah-How Trailer Court* (226-2676); Bayview, *Redman's Resort* (683-2214); Blackfoot, *Parkside Mobile Manor* (785-2810); Boise, *A Rogers Trailer Park* (343-0401), *Broadway Trailer Park* (342-6161), *Fiesta Mobile Home & Trailer Park* (375-8207), *KOA Kampground* (342-9714); Buhl, *Manor Drive Mobile Home Park* (543-6431); Burley, *Bel Aire Trailer Park* (678-9302), *Riverview Trailer Court* (678-3223); Caldwell, *Coffey Grounds Trailer Park* (459-7712), *KOA Kampgrounds* (454-0279); Coeur d'Alene, *Friendly Acres Mobile Park & Campground* (773-5681), *Lucky Pines Trailer Court* (773-5393); Driggs, *Larsen's Service Motel & Trailer Park* (354-9981); Eden, *The Campground* (733-6756); Emmett, *Capital Mobile Park* (365-3889); Garden City, *Bear Lake KOA* (946-3454); Garwood, *Flying H Guest Ranch Kamp KOA* (772-5602); Gooding, *Hacienda Motel & Trailer Park* (934-4792); Hagerman, *Sportsman Lodge* (837-6364); Hauser Lake, *Woodland Beach Resort* (773-4360); Hayden Lake, *Brunners Mobile Park* (772-3564), *Mountain View Park* (772-3327); Homedale, *Homedale Motel & Trailer Court* (337-4288), *Sunset Village Mobile Home Park* (337-4585); Hope, *Chris & Mary's Pend Oreille Resort* (264-5505); Idaho Falls, *KOA* (523-3362), *Sunnyside Acres Park* (523-8403); Island Park, *Valley View Trailer Park* (558-9935); Jerome, *Big Trees Mobile Park* (324-8265); Ketchum, *Mountain Meadows Mobile Home Park* (726-5656); Kingston, *Kingston Trailer Park* (682-2755); Kooskia, *Flying R Lodge* (926-4377); Lava Hot Springs, *Mountain View Trailer Court* (776-5611); Lewiston, *Terrace Mobile Home Park* (758-7167); Mackay, *Wagon Wheel Motel & Mobile Home Park* (588-3331); Meridian, *Knotty Pine Motel* (888-2727); Moreland, *Johnson's Mobile Village* (684-3434); Moscow, *Greenstreet Trailer Court* (882-9906), *Terrace Gardens Mobile Homes Court* (882-7134); Mountain Home, *Golden Rule KOA Trailer Park* (587-5111), *Ranchette Trailer Park* (587-4030), *Rose Garden Trailer Park* (587-3455); Nampa, *Evergreen Mobile Home Park* (467-1578); Orofino, *Clearwater Trailer Court* (476-5423), *Hidden Village Mobile Home Park* (476-3416), *KOA Kampground* (476-3911); Payette, *Riverside Mobile Court* (642-2053); Pocatello, *Barret Trailer Park* (237-0410), *KOA Kampground* (233-6851), *Sullivan's Mobile Manor* (233-0661); Rathdrum, *Twin Echo Resort* (687-3411); St. Anthony, *Targhee Trailer Court* (624-3054); St. Maries, *Ragan's Golden 20's Musical Museum* (245-3462), *Torchie's Chevron Service* (245-9210); Salmon, *Highway 28 Motor Court* (756-3443), *Riverside Club & Trailer Court* (756-3513); Sandpoint, *Sunset Beach Resort & Trailer Park* (263-2944), *Travel America Parks* (263-6522); Shelley, *Mobile Home Estates* (523-6930); Shoshone, *McFall Hotel Bar Trailer Court & Restaurant* (886-2032); Soda Springs, *Brigham Young Lodge & Trailer Court* (547-3564), *Lava View Motel & Trailer Park* (547-4351); Spirit Lake, *Fireside Lodge* (623-2871); Stanley, *Hansen's Summer Home Trailer Park* (774-3310), *Smiley Creek Resort* (774-3547); Twin Falls, *Bergerville* (734-2175), *Curry Trailer Park* (733-3961), *Graceman Auto*

Court & Trailer Park (733-8841); Wallace, *Cedarvale* (753-7111); *Silver Leaf Motel & Trailer Court* (752-0222); Wendell, *Atkins Trailer Park* (536-2227); Weston, *Caribou KOA* (747-3910).

GUEST RANCHES. Idaho has many outstanding guest ranches. Some specialize in pack trips for hunting or fishing, some offer more leisurely enjoyment of the big-sky country, and most are a combination of the two. Because rates change due to inflation, they are not listed here; but it can be said that Idaho guest-ranch rates are no more expensive than most guest ranches in other states. Among the better-known guest ranches are these: *Boulder Creek Pack Camp*, at the gateway to the Selway-Bitterroot Wilderness Area. Family vacation, summer fishing, photography trips, big-game hunts in season. (Address: Rt. 1, Box 12-0, Peck, ID 83545; tel. 208-486-7523.) *China Bar Lodge*. Jet boat and float trips, steelhead and trout fishing, family style meals. (Address: P.O. Box 1185, North Fork, ID 83466; tel. 208-865-2512.) *Cool Water Ranch*, on lower Selway River in the Selway-Bitterroot Wilderness. Modern cabins, campground, fishing, camping, backpacking, big-game hunting in season. (Address: 1376 Walenta Drive, Moscow, ID 83843; tel. 208-882-5367.) *Elk Creek Ranch*, located on South Fork of Salmon River, 64 miles north of McCall. Trips to high mountain lakes, fishing, sightseeing, camping in Payette National Forest, horseback riding. (Address: Box 987, McCall, ID 83638; tel. 208-634-5173.) *Happy Hollow Camps*, in the mountains of the Salmon River Country. Youth camp, fishing, wild water boating, trail rides, pack trips. (Address: Box 694, Salmon, ID 83467; tel. 208-756-3954.) *Indian Creek Guest Ranch*, located 10 miles down Salmon River from Northfork, ID. Small ranch specializing in individual attention. Family-style meals, 3 miles of trout fishing on property, horseback riding, hiking. Flying customers picked up at Salmon Airport. (Address: Box 109, Salmon, ID 83467; tel. 208-756-2712. *Mackay Bar Lodge*, on the "River of No Return," the big Salmon, in the heart of the Chamberlain Basin primitive area. Guest rooms and tent cabins. (Address: Drawer F, Suite 1010, One Capital Center, Boise, ID 83702; tel. 208-344-1881. *Salmon River Lodge*, located across the Salmon River from the end of the road, 30 miles below Shoup. Middle Fork and Salmon River float trips, steelhead fishing, primitive area pack trips, Salmon River jet boat trips, big-game hunting in season. (Address: Box 58, Salmon, ID 83467; tel. 208-756-2646.) *Mystic Saddle Ranch*, in the Sawtooth Wilderness. Pack trips, trout fishing, big-game hunting in season. (Address: Stanley, ID 83340; tel. 208-774-3591.) *Triangle C Ranch*, with new lodge on Cummings Lake. White-water float trips, big-game hunting in season. (Address: 1155 North Locust, Twin Falls, ID 83301; tel. 208-733-0699.) *Whitewater Ranch*, located on the main Salmon, "River of No Return." Only one family or party at a time, by reservation. Boat trips, trail rides, lake pack trips, big-game hunting in season. (Address: Salmon River Air Route, Cascade, ID 83611; tel. radio phone 208-382-4336.)

CONVENTION SITES. National and international conventions (as well as regional gatherings) are held at Sun Valley. Small national conventions and regional conventions are held at Boise. Scholarly-technical meetings and conventions are held at the University of Idaho (Moscow) and Idaho State University (Pocatello). Regional conventions are staged at McCall, Burley, Idaho Falls, Pocatello, and at the North Shore Convention Center in Coeur d'Alene.

HOT SPRINGS. Idaho has more than a hundred mineral springs, with a variety of facilities and accommodations at the most popular of them. At *Lava Hot Springs*, on the Portneuf River, the state operates a resort. Probably the best-known of the mineral springs are at *Soda Springs*, famous in Oregon Trail lore. The waters of these springs are reputed to contain 22 different kinds of minerals and to possess curative powers. One of the soda springs in this area is Steamboat Spring, which boils up through 40 feet of water and explodes at the surface; another is Mammoth Soda Spring, which is nearly the same size as Mammoth Hot Springs in Yellowstone Park. At *American Falls* there is bathing in mineral pools fed by 30 different springs, from hot to cold. At *Hot Creek*, near Bruneau Canyon, in southwestern Idaho, hot springs boil out of a ravine, and for a mile the steaming water froths in fury until it tumbles over a fall into a scoured-out cavity, 15 feet across, called Indian Bowl. Near the area are campground and dressing facilities for swimmers. Other hot springs in the state include *Red River*, 27 miles east of Elk City, Idaho 14; *Boulder Creek*, 8 miles south of Pollock, US 95; *Riggins*, 9 miles east of Riggins, US 95; *Sulphur*, 14 miles north of New Meadows off US 95; *Zim's Plunge*, 7 miles north of New Meadows off US 95; *Meadows Valley*, 5 miles north of New Meadows, US 95; *Kreigbaum*, at Meadows, 2 miles east of New Meadows, US 95; *Starkey*, 8 miles north of Council, US 95; *Burgdorf*, 30 miles north of McCall, Idaho 55; *Givens*, 12 miles south of Marsing, near US 95; *Warm Springs Plunge*, 2 miles south of Idaho City, Idaho 21; *Silver Creek Plunge*, 10 miles east of Banks, Idaho 55; *Kirkham*, 4 miles east of Lowman, on Idaho 21; *Grandjean*, 30 miles east of Lowman, Idaho 21; *Hot Spring* at Weatherby Sawmill, near Atlanta, on dirt road near southern edge of Sawtooth Wilderness Area; *Baumgartner*, near Featherville, on gravel road 22 miles south of Atlanta; *Paradise*, on South Fork of the Boise River near Featherville; *Salmon*, 3 miles southeast of Salmon, US 93; *Beardsley*, south of Salmon along US 93; *Sharkey*, 20 miles southeast of Salmon, US 93, and near Idaho 28; *Challis*, on Warm Springs Creek east of Challis, Idaho 75; *Sunbeam*, on Idaho 75, 13 miles east of Stanley; *Robinson Bar Ranch*, 16 miles southeast of Stanley, Idaho 75; *Mineral*, 2 miles south of Stanley on Idaho 75; *Stanley*, at junction of Valley Creek and Idaho 75; *Clarendon*, 7 miles northwest of Hailey, Idaho 75; *Banbury*, between Buhl and Hagerman on US 30; *Nat Soo Pah*, 6 miles east of Hollister, US 93; *Cedar Creek*, west of Rogerson (US 93) at intersection of road and Cedar Creek; *Murphy*, near Rogerson, US 93; *Magic*, 24 miles southeast of Rogerson, US 93; *Lidy*, 16 miles west of Dubois on Idaho 22; *Green Canyon*, 33 miles southeast of Newdale, Idaho 33; *Heise*, 5 miles east of Ririe, near US 26; *Hooper*, one mile north of Soda Springs, US 30; *Champagne*, near Hooper Spring; *Sulphur*, 8 miles southeast of Soda Springs, US 30; *Vincent*, near Idaho 36 midway between Preston and Mink Creek at southern end of Oneida Narrows; *Downata*, 5 miles south of Downey, US 91; *Pleasantview*, 5 miles west of Malad City, Interstate 15; *Indian*, 3 miles southwest of American Falls, Interstate 15W.

 MUSEUMS AND GALLERIES. Most of Idaho's museums and galleries in the larger towns are open daily in the summer, from 9 a.m. to 5 p.m., and most are free. In the smaller towns, schedules are often erratic. Idaho has no really great museum or gallery, but local history and culture are reflected in the smaller town museums.

Historical: Blackfoot, Brigham County Tom Bond Pioneer Museum. Boise, Idaho State Historical Museum, best historical museum in state, in Julia Davis Park; Old Idaho Penitentiary Museum. Bonners Ferry, Boundary County Historical Society Museum. Burley, Cassia County Historical Museum, in Fairgrounds. Caldwell, Odd Fellows Historical Museum. Cambridge, Cambridge City Museum. Coeur d'Alene, Museum of Northern Idaho. Cottonwood, St. Gertrude's Museum. Sunbeam, Custer Museum, located 11 miles north of Sunbeam on Yankee Fork forest road. Franklin, Pioneer Relic Hall, tracing the past of oldest town in Idaho. Hailey, Blaine County Historical Museum, contains an American Political Items Collection—more than 50,000 badges, pennants, buttons, and other memorabilia from political campaigns beginning in the late 1800s. Idaho City, Boise Basin Museum, exemplary collection of early mining-camp artifacts. Juliaetta, Arrow Museum. Kooskia, Nee Moo Poo

Museum. Lewiston, Luna House, Third St., displays Indian artifacts and other relics, some going back 2,000 years; H.L. Talkington Collection, Lewis-Clark State College. Malad City, Oneida County Relic Room, corner of Main & Bannock. Marsing, City Museum, 430 Clay. Moscow, Latah County Pioneer Museum, 110 S. Adams; University of Idaho Museum. Murphy, Owyhee County Historical Museum, in ancient structure of old mining town that would be a ghost if it weren't the county seat (with a population of 75!). Nampa, Cleo's Ferry Museum. Orofino, Clearwater Historical Museum. Pocatello, Bannock County Historical Museum, corner of Garfield & Center; Idaho State University Museum, Library Building, University Campus; replica of Ft. Hall, re-creating the fur-trading and provision post that operated from 1834 into the late 1850s. Rupert, Minidoka County Historical Museum. Salmon, Lemhi County Historical Museum. Sandpoint, Bonner County Museum. Silver City, Old Schoolhouse Museum, in genuine ghost town. Twin Falls, Twin Falls County Historical Museum, 3 miles west of Addison Ave. Weiser, Fiddler's Hall of Fame & Historical Museum, 46 W. Commercial. Many of Idaho's ghost towns—and the state is dotted with them, especially in the backcountry—are living museums. Among them are Murray, Florence, Bonanza, Custer, Warren, Silver City, Rocky Bar, Atlanta, Shoup, Gibbonsville, Leesburg, Blackbird, Yellowjacket, Roosevelt City, Thunder City, Bullion, Vienna, Sawtooth City, Galena, Eagle City, Moose City, Nicolia, Mount Idaho, and Springtown. Many of the old mining towns are still inhabited, though sparsely, so please respect private property and the rights of others when you come a-visiting.

Art: Boise, Boise Gallery of Art, in Julia Davis Park, is finest in state. Pocatello, Idaho State University Art Gallery, Fine Arts Building, University Campus, displays works of regional artists. Twin Falls, Herrett Arts & Science Center, East Five Points & Kimberly Rd., is focal point of Snake River Valley artists.

Special Interest: Craters of the Moon National Monument, south of Arco, has exhibits explaining the volcanic features, flora and fauna of the area. Boise, Idaho Wild Birds, Science Building, Boise State College. Idaho Falls, Intermountain Science Experience Center. Massacre Rocks, 20 miles southwest of American Falls, has a museum containing displays of fossils and Indian objects. Pollock, Little Canyon River Museum, has exhibits on natural history of area. Shoshone, Shoshone Ice Caves Museum. Stanley, Visitor Center, off US 93, at Redfish Lake, in Sawtooth National Forest, contains exhibits of the flora, fauna, geology, and history of area. Wallace, Coeur d'Alene Mining Museum, has displays of mining equipment and models of famous mines of the area.

 HISTORIC SITES. Many of Idaho's historic sites parallel the trails of history through the state—the *Oregon Trail* in the south, *Lewis and Clark Route* in the north-central section, and *Mullan Road* in the panhandle. The visitor may retrace these famous routes on modern highways, guided by the state's fine graphic historical-sign program.

In the north, along US 10, I-90, the visitor should pause at Cataldo, between Kellogg and Coeur d'Alene, to see the *Mission of the Sacred Heart*, oldest building in Idaho. Construction of this church began in 1846, after the black-robed Jesuits abandoned an earlier mission, founded in 1842 on the shores of Lake Coeur d'Alene. "The Old Mission," as the Cataldo structure is called, is honored by an annual pilgrimage. A few miles west, and just a short walk from the highway, is the stump of the tree blazed with his name by wagonroad-builder Capt. John Mullan on July 4, 1861, which gives the *Fourth of July Canyon* its name. Eighteen miles east of Sandpoint, and near the village of Hope (Idaho 200) and on the shore of Lake Pend Oreille, is the site of *Kullyspell House*, built in 1809 by David Thompson, who opened Idaho's fur trade by constructing the post.

Lewiston, at the junction of US 12 and US 95, was the site of the *first capitol of Idaho Territory* in 1863. Only a marker indicates the location. *Luna House Museum*, one of the oldest residences in north Idaho, is a rich repository of Indian artifacts. *Old Fort Lapwai*, at Lapwai, near Lewiston, is one of the sites in *Nez Percé National Park*, the first decentralized park in the nation. Open 8-4:30 weekdays, 9:30-6 weekends in winter. Open daily 8-4:30 in summer. Closed Thanksgiving, Christmas, and New Year's. Other historical sites in the area are the *Craig Donation Land Claim*, five miles south, along US 95, and *St. Joseph's Mission*, 14 miles southeast.

In 1840, a veteran mountain man, Col. William Craig, of Greenbrier, Virginia, beat his way west, until he came to the confluence of the Snake and Clearwater rivers. He liked what he saw and built a good home a few miles from the Spaldings. So he became the first settler and homesteader in Idaho and received the earliest title for a land patent issued. The nearby town of Craigmont was named for him.

Spalding Memorial Park, 11 miles east of Lewiston, is the site of the second mission built by the Rev. Henry Harman Spalding and his wife, Eliza, the first missionaries in what is now Idaho. They came in 1836 with famed Dr. Marcus Whitman (see chapter on *Washington*). The Spaldings built the first church, school, and mills in what is now Idaho and set up the first printing press. Sent originally from Boston to Honolulu, the press arrived at Ft. Vancouver (across the Columbia from present Portland) in 1839 and was delivered to Spalding at Lapwai Mission. There it was set up, and that same year of 1839 the first book was run off, a Nez Percé primer. The memorial park contains the site of the original Nez Percé Indian Agency and the graves of the Spaldings, as well as monuments to them. The memorial park is also the headquarters of the Nez Percé National Historical Park.

Each section of the national historical park reflects in its own unique way the prewhite culture of the Nez Percé people and the emergence of white domination following the Lewis and Clark expedition. *Visitor centers* at *Spalding, East Kamiah* (US 12) and *White Bird Battlefield* present interpretive displays to reveal the influences significant in the molding of this part of the great Pacific Northwest.

Pierce, in 1860 the *scene of the first significant gold discovery in Idaho*, an event that had the most far-reaching effects, including the creation of Idaho as a state, is 80 miles east of Lewiston, reached by US 12 and Idaho 11. Mementoes of the glory days of the 1860s remain.

US 12 parallels the *Lewis and Clark trek from Lewiston to Lolo Pass*, on the Montana border. To the north is the perilous Lolo Indian Trail, which put the elkskin explorers to their severest test. *Visitors' Center*, at Lolo Pass, has graphic displays about this portion of the Lewis and Clark trail.

Grangeville, 65 miles below Lewiston, on US 95, was the jumping-off point to many mining communities. *Mt. Idaho*, a few miles southeast, hosted the state's first Republican convention and boasted a hotel. The population is now 75. *Elk City*, 45 miles east of Mt. Idaho, and also on Idaho 14, was a booming gold town, with miners thronging the creeks, ravines, and streets. Today the settlement has fewer than 500 people, and there is more interest in farming than in mining. *Dixie* and *Orogrande*, also born in the gold boom of 1861, are practically ghost towns now, each with a population of about ten. Both are reached by gravel roads from Elk City.

White Bird Battlefield Area, 15 miles south of Grangeville, along US 95, is the site of the first battle of the Nez Percé War.

Six miles northwest of Parma (US 95, 20, and 26) is the site of *Ft. Boise*, established in 1834 as a trading post and later prominent in the annals of Oregon Trail emigrants.

In Caldwell, *Memorial Park* has a pioneer cabin.

In Boise, the *O'Farrell Cabin*, between 5th and 6th on Fort St., is the city's best-known pioneer building. A *pioneer log cabin* stands in Boise's Julia Davis Park.

Idaho City (Idaho 21), 40 miles north of Boise, was the state's biggest *gold-rush* town. In the 1860s it had a population of 40,000 and was the capital of Idaho Territory. It boasts many state firsts, including publication of the first newspaper. The population today is fewer than 200. Pioneer buildings and miles of dredges remain.

Near Idaho City are the *gold ghost towns* of Centerville, Placerville, and Pioneerville, reached by slow, but not exasperating, gravel and dirt roads.

Custer, 24 miles northeast of Stanley (11-mile dirt road from Sunbeam, on US 93), is a shadow of its past as febrile *gold-mining town*. A tintype of a century gone.

Settlers Cave, on a gravel road southeast of Bruneau (21 miles south of Mountain Home), contains several rooms hollowed from a hardclay hillside by settlers as a retreat from unfriendly Indians.

The *California Land Trailmark*, where the California Trail and a branch of the Oregon Trail divided, is at the Silent City of Rocks, southeast of Oakley (Idaho 27).

A replica of *Ft. Hall*, built in 1834, stands in Pocatello. The original site of Ft. Hall was 11 miles west of the present town of Ft. Hall, which is 10 miles north of Pocatello.

In 1860 a band of Mormons, looking for land to call home and under the impression that they were still within the boundaries of Utah, established the *first agricultural settlement* in Idaho, at Franklin (US 91). The town, regarded as Idaho's oldest, has a pioneer flavor even now.

Pierre's Hole, south of Diggs, was a famous rendezvous of the Mountain Men. It was on the direct road from Jackson Hole, Wyoming, to the Snake River. Through here passed Capt. Bonneville, Nathaniel Wyeth, William Sublette, and a host of other figures famous in Western exploration.

Salmon has history all around it. To the north is the pass where the Nez Percé, led by Chief Joseph, crossed the Continental Divide as they fled pursuing soldiers. Fourteen miles south of Salmon, on Idaho 28, is the *Sacajawea Monument*, marking (approximately) the birthplace of the only woman with the Lewis and Clark party. Six miles below the monument is the village of Tendoy. Ten miles east, on a gravel and dirt road, at Lemhi Pass, is *where Lewis and Clark crossed the Continental Divide* in 1805. Just northwest of Tendoy is the site of *Ft. Lemhi*, a Mormon community established in the 1850s. Two years later, after a grasshopper plague and Indian attacks, the Mormon missionaries were recalled to Utah, putting an end to the colony.

One of the most interesting historical sections of the state is in the southeast, where a tide of gold seekers flooded the Owyhee hills in the 1860s. After the precious metals ran out, or the miners thought they did, or they became too expensive to extract, the miners left, and towns they had populated and frenzied stayed behind, empty and silent. From the top of 8,065-foot War Eagle Mountain, the scene is a panorama. Silver City at 6,719 feet, is the most unblemished ghost town in the state and has the best representation of the past. Other ghost towns in the area are not as large and picturesque, but all are fascinating.

For a list of historical landmarks by town, write: Idaho Divison of Tourism and Industrial Development. (See *Tourist Information Services*.)

LIBRARIES. All of the major schools of higher learning have excellent libraries. This is particularly true of the University of Idaho, Idaho State University, Boise State College, and College of Idaho. Idaho State Library, in Boise, founded soon after the turn of the century, is largest in the state. All major cities have good public libraries.

TOURS. *By boat*. Boat trips from Lewiston go into Hells Canyon on 220-mile round trips, on 2-, 3-, or 4-day cruises, with accommodations and meals furnished at Willow Creek Camp, 90 miles up the Snake River. (For specifics, write: Chamber of Commerce, Lewiston, ID 83501.)

The adventurous can go down the Snake through Hells Canyon on 5-day float trips (rubber rafts) or on 2-day jet boat excursions. The floaters make camp on shore; the jet boaters put up at a lodge. There are also exciting jet and paddle rides on the Middle Fork of the Salmon and on the swift Selway River. (See next section, *Special Interest Tours*.)

On a more placid note, an excursion boat operates daily in the warm months from the city dock of Coeur d'Alene for short cruises on Lake Coeur d'Alene. Seven- and eight-hour boat journeys are available Sun. and Wed. Seaplane flights also available. (For up-to-date schedules, write: Chamber of Commerce, Coeur d'Alene, ID 83814.)

 SPECIAL-INTEREST TOURS. With so much of Idaho swift stream, high lake, and mountain country, it is natural that most special-interest tours feature the rugged and the off-the-beaten path. Practically every guest ranch offers a variety of these trips. Rates vary and are, of course, subject to change. St. Joe Lodge (Springdale, WA 99173) charges as low as $30 a day, including meals and saddle horse, on fishing trips. Chamberlain Basin Outfitters (Wells, Nev. 89835; tel. 802-752-3697) charges up to $1,500 per day for 9 days on individually guided hunts for elk and deer.

Few guides list prices. For these, you have to contact them individually. Guides available for special trips other than guest ranches listed earlier include: Fog Mountain Outfitters, for big-game hunting and summer family vacations (c/o S.C. Miller, Box 851-B, Salmon, ID 83467; tel. 208-756-3388). Lochsa River Outfitters, for fishing trips and big-game hunting (Rt. 2, Box 30, Potlatch, ID 83855; tel. 208-875-5201). Wilderness River Outfitters, for oar-powered float trips on the Main Salmon River, Bruneau River, and Hells Canyon of the Snake, as well as backpacking (P.O. Box 871, Salmon, ID 83467; tel. 208-756-3959). Salmon River Expeditions, for floats on the Middle Fork and Mail Salmon River and Hells Canyon of the Snake (Box 015, Jerome, ID 83338; tel. 208-324-4339). Whitewater Adventures, for float trips on Hells Canyon of the Snake, Main Salmon, and Selway River (P.O. Box 184, Twin Falls, ID 83301; tel. 208-733-4548). Bill Guth & Sons, for big-game hunts and 5-day float trips on the Middle Fork of the Salmon (Box 705, Salmon, ID 83467; tel. 208-756-3279). Nez Percé Outfitters & Guides for float trips on the Middle Fork and Main Salmon River and pack trips into Salmon River Breaks and Idaho Primitive Area (P.O. Box 1454-A, Salmon, ID 83467; tel. 208-756-3912). Idaho Adventures for float trips on the Middle Fork, Main Salmon, and Hells Canyon, and steelhead fishing by jet boat on the Salmon (P.O. Box 834-1, Salmon, ID 83467; tel. 208-756-2986). Elk Creek Ranch for big-game hunting, trout fishing, and summer pack excursions (Box 987, McCall, ID 83638; tel. 208-634-5173). Wilderness World, for float trips through Hells Canyon and on the Middle Fork and Main Salmon (1342 Jewell Ave., Pacific Grove, CA 93950; tel. 408-373-5882). Quarter Circle A Outfitters, for big-game hunting in the Middle Fork Primitive Area and Selway-Bitterroot Wilderness (Star Route, Salmon, ID 83226). Western River Expeditions, Inc., for float trips down the Selway, Middle Fork of the Salmon, and Main Salmon (P.O. Box 6339, Salt Lake City, UT 84106; tel. 801-486-2323). Nitz Brothers Outfitters, for big-game hunting and fishing in the Selway-Bitterroot Wilderness (Elk City, ID 83525; tel. 208-842-2424). Primitive Area Float Trips, for wilderness float trips, summer pack trips, Salmon River jet boat trips, backpacking, and steelhead and salmon fishing (Box 585, Salmon, ID 83467; tel. 208-756-2319). Rawhide Camps, for horseback trips to high lakes and streams (Box 5461, Boise, ID 83705; tel. 208-344-6565). Teton Expeditions, for floating, fishing and packing (427 East 13th St., Idaho Falls, ID 83401; tel. 208-523-4981). Gillihan's Guide Service, for fishing, high mountain lakes, scenic trail rides, and big-game hunts (Rt. 2, Box 242, Emmett, ID 83617; tel. 208-365-5384). Bruce Henderson, for whitewater floats, jet boat trips, big-game hunting, high mountain lake packing (Star Route, Lucile, ID 83542; tel. 208-628-3465). Ronald Vaughn, for big-game hunting, fishing, family vacation saddle trips (P.O. Box 401, Emmett, ID 83617; tel. 208-365-4946). Hatch River Trips, for float trips on the Middle Fork, Salmon, and Selway (411 E. 2nd North, Vernal, UT 84078; tel. 801-789-3813). Ora Lee Medlock, for bear and mountain-lion hunting (Box 662-A, Bovill, ID 83806; tel. 208-826-3237). Gladys L. York, for big-game hunting and fishing in the Salmon River primitive area. (Box 355, Elk City, ID 83523.)

(For more detailed information, write: Idaho Outfitters and Guides Association, P.O. Box 95, Boise, ID 83701.)

Ice Caves: Minnetonka Cave in the Cache National Forest, near Paris, in the southeast corner of the state, is open daily from mid-June through Labor Day. Guided tours begin on the hour from 10-5. Jackets advisable, temperature in cave is 40°F. Shoshone Ice Caves, Idaho 75, 17 miles north of Shoshone, is open May thru Sept. from 8 a.m. to 8 p.m. Guided tours every 20 minutes. Crystal Ice Cave, North Pleasant Valley Road, American Falls, is open daily May-Oct. from 7 a.m.-sunset. Guided tours. Mammoth Cave, located 7 miles north of Shoshone on Idaho 75, has similar schedule to Shoshone Ice Caves.

Old Idaho Penitentiary, built in 1870, has guided 30-minute walking tours of the former state prison and grounds. Sat. 10-4; all other days, noon-4. Comfortable walking shoes suggested.

Idaho State Capitol, built in 1905, and constructed of native sandstone and marble from Alaska, Georgia, and Vermont, has weekday tours, with emphasis on exhibits of agricultural, mineral, and timber products.

 INDUSTRIAL TOURS. A visitor interested in Idaho's economy should plan to visit at least one mine, one mill or wood-products plant, and one food-processing plant. Food-processing plants are all through the Snake River Valley and can be visited informally.

Boise: *Idaho Power Company*, 1220 Idaho St., has tours of Hells Canyon Dam, Brownlee Dam, and Oxbow Dam, all located in North America's deepest gorge. Tours daily at Hells Canyon Dam, 1 p.m., and Brownlee Dam, 11 a.m., and weekdays at Oxbow Dam, 3 p.m. Tour length: 1 hour. Advance notice of 2 days required. Contact Power Plant Operating Superintendent, phone: 208-345-7210. *The Idaho Statesman*, 1200 N. Curtis Rd. Visitors will discover how the newspaper is produced every 24 hours, will see original first edition (July 26, 1864), and learn how stories and pictures become news. Tours Mon., Tue., Wed., and Fri., 9:30-noon and 1:30-4 p.m. Tour length: 1 hour. Advance notice of 1 week required. Phone: 208-376-2121, Ext. 329. *Lucky Peak Nursery*. U.S. Forest Service, c/o Idaho City Stage (17 miles northeast of Boise on Idaho 21). Growing bare-root tree seedling stock from seed and seed extraction. Tours weekdays, 7:30 a.m.-4:30 p.m. Tour length: 1 hour. Advance notice of 1 week required. Contact Nurseryman, phone: 208-343-1977. *Shelterex Corporation*, 3210 East Amity Rd. Mobile Home manufacturer. Tours Mon. thru Thur., 10-noon and 1:30-3:30. Tour length: 1 hour. No tours week of July 4 and week of Christmas. Children not admitted. Advance notice of 1 week. Phone: 208-345-5500. *Interagency Fire Center*, 3905 Vista Ave., has tours 10 a.m., Mon.-Fri., of training facilities, equipment, infrared mapping unit, and meteorological data center.

Coeur d'Alene: *Forest Service Tree Nursery*, June thru Aug., daily, 8-4:30 p.m.

Emmett: *Boise-Cascade Corporation*. Processing of logs from mill pond to finished products. Tours Mon. thru Fri., 10 a.m. and 1:30 p.m. Tour length: 2 hours. No tours the first 2 weeks in July. Written advance notice of 6 weeks required. Contact Plant Manager, phone: 208-365-4431.

Grangeville: *Ray Holes Saddle Company*, 213 W. Main. Custom-made saddles, pack equipment for horses and mules, and riding equipment. Tours Mon. thru Sat., 9-5. Tour length: 30 minutes. Advance notice of 1 day required. Children under 6 not admitted. Phone: 208-983-1460. *Wickes Forest Industries*, Highway 95 North. Manufacturing and selling wholesale lumber. Tour of main sawmill, from log infeed thru bin sorter and automatic stacker. Tours Tue. thru Thur., 10:30-11:30 a.m. and 3:30-4:30 p.m. Tour length: 30-45 minutes. Written advance notice of 6 weeks required. No cameras or sketches permitted. Children under 6 not admitted. Contact Safety and Personnel Director, phone: 208-983-1290.

Hagerman: *Snake River Pottery*. Daily, 9-6.

Kamiah: *Potlatch Corporation*, Star Route. Tours begin at log pond and go thru the sawmill. Tours Mon. thru Fri., afternoons only. Tour length: 45 minutes. No cameras or sketches permitted. Advance notice required. Children must be accompanied by an adult. Contact Personnel and Safety Director, phone: 208-935-2577.

Kellogg: *Bunker Hill Company*, 834 W. McKinley. Mine and smelter. Products include lead, zinc, silver, cadmium, and various by-products. Walking tours of the mine surface, concentrator, and lead smelter. Mine tour consists of the mine portal, a mine model, and the mill. The smelter tour consists of the blast furnace, lead refinery, and casting area. All necessary safety equipment provided. Tours weekdays during June, July and August. Mine tour, 9 a.m. and 1 p.m.; smelter tour, 10:30 a.m. and 2:30 p.m. Tour length: 1 hour. No cameras or sketches permitted. Children under 5 not admitted. Contact Public Relations Administrator, phone: 208-784-1261, ext. 422.

Lewiston: *Potlatch Corporation*. Lumber, plywood, and tissue products. Weekday tours during June, July and August, 9 a.m. and 1 p.m. Weekday tours from Sept. thru May at 1 p.m. only. Tour length: 2 hours and 30 minutes. No cameras or sketches permitted. Children under 8 not admitted. Phone: 208-799-1483.

McCall: *Boise Cascade Lumber Mill*. Daily, 12 noon to 3.

Mullan: *Lucky Friday Mine*. Surface tour of facilities. June 1 thru Sept. 1, Mon. thru Fri., 12:30 and 1:30.

Nampa: *Idaho Concrete Pipe Company, Inc.*, 222 Caldwell Blvd. Asphalt-prestress concrete building components. Tours Mon. thru Fri., 8-4. Advance notice required. Spanish translation available. Hard-hats provided. Phone: 208-466-8971.

New Meadows: *Evergreen Forest Products, Inc.* Highway 95 between New Meadows and Council. Lumber manufacturing. Tours Mon. thru Fri., 7 a.m.-4 p.m. No tours from mid-Dec. thru Feb., over 4th of July, and first week of hunting season. Advance notice required. Contact Mill Superintendent, phone: 208-347-2111.

Pocatello: *American Microsystems, Inc.*, 2300 Buckskin Rd. Semi-conductor and integrated circuits. Tours Mon. thru Fri., 9 a.m.-3 p.m. Tour length: 1 hour. Advance notice of 2 weeks required. No cameras permitted. Children under 14 not admitted. Contact Personnel Administrator, phone: 208-233-4690. *J.R. Simplot Co., Minerals & Chemicals Division*. Fertilizer. Tours by appointment only; advance notice of 2 weeks required. Japanese translation available. Children under 14 not admitted. Contact Plant Manager, phone: 208-232-6620.

St. Maries: *Potlatch Corporation*, Mill Road. Tours Mon. thru Fri., 9 a.m. and 1 p.m. Tour length: 1 hour. Children under 10 not admitted. Contact Tour Guide, phone: 208-245-2585.

Sandpoint: *Louisiana-Pacific Corp.*, 808 N. Boyer. Lumber mill. Tours Mon. thru Fri., 9-2. Tour length: 1 hour. Advance notice required. Children under 10 not admitted. Contact Plant Manager, phone: 208-263-3145.

Troy: *Idaho Winery & Grape Growers*. June thru Sept. Daily except Sun., 10-6.

 GARDENS. Idaho residents like to boast that their garden is on the mountainsides and across the prairies in nature's setting. Driving through the relatively sparsely populated state, the visitor will see specimens of more than 3,000 different plants growing without cultivation, but few formal gardens. In Boise, Ann Morrison Memorial Park has flower gardens and an unusual illuminated pool with fountain. Howard V. Platt Gardens, at the railroad depot, in Boise, is especially beautiful at night. Ross Park, south along the Portneuf River, in Pocatello, has lovely gardens.

 MUSIC. Music blooms in Idaho all year-round and literally fills the air in summer. For such a small state, population-wise, there is a wide variety of music—and a lot of it. Early in May Boise puts on Music Week, with citywide music programs daily in schools, churches, and colleges. The Boise Philharmonic Orchestra performs not only in its home city but in other major communities. The Boise State College-Community and College of Idaho-Community orchestras have justifiably achieved regional recognition. Northwest Nazarene College (Nampa) has sent its madrigal choir overseas to give USO performances. The music departments of the University of Idaho (Moscow) and Idaho State University (Pocatello) present concerts featuring almost anything from the classics to jazz and pop, and a number of groups tour Idaho annually to offer this musical fare to those unable to attend the on-campus performances. Summer concerts are provided in an inspiring setting by the Sun Valley Creative Arts Center. Summer-evening band concerts are held at Julia Davis Park, in Boise; in Ross Park, Pocatello; and in City Park, Twin Falls. At Macks Inn, from mid-June thru Labor Day, Mon. thru Sat., the Island Park Music Circus presents musical productions. At Bannock Creek and Ross Fork, Indian chants pierce the air at the Shoshone-Bannock Dances, held in July; and Nez Percé soul music pours out in the mid-August Pi-Nee-Waus Days held at Lapwai.

McCall is the scene of the 3-day annual Square and Round Dance Funstitute, held in early July, Coeur d'Alene is the site of the late July annual Scottish Highland Festival & Tatoo, featuring classic and general bagpipe competition, and, also in late July, the music-filled Idaho State Square & Round Dance Festival is held at the University of Idaho Student Union Building in Moscow. The Fairgrounds at Burley is the stage in mid-August for the Country-Western Jamboree, with top country-western recording artists performing.

Much of the music heard in Idaho is folk, reflecting the largely small-town character of the state. One form of folk music has been deep-seated in southwestern Idaho for about a century now. It is that of the Basques, who came to this far land from the Pyrenees of Spain. Although Basques are better known as dancers than singers and instrumentalists, Basque music does exist, and is due for popular exposure.

The most widespread folk music is fiddling. All around Idaho, and in every month of the year, fiddling contests are held, and local fiddlers are featured at many events, ranging from county fairs to fund-raising activities. The big happening is at Weiser, where in late June the town is practically set aside for the National Old-Time Fiddlers' Contest.

 STAGE AND REVUES. As in every other state, dramatic groups are springing up all over Idaho. Not since the W.P.A. in the Great Depression of the 1930s has there been such a renaissance. Most of the new groups border on the ephemeral, and some are so intimate that only their small circles of friends know them. But, wherever they have sprouted and however long they last, they are adding more strands of culture to the state.

Any place you go in Idaho you may come across the ubiquitous Antique Festival Theatre. Antique plays anywhere—performing in American Legion and Grange halls, state parks, football fields, barns, ranchhouses. It performs not only in the major cities of Idaho but the outposts as well.

Boise, as to be expected, has the largest number of theatrical groups, including those at or emanating from Boise State College, the cultural pillar and wellspring of the city. The most important new company is the Morrison Foundation, which in November, 1977, staged *Shenandoah* in Boise and Twin Falls. Boise Little Theatre, performing in a unique 24-sided building, is a self-supporting community theater that puts on a wide variety of plays.

The Coeur d'Alene Summer Theatre aspires to bring quality musical repertory to north Idaho. The season runs from mid-June thru Labor Day, except Mondays. The University of Idaho Summer Theatre in the Kiva, at Moscow, produces several shows over the summer (late June thru July, Tue. thru Fri.), each playing for several nights. The Lewiston Divic Theatre starts its season in September and runs until the last week of May, with a broad program of presentations. Lewis-Clark State College, also in Lewiston, has a summer theater schedule. In the fall a Children's Theatre tours northcentral Idaho. Valley Dramatists, a Nampa-Caldwell community group, stages fall plays, usually melodramas, at the Nampa High School Little Theater. Fairyland Park Marionette Theater, in Jerome, is unique in its casting; the actors are not local talent but are manufactured by local talent. The group has been presenting summer marionette shows since 1967; during the winter it tours neighboring towns. The Magic Valley Dilettantes have produced a musical comedy in Twin Falls annually since 1958. The Magic Valley Little Theatre, also in Twin Falls, is devoted to legitimate drama; it tries to do two shows a year, one in winter and one in May. College of Southern Idaho, also in Twin Falls, has a variety of dramatic entertainment, including the Summer Mummers, a training program for Magic Valley High School students. During the fall and winter the drama and music departments frequently combine to produce musicals, and the Readers Theater offers an opportunity for informal readings-in-the-round of many plays. Theatre I.S.U. at Idaho State University, in Pocatello, presents comedies in its summer season, and in the fall and winter turns to more-serious drama. Frazier Little Theatre, on the university campus, is one of the finest in the state. The Theater Department of Ricks College, in Rexburg, offers a variety of plays during the fall and winter season. Pierre's Summer Playhouse, in Victor, whoops it up with summer melodrama. Island Park Music Circus, at Macks Inn, stages musicals from mid-June thru Labor Day.

BARS. A Boise favorite is *The Gamekeeper* in the Owyhee Plaza Hotel, 11th & Main, downtown. Also popular with the Boise chic set is the lounge in the Sheratown Downtown, 1901 Main. For local folk-color, try *Louie's Liquid Hide-Away*, 1607 Federal Way, and *The Beerhouse*, 9751 Cory Lane. In Coeur d'Alene, enter the *Sourdough Club*, 2600 E. Sherman, thru a mine shaft; everyone taller than 5 feet has to duck. The place is a virtual museum of curiosities and oddities. Also in Coeur d'Alene, *North Shore Motor Hotel*, 115 S Second, and *Templins*, 122 Sherman, have lake views. In smaller towns, the bar is sometimes the cultural center, especially for loggers, miners, and farmers. Good example: *State Line Tavern*, at Oldtown, on the Idaho-Washington border, 40 miles north of Coeur d'Alene.

NIGHTCLUBS. Night life in much of Idaho tends to be loud and lively. There are some communities where casual conviviality seems to be the principal industry. Like wildflowers, many nightclubs appear to jump up overnight and as quickly disappear. In the Ketchum-Sun Valley area the names and decors change almost with the seasons.

Boise: *Sheraton Downtown*, 1901 Main, draws patrons to its lounge with a congenial atmosphere and live entertainment. *Iron Gate Lounge* of University Ramada Inn, near Boise State College, attracts a young, bright clientele with its crisp entertainment. *Cock O' The Walk*, Rodeway Inn, 29th & Chinden Blvd., combines good food and entertainment. Live entertainment nightly in *The Gamekeeper* of the Owyhee Plaza Hotel, 11th & Main, downtown. "Happy Hour" Mon. thru Fri. *Holiday Inn-Airport* draws more than travelers with its live entertainment nightly in the decorative lounge. Dancing and good music nightly in the *Purple Jester Lounge* of the Jolly King Restaurant, 1115 N. Curtis.

Coeur d'Alene: Nightly entertainment combines with lake breezes to make life pleasurable at *Holiday Inn*, 414 W. Apple Way. Live entertainment and dancing at the *North Shore Motor Hotel*, near the marina of Coeur d'Alene Lake. North Shore Plaza, Second and Sherman, features *Cloud 9*, Idaho's only rooftop lounge. Dancing and exciting live entertainment.

Grangeville: Live entertainment in lounge of *Charcoal Broiler Restaurant*, 111 E. North, Tue. night.

Idaho Falls: *Stardust Restaurant*, 680 Lindsay Blvd., has live entertainment 6 nights weekly in lounge.

Pocatello: *Holiday Inn*, Bench Rd., has lounge with live music and dancing nightly.

Twin Falls: *Coy's at the Holiday Inn*, 1350 Blue Lakes Blvd., offers live entertainment in lounge.

Worley: *Leo's Worley Motel* offers live entertainment on weekends, dancing from 8:30 p.m.-12:30 a.m. each Fri. and Sat.

DRINKING LAWS. The legal age for consumption of alcoholic beverages is 19. Liquor can be obtained from state liquor stores or by the drink from 10 a.m. to 1 a.m. The sale of liquor is prohibited on Sundays, Memorial Day, Labor Day, until the polls close on Election Day, Thanksgiving, and Christmas.

SUMMER SPORTS. Idaho is a state of mountains, forests, lakes, and streams. Sports are generally of the outdoor type—fishing, hunting, hiking, boating and skiing in season.

Fishing: The fishing is good in all parts of Idaho. The rivers, smaller streams, large lakes, mountain pools, and ponds all produce excellent catches. Record-size trout are taken from Lake Pend Oreille, in the north, and the average is also heavy in nearby Priest and Coeur d'Alene lakes. Steelhead and sturgeon challenge the anglers along the Snake and Clearwater Rivers, while the Salmon and its Middle Fork offer solitude as well as top fly fishing.

The general fishing season usually runs from the Saturday before the Memorial Day holiday thru November, when trout and other species may be taken. Special seasons also apply to trout, salmon, steelhead, and a number of other species. Bag limits vary with different species. Non-resident season fishing license is $20; non-resident seven-day fishing license is $7; non-resident one-day fishing license is $3. Fishing licenses may be obtained from vendors in nearly every town in the state.

Forest Service public campgrounds are available along many streams and lakes. Packers and guides may be hired to go into the back country. Idaho has over 1,800 lakes, in addition to rivers, reservoirs, and smaller streams.

For list of regulations and further information, write: Idaho Fish & Game Dept. (see *Tourist Information Services*).

Boating: The lakes and rivers provide water highways for small-boat operators. Days can be spent on inland waters in the north, and Snake River reservoirs provide more-than-adequate water space in the south. Waterskiing is popular at Lucky Peak Reservoir, a short drive east of Boise. Sailboats abound on the Payette Lakes, at McCall, and on Coeur d'Alene Lake, where there is sailboat racing. Dangerous storms can whip up on huge Pend Oreille and other lakes of the panhandle. Boatmen unfamiliar with the lakes should stay within shouting distance of shore. Special thrills are offered on the white-water trips down the Snake, Middle Fork of the Salmon, Main Salmon, and Selway, but these are for the skilled and experienced only. (For guided float and jet boat trips down these rivers, see *Guest Ranches*, *Tours*, and *Special Interest Tours*).

Golf: The Sun Valley Golf Club has a beautiful 18-hole course, open May to Oct. One of the most picturesque courses is Blue Lakes Country Club in the Snake River Canyon near Twin Falls. All major cities have golf courses, along with golf shops.

Hunting—big game: The many miles of wilderness and age-old forests provide a special opportunity for big-game hunting. The inexperienced hunter would be little short of insane not to hire a professional guide before striking out into treacherous terrain. General seasons for deer, elk, and bear extend from mid-Sept. until Nov., though areas and seasons vary throughout the state. Controlled hunts are sometimes established for moose, antelope, mountain goat, and bighorn sheep. Non-resident big-game hunters should contact the Idaho Fish & Game Dept., beginning in Jan., since licenses are obtained on a quota basis. Copies of the official regulations may be obtained without charge from license vendors or from the Idaho Fish & Game Dept. Big-game seasons are set about May 20, and hunting maps are available from the

Department after July 1 each year. License fees are more than $100 for some species; game tags are additional. Since fees are subject to change, for up-to-date information, write: Idaho Fish and Game Dept. (see *Tourist Information Services*). For hunting trips and guides, see *Guest Ranches* and *Special Interest Tours*, and write: Idaho Outfitters and Guides Association, P.O. Box 95, Boise, ID 83701.

Hunting—birds: Hunting seasons of varying length are set for partridge, quail, and grouse, usually in Sept. and Oct.; for pheasant, in specified areas from late Oct. thru most of Nov.; for waterfowl, usually from mid-Oct. thru Dec. Opening dates for upland bird seasons are set in May, with complete regulations established in late August. Licenses may be obtained from vendors in nearly every town in the state. A non-resident bird hunting license is $50. For regulations and up-to-date information, write: Idaho Fish & Game Dept. For guides, write: Idaho Outfitters and Guides Association.

WINTER SPORTS. *Skiing:* The fastest-growing sport in Idaho, at least as far as facilities are concerned, is skiing. Tow lines and chair lifts now run up many slopes in the state, and the facilities attract skiers from a wide area outside Idaho.

The most famous ski resort is *Sun Valley*. Western Airlines, which flies to many ski areas in the West, says of Sun Valley, "The first complete ski resort remains the best. The two mountains are the finest in America." Ten miles of additional intermediate skiing were opened in 1977 by a new triple chairlift on Seattle Ridge. With 200 ski instructors, "Sun Valley continues to offer the finest learn-to-ski and ski-improvement program available anywhere," says Western Airlines. *Elkhorn* at Sun Valley is located adjacent to Dollar Mountain, while still convenient to the slopes of Mt. Baldy. Sun Valley offers 3 ice rinks, supervised child-care, and a romantic horse-drawn sleigh ride, in addition to skiing. Elkhorn has its own ice rink. Both have lodging, dining, and entertainment facilities. Ketchum (Idaho 93) is close by, and some people stay there. The city of Ketchum operates buses to Sun Valley and Elkhorn between 7 a.m. and 11 p.m.

One of the most spectacular scenic ski areas in the nation is *Grand Targhee*, 12 miles east of the Driggs (Idaho 33) on the western slope of the Tetons, with panoramic views of the awesome range. Although actually in Wyoming, Grand Targhee is included in Idaho because of its proximity to Idaho Falls and nearby communities. Snow here is described by Western Airlines as "limitless in its profusion of Rocky Mountain powder." Snowfall often exceeds 140 inches at the base of the mountain. Because snow comes early to Grand Targhee, skiing begins in October and lasts into June. Helicopters fly powder enthusiasts to untracked areas in the high mountains. Accommodations at Targhee Lodge & Melehes' Teton Tee Pee, and in Driggs. Ski shop, equipment rental, and full-time nursery. Restaurant at base of chairlifts.

Bogus Basin, 16 miles north of Boise, and a favorite with western Snake River Valley winter sports-minded men and women, is one of the major ski areas in the Pacific Northwest. Copious snowfall and moderate temperatures from Thanksgiving deep into April make Bogus Basin a true winter wonderland. The longest illuminated slope in the country is here—over 1,000 acres; 20 major runs offer a variety of ski terrain with packed and powder slopes. Day and night skiing. Ski area has ski rental shop, day lodge, cafeteria, full-time nursery, and professional ski school.

Another magnificently-located ski area is *Brundage Mountain*, 7 miles north of McCall, on Idaho 55. The slopes overlook Payette Lakes and out to a world of silver forests and high, rugged terrain. Two riblet double chairlifts transport skiers a mile to the top of the mountain in approximately 10 minutes (no lift lines here). Total vertical drop on Brundage Mountain is 1,600 feet. An alpine T-bar lift, 1,800 feet long, 450-foot vertical rise, services the more gentle beginner and intermediate slopes. At this high, dry altitude, powder snow is the rule rather than the exception. Ski shop, rentals, snack bar, ski school. Open 7 days a week. Overnight accommodations in McCall.

Other principal ski areas include:

Bald Mountain, 6 miles northeast of Pierce on Idaho 11. Has 3,000-foot T-bar and 3 main runs. Day lodge, snack bar, ski shop, equipment rental. Open weekends and holidays. Overnight accommodations in Pierce and Orofino.

Bear Gulch, 13 miles northeast of Ashton (US 20-US 191) and off Idaho 47. From the top of the 5,300-foot mountain, downhillers have 6 slopes and a trail to attack. Day lodge with snack bar. Ski school has family rates. Open daily except Mon. Overnight accommodations in Ashton.

Blizzard Mountain, 18 miles west of Arco on US 93-US 20-US 26, and 2 miles from Craters of the Moon National Monument. A 2,500-foot poma lift and rope tow handle the mountain. Day lodge, snack bar, and ski school. Open weekends and holidays. Overnight accommodations in Arco.

Caribou, 6 miles east of Pocatello. Two main slops and three trails are served by a chairlift and rope tow. Night skating Wed. thru Fri. Olympic-size ice rink and skating instructor. Day lodge and snack bar, equipment rental, ski school. Open weekends. Overnight accommodations in Pocatello.

Cottonwood Butte, 5 miles west of Cottonwood off US 95. Six miles of crosscountry runs open off the north slope of Cottonwood Butte. Downhill skiers have 3 open slopes, the longest just under 1 mile. Open Wed. afternoons, weekends, and holidays. Day lodge, snack bar, equipment rental, ski school. Overnight accommodations in Cottonwood, Grangeville, and Craigmont.

Flying H Ski Resort, 12 miles north of Coeur d'Alene off US 95. A novice and intermediate ski area with gentle slopes illuminated for night skiing. Open slopes with the longest trail 1,200 feet and 250 feet of vertical drop. Day lodge and snack bar. Rental equipment available. Fri., Sat. & Sun. Overnight accommodations.

Hitt Mountain, 14 miles west of Cambridge (US 95) on Idaho 71. Five trails branch off the top of the 2,500-foot T-bar lift. Day lodge, snack bar, ski school, rental equipment. Open weekends and holidays. Overnight accommodations at Cambridge and Weiser.

Kelly Canyon, 25 miles northeast of Idaho Falls. Three double chairlifts and 2 rope tows. Six open slopes are served by 3 chairs. Longest run is 1 mile in length with a vertical drop of 870 feet. Day lodge, ski school, equipment rental. Open daily except Mon.; night skiing 3 evenings a week. Overnight accommodations in Idaho Falls.

Lookout Pass, 14 miles northeast of Wallace on I-90 at Montana border. Excellent snow and gentle (700-foot vertical drop) slopes make it a fine teaching area. Day lodge, cafeteria, and ski rental shop. Open weekends and holidays with night skiing each Fri. Overnight accommodations in Wallace and Mullan.

Lost Trail, 42 miles north of Salmon on US 93, near Montana border and Continental Divide. Double chairlift. Seven open runs, the longest 6,600 feet in length, and a 10-mile crosscountry area. Day lodge, snack bar, ski school, equipment rental. Overnight accommodations in Salmon and Gibbonsville.

Magic Mountain, 35 miles southeast of Twin Falls. Two separate mountains, 15 runs and 4 trails, with the longest 2 miles in length. Main lift is a 3,000-foot double chair; it and the adjacent 2,500-foot T-bar offer excellent powder runs for advanced skiers. The second mountain is primarily a ski-school slope; skiers move up on a 2,000-foot poma lift. Day lodge with cafeteria, ski school, equipment rental. Open Wed., Thur., weekends, and holidays. Overnight accommodations in Twin Falls.

Montpelier Ski Area, at the edge of city limits of Montpelier, on US 30. Recreation area for children and teenagers. One rope tow climbs an 800-foot hill with slopes for skiers, sleds, and toboggans. Open weekends and holidays. Accommodations in town.

North-South Bowl, 60 miles south of Coeur d'Alene and 45 miles north of Moscow (US 95) on US 95 Alt. Popular with students from University of Idaho and Washington State University. Double chairlift and 2 rope tows. Open Thur. thru Sun., with night skiing Fri. and Sat. Day lodge, ski school, rental equipment. Accommodations at St. Maries.

Pine Basin, 7 miles north of Swan Valley (US 26) off Idaho 31. Basically a teaching and intermediate area, with 7 ski trails, 4 beginner and intermediate slopes, 1 intermediate run, and 2 advanced runs. Day lodge and ski school. Overnight accommodations at Swan Valley.

Pomerelle, 29 miles southeast of Burley (US 30) off Idaho 77. A variety of challenging runs over open slopes and trails winding down through the timbered slopes of 8,020-foot Mt. Harrison. A 4,600-foot double chair and a poma lift move skiers up the mountain. Day lodge has cafeteria, lounge, and ski shop with equipment rental. Open Wed. thru Sun. Overnight accommodations in Burley.

Robinson Bar Cross Country Ski Resort, 15 miles east of Stanley off Idaho 75. Experience begins with sleigh ride into the Robinson ranch from the highway. Crosscountry skiing in Idaho wilderness. Experienced guides for half-day, full-day, or overnight runs into the White Clouds or Sawtooth Mountains. Accommodations at the ranch include family-style meals and heated swimming pool.

Schweitzer Ski Basin, 11 miles northwest of Sandpoint off US 95-US 2. Has an 8,000-skiers-per-hour capacity. Six double chairlifts and 4 T-bars move skiers uphill into 2 huge bowls, Schweitzer and Colburn. More than 30 runs and trails up to 3 miles long. The Lodge, the Outback Inn, and the Powder House serve food and beverages. The Beer Stube in the Lodge is a popular after-ski stop. Ski shop and equipment rental in the Alpine Shop at Lodge. Open daily.

Silverhorn, 6 miles south of Kellogg off I-90, has 14 major runs which lace Silverhorn's twin peaks, providing deep powder as well as packed powder skiing through wooded and open terrain. Runs range from Stemwinder's 2-mile tour and the winding, gentle Success to free-fall skiing down the Last Chance. No lift lines, but a mile-long double chairlift with 2 loading points. Day lodge, with cafeteria. Nursery service available on weekends and holidays. Ski shop, complete with rentals and repair service. Brown-bag lounge in the lodge. Flanking the lodge are 18 electrical hookups for recreation vehicles. Overnight accommodations in Kellogg.

Skyline, 15 miles southeast of Pocatello at I-15 Inkom Exit. Great for downhill skiers with a 1,650-foot vertical drop in its 5,000-foot length. Ten open slopes and 4 trails. Day lodge at the 6,700-foot level on Mt. Bonneville. Ski shop and restaurant. Overnight accommodations in Pocatello.

Snowhaven, 7 miles south of Grangeville (US 95). Local area, with gentle slopes, serving residents of the Camas Prairie. Emphasis on instruction for beginning and intermediate skiers. Four open slopes and 2 trails. Day lodge, snack bar, equipment rental, ski school. Open Wed. afternoons and weekends. Overnight accommodations in Grangeville.

Soldier Mountain, 11 miles north of Fairfield off Idaho 68. Excellent skiing from mid-Dec. thru April on the open slopes of the 10,000-foot mountain. More than a dozen packed and powder runs. Day lodge, snack bar, equipment rental, ski school. Open Thur. thru Sun. Overnight accommodations at Fairfield and Gooding.

Tamarack, 17 miles northeast of Moscow (US 95); 5 miles north of Troy (Idaho 8). Novice, intermediate, and advanced runs on 2 open slopes and 2 trails serviced by 2 surface lifts. Day lodge, snack bar, equipment rental, ski school. Overnight accommodations at Troy or Moscow.

Taylor Mountain, 16 miles southeast of Idaho Falls, has 6 open slopes and 12 trails. Longest run is 3,500 feet, with 800 feet of vertical drop. Day and night skiing Wed. thru Sun. Day lodge, cafeteria, ski school, equipment rental. Overnight accommodations in Idaho Falls.

Torarun, 2 miles west of Hailey off Idaho 75. Basically a developing ground for junior racers. The open slopes are just 12 miles from Sun Valley. Day lodge and snack bar, ski school and equipment rental. Open weekends and holidays; night skiing on Tue. and Thur. Overnight accommodations in Hailey.

SPECTATOR SPORTS. Rodeos are scheduled throughout summer and early fall, providing excitement for many. (See *Seasonal Events.*) Many colleges as well as the University of Idaho and Idaho State University field football, basketball, baseball, and track teams, along with teams in other sports, with women moving forward strongly in the area of athletics. Idaho State University, a power in the Big Sky Conference, achieved national recognition when its basketball team defeated UCLA in the regional NCAA playoffs in 1977. Boise State College attracts large crowds with its always-formidable football teams. Motorcycle and drag races are held throughout the state. Blackfoot has a Sportsman's Speedway, Boise a Firebird Speedway (as well as Owyhee Motorcycle Races at Peaceful Cove), Lewiston a Banana Belt Speedway, and Meridian a Meridian Speedway. There is horse-racing from mid-May thru Labor Day at the Fairgrounds in Boise and in summer at Coeur d'Alene and Pocatello. Swimming meets and tennis tournaments are held in Boise during the summer.

 SHOPPING. The visitor will find interesting craft and gift shops scattered around Idaho, especially at or near major resort areas. Antique hunters will do best at second-hand stores and auction houses in smaller communities. There is no concentration of population to support a metropolitan range of specialty shops, but most Idaho cities offer an adequate selection. Best buys: Western styles. (Caution: Check labels. As in every other state, some "native" products are actually from Japan, Taiwan, and South Korea.)

In Boise, popular general stores are the Bon Marché, 918 W. Idaho, and Falk's Idaho Department Store, 100 N. 8th. The style-conscious might try Mode Ltd., 802 W. Idaho, and Carroll's, 816 W. Bannock. Unusual shops include World Toy and Hobbycraft, 7820 Fairview; Sawtooth Mountaineering, 5200 Fairview; and The Art Mart, 711 S. Latah.

In Idaho Falls, the L.D.S. Ladies Relief Society sells local crafts, and Marketplace Books & Art has a good display of Idaho arts and handcrafts. Karcher's Mall, Nampa, boasts Idaho's largest shopping center; 60 stores, including fine restaurants.

 WHAT TO DO WITH THE CHILDREN. In a state abounding with lakes, streams, woodland trails, ghost towns, deer, old barns, picturesque farmsteads, and charming fences, children will find activity or interest nearly every time the family car pauses. In addition, public parks in Blackfoot, Boise, Caldwell, Coeur d'Alene, Idaho Falls, Pocatello, and other major cities provide playgrounds and pools. There are zoos at Boise, Idaho Falls, and Pocatello, and amusement rides in the parks at Boise, Coeur d'Alene, and Idaho Falls. Children are fascinated by the miniature power station at Trenner Memorial Park at American Falls. Then, of course, there are the county fairs (which always have a lot of things for children), rodeos, horse shows, and Indian festivals, as well as fun theaters popping up here and there. Square dancing, which delights many youngsters, seems to be going on all over the state all the time. Sun Valley is a children's paradise. At Macks Inn, in eastern Idaho's legendary Mountain Man country, the Island Park Music Circus has Mon. thru Sat. performances from mid-June thru Labor Day. Pierre's Summer Playhouse, at Victor, stages "old-fashioned melodramas" Thur. thru Sat., July thru Labor Day—and any one of those ought to send the kids into titters and screams. Finally, there are the magnificent backpacking and trail pack trips deep into the wilderness, where the children come close to nature and, with reasonable luck, will see a variety of wildlife.

INDIANS. Idaho has a rich Indian heritage. The Indians lived almost entirely upon fish and plants, preferred the portable tepee, used skins instead of cloth, made little pottery, and did not practice agriculture. The horse probably reached the Idaho region before 1751. These tribes were able to become excellent nomadic horsemen, and the acquisition of horses was the most important factor in Indian life before the coming of the whites. Horses revolutionized Indian warfare and transportation; permitted wider and more frequent migration, leading to tribal wars—though these have been grossly exaggerated by white historians; and, especially, enabled Indians to fight the whites in more equitable battles. The horse also changed the Indian mode of hunting and could not help but have a strong effect upon Indian culture.

The friendliest and most helpful Indians Lewis and Clark met on their long trek to the Pacific and back to St. Louis were the Nez Percé.

Not until hordes of white settlers began usurping the Indian lands did Idaho's Indians retaliate with gun and arrow.

However, only three red-white wars were fought in Idaho, and all were caused by forcing the Indians to move to reservations. The Nez Percé War in 1877 was the largest. The next year the Bannocks, under Chief Buffalo Horn, fought to retain rights on the Camas Prairie, near Fairfield. The last battle was fought in the Sheepeater War in the Lemhis in 1879.

The Nez Percé have been eulogized by historians since the journals of Lewis and Clark were made public, and their heritage is honored and preserved in this nation's first National Historic Park, unique in that it is a scattered sanctuary of 22 bits and parcels of land, all in Idaho.

Spreading from Spalding on the west to Lolo Pass on the east, and as far south as the White Bird Battlefield (US 95), the park, with headquarters at Spalding, near Lewiston, brings together separate sites of historical significance.

In recent years, Idaho archeologists have discovered "buffalo jumps" in the Owyhee breaks and near Challis, some dating back less than 150 years. Excavations of ancient campsites have been made by researchers from the University of Idaho, Idaho State University, and Boise State College. These official digs throughout the state have found layered remains dating back some 10,000 years, to the time of the atlatl. To preserve this Indian heritage, only surface finds may be kept by individuals, and digging is prohibited by law.

Indian petroglyphs are found primarily along the Snake River and to the south and west. Near Melba is a "map rock" which has been studied by ethnologists.

There are many small collections of Indian artifacts spread about Idaho. Major collections include: Spalding Museum, Juliaetta Arrow Museum, Owyhee County Historical Museum at Murphy, Herrett Arts and Science Center in Twin Falls, and Idaho State University at Pocatello. Tepees of the Bannock tribe are on view at the replica of Old Fort Hall in Pocatello's Ross Park.

Idaho's Indian people have six languages, spoken with numerous dialects. One, the Salishan, ties the Coeur d'Alene—whose own name was Skitswish—with tribes as far away as southeastern Alaska. Culturally, the Indians of Idaho were closely identified with those of neighboring areas: Great Basin, Columbia Plateau, and Great Plains.

Five tribes can be found today in Idaho: Kutenai, Coeur d'Alene, and Nez Percé in the north, and Shoshone-Bannock and Paiute in the south.

The Lower Kutenai own 3,985 acres of treaty land in he Bonners Ferry area, and have a population of 75.

Of the four reservations in the state, the largest is Fort Hall, in southeastern Idaho, where a treaty signed more than 110 years ago set aside 1.8 million acres for the Shoshone and Bannock tribes. The reservation has dwindled to 524,557 acres, including government-owned land within the boundaries. In addition, about 50 miles of the Old Oregon Trail cross the reservation. Present population is about 3,000. In July the reservation Indians hold their Sun Dances and religious observances, at Ross

Fork and Bannock Creek. Both include a buffalo feast. In August, the Shoshone-Bannock Indian Festival, at Fort Hall, includes 4 days of activites: historical pageant, war and social dancing, Indian games, parade, all-Indian rodeo, displays, buffalo feast, and the crowning of Miss Shoshone-Bannock. In September, Indian Days is held at Fort Hall, with a varied program. Indian exhibits, dances, and horse races are featured at the Eastern Idaho State Fair (in Blackfoot) in early September, with strong Shoshone and Bannock participation.

In the panhandle, about 35 miles south of the city of Coeur d'Alene, is the Coeur d'Alene Reservation, with some 69,000 acres mingled in a checkerboard pattern with non-allotment lands. Current population is about 500. In mid-June, Whaa-Laa Days, a celebration centered on Indian games and dancing, is held in the reservation town of Worley. In late July or early August, Plummer, the reservation headquarters, is the site of Indian Days, a Pow-wow and festival, with a parade, and held in conjunction with Plummer Days. The big attraction is the annual Tepee Town gathering. Also in August, at the yearly Pilgrimage to Old Cataldo Mission, the first Catholic Mission in Idaho, a Catholic Mass is held by the Coeur d'Alene in their ancient tongue. The public is welcome to the services and to the "friendship" lunch that follows.

Northcentral Idaho is the home of the Nez Percé tribe, which once ranged over the entire region. With headquarters at Lapwai, the reservation contains almost 93,000 acres, and has a population of about 1,600. Lincoln's Birthday Celebration, with Nez Percé games and war dances, is held at Kamiah. From late July to early August, the Talmaks Annual Camp Meeting is held at Craigmont. Religious services begin at 6 a.m. and continue all through the day and evening. Games and races are held on July 4. The meeting includes all six reservation churches. In mid-August, at historic Lapwai, the Nez Percé hold their Pi-Nee-Waus Day, with soul music—Indian style—for the modern touch, plus dancing, Friendship Feast barbecue, parade, races, exhibits, and Indian games. In late August the Nez Percé go to their Mud Springs Camp, near Craigmont, for Indian games and feasting. And late in November they hold a Thanksgiving Celebration at Lapwai, with traditional games and war dances.

The Paiute occupy some 293,000 acres in Duck Valley, part of which lies in southern Owyhee County. Headquarters are at Owyhee, Nevada. About 200 Paiutes live on the Idaho part of the reservation. No Paiute ceremonials are held in Idaho.

RECOMMENDED READING. Undoubtedly the best single volume on the state is *Idaho*, almost completely researched, written, and edited by the late Vardis Fisher, the most creative literary talent in the state's history. A product of the Writers' Program of the Works Project Administration, the book has long been out of print but can be found at many libraries. Though much of it is outdated, it still provides excellent historical background and a sparkling flavor that reflects the state's origins, development, and culture.

For detailed information, the Territorial Centennial Edition of the *Idaho Almanac*, also out of print—and parts of it outdated—is invaluable in getting a broad picture of the state. (For possible copies, write: Idaho Division of Tourism and Industrial Development; see *Tourist Information Services*.)

Other books: *Northwest Passages: A Book of Travel* by Ralph Friedman (Ballantine, $1.50); *This Land Around Us*, edited by Ellis Lucia (Doubleday, $12.50); *Indian Legends of the Pacific Northwest* by Ella E. Clark (University of California Press, $2.85); *Snake River Country* by Bill Gulick, photography by Earl Roberge (Caxton, $30.00); *Home Below Hells Canyon* by Grace Jordan (University of Nebraska Press, $2.45); *War Chief Joseph* by Helen Addison Howard and Dan L. McGrath (University of Nebraska Press, $2.45); *Lost Mines and Treasures of the Pacific Northwest* by Ruby El Hult (Binford and Mort, $6.50); *Ghost Towns of the Northwest* by Norman D. Weis (Caxton, $7.95); *Gold Rushes and Mining Camps of the Early American West* by Vardis Fisher and Opal L. Holmes (Caxton, $17.95); *Wilderness Trails Northwest* by Ira L. Spring and Harvey Manning (Touchstone,

$5.95); *Gem Minerals of Idaho* by John A. Beckwith (Caxton, $3.95); *Indian Wars of the Pacific Northwest* by Ray H. Glassley (Binford and Mort, $6.95).

 HOTELS AND MOTELS. In addition to the many hotels and motels that are operated by regional and national chains, there are a number of attractive independent hostelries in Idaho. They cater, with equal enthusiasm, to vacationers and traveling business people. Rates tend to be less expensive than in heavily populated states, so you may well find deluxe accommodations for less than deluxe prices. Based on double occupancy, categories and price ranges are as follows: *Deluxe* over $30; *Expensive* $21 to $30; *Moderate* $14 to $20; and *Inexpensive* under $14.

AMERICAN FALLS

Hillview Motel. *Moderate.* Single- and two-story sections, spacious, comfortable units. Heated pool. Near cafe.

ARCO

D-K Motel. *Moderate.* Smaller motel providing comfort and convenience.

ASHTON

Four Seasons Motel. *Moderate.* Small motel on main business route, with some units with kitchens. Seasonal rates.

Log Cabin Motel. *Moderate.* Small motel with charming, individual log-cabin units, a few with kitchens. Seasonal rates.

BLACKFOOT

Sunset Motel. *Moderate.* Small motel with comfort and convenience, some units with kitchenettes.

BOISE

Rodeway Inn. *Deluxe.* Excellent accommodations, beautiful grounds near the banks of the Boise River. Heated pool, therapy pool, two restaurants, coffee shop, cocktail lounge, entertainment.

Holiday Inn. *Expensive.* Huge motel near airport with elevator, heated indoor pool, therapy pool, sauna, play area, recreation rooms, exercise room. Dining room, cocktail lounge, entertainment.

Owyhee Plaza. *Expensive.* Large, multi-story motel with some rooms with balconies. Fine restaurant with lounge and nightly entertainment.

Ramada Inn-University. *Expensive.* Large motel with heated pool, restaurant, bar, dancing, and entertainment. Near Boise State University.

Royal Inn Motor Hotel. *Expensive.* Large establishment with heated pool, sauna, therapy pool, putting green. Dining room, coffeeshop, cocktail lounge.

Sheraton Downtown. *Expensive.* Large motor hotel, many conveniences, including heated pool, dining room, coffee shop, cocktail lounge, entertainment. Beauty salon, barber shop. Free in-room movies. Close to all downtown facilities.

Boise TraveLodge. *Moderate.* Good family motel, near downtown, with heated pool.

Boisean Motel. *Moderate.* Opposite Boise State College. Medium-size motel with play area, oversize beds, heated pool. Near restaurant.

Cabana Motel. *Moderate*. Extremely comfortable, well-appointed, medium-size motel with variety of unit sizes and some suites. Close to downtown.

Capri Motel. *Moderate*. Medium-size motel with sauna. Cafe close at hand.

Safari Motor Inn. *Moderate*. Comfortable units, heated pool, free continental breakfast. Near State Capitol, museums, parks.

Idanha Motel. *Inexpensive*. Comfortable, roomy units. Coffee shop, cocktail lounge, coin laundry.

Sands Motel. *Inexpensive*. Comfortable small motel with all basic conveniences. Airport limousine available.

Skyline Motel. *Inexpensive*. Small motel with comfortable units.

BONNERS FERRY
Deep Creek Motel. *Moderate*. Small motel on shady grounds near a cool mountain stream. A few 2-room units. Most units with kitchenettes. Heated pool, playground, restaurant, cocktail lounge. Seven miles south of town.

City Center Motel. *Inexpensive*. Very small motel near cafe. Kitchenette facilities.

BUHL
Siesta Motel. *Moderate*. Small motel, with some units having kitchen facilities, some queen-size beds.

BURLEY
Ponderosa Inn. *Expensive*. Large motel with well-furnished units, beautiful grounds, wide choice of accommodations. Two heated pools, 24-hour cafe, dining room, cocktails, dancing, entertainment.

East Park Motel. *Moderate*. Small, comfortable motel, across from city park. Restaurant nearby.

Greenwell Motel. *Moderate*. Another small motel with pleasant, comfortable units, refrigerators in rooms.

Ramada Inn. *Moderate*. Large facility with excellent accommodations. Heated pool. Dog kennel. Airport transportation available. Restaurant, cocktails, entertainment, dancing. Coin laundry.

Y-Dell Motel. *Moderate*. Small motel, a few units with kitchens, near bowling and golf facilities. Heated pool, play area. Children under 6 free. Seasonal rates.

CALDWELL
Sundowner Motel. *Moderate*. Fairly large motel with pool. Easy access to restaurant.

Frontier Motel. *Inexpensive*. Smaller motel with heated pool, accessible to cafe, and fishing and golf facilities.

CHALLIS
Holiday Lodge. *Moderate*. Small motel with comfortable units. At north end of town. Seasonal rates.

Village Inn. *Moderate*. Somewhat larger motel a bit southeast of town, with a few kitchen units. Seasonal rates.

COEUR D'ALENE

Holiday Inn. *Expensive*. Very large, two-story motel with family-size units available. Heated pool, restaurant, cocktail lounge. Seasonal rates.

North Shore Motel. *Expensive*. Posh facilities at this lakeshore-front lodge. Large motor hotel with three heated pools including a wading pool; therapy pool; playground. Marina. Restaurant, cocktail lounge, entertainment. Tennis and golf available. City beach less than a block away. Seasonal rates.

Lamplighter Motel. *Moderate*. Small motel on pleasant grounds. Heated pool, playground. In-room coffee. Cafe near. Seasonal rates.

State Motel. *Moderate*. Small motel with several 2-room units. Seasonal rates.

Talk of the Town Motel. *Moderate*. Medium-size motel with many conveniences. In-room coffee and tea, heated pool, heated garage. Near restaurant and cocktail lounge.

Travels 9 Motel. *Inexpensive*. Medium-size motel with comfortable units, extra long beds. Cafe near.

DRIGGS

Teton West Motor Inn. *Moderate*. Modest size but a variety of accommodations, including some family-size units with kitchens. Twelve miles from Grand Targhee Ski Resort; 35 miles to Jackson Hole, Wyo.

GRANGEVILLE

Downtowner Inn. *Moderate*. Small motel with comfortable units. Restaurant, bar.

IDAHO FALLS

Driftwood-Falls View Motel. *Moderate*. A large motel overlooking river and falls and offering many conveniences. Two heated pools. Guest laundry. Restaurant near. Seasonal rates.

Haven Motel. *Moderate*. Varied accommodations. Heated pool, morning coffee, cafe nearby. Seasonal rates.

Stardust Motor Lodge. *Moderate*. Huge motel located on river bank, offering fine view of LDS Temple. Heated pool. Restaurant and cocktail lounge. Seasonal rates.

Westbank Motel. *Moderate*. Huge motel with varied accommodations, lovely view of park and falls. Heated pool. Popular coffee shop, restaurant and lounge on premises. Seasonal rates.

Idaho Falls Thrifty Lodge. *Inexpensive*. Medium-size motel near downtown. Restaurant close by.

JEROME

Holiday Motel. *Moderate*. Medium-size motel with heated pool, some family-size units.

KETCHUM-SUN VALLEY

Sun Valley Lodge Inn. *Deluxe*. Huge facility with hundreds of units and wide variety of accommodations, including many sizes of apartments and suites. Many kitchens. 3 swimming pools, indoor and outdoor. Varied recreational facilities available, including ice-skating, fishing, skiing, golf, tennis, riding. Dining room, cocktail lounge, entertainment. Seasonal rates.

Christiania Motor Lodge. *Expensive*. Fine motel in center of Ketchum, with heated pool, variety of accommodations, some with fireplaces, several with kitchens. Restaurants and other city facilities within a few blocks. Seasonal rates.

Heidelberg Inn. *Expensive*. Attractive motel built in Bavarian style; refrigerators in all units. Coin laundry. Heated pool, enclosed in winter. Seasonal rates.

Tamarack Lodge. *Expensive*. Medium-size motel with enclosed courtyard, units with private balconies or patios, some with fireplaces. Glassed-in heated swimming pool. Seasonal rates.

Tyrolean Lodge. *Expensive*. Very convenient medium-size motel with heated pool, saunas, recreation room. Free coffee and hot spiced wine. Continental breakfast. Restaurant nearby. Seasonal rates.

LAVA HOT SPRINGS

Lava Spa Motel. *Moderate*. Medium-size motel near park and recreation areas, and across from hot baths.

LEWISTON

Tapadera Motor Inn. *Expensive*. Large, multi-story motor inn with comfortably furnished rooms and some suites. Heated pool. Cocktail lounge overlooking pool. 24-hour restaurant adjacent.

El Rancho Motel. *Moderate*. Quiet, modest-size motel with heated pool. Some units with kitchens.

Royal Motor Inn. *Moderate*. Larger-size downtown motel with heated pool, a few units with kitchen facilities.

Sacajawea Lodge. *Moderate*. Large motel with variety of units, many with refrigerators; some two-room units, some suites. Heated pool. Restaurant.

MCCALL

Shore Lodge. *Expensive*. Large resort facility with both winter and summer recreational opportunities. Pool (heated), skiing, boating, tennis, golf. Playground. On lake shore. Several kitchens. Dining room, coffeeshop.

MALAD CITY

Southgate Motel. *Moderate*. Medium-size motel with well-furnished units.

MONTPELIER

Crest Motel. *Expensive*. Medium-size motel with pleasant, comfortable rooms. Restaurant near. Shuffleboard. Seasonal rates.

Park Motel. *Moderate*. Smaller motel in downtown location, near restaurant.

Sunset Motel. *Inexpensive*. Small motel near cafe.

MOSCOW

Moscow TraveLodge. *Expensive*. Large motel with heated indoor pool, therapy pool. Restaurant and cocktail lounge.

Hillcrest Motel. *Moderate*. Medium-size motel with several two-room units, a few kitchenettes. Heated pool.

Royal Motor Inn. *Moderate*. Medium-size motel with comfortable units, heated pool.

MOUNTAIN HOME

Hilander Motel. *Moderate*. Medium-size motel with pool, restaurant, and cocktail lounge.

Thunderbird. *Moderate*. Smaller motel, conveniences and comfort throughout. Pool. Restaurant short walk away.

Towne Center Motel. *Inexpensive*. All the comforts and convenience of more expensive facilities. Pool.

NAMPA

Desert Inn Motel. *Moderate*. Medium-size motel with heated pool, restaurant nearby. Seasonal rates.

POCATELLO

Holiday Inn of Pocatello. *Expensive*. Huge motel with variety of units, free transportation from airport. Heated pool. Restaurant, coffee shop, cocktail lounge, entertainment.

Imperial "400" Motel. *Expensive*. Medium-size motel. Long and queen-size beds, waterbed. Heated pool.

Weston's Lamplighter Motel. *Expensive*. Large motel across from Idaho State University. Indoor heated pool. Near restaurant.

Bidwell Motel. *Moderate*. Medium-size motel across from Idaho State University. Indoor heated pool. Restaurant nearby.

Thunderbird Motel. *Moderate*. Medium-size motel near city park. Heated pool.

REXBURG

Viking Motel. *Expensive*. Medium-size motel near city park. Heated pool.

ST. ANTHONY

Riverview Inn. *Moderate*. Snake River locale, across from city park, gives this motel special attractiveness. Restaurant near.

ST. MARIES

Pines Motel. *Moderate*. Located downtown, this medium-size motel is comfortable and convenient to city facilities, restaurants. Municipal park and pool across street.

SALMON

Stagecoach Inn. *Expensive*. Comfortable units in this medium-size motel with heated pool. Cafe near.

Suncrest Motel. *Moderate*. Smaller motel with a few kitchen units. Playground for youngsters. Near cafe.

Herndon Hotel and Motel. *Inexpensive*. Variety of units in this medium-size facility with heated pool, cafe and dining room, cocktail lounge.

SANDPOINT

Edgewater Lodge. *Expensive*. Located on Lake Pend Oreille, and close to downtown, this medium-size motel affords comfortable units and convenient access to shopping, restaurants, beach, boating facilities. On-premises conveniences include health spa, sauna, therapy pool, dining room, cocktail lounge. Seasonal rates.

Lakeside Motel. *Moderate*. A block from downtown business area, this medium-size motel has large, comfortable units, easy access to city beach and park, and to tennis courts. Some units have kitchens. Recreation room. Cafe nearby. Seasonal rates.

Travelers Motel. *Moderate*. At north edge of town. Somewhat smaller than other two motels listed. Comfortable rooms; dining room and cocktail lounge. Seasonal rates.

SODA SPRINGS

J-R Inn. *Moderate*. Medium-size motel two blocks west of town, cafe a few minutes away.

Trail Motel. *Moderate*. Medium-size motel with family-size units, family rates, cafe open 24 hours a day, coin laundry half-block away.

STANLEY

Armada Motel. *Moderate*. Comfortable, medium-size motel, between Salmon River and the Sawtooth Mountain Range, with good view of mountains. Near cafe. Seasonal rates.

Redwood Motel. *Inexpensive*. Small motel on Salmon River, in lovely picnic spot. Several units with kitchens.

SUN VALLEY (See KETCHUM-SUN VALLEY)

TWIN FALLS

Blue Lakes Inn. *Expensive*. Very large motel with heated pool, restaurant, cocktail lounge, entertainment, dancing. Seasonal rates.

Holiday Inn. *Expensive*. Another huge facility, with heated pool, health club facilities, cafe, dining room, bar, dancing, entertainment. Seasonal rates.

Weston's Lamplighter. *Expensive*. Large, two-story motel with heated pool. Free coffee. Near cafe. Seasonal rates.

Apollo Motor Inn. *Moderate*. Medium-size motel with heated pool. Golf. Cafe nearby. Seasonal rates.

Holiday Motel. *Moderate*. Small, comfortable motel with easy access to restaurant, coin laundry. Picnic facilities. Seasonal rates.

Imperial "400" Motel. *Moderate*. Medium-size motel in downtown location. Family units. Heated pool. Near restaurant.

Monterey Motor Inn. *Moderate*. Quiet, medium-size motel on spacious two acres. Family units. Heated pool, picnic and playground areas. Seasonal rates.

Twin Falls TraveLodge. *Moderate*. Medium-size motel with heated pool, coffee free, near cafe. Seasonal rates.

WALLACE

Stardust Motel. *Moderate.* Downtown motel, medium-size, convenient to restaurant and coin laundry. Family units. Ski-waxing room.

WEISER

Colonial Motel. *Moderate.* Smaller motel with comfortable units, some kitchens, and located close to restaurant and coin laundry.

 YOUTH ACCOMMODATIONS. Many youngsters traveling through Idaho on their own make full use of the numerous campgrounds in national forests and state parks. But there is a scarcity of established inexpensive lodgings. There are no hostels, and only two YWCAs which have rooms for transient women. These are in Boise (at 720 Washington) and in Lewiston (at 300 Main St.). None of the YMCAs has a hotel, but they are usually good sources of recommendations of local spots where one may secure inexpensive overnight accommodations.

 DINING OUT. Idaho exudes Western informality, and dining out in Idaho is an experience in keeping with that atmosphere. The emphasis is on good-sized portions of hearty, tasty fare, cheerful atmosphere, and quick service, rather than on exotic dishes and extensive imported wine lists. Sport or casual dress is acceptable in all but the top clubs and city restaurants. High on the popularity list for native Idahoans is a thick, juicy steak with potatoes (Idaho, of course), vegetable, and salad, topped off with a slab of homemade pie. Of course, there are exceptions. For decor, many Idaho restaurants take advantage of the state's natural beauty by providing luscious views of the immediate area to whet the appetite of their patrons and to complement the good food. There is often fine food and relaxing atmosphere in restaurants connected with hotels or motels. Restaurants are listed by categories: *Expensive* $8 to $12; *Moderate* $4 to $8; *Inexpensive* under $4.

BOISE

The Gamekeeper. *Expensive.* Located in the Owyhee Plaza Hotel, this restaurant offers top quality steaks, seafood, wines. Live entertainment nightly.

Cock o' the Walk Restaurant. *Moderate.* One of two restaurants at the Rodeway Inn. 24-hour coffee shop, dining room, cocktail lounge, entertainment nightly. Features include tempting salad bar, steak and seafood specialties.

The Royal. *Moderate.* Good downtown restaurant with turn-of-the-century decor, featuring broiled steaks and "smokqued" spareribs, plus delicious pastries. Several dining rooms. Bar.

The Sandbar. *Moderate.* This is the other restaurant at the Rodeway Inn. Special features are its poolside location, outdoor patio with lovely river view, barbecued shrimp and "open hearth" steaks. Cocktails, too.

Stagecoach Inn. *Moderate.* From informal cafeteria luncheons to gracious evening dinners, this establishment provides a warm, cozy background to enjoy steak, seafood, and great spaghetti.

COEUR D'ALENE

The Cedars. *Expensive.* Located on Lake Coeur d'Alene, this floating restaurant and cocktail lounge features Hawaiian-style broiled chicken and biergarten steak among its specialties.

North Shore Plaza Restaurants. *Moderate.* Whether you want plush rooftop dining as offered by the Cloud 9 restaurant atop the North Shore Motel, or the more casual atmosphere of the Shore Restaurant where pancakes and a salad bar are among the features, or chicken-to-go from Templin's, you'll find it at this lakeshore complex.

GRANGEVILLE
Charcoal Broiler. *Moderate*. Specialties are charcoal broiled steaks and prime ribs. Cocktail lounge with live entertainment.

IDAHO FALLS
Stardust Restaurant. *Moderate*. Informal coffee shop and full dining room, along with cocktail lounge featuring live entertainment.

Westbank Coffee Shop. *Moderate*. Located in Westbank motel, this 24-hour coffee shop, plus dining room and lounge, offers exhilarating river view as well as fine food.

KETCHUM-SUN VALLEY
Warm Springs Ranch Inn. *Moderate*. Outdoor dining with a mountain view, and specialties which include trout, sourdough scones, and barbecued ribs.

LEWISTON
Helm Restaurant. *Moderate*. Steaks and seafood specialties served against attractive marine decor.

Spencer's Restaurant. *Moderate*. The chef-owner of this restaurant specializes in preparing mouth-watering prime ribs, steaks, and shrimp.

NAMPA
Thoroughbred Restaurant. *Moderate*. Located in Karcher Mall shopping center, this restaurant and cocktail lounge is open for breakfast, lunch, and dinner.

POCATELLO
Elmer's Pancake and Steak House. *Moderate*. Twenty-one varieties of pancakes to choose from, as well as ever-popular steaks, chicken, seafoods, and salads. Across from Idaho State University.

SALMON
Salmon River. *Moderate*. Home baking here, which makes the cinnamon rolls just about irresistible. Fine steaks and seafood. Music, dancing, entertainment.

Shady Nook Inn. *Moderate*. Steaks, seafoods (a specialty is shrimp in a beer batter), and home baking make this cafe on motel premises a popular dining spot.

SANDPOINT
Garden Restaurant. *Moderate*. Outdoor dining, homebaked breads and desserts are among the attractions here, where the chef-owner takes pride in serving specialties ranging from fresh seafoods to roast duck and Oriental-style dishes. Lakeside view.

TWIN FALLS
Coy's at the Holiday Inn. *Moderate*. 24-hour coffee shop, dining room, cocktail lounge with live entertainment. Prime ribs and steaks are specialties.

Rogerson Restaurant. *Moderate*. Long-established reputation for good food, good service at this restaurant in Rogerson Hotel. Home-made soups and baked goods.

MONTANA

Riches in the Hills

by

BILL OWEN

Bill Owen is a graduate of the University of Montana where he was editor of the Montana Kaimi, *the student daily newspaper.*

Nature's unmistakable supremacy over man is evident from your first glimpse of Montana. If you come from the East, as did explorers Meriwether Lewis and William Clark, early fur trappers, prospectors, mountainmen and, later, the railroad builder, you are awed by the natural beauty and solitude found nowhere else. This is what the last frontier must have looked like when Lewis and Clark brought their boats up the Missouri River into present-day Montana. Against the background of "badland" rock formations, Hereford, Angus, and Charolais cattle and sheep graze where there were once great buffalo herds. Alternate plowed and planted, brown and gold strips of wheatland turn the countryside into a checkerboard. Along Interstates 90 and 15, which crisscross the state, only a grove of cottonwood or an occasional farmhouse breaks the regularity of the countryside, while the glint of a distant grain elevator signals the location of a town. The emptiness of Montana, however, will impress you even more. One can drive for thirty miles without seeing another soul.

Then, as you move westward, the thin blue line of the horizon is serrated by the jagged crests of the Rocky Mountains—home of early-day miners, trappers, and lumbermen, and modern-day sportsmen. Here are ghost towns and mining gulches, thick stands of fir, larch (tamarack), and pine, wilderness areas ideal for the outdoor enthusiast, national forests and parks for family camping, mountain lakes, and, most importantly, the immense snow-capped peaks of Glacier National Park.

This is "Big Sky Country." The people here are a tough, independent lot, raised to accept others for what they are, not who they are. A close-knit society, they take an almost nationalistic pride in their state. But it is a pride that visitors find justified. John Steinbeck once wrote, "For other states I have admiration, respect, recognition, but with Montana it's love, and it's difficult to analyze love when you're in it." Ernest Hemingway too seemed to feel this love and spent long periods of time here.

The beauty of this region is inextricably bound up with its history. The Blackfeet, Crow, and Sioux fought many bloody battles trying to preserve their land. In the 17th and 18th centuries the Indians believed that this great buffalo ground was the promised land. Indeed it was, until the white man began pushing westward. The Blackfeet saw the beauty of what is now Glacier National Park and made it sacred ground. Montana's battlefields and reservations attest to the tragic struggle that followed.

At the turn of the 19th century (1804) Lewis and Clark poled and hauled a fifty-five-foot keelboat and two pirogues westward to the headwaters of the Missouri near Three Forks, Montana, keeping one eye open for Indians and wild animals and the other in search of the mountains. It is well they were alert. Lewis later had an encounter with "the great white bear (Grizzly)" three miles southwest of what is now Great Falls, Montana. Favoring discretion over valor, he ended up in the Missouri River, and later logged the incident in his journal as a "curious experience." Lewis and Clark's initials can still be seen carved in Pompey's Pillar near Billings, but the extent of their feelings for Montana have been left to later writers. Bernard De Voto's *Journals of Lewis and Clark* and *Across the Wide Missouri* and Don Barry's *A Majority of Scoundrels* recapture the flavor of those days.

After this exploration, the fur trade began in earnest and changed the course of Montana history. Eastern money was used to sponsor expeditions into the Northwest, and the profit from the sale of fur went back to the East. Little remained in the territory. Men like Jim Bridger, Jedediah Smith, and "Liver Eatin' " Johnson trapped beaver, mink, and otter for the fur hats of eastern moneymen. They also mapped and charted the area for the miners and settlers who were to follow.

They were a rugged breed, these early Montanans, and tales of their courage, daring, and hardship make fascinating reading. Montana novelists A. B. Guthrie in *The Big Sky* and Frank Linderman in *Lige Mounts, Free Trappers* have successfully re-created the scene, while K. Ross Toole, the leading authority on Montana history, gives an accurate account of the early days in *Montana: An Uncommon Land*.

The era of the mountainmen and fur trapper had ended by 1840, and the westward expansion along the Oregon Trail had begun. Guthrie's *The Way West* describes the struggles of the pioneers. For twenty years travelers along the Oregon Trail, which crossed to the south of Montana, left the state relatively untouched. Occasionally a steamboat made a brief excursion up the Missouri River to replenish supplies of the few remaining fur trappers. By 1932 riverboats had reached Fort Union, and by 1859 the boats had reached Fort Benton, Montana, head of navigable waters.

Gold and Every Man's Last Chance

Then came the Civil War, with its stream of refugees headed west for a new life. The discovery of gold in the Montana hills in 1862 helped to spur that migration. Mining camps such as Bannack and Virginia City mushroomed overnight. Sweating miners and snorting burros traveled up the craggy valleys of western Montana in search of the precious ore. A hundred ghost towns commemorate this period, and Helena, the capital, still has the main street, named "Last Chance Gulch."

These early settlers were courageous people with strong beliefs and the ability to set up communities overnight. Slow, steady growth is not typical of Montana. Merchants shipped their goods by steamboat up the Missouri, or overland by wagon from Utah and Wyoming. Cattlemen from Texas brought huge herds of longhorns to graze on the lush prairie grasslands. They all came—the reverends, womenfolk, lawyers, doctors, merchants, miners, trappers, horse thieves, murderers, and scoundrels.

Each community set up its own brand of law. Vigilantes dispensed "hemp" justice in the Virginia City area to such undesirable elements as Henry Plummer and his gang, called "The Innocents." Henry and his twenty-four followers were road agents, killing a recorded 102 victims between the winters of 1862 and 1864. Henry was the sheriff of Bannack, Montana, when he assembled his unholy crew. All of The Innocents were caught and hanged between December 21, 1863, and January 11, 1864.

Meanwhile, the U.S. Army was having a tougher time in its role as judge and jury trying to keep apart the alarmed Indians and the pushy settlers. The Indians saw their buffalo and game driven off, their lands taken, and their treaties broken. Finally, in 1876, they made their views known to General George Custer on the Little Bighorn River, just south of what is now Billings. But it was too late. The white man was here, and there was no driving him out.

Other kinds of people began to enter the Montana story in the decades following the Civil War—the steamboat captain, the wagon master, the frontier storekeeper. (Up until a few years ago, all the streams that flowed from the mountains were named after famous ladies of that day.)

The frontier was being conquered. The kid in the army blanket, lying on the prairie, wondered if that rustle beyond the firelight was just a breeze. The cowboy up from Texas rode herd on the longhorns and doubted if anything could be as cold as this Montana blizzard. And the settlers continued to eke out a living on the land. A sense of this period is reflected in the work of Charley Russell, Montana cowboy, who has gained a reputation as one of the foremost western artists. Two museums, one in Great Falls and the other in Helena, display his paintings, bronzes, and wax models. And a display of early photographs taken by L. A. Huffman, a pioneer, is in Miles City.

Then came the railroad. As it pushed westward across the "Hi Line" (Highway 2), farming and ranching communities began to appear. The railroad named these new towns. According to legend a group of railroad men took turns spinning a world globe. Wherever they put their finger when it stopped became the name of the next town—Glasgow, Havre, Malta, Inverness, Harlem, Hinsdale. Some retained Indian names; others such as Cut Bank and Wolf Point were named after early residents.

The coming of the rails meant huge profits for eastern financiers and, once again, little was returned to the state. The railroads were given choice land by the government for their right of ways, and the railroads, in turn, made fantastic promises to lure people into the new "Garden of Eden." Butte became a capital of labor and political strife as verbal and physical wars waged between the mining factions. The disillustioned immigrant farmer began to discover that things don't grow so fast in the "Garden of Eden" as the promotional brochures said they would. Buffalo hunters left huge piles of rotting carcasses, the only evidence of the once-great herds of plains buffalo. The Crow, Blackfeet, and Sioux were pushed onto governmental reservations and forgotten.

The 20th-Century Montanan, A New Breed

In the 20th century new types of Montanans appear: forest rangers, environmentalists, grazing and agricultural experts; oilmen finding new mines under the prairie; dam builders harnessing the rivers at Fort Peck, Hungry Horse, and Libby; men piloting jet planes from Great Falls; small-time farmers forced, because of scientific advances and economic factors, into conglomerate farming; and politicians who have a feeling for the aesthetic beauty of Montana and are willing to say no to a rapidly advancing industrial complex. Bolstered by a knowledge of the history of Montana, each holds a new awareness of what Montana is and can become.

K. Ross Toole, in *Montana: An Uncommon Land,* says "Politically Montana did not evolve by trial and error. Politics sprang forth the hand-maiden of men battling both the wilderness and each other. And the combat was ruthless. These men, too, were literally wresting wealth from the earth. There were no theorists among them. And so almost before it had begun, Montana's political story was characterized by violent feuds, open corruption, and personal schisms among the "copper kings" which shook the very foundations of the new land and set the course of political events for many years to come." And set the course they did. Montana was controlled by industry until the mid-1950s and industry still holds a strong grip on the workings of the state. However, many people became active in state issues and opposed the vested business interests—thinking of what was best for the state rather than who would profit most by the transaction.

The fuel shortage brought tremendous pressure to bear on eastern Montana because of the 1.5 trillion tons of coal buried under the prairie of the Powder River and Williston Basins. The conflict between consumption and conservation has plagued the state for years. Only thirty percent of the land is owned by private individuals, while the other seventy percent is controlled by the Federal government or private corporations. As of this writing, almost thirty major corporations have leased land or mineral rights in eastern Montana. The individual cannot prevent a corporation from strip mining on his land: Mineral rights are retained by the state, and condemnation procedures can be quickly brought against those that try to oppose a mining process.

Another problem is an ever-increasing flow of people who once traveled through on the way to the West Coast but are now beginning to return and become residents. This influx is causing land prices to soar, and many people have come to realize that the slowness that once characterized Montana's growth was really a blessing in disguise. Caught unprepared for the vast amount of subdividing, especially in the recreational areas around Flathead Lake, the state has had to scramble to stay on top of the situation. This is one of the most crucial problems Montana must face, for on it hinges the preservation of the state's unspoiled beauty and of the citizens' well-being.

Still a Land of Wide-Open Spaces

In this largest of the Rocky Mountain states—a little over 575 miles east to west and 275 miles north to south—there are fewer than 700,000 people spread over 147,138 square miles. The largest cities are Billings and Great Falls—each with approximately 60,000 people. But although the Montanan may seem isolated, he enjoys his wide-open spaces. He knows about economic development and recognizes that Montana cannot remain forever as it is today. He may have come to enjoy the elbow room or he may be descended from the stock that came here over one hundred years ago. Whether his ancestors found gold or not, local people tended to figure that too many folks could mess things up. A lot of Montanans, despite the exhortations of their Chamber of Commerce, still think the same way.

But the friendliness of Montanans holds true. In the mining camp they tended to judge a man by what he was, not what he was worth. Money meant very little. It couldn't improve your aim, or tell you where to sink your pick. Personal characteristics were more important than show, and even today affluent Montanans of the old school step softly.

Don't be deceived by Montana's wide-open spaces or the apparent simplicity of the people. Distance means very little out here—a hundred miles for a high school ball game or an evening of bridge is nothing. And a few of these homespun types in Stetsons and jeans are equally at home in Tiffany's—when they choose to be.

We are proud of our state and learning to be protective of its wealth and beauty. We can promise one thing: if you come to enjoy Montana, Montana and its citizens will enjoy you.

EXPLORING MONTANA

A good starting point for visitors coming from the east is Wibaux on I-94. Throughout the state, highway signs tell you about historical happenings in the area. For example, four miles east of Wibaux a sign indicates that less than a century ago this was buffalo and Indian country. From here to Billings you drive your car through the area where the U.S. Cavalry fought the Cheyenne and Sioux tribes in the late 1870s. The trail was opened by the white buffalo hunters, and after 1866 was used by the Army and cattlemen driving their herds up from Texas to new grazing lands. From Glendive on, the route parallels the Yellowstone River and the Northern Pacific Railroad that brought sod-busters and gave life after 1880 to most of the towns you will pass.

T.R. Got Vigor

Wibaux (pop. 644) was once the preserve of a dreamer. Pierre Wibaux left a textile fortune in Napoleon II's France to become one of the biggest cattle barons of the late 1880s. His statue is just west of town. To the south Teddy Roosevelt's cattle used to drift over from their North Dakota base. T. R. accumulated some of his well-known vigor in these badlands. Today, however, a stray drilling rig is as common as a drifting cow, for this is in the Montana portion of the famous Williston Basin, and the oil boom after World War II hasn't abated. The old fortunes were made in cattle; now new men dreaming of riches are jeeping around, hunting for leases and inspecting geological strata.

Glendive, where the highway crosses the Yellowstone River, was named by one of Montana's first "dudes." Sir George Gore was guided into the area by Jim Bridger in 1855. He had with him several six-mile wagons, three-yoke ox wagons, twenty-one French carts painted red, forty employees, 112 horses, seventy rifles, fifteen shotguns, a linen tent, bottles of French wine, and a heavy volume of Shakespeare. After killing 105 bear and two thousand buffalo, elk, and deer, Sir George withdrew to St. Louis. He named Glendive Creek after a stream in his native Ireland, and left Montana a tradition of trigger-happy hunters that eventually led to an active Fish and Game Commission. This area is still fine hunting ground for antelope and deer, but the bear and most of the fine dude ranches are in higher country now.

Glendive is a division point on the Northern Pacific Railroad, a county-seat shipping center for grain, beef, and oil. It has a fine museum of prehistoric reptile fossils. Makoshika State Park, three miles south of town, will give you a good idea of what the badland rock formations of the region look like. Try to see these twisted remains of geologic change near sunrise or sunset, when the Sioux thought they looked like Makoshika—"hell cooled over."

Yellowstone Country

The Yellowstone River, called the *Roche Jaune* by the Indians because of its occasional yellowish boulders, has been the dominant highway of the region for years. Captain William Clark followed it on his way back from the Pacific, and generations of Montanans have looked to it for protection, direction, and a sometimes reliable drink for man, cow, or crop.

From Glendive down I-94 to Miles City, you pass a number of streams flowing northward into the Yellowstone. There's the town of Fallon near O'Fallon Creek, named for Clark's nephew, and Terry, named for General Alfred H. Terry who was Custer's commander. Then comes the Powder River, so named because it often is dried up and dusty. The 91st Division in World War I immortalized the cry, "Powder River, Let 'er Buck." Along the Powder and through all this country were the really big cattle spreads like the LO, Niobarra, Rafter Circle, Diamond Bar, and XIT. Their successors are still there, and water is still their lifeblood.

The Tongue River forks into the Yellowstone at Miles City. Clark camped on its banks in 1806, and Fort Keogh was established here in 1877, the year after Custer's fall. Keogh was a captain who fell with him. From Fort Keogh, General Nelson Miles ranged out after the Custer debacle eventually to defeat the Indians.

In Miles' honor, the civilian shacks near the fort took his name, and the settlement grew into a great cowtown. After the Indian wars, it became a northern terminus for longhorn drives up from Texas. Beneath these cotton-woods that Western tradition is still alive. At the stock yard or on Main Street, Stetsons and sharp-toed boots are part of a Montanan's everyday wardrobe.

Miles City was the home of frontier photographer L. A. Huffman. Coffrin Photo Studio, Red Rocks Inn, and Range Riders Museum (west of the city) have good collections of his work as well as range and Indian memorabilia. The U.S. Livestock Experiment Station is at the western city limits, and nearby is a seismic station where the U.S. monitors nuclear blasts around the world.

Fort Peck and the Missouri

Miles City and Glendive offer you the most convenient takeoff for a roundtrip to the north to see Fort Peck Dam and the Missouri River where Lewis and Clark first entered Montana.

Fort Union, one of the three or four important forts of the trapper's West, stood where the Missouri and Yellowstone Rivers join northeast of Sidney, a center of irrigated sugarbeet farming and an extensive coal field. Fort Union is being restored as a national historic landmark.

On US 2, "The Hi-Line" westward to Fort Peck Dam, you pass Culbertson, named for an old fur trapper. Its economy now is based on wheat, some cattle—although beef ranching is not extensive north of the Missouri—and a new plant to crush oil from safflower seeds. If you have time, drive north of Culbertson to the area of Froid and Medicine Lake where you will see the best examples of the extensive, highly mechanized wheat farming which characterizes this section of Montana. Note the strips of alternately plowed and planted land, widely adopted after the dust storms of the Depression 30's. Alternate planting conserves moisture in the non-planted strip, while the planted strip forms a break to slow wind erosion. The zebra-striped land pattern extends across northern Montana to the mountains.

On US 2, west of Culbertson, you will pass Poplar, headquarters of the Fort Peck Indian Reservation. The agency, as Indian reservation headquarters is called, was set up here in 1876, and it was here that Sitting Bull finally surrendered. The Indians are remnants of the Assiniboine tribes who lived in the vicinity when Lewis and Clark first arrived. The reservation is one of seven in the state.

Past Poplar you come to Wolf Point, a former fueling station for steamboats. Now a county seat, Wolf Point gets its name from its early reputation as a hunting spot for wolves. Its Wild Horse Stampede in July is one of the toughest rodeos in the nation.

Fort Peck Reservoir, seventeen miles southeast of Glasgow, off the main highway, is formed by the waters of the Missouri River retained by the world's second largest earthfill dam, 250 feet above the river surface. The lake is 180 miles long, with 1,600 miles of shoreline, most of which is surrounded by a wildlife refuge. Rock Creek State Park on the eastern shore and Hell Creek State Park on the south offer good camping and picnicking facilities, but make local inquiry about road conditions. Drive south to join I-94 either at Glendive or Miles City.

Custer Stood Here

Continuing westward from Miles City, detour to Custer Battlefield National Monument. From I-94, turn south about forty-seven miles west of Forsyth onto Route 47. This highway turns off near the mouth of Big Horn River where Manuel Lisa founded the first Montana fur post in 1807. The battlefield is thirteen miles southeast of Hardin. As an alternative, you may want to continue on I-94 to see the initials Clark left on Pompeys Pillar, a 200-foot towering landmark on the Yellowstone from which the Indians used to send smoke signals. A gravel road straight south from the Pillar will also take you to Hardin and the battlefield area.

Custer's Last Stand is the Montana incident most familiar to Americans. The government's museum tells the story of the ill-fated Yellow Hair, as the general was called. The battlefield is two miles southeast of Crow Agency, headquarters for the Crow Indian reservation. The Crow reservation is open to the public, in August, the battle is reenacted, and visitors can take in a rodeo, dances and tours.

On June 25, 1876, George Armstrong Custer, flamboyant Civil War hero and—his detractors claim—a headstrong glory-seeker, led 225 cavalry troopers into an attack on some four thousand Sioux and Cheyenne warriors, one of the largest Indian armies ever assembled. His defeat affected the whole area. The Indians won that battle but lost the war when a shocked nation demanded that the Army, based mostly at Miles City, end the Indian threat once and for all. In 1915, Chief Yellow Hand of the Cheyenne, a participant in the Little Big Horn Battle, described seeing Custer just before he fell. Custer's eyes, he said, showed insanity and hatred, but no fear. The guns, maps, and dioramas of the museum, and the many white headstones on the skyline marking the areas of battle, will help you understand what happened on that fateful day.

From Hardin you may wish to take a side trip southwest on Route 313 forty-five miles to Yellowtail Dam. The dam underscores the importance of reclamation in this barren area. For many years, reclamation of land by storage of water has been a major theme in Western politics. The dam provides irrigation for 43,500 acres, while the power plant generates nine hundred million kilowatts.

Near the dam is old Fort C. F. Smith. Ten years before Custer put the area on the map, this was one of a string of important posts that were built to protect the Bozeman Trail which led up from the Oregon Trail near Casper, Wyoming. The Bozeman Trail later was avoided because of the continued hostility of the Indians.

The Range Rider Rides Again

Billings, northwest of the Custer Battlefield, is the largest city of Montana. Named for the president of the railroad that gave it life, Billings has sugarbeet and oil refineries, livestock yards, and two small colleges. They say of its Northern Hotel that if you wait long enough in the lobby, you'll meet everyone in the state you know.

Among the Billings' sights is the statue of the Range Rider of the Yellowstone, William S. Hart, cowboy hero of silent movies. This is along Black Otter Trail, which follows the rim above the city to the north. Five miles from Billings there's a Pictograph Cave with the most important scratchings of prehistoric man on the Great Plains.

Billings is a modern shopping mecca and the banking hub for the eastern region. Its Midland Empire Fair in August is one of the state's largest. See the Brown Barn for Western art.

From Billings turn south on US 212 for a ride along the Beartooth Scenic Highway, which cuts through the western portion of Custer National Forest.

If you have the time, call at U.S. Forest Service headquarters in Billings to get information on the many hiking, horseback, and camping possibilities. You will begin to climb sharply after passing the town of Red Lodge. You get to Beartooth Pass (elev. 10,940 ft.) passing alpine meadows and mountain lakes and viewing, off to the west, Granite Peak, Montana's highest at 12,799 feet. The road dips into Wyoming and into Yellowstone Park. Here is an excellent opportunity to include this important national park in your tour of Montana. The mountains you spiral around on this trip are the Absaroka, from the Indian word other tribes gave to the Crows: Up-sa-rah-qu, or sharp people. Southeast of Red Lodge, you will pass one of Montana's top winter sports areas. And in Red Lodge there's an outstanding August International Festival of Nations.

Return to Montana from Yellowstone

You may return to our route swiftly from the Gardiner entrance toward Livingston on I-90. (Or cross the park to the West Yellowstone entrance where, incidentally, an airport receives scheduled service during the summer months.) If you take the Gardiner route (US 89), the area around Emigrant was the site of Yellowstone City, where gold was discovered in 1862. You're getting into ghost town country; the State Advertising Department has a fine list.

Back to Livingston, named for a Northern Pacific official. This is a great fishing center. Drive west over Bozeman Pass into the Gallatin Valley, called Valley of the Flowers by the Indians. They weren't far wrong; this is one of the richest agricultural valleys in Montana. Bozeman Pass was the divide between mountain and plains Montana in the old days. East of the pass was Indian country, where white settlement proceeded with great risk; west was mountain country, where mining boomed and brought in trade and towns.

Bozeman, settled in 1864, was named for a frontiersman who founded that short-lived trail north from Wyoming. Today it's the home of Montana State University (with an enrollment of nine thousand students), headquarters for the 1,700,000-acre Gallatin National Forest, and the center of purebred livestock, small grain, and dairying. The college fieldhouse and the museum on the southwest corner of the campus are worth a side trip. If you are interested in grain or cattle farming, the Montana Agricultural Experiment Station is one of the best in the country.

Bozeman is also headquarters for the Montana Wilderness Association which every summer conducts numerous walking and riding trips for visitors into the remote wilds of the state.

Follow I-90 west from Bozeman to Three Forks. Just north of the town you'll find the Missouri River Headquartesr State Monument, where three rivers meet: the Jefferson, the Madison, and the Gallatin. The rivers were named by Lewis and Clark for their bosses—the President and the Secretaries of State and Treasury—when they reached the forks in late July 1805 after their long struggle upriver. This juncture is the beginning of the Missouri River proper, which then flows east 2,500 miles to the Mississippi at St. Louis.

The Three Forks of the Missouri was a bloody battleground in the early days. Blackfoot Indians from the north, Crows from the east, Snakes from the south, and the Nez Percé and Flatheads from over the divide to the west, all converged on the forks at various times to fight over game or to discourage trappers. Manuel Lisa, aided by John Colter of the Lewis and Clark party, tried to build a post as early as 1810, but this was only one of many attempts that failed because of the Blackfeet.

One of Montana's leading natural attractions, Lewis and Clark Caverns, is thirteen miles further west on your interstate route. This is a safe, underground limestone cavern where guided tours operate daily from May 1 to September 30. The 90-minute walk through this fantasia of stalactites and stalagmites fascinates children and is a refreshing change from Indians, cows, and history.

Turn south from the caverns on US 287. You are following the Madison River trout stream. The most important turnoff is at Ennis west to Virginia City. But if you haven't already visited it on your trip up from Yellowstone, first go on south to the site of the 1959 earthquake on the shores of Hebegen Lake. The U.S. Forest Service has excellent displays and campgrounds here. An 80-million-ton rockslide blocked the river, created Quake Lake, and killed at least twenty-eight people in one of the West's most dramatic natural disasters.

Williamsburg of the West

Now back to Virginia City, a boom town that has been carefully restored. Here you can recapture the feel of those post-Civil War gold rushes which first drew large numbers of people upriver and overland to the mountainous West.

Six prospectors fleeing from the Indians tried to change their luck in Alder Gulch on the Stinkingwater, now more decorously called the Ruby River. It was May 26, 1863. They discovered gold. Within a month, ten thousand people were sweating and snorting in the area. Within a year thirty-five thousand people were working within a ten-mile radius. In the months and years to come, $300 million in gold dust came out of this provincial gravel. Mining operations didn't end until 1937.

Virginia City was the territorial capital for ten years. Here the vigilantes took the law into their own hands after outlaws had murdered two hundred residents. More important, this was the first home for many of the families, businesses, churches, and lodges that later spread over Montana.

At Virginia City, the visitor will see many authentic details of the West's mining frontier, thanks to a dedicated couple, State Senator and Mrs. Charles Bovey. They have spent a fortune in restoring both Virginia City and neighboring Nevada City. A narrow-gauge railroad operates in the summer months to ferry tourists between the two cities and provide the chance to see some beautiful, untamed country. You can enjoy wooden sidewalks, real saloons, good museums, an old assay office, a Wells Fargo office, and Boot Hill Cemetery—where six of the vigilantes' guests rest. Nearby is the original Robbers' Roost, where the gang of Henry Plummer, the sheriff who turned outlaw, lay in wait.

From Virginia City, rejoin the interstate route for a visit to Butte. Follow Route 287 west from Virginia City to Twin Bridges, drive south on Route 41 to Dillon. This is the site of Western Montana College and headquarters for the Beaverhead National Forest, one of the great hunting and fishing areas of the West. Join I-15 at Dillon and proceed north to Butte.

Bannack, a ghost town twenty miles to the west of Dillon on Route 278 is now a Registered Historic Landmark. The very first capital, it was also the first camp of any note: gold was struck here in 1862. Lewis and Clark pushed southward into this area from the Three Forks, and it was here that they decided to turn west to cross the Continental Divide. This is less developed than Virginia City, but quaint and quiet.

Butte—the Richest Hill on Earth

Butte was settled in 1864 and is the historic homebase for the mighty Anaconda or "The Company," as it is known to Montanans. It was named Anaconda after the snake capable of great, but constricting, embrace.

First gold and then silver were discovered around Butte, but the big fortunes were made after 1870 in copper. The "war of the copper kings" dominated Montana politics for the next three decades.

From beneath these five square miles of bleak hilltop have come more than 17 billion pounds of copper. More than ten thousand miles of mine shafts run below Butte. The underground operations closed some years ago. The huge Berkeley Pit gives an excellent view of modern open-pit mining methods, where scrapers and earth movers replace the sweating worker, the burro, and the rickety hoist.

Today Butte is an industrial and distributing center, and an international Port of Entry. While you are there, be sure and visit the Old Town and the World Museum of Mining. The early-day displays on the 33-acre mine site will take you back to the frontier days of Montana.

Three big names in Montana history were the copper kings: Marcus Daly, William Andrews Clark, and F. Augustus Heinze. Clark eventually made the U.S. Senate in 1900 after a corrupt election that put Montana on the national political map. Daly, a founder of ACM, lost to Clark in his battle to have nearby Anaconda named capital over Helena, but nonetheless his company was the power in Montana for a half century. Heinze gave the other giants fits with his court cases. He eventually pulled out with $10.5 million, which he later lost in the Wall Street panic of 1907.

Anaconda has produced the biggest share of the state's wealth in the form of copper, zinc, silver, and gold, as well as playing a dominant role in its lumber industry. Today it has diversified with an aluminum plant at Columbia Falls near the west entrance to Glacier Park.

Anaconda, practically a western suburb of Butte, is the site of the Anaconda Smelter, with its 585-foot smokestack, highest in the world. The smelter tour offered in the summer is an excellent companion tour to underground mine and open-pit excursions in Butte. Marcus Daly was determined that Anaconda should be the queen city. One of the monuments to that dream was the Hotel Marcus Daly, opened in 1889, the year Montana became a state. The splendid Victorian bar is a mahogany and gilt showpiece, and the floor features an inlaid mosaic head of Tammany, Daly's favorite racehorse. No patron was allowed to step on that head. The hotel closed in 1976.

Ghost Towns Galore

From Anaconda, drive north on I-90 through Warm Springs to Deer Lodge, one of the earliest mining camps but now the home of the state prison. Here is W. A. Clark's old mansion, at 311 Clark Street. Follow the interstate to Garrison, where you turn eastward on US 12 to climb over McDonald Pass to Helena, the state capital. (You slipped over to the west side of the Continental Divide north of Dillon; now you go back over it.) Just over the Divide you might enjoy Frontier Town, Old West museum, restaurant, stockade, jail, store, chapel, and bar.

If you are enthusiastic about ghost towns, swing west from Anaconda on Route 10A to Philipsburg, a famous silver-mining center, East of Philipsburg is Granite, an old silver town. Between 1865 and 1913 it produced $32 million. Drive north from Philipsburg between the Flint Creek Range and the John Long Mountains to Drummond. You'll be back on the interstate and can turn east to pick up the route at Garrison, passing Gold Creek, scene of the very first Montana gold strike in 1850. It was developed by the Stuart brothers. Granville Stuart became a leader in mining and cattle and was later appointed Minister to Uruguay. If you should choose the direct route north from Butte to Helena, don't miss the Elkhorn ghost town, just south of Boulder on I-15 and one of the best preserved.

Helena got its start when some discouraged miners took their "last chance" in 1864 on what is now the main street of the city—and made a strike. The area subsequently produced $20 million in gold. It is said that by 1888 Helena had fifty millionaires and was the richest city per capita in the country.

The American Smelting and Refining Co. has a plant in East Helena, and the city is a prosperous distributing center for the surrounding Prickly Pear Valley. But the main business of Helena is government, and the trappings of politics are the real attraction. The state capitol is faced with Montana granite, topped by a copper dome, and adorned by Western artists, most notably the Russell masterpiece, *Lewis and Clark Meeting the Flatheads,* on the third floor. In front of the capitol is a statue of Thomas Francis Meagher, an Irish revolutionary of note who somehow harangued his way West to become an "acting" territorial governor of Montana. Amid great mystery, he eventually fell into the Missouri River at Fort Benton and presumably drowned. Some say the vigilantes pushed him.

Some Montanans from time to time bemoan what they consider a cultural lag. But the State Historical Museum, east of the capitol, takes second place to none. It has good dioramas covering the complete story of Montana, an excellent collection of Charlie Russell's art, and a comprehensive gun collection. If you get Montana fever, ask to see a copy of the *Montana Magazine of Western History.* The museum offers an excellent research library, too. The Cathedral of St. Helena, replica of the Votive Church of Vienna, is worth seeing.

Politics remains important in Montana. When the legislature is in session, the town fills up with performers and spectators. There are company lobbyists, cattlemen from the plains, grain growers—both the conservatives and the more liberal Farmers Union agents—timbermen, the Butte and Great Falls labor leaders, conservationists and recreationists from the mountainous West, educators and students, plus the ever-watchful eyes of the railroads, oil, mining and trucking interests. The political fates of the state in the past have often matched a conservative, Republican plains group against the more urban, labor-conscious mountain men who are often Democratic. Political generalizations are difficult, but for the past few decades the Democrats have had the two U.S. Senators and the one western Congressman, while the Republicans have held the governorship and the one plains congressional seat to the east. But victory margins often are narrow and tempers can wear thin in a state which takes its politics and individualism seriously. (The present governor is a Democrat.)

Helena has been the stomping ground for several great Senators, including Thomas Walsh, the prosecutor of the Teapot Dome scandals; Burton K. Wheeler, FDR's isolationist opponent of the '30s; Mike Mansfield, former long-time Senate majority leader who came up from the Butte mines; and Jannette Rankin, the country's first congresswoman. If that seems too political, reflect that Gary Cooper and Myrna Loy were born in the area.

Gates of the Mountains

Sixteen miles north of Helena, on I-15, you come to the Gates of the Mountains, a 2,000-ft. gorge in the Missouri River named by Lewis. Nervous about what he would find in the Rockies (remember he had been trudging upriver and hadn't been in the mountains, yet), he thought the gorge "the most spectacular" he had seen, but of "dark and gloomy aspect." A two-hour summer river cruise lets you check his opinion in almost the same setting.

You should also explore Canyon Ferry Dam and Reservoir. The best route is to go southeast out of Helena on Route 287, then turn northeast on Route 284. This road will take you across the 210-foot-high dam, which has created a 24-mile-long lake. As you drive on its east shore, the lake will be on your right hand. To the left you will come to the turnoff for Diamond City which will take you to yet another ghost town and, if you persist, to the old site of Fort Logan, where one building still stands. Return to Helena by way of White Sulphur Springs and Townsend.

North from Helena, keeping to I-15, we approach Montana's second largest city, Great Falls, with 58,500 residents (Billings, pop. 68,800, is actually the largest). Great Falls was named for the falls in the Missouri to the northeast. It is the site of Malmstrom Air Force Base, one of the important links in the SAC and Air Defense Command system protecting North America. Minutemen missiles abound hereabouts. Hydroelectric plants near the falls, an Anaconda Company smelter and plant which produces copper and aluminum rods and wire, and a fertile winter wheat and livestock area have made Great Falls a boom bown.

Great Falls was home base for cowboy artist Charley Russell. A fine gallery of Russell's work may be seen in his old studio at 1201 4th Avenue North. From this town his fame spread even to Hollywood, but he preferred the Mint Saloon and the leathery cronies of the open-range days. The Rainbow Hotel was a Great Falls landmark similar to other Montana hotels such as the Northern in Billings, the Placer in Helena, or Butte's Finlen. See the great falls themselves and the nearby springs which flow at a rate of 388 million gallons daily.

If you want to make a side trip to Russell's country, take US 87 southeast of Great Falls to US 191, then drive northward across the Missouri River to join US 2 at Malta. From Great Falls, you will be traveling through the heart of the Judith Basin cattle country, the Russell National Wildlife Refuge, and, in the Little Rocky Mountains, the outlaw camps of Landusky and Zortman. Until recently this area was not accessible by good roads. When you get to US 2, the Chief Joseph Battleground, south of Chinook, recalls the last of the Montana Indian Wars. The Nez Percé chief, Joseph, led the U.S. Army on a chase across the breadth of Montana but was finally caught by General Miles coming up from the Yellowstone. Chief Joseph lost the last round here in the Bear's Paw Mountains in 1877, and said, "Where the sun now stands I will fight no more forever."

Return by US 87 from Havre to Fort Benton or proceed northeast from Great Falls if you skipped the side trip.

Fort Benton, pop. 1,863, now a sometimes bypassed county seat, was once the economic capital of the Rocky Mountain West. For two decades, it was the center of steamboat travel on the Missouri River—a direct link with St. Louis and the "States."

After Lewis and Clark passed by, Fort Benton slumbered until an American Fur Company post was established in 1846 by Alexander Culbertson, a great trader. The steamboat on the Missouri had reached this point by 1860. So when the mining camps sprouted in the mountains to the southeast, Fort Benton merchants were ready with goods to be wagon-hauled to the camps. Hundreds of boats puffed up the Missouri River to serve the gold camps and to link up with the Mullan Road wagon trail over the Rockies to Walla Walla, Washington. In its peak year (1879) Fort Benton docked forty-nine steamboats.

Today Fort Benton has an excellent museum, and you can visualize from its old levees the days when it was a bustling port. Not until the Northern Pacific Railroad pushed through to reach the Pacific Coast in 1883 did Benton and the steamboat era begin to decline. Guthrie's *Three Thousand Hills* or Paul Sharp's *Whoop-Up Trail* are good reading on Benton.

From Fort Benton, the Missouri moves eastward 180 miles through the untouched Missouri River Breaks to the beginning of Fort Peck Reservoir. Some years ago, a national battle took place over whether this relatively wild waterway was to be preserved as a refuge or dammed for waterpower and irrigation. One part of the land still remains wild and scenic. For the canoeing enthusiast, this stretch of river provides a rare opportunity.

Blackfeet Country

From Fort Benton, turn north and west for the Blackfeet Indian country around Browning, which also is the gateway to Glacier National Park, the Alps of America. You take Route 223 north from Fort Benton to Chester, and then go west on US 2. Near Shelby—where Dempsey fought Gibbons in 1923—and Cut Bank, you pass through one of Montana's prolific oil areas. More than 1,100 oil wells and one hundred gas wells dot the dryland wheat farms of the area.

Browning is the headquarters for the 2,400-acre Blackfeet Indian Reservation. In the summer months, the town is alive with the colorful tribesmen, and each first week of July they celebrate North American Indian Days with traditional dances. It's the Montana event the U.S. State Department feels is of most interest to foreign tourists.

The Museum of the Plains Indians, a half mile west of town, was opened in 1941 and has been continuously improved. It is now under the wing of the Smithsonian Institution in Washington. The carvings and costumes, murals and dioramas are first class; so, too, is the crafts shop. Operated by the Bureau of Indian Affairs, the museum is only open from June 1 to September 15.

Located 129 miles north of Great Falls, Glacier National Park remains Montana's great natural "spectacular." Since 1910, the more than 1,500 square miles of jagged mountain scenery have drawn travelers, lured by its many glaciers and alpine lakes, well-developed campgrounds, and motel and hotel accommodations of all types. A quick drive through the park can touch only the highlights, but there are endless opportunities for hiking, camping, and fishing to meet each vacationer's taste and time. The park season runs from June 15 through September 10, when most hotels and cabin camps are open. The main roads, however, may stay clear until mid-October, depending on the weather.

Most of Glacier Park is accessible only by its seven hundred miles of foot and horse trails; on-the-spot inquiry and attention to park regulations is essen ial—this is rugged country. When the park itself is closed, US 2 may be used to the south from Browning to West Glacier. Local inquiry is advisable if the weather looks bad. And, don't feed the bears.

Starting from Browning, you'll visit the Glacier Park Lodge at East Glacier on US 2. This is typical of the huge log hotels developed by the Great Northern Railway in the early days of the century to handle what was primarily a time-to-burn railroad trade. This hotel, like its sister, Many Glacier Hotel, offers a variety of riding, hiking, golf, and fishing. Be sure to inquire about guided tours and lectures offered by the National Park Service naturalists. They will increase your enjoyment of this alpine beauty spot.

From St. Mary you can also swing north to Waterton-Glacier International Peace Park in Canada, an extension of the same kind of mountain terrain as you find on the American side, but perhaps less crowded in the peak months. Also note on the north route the access road to Many Glacier Hotel on Swiftcurrent Lake; you leave the highway at Babb and drive a few miles west to what many consider the park's most varied center of activity. All of the recreation activities are developed here, with trails to Grinnell Lake and Glacier. George Bird Grinnell, the naturalist, was instrumental in the establishment of the park.

On a quick tour, you'll want to see Two Medicine Valley and Lake. Turn west about four miles north of East Glacier on State 49. A seven-mile road leads to a lake (launch trips during the season) ringed by high peaks. There is a self-guiding, well-marked nature trail at Trick Falls, a safe, quick introduction to Glacier.

There's a good campground at St. Mary Lake and another at Rising Sun on the north shore highway. Four miles west of the latter at Sun Point there are an information station and self-guiding trails. The frontal range of the Rockies at this point is known as Lewis Range.

The most spectacular drive through Glacier is over the Continental Divide via the Going-to-the-Sun road. From Browning and East Glacier, drive north on State 49 and 287 to St. Mary, and then turn westward for the 50-mile drive over Logan Pass to the west end of the park. If you are hauling a camper, and your rig is over thirty feet in length—including your car—you had better make arrangments to leave your camper and pick it up later. In July and August park rules forbid vehicles over thirty feet long on this highway. After August 3, overall length limit is 35 feet. You will realize why when you begin your climb.

From St. Mary Lake in the east to Lake McDonald in the west the highway crosses 6,664-ft. Logan Pass. It is the great spot to stop and view the park: from here you have 100-mile vistas. There is a large Information Center atop Logan Pass. Ask about the trail to Granite Park Chalet.

After Logan Pass, descend west along the Garden Wall, one of America's greatest mountain highways. Below, at Avalanche Campground, there is an easy two-mile trail to Avalanche Basin, a natural amphitheater with walls two thousand feet high and waterfalls for a backdrop. The red cedars and the rushing streams give you a sense of what the park must be like deep in the interior, if you haven't the time for longer hikes or rides.

Lake McDonald is ten miles long and a mile wide. Lake McDonald Lodge near the head of the lake on our highway is the center. There are public campgrounds here and at the foot of the lake at Apgar, as well as several classes of accommodations at both spots. The hike to Sperry Glacier and Chalet is popular.

Flathead Country

Coming over Logan Pass you cross to the west side of the Continental Divide again. Both the North and South forks of the Flathead River flow southwestward through Flathead Lake to join eventually the Columbia River and drain into the Pacific Ocean.

At this point in your exploration, you can view one of the biggest of the hydroelectric power projects which have played an important role in the recent history of the area. Eight miles west of the exit from Glacier Park on US 2 is the turnoff for Hungry Horse Dam. Leave the main highway at Martin City for a quick glance at this huge concrete dam which backs up the South Fork of the Flathead River. The dam is 564 feet high, the reservoir is thirty-four miles long. The road around the reservoir passes through beautiful wilderness. You may meet some logging trucks, for this is big timber country; most of it is cut in the Flathead National Forest administered in nearby Kalispell.

Back on US 2, you can reach Kalispell via Columbia Falls, where the Anaconda Company has built a huge aluminum plant powered by electicity from Hungry Horse Dam. Visitors may tour the plant. Kalispell is a lumber and vacation center. Each year 1,500,000 Christmas trees are shipped from here. The region is also noted for potatoes, sweet cherries, and lovely Flathead Lake, on US 93 to the south. Many people from the eastern plains have come here to retire where nature is bountiful and there's enough water. You can't help notice lumbering in the area. The big logging trucks bring loads of Ponderosa pine, Douglas fir, larch (tamarack), and spruce from the hills to the mills. It's all power-tool work now—chain saws, big tractors, and steel helmets. Plywood mills and paper plants are moving in.

If you want to see more beautiful scenery and get a feel for the lumber industry, take a circular side trip from Kalispell west along US 2 to Libby, where the St. Regis Paper Company has one of the largest lumber mills in the state. Tours of the operations are possible. Then swing north along 37 to Eureka, but make local inquiry first because this Kootenai River Valley will shortly be flooded by the new Libby Dam, another major part of the Columbia Basin development which will back water into Canada.

From Eureka drive back south to Kalispell along Route 93, passing Whitefish, site of the well-known vacation lake. On the mountainside above is Big Mountain Ski Area, one of the best developed in the West. It's served by the Great Northern Railway and appreciated by skiing sophisticates because of its relative lack of crowds and its reliable snow. If you come in early spring be sure and catch the Whitefish Winter Carnival. It will provide entertainment for the whole family.

Flathead Lake and the Mission Valley

South from Kalispell, go around Flathead Lake by either the west shore, US 93, or east shore, Route 35; both give excellent views of this largest freshwater lake west of the Mississippi, twenty-eight miles long and from five to fifteen miles wide. On the east shore the lake nestles up to the white-topped Mission Range. On the west it blends into the foothills of the Salish Mountains. On the east shore you'll find at Yellow Bay a state park and the Montana State University Biological Station (its museums open in summer). On the west shore, there are two good state parks and numerous commercial accommodations. The east shore is also the home of the annual Cherry Blossom Festival in May. Cherries from this area reach the entire United States.

South from the lake by US 93 brings you into the heart of the Mission Valley, site of the Flathead Indian Reservation. There's an especially interesting stop at St. Ignatius, where one of the early Jesuit missions to the Indians is still preserved. This was a headquarters for Father DeSmet, the "blackrobe" who influenced the early West in both Wyoming and Montana.

Southwest of St. Ignatius near Ravalli, you may see from the highway some of the herd kept at the National Bison Range. Drive from Ravalli along Route 200 to Dixon and then turn off on the gravel road to range headquarters at Moiese. During the summer months there are daily self-guided auto tours to search out the herd of between three and five hundred bison, with their accompanying bands of deer, antelope, elk, and bighorn sheep. The range covers 19,000 acres and is one of the oldest wildlife preserves in the country.

In the year 1800, an estimated sixty million buffalo roamed the prairies of the continent in both the United States and Canada. A century later that number had been cut to fewer than three hundred. Today, because of conservation there are about 20,000 in both countries. May and June are good wildflower months on the range; in October there is a horseback roundup of the bison herd which draws many visitors.

US 93 returns us to the I-90 system near Missoula, the prosperous home of the University of Montana (beneath the "M" on the mountain). The University has 8,000-plus students and leading forestry, law, and journalism schools. This is headquarters for Region I of the U.S. Forest Service, as well as a lumber and distributing center. From Hell Gate Canyon on the Clark's Fork River to the east of town, the Blackfeet raided the more peaceful Flatheads, hence the canyon's name. Missoula is the home base for novelists A. B. Guthrie, Jr., and Dorothy Johnson, author of *The Hanging Tree* and *A Man Called Horse,* and the Montana States of the Nation Series.

Seven miles west of Missoula, on the main highway, is the center of forest fire-fighting activities for the northern Rocky Mountains. Here parachutists are trained to "smoke jump" into the bad fires. Research on how to prevent and fight these disasters is carried on. During the summer season the center is open daily for tours.

At Bonner, seven miles east of Missoula on I-90, U.S. Plywood maintains a major lumber mill (tours), and to the south on US 93 the visitor can make a one-day swing of the Bitterroot Valley. Just east of Stevensville is the St. Mary's Mission at Fort Owens State Monument, oldest mission in the Northwest. This is well preserved and a lovely reminder of the early-day missionary efforts of the Jesuits among the mountain tribes. Here was the first permanent white settlement in the state, in 1841.

Indian-history fans may wish to push out of the valley southeastward along US 93 and Route 43 to the Big Hole Battlefield National Monument. Chief Joseph and his Nez Percé fought one of their great delaying actions at this poin .

Also stemming off the Bitterroot Valley is highway US 12, west off US 93 from Lolo. This follows closely the final westward swing of Lewis and Clark down into the Columbia Basin. The terrain is wilderness forest at its best, with good camping and picnic spots. A grove along the way is named for Bernard De Voto, Harvard historian of the Lewis and Clark journeys. Travellers Rest near Lolo was a stopping place for the explorers on both westward and eastward journeys.

This Lewis and Clark Highway is the most interesting summer exit from Montana if you have time. However, I-90 also leads directly west from Missoula into the Idaho panhandle and on to Spokane, major economic center for the entire region west of the Divide.

PRACTICAL INFORMATION FOR MONTANA

 MONTANA FACTS AND FIGURES: Montana takes its name from the Spanish montaña, meaning mountain. The state's nickname is the *Treasure State.* Th e state flower is the bitterroot; the state tree the Ponderosa Pine; the state bird the western meadowlark. "Oro y Plata" ("Gold and Silver") is the state motto; "Montana," the state song.

Helena is the state capital. The state has a population of 694,409 and encompasses 147,138 square miles. It is the fourth largest state in the union, following Alaska, Texas, and California.

The climate on the east side of the Divide is harsh during the winter months; it is milder on the west side, which is protected by the mountains. There is usually heavy snowfall on the higher elevations and on the unprotected plains. The summers are generally cool. If traveling in the mountains, it is advisable to bring along some warmer clothing.

 HOW TO GET THERE. *By air:* Western, Eastern, Northwest, Frontier, and Hughes Airwest serve Montana, flying principally into Billings and Great Falls.

By train: Amtrak provides service to Billings, Butte, Helena, Missoula, Glacier Park, and Havre from Chicago and Seattle.

By bus: Continental Trailways, Greyhound, Mid-Continent, and Intermountain Transportation have buses running to major cities in Montana.

By car: I-94 enters Montana from North Dakota in the east, I-90 from Wyoming in the south and from Idaho in the west, and I-15 from Alberta, Canada, in the north and Idaho in the south.

HOW TO GET AROUND. *By air:* Frontier flies to Missoula, Kalispell, Bozeman, Billings, Miles City, Glendive, Sidney, Wolf Point, Glasgow, Havre, Lewiston, Helena, and Great Falls. Northwest lands in Billings, Bozeman, Butte, Missoula, Great Falls, and Lewiston. Western has service to Butte, Great Falls, West Yellowstone, and Billings. Eastern flies between Helena and Billings. Hughes Airwest has flights between Kalispell and Great Falls.

By train: Amtrak has two lines serving Montana. The "Empire Builder" (which parallels US 2) serves Havre and Glacier Park. The "Northcoast Hiawatha" (running near I-90 and 94) stops at Billings, Butte, Helena, and Missoula.

By bus: Greyhound, Continental Trailways, and Intermountain Transportation are the principal carriers serving the major cities. Glacier Transportation serves Great Falls, Choteau, Glacier Park, and Kalispell; Clark Fork Valley Express—Bozeman, Helena, Missoula; Brown Bus Lines—Kalispell, Libby, Troy.

By car: I-94 runs east-west from Glendive through Miles City to Billings, where I-90 continues to Bozeman, Butte, and Missoula. The northern east-west route, US 2, is the principal access to Glasgow, Havre, Shelby, Glacier National Park, and Kalispell. I-15 and US 91 run north-south through Butte, Helena, and Great Falls to Shelby.

TOURIST INFORMATION. For information and brochures about points of interest, travel, and campgrounds in Montana, write the Advertising Unit, Montana Dept. of Highways, Helena 59601.

SEASONAL EVENTS. The State Advertising Department in Helena furnishes on request a *Montana Vacation Events* folder which gives the exact dates and location of the current year's activities.

Principal annual events are:

January: Montana Winter Fair, Bozeman; *Snowmobile Races,* Butte.

February: Winter Carnival, Whitefish; *Dogsled races,* Lincoln.

March: Music Festival, Butte; *Winter Snowmobile Rally,* West Yellowstone.

April: Figure Skating Club Annual Ice Show, Great Falls; *Missoula Festival of the Arts.*

May: Figure Skating Annual Ice Show, Butte; *Vigilante Parade,* Helena; *Mon-Dak Wagon Train,* a twenty-mile trip, Sidney; *fishing season* opens the third weekend; *Gates of the Mountains launch trips* open mid-month, Helena; *Cherry Blossom Festival* on the east shore of Flathead Lake; *rodeo season* begins last week.

June: Glacier National Park and main roads into *Yellowstone* open, and park accommodations are available beginning mid-month; *Missouri River Cruise* from Fort Peck to Fort Benton (participants supply their own boats) takes place mid-month from boat docks in Glasgow; *Jeep tours* of Helena; *Horse Show* at Forsyth; *Cherry Blossom Festival* including regatta, blossom viewing, Polson; *National Intercollegiate Rodeo Finals,* Bozeman, third week; *Pioneer Days,* Ronan.

July: Fair season begins: *Whitefish Lake Regatta,* Whitefish; *Diamond Jaycee Rodeo,* Polson; *Wild Horse Stampede* at Wolf Point attracts riders from throughout the nation; *Home of Champions Rodeo,* Red Lodge; *Western Montana Quarter Horse Show,* Missoula, mid-month; *Indian Powwows* throughout the month; *North*

American Indian Days at Browning, the Blackfeet invite other Indians to join a four-day encampment featuring dances, games, races, and a rodeo; *Gallatin Saddle Club Horse Show,* Bozeman; *River Raft Race,* Terry; *Boat Float,* Livingston; *Montana State Fiddlers Contest,* Polson; late July or early August, *North Montana State Fair and Rodeo,* Great Falls.

August: Copper Cup Regatta, Polson; *Festival of Nations,* Red Lodge; *Rodeo,* Billings; *Rodeo High School Finals,* Helena; *National Trout Derby* at Livingston offers a heavy purse for the largest trout caught; *Crow Indian Fair and Rodeo,* Crow Agency; *Bozeman Roundup Rodeo,* Bozeman; *Western Montana Fair,* Missoula; *Mineral County Fair,* Zortman.

September: Milk Wagon Train from Landusky to Malta. *Jaycees Rodeo,* Dillon.

October: War Dance Championships, St. Ignatius; *hunting season* begins; *Northern International Livestock Exposition,* Billings.

November: Ski season begins.

December: Snowmobile Roundup at West Yellowstone, through Mar.

 NATIONAL PARKS AND FORESTS. *Glacier National Park,* crowning the continent across the Rocky Mountains of northwestern Montana, contains one of the most spectacularly scenic portions of the entire range. Although today there are still some forty glaciers, the park is named for the Ice Age glaciers which carved out the rugged scenery. Covering over 1,600 square miles, it is the U.S. section of the Waterton-Glacier International Peace Park (the rest lies across the Canadian border in Alberta).

The Going-to-the-Sun Road, which links the east and west sides of the park by crossing the Continental Divide at Logan Pass, is one of the most beautiful drives in the world, but the over nine hundred miles of well-kept trails throughout the park are the only access to many isolated and magnificent areas.

For detailed information write Superintendent, Glacier National Park, West Glacier 59936.

Yellowstone National Park. Three of the five entrances are in Montana: at Gardiner on US 89, the Beartooth Highway (US 212), and US 191 and 287. (See section on Wyoming for detailed information about the park.)

Bighorn Canyon National Recreation Area. Focal point of this 63,000-acre area in northern Wyoming and southern Montana is the 71-mile-long Bighorn Lake. Boating, camping and picnic facilities are available. (See also section on Wyoming.)

Beaverhead National Forest, in southwestern Montana east of Divide, is a great hunting and fishing area and one of the few places in the nation where grayling can be caught. In addition to scenic rugged mountains and alpine lakes there are hot springs and winter sports here. Park headquarters are at Dillon.

Bitterroot National Forest, west of the Divide in southwestern Montana, contains the Selway-Bitterroot Wilderness, largest in the U.S. Mountain lakes, hot springs, scenic drives, fishing, hunting, and winter sports are also available. Headquarters are in Hamilton.

Custer National Forest, located in the southeast, partly in Montana, partly in South Dakota, offers winter sports, trout fishing, and big-game hunting. Granite Peak, at 12,799 feet, is the highest point in Montana. There are also primitive areas, alpine plateaus, glaciers, and hundreds of lakes. Grasshopper Glacier has millions of grasshoppers imbedded within its depths. Headquarters are at Billings.

Deerlodge National Forest headquartered at Butte has wilderness areas, alpine lakes, fishing, hunting, and winter sports.

Flathead National Forest, south and west of Glacier National Park, is a heavily timbered area of rugged, glaciated mountains. There are wilderness and primitive areas here and fishing, hunting, boating, swimming, winter sports, and scenic drives. Headquarters are in Kalispell.

Gallatin National Forest in south central Montana includes dramatic quake area camps and the beautiful Beartooth Scenic Highway. One of the gateways to Yellowstone. Headquarters are in Bozeman. The Big Sky ski area is here.

Helena National Forest, straddling the Continental Divide in west central Montana offers almost 1 million acres of fishing, hunting, and wilderness areas. The Gates of the Mountains Wilderness, where the Missouri River pushes through the Big Belt Range, contains a deep gorge lined with 2,000-foot limestone walls. Headquarters are in Helena.

Kootenai National Forest, in the northwest corner of the state, offers wilderness, beautiful timber (including Giant Cedars), hunting, fishing, and winter sports. Headquarters are in Libby.

Lewis and Clark National Forest in north central Montana contains nearly two million acres of canyons, mountains, meadows, and wilderness. The 1,000-ft.-high, 15-mi.-long Chinese wall is here. Headquarters are in Great Falls.

Lolo National Forest, mostly west of the Divide in west central Montana, includes the famed Lewis and Clark Highway over the Bitterroot Mountains, and fishing, hunting, scenic drives, and winter sports. Headquarters are in Missoula.

STATE PARKS. The *Lewis and Clark Caverns State Park,* just off I-90 forty-seven miles east of Butte, contains the largest limestone caverns in the northwest. Delicate, varicolored stalactites and stalagmites make this one of the most beautiful caverns in the country. Guide service through the caverns is available.

Giant Springs State Park, four miles northeast of Great Falls on Missouri River Dr. Here, one of the world's largest freshwater springs flows at a rate of 338 million gallons of water per day.

James Kipp State Park, northeast of Lewistown off US 191, is the area said to have provided a hiding place for Kid Curry. Drinking water, stoves, tables, sanitary facilities, fishing, boating, and boat ramp are available.

Long Pine State Park is located west of Kalispell off US 2.

Lost Creek State Park, northwest of Anaconda off I-90, offers fishing, sanitary facilities, stoves, and tables in the ghost town country near big mining centers.

Medicine Rocks State Park, north of Ekalaka off State 7, provides drinking water, stoves, tables, and sanitary facilities amidst 220 acres of weird sandrock formations.

Makoshika State Park, out of Glendive off I-90, is set in colorful badlands created by wind and water erosion. Stoves, tables, and sanitary facilities are available.

West Shore State Park is located south of Kalispell on Flathead Lake off US 93.

HOT SPRINGS. *Sleeping Child Hot Springs,* 3 mi. S of Hamilton on US 9, then E on State 38, then 11 mi. SE on County 501, offers swimming in natural hot springs and pool.

In addition there are hot springs in the Bitterroot National Forest near Hamilton, in the Beaverhead National Forest near Dillon, and locally around such towns as White Sulphur Springs, Hot Spring, and Camas.

CAMPING OUT. State Parks and Recreation areas are open from May to Sept. Camping is limited to fourteen consecutive days. Fees in some areas range from $1 to $2 per night per person. Complete information and brochures are available from the Montana Fish and Game Dept., State Parks Division, Helena 59601.

Montana has far too many recreation areas to list all of them here conveniently, so only information on the principal areas will be given (see also section on State Parks). "Complete facilities" as used here will mean that drinking water, stoves, tables, sanitary facilities, fishing, boating, swimming, and boat ramps are all available at the area.

Ashley Lake, fifteen miles southwest of Kalispell on US 2, then thirteen miles north on an unnumbered road. Complete facilities.

Big Arm, fifteen miles north of Polson on US 93 along the west shore of Flathead Lake. Complete facilities except no boat ramp.

Bitterroot Lake, twenty-three miles west of Kalispell off US 2. Complete facilities.

Canyon Ferry, ten miles east of Helena on US 12, then nine miles north on State 284. Complete facilities.

Clark Canyon Reservoir, twenty miles south of Dillon on US 91, I-15. Complete facilities.

Cooney Lake, twenty-two miles south of Laurel on US 212 to Boyd then nine miles west. Complete facilities except boat ramp.

Deadman's Basin, twenty-three miles east of Harlowton off US 12. Complete facilities except drinking water.

Elmo, sixteen miles north of Polson off US 93 on the shore of Flathead Reservoir. Complete facilities.

Finley Point, twelve miles north of Polson off State 35, Complete facilities including golf course.

Fort Peck Dam and Reservoir, twenty miles southeast of Glasgow on State 24, is the world's second largest earth fill dam. Complete facilities.

Hell Creek, twenty-six miles north of Jordan off State 200. Complete facilities including rockhound areas.

Hooper, seventy-three miles east of Missoula off State 200. Drinking water, stoves, tables, sanitary facilities, and rockhound areas.

Lake Mary Ronan, twenty-three miles north of Polson on US 93, then seven miles northwest on unnumbered road. Complete facilities.

Logan, forty-five miles west of Kalispell off US 2. Complete facilities.

Nelson Reservoir, seventeen miles northeast of Malta on US 2, then north. Complete facilities.

Painted Rocks, twenty miles south of Hamilton on US 93, then twenty-three miles southwest of State 483. Complete facilities.

Rock Creek, fifty miles south of Glasgow off State 54. Complete facilities.

Rosebud, at Forsyth on the Yellowstone River. No swimming or drinking water.

Thompson Falls, two miles northwest of Thompson Falls on US 10A. No swimming.

Tiber Dam Reservoir, thirty-eight miles east of Shelby on US 2 to Tiber then south on unnumbered road. Complete facilities.

Wayfarer, south of Bigfork off State 35. Complete facilities.

Whitefish Lake, out of Whitefish on west shore of lake off US 93. Complete facilities.

Woods Bay, one mile west of Bigfork off State 35. Complete facilities.

Yellow Bay, fifteen miles south of Bigfork on State 35 along east shore. Complete facilities.

 TRAILER TIPS. For information about trailer and campground sites, contact Montana Fish and Game Dept., State Parks Division. Helena 59601 or Montana Dept. of Highways, Helena 59601.

West Yellowstone: Beaver Creek National Forest, 8 mi. N on US 191, has 65 sites with flush toilets and boating. Open June 1 to Oct. 1.

Kalispell: Bitterroot Lake State Park, 20 mi. W on US 2, then 5 mi. N on Marion Rd., has 15 sites and swimming, boating, and fishing. Open May 1 to Oct.

East Glacier Park: Two Medicine National Park, 8 mi. NW on State 49 then 4 mi. W on County Rd., has 125 sites, store, snack bar, swimming, boating, fishing.

Fort Peck: Rock Creek, 31 mi. S on State 24 then 5 mi. W on dirt road, has 25 sites and swimming, boating, and fishing.

West Glacier Park: Fish Creek National Park, 4 mi. NW on Park Rd., has 180 sites, flush toilets, swimming, and fishing.

 FARM VACATIONS AND GUEST RANCHES. Montana has hundreds of guest or "dude" ranches which are either working ranches with crops and livestock where guests are another source of income, or mountain ranches primarily for guests which run only horses for that purpose. Either type of ranch is an excellent way to get the best of Montana for you meet congenial and characteristic local types. Ranches furnish the necessary guides for pack trips, fishing, hunting, etc., and can make sidetrips to points of interest. Yet, you have thoroughly modern accommodations on the whole.

Most "dude" ranches require advance reservations. The best source of information are the railroads or airlines serving the state or the *Montana Dude Ranchers Assn.,* Billings, Montana 59101, which will be glad to furnish an up-to-date list of ranches. Most ranches open for June-Sept. season only, and most will meet you at train or plane.

For those of you on the road, what follows is a list to which you can write or call.

Yellowstone Park Area. *Bar-N Ranch* at Yellowstone has fishing, hunting, horseback rides.

Covered Wagon Ranch, Gallatin Gateway, Montana, four miles from northwest corner of Yellowstone on Gallatin River.

Four K Ranch, Fishtail, Montana. Working ranch (you can help brand!). Thirty-two miles southwest of Columbus, off I-90.

Flying Cloud Guest Ranch, Wise River, Montana, forty-five miles southwest of Butte in Beaverhead National Forest.

G Bar M Ranch, Clyde Park, Montana, operating stock ranch some thirty miles off I-90 northwest of Livington. Horses and fishing.

Hawley Mountain Guest Ranch at McLeod offers pack trips, river floats among other activities.

Hidden Hollow Ranch at Townsend is a working cattle ranch which takes guests. Horses, of course, along with gold panning and other recreation.

Lazy K Bar Ranch, Big Timber, Montana. In the Crazy Mountains north of Big Timber.

Lion's Head Ranch at Big Timber offers all the dude-ranch pleasures.

Lone Mountain Guest Ranch, forty miles south of Bozeman. Part of the Big Sky complex, this resort provides summer and winter recreation in an atmosphere typical of a western ranch.

Ox Yoke Ranch, Emigrant, Montana. North of Livingston off I-90. Working ranch, not resort. Fishing, riding.

Rockin' Horse Ranch, Gallatin Gateway, Montana, forty-two miles south of Bozeman.

Sawtooth Ranch at Hamilton provides plenty of opportunities for good fishing and enjoyable hiking.

Shining Mountain Ranch, Sula, specializes in putting up young girls, ages 10 to 14. Horseback riding.

Sixty Three Ranch, Livingston, Montana. Specialize in pack trips and big-game hunting.

S/R Ranch, Big Timber, Montana. Cattle ranch with 13,000 acres. Guests can help on normal ranch operations if they choose.

Watkins Creek Ranch, Hebegen Lake near West Yellowstone. Lake sports.

Willow Ranch, Jackson, Montana. Western vacation ranch for *boys and girls.* In Big Hole Basin southwest of Butte on Route 278.

X Bar A Ranch, Big Timber, Montana, operating ranch north of the park.

Glacier Park Area. *Bear Creek Ranch,* East Glacier Park, Montana, five miles west of the Divide off US 2 to the south. Open all season and for fall hunting. Trail rides into the park and Flathead National Forest.

Black Tail Ranch at Wolf Creek consists of 8,000 acres, for horseback riding aplenty.

Western Mountain Area. *Flathead Lake Lodge,* one mile south of Bigfork on the east shore of Flathead Lake. This dude ranch on a lake has pools, lake sports and rides, horseback riding, barbecues, square dancing.

Rocky Bar O Ranch, Bigfork, Montana, special for girls 13-17 and for boys and girls 8-12. Special children's pack trips.

Diamond L Bar Ranch, near Lake Lindbergh on edge of Mission Range Wilderness Area, northeast of Missoula on Route 209. P.O. address: Seeley Lake, Montana. All facilities except you prepare own meals in cabin kitchen to cut costs. Food available at ranch store.

Whitetail Ranch, near Ovando south of Lincoln, specializes in pack trips and big-game hunting.

Double Arrow Ranch, Seeley Lake, Montana. Northeast of Missoula. Pack trips into Bob Marshall Wilderness Area.

Bar A Ranch, Seeley Lake, Montana. Operating ranch in Swan Valley.

Other Areas. *Circle 8 Ranch,* Choteau, Montana. Horse ranch roughly twenty-six miles from Choteau on eastern face of Rockies. Nearest area to Great Falls. Licensed guide into wilderness areas: fall hunting.

Bar 34 Ranch, Geraldine, offers actual ranching on 6,000 acres, while the *Hell Creek Ranch,* at Jordan, has good programs for hunters, hikers, fishermen.

Homestead Ranch, Utica, is a general ranching operation with many possibilities for vacationers, including fossil and rock hunting.

 MUSEUMS AND GALLERIES. The *Montana Historical Museum & C. M. Russell Art Gallery* at 225 N. Roberts St. in Helena presents a capsule history of Montana in dramatic dioramas and a notable collection of Charles M. Russell's art.

Charles M. Russell Gallery & Original Studio at 12th St. and 4th Ave. N. in Great Falls exhibits Russell paintings, bronzes, and wax models including the Trigg collection. There are also Russell's own collection of Indian costumes and gear, watercolors and changing exhibits, lectures, films and children's theatre.

Museum of the Rockies, on the campus of Montana State University, contains Indian and pioneer relics.

Range Riders Museum and *Pioneer Memorial Hall,* on US 10, 12 in the west end of Miles City, presents exhibits and memorabilia from the era of the open range.

J. K. Ralston Museum & Art Center, 221 5th St. S.W. in Sidney, exhibits historical artifacts from the region and original Ralston paintings.

The Central Montana Museum, on Main St. in Lewistown, casts a light on early Montana history via photos and dioramas.

World Museum of Mining, W. Park St., one mile west of Butte at Golden Girl Mine, has indoor and outdoor displays of mining tools, equipment, relics, and an old-time mining town.

Big Sky Historical Museum, south of Red Lodge on US 212, has a large collection of western frontier guns, Indian artifacts, and antiques. Open 8 a.m. to 9 p.m. June to Sept. 15. Closed rest of year.

Fort Benton Museum, 1800 Front St. in Fort Benton, has dioramas and displays on steamboats, Indians, and agriculture. Open 10 to 6, June to Aug.; May 19 to 31 and Sept. 1 to 15. 1 to 5 p.m. Closed rest of year.

Beaverhead County Museum, 15 S. Montana St. in Dillon, offers Indian artifacts, geological displays, and memorabilia of frontier and mining days.

H. Earl Clack Memorial Museum, one-half mile west of Havre on US 2 on the Hill

County Fairgrounds, presents exhibits on the history, development, geology, and archeology of the area.

Range Riders Museum, on US 10, Miles City, highlights the days of the open range.

Gallery '85, on Emerald Dr. two miles northeast of Billings in Billings Heights, has permanent and changing exhibits of works by contemporary Montana artists and craftsmen as well as art of the pioneer west. Open daily except Sun.: Apr. to Dec. 10 to 5; June to Aug., also 7 to 9 p.m.

 HISTORIC SITES. *Fort Union Trading Post National Historic Site,* twenty-three miles north of Sidney via State 200 on an unnumbered road at the fork of the Missouri and Yellowstone Rivers. The American Fur Company built this fort in 1828, and for a long time it served as one of the most important frontier outposts.

Custer National Monument. Located in southeastern Montana, this scene of the famous Last Stand memorializes one of the last armed efforts of the Northern Plains Indians to resist the westward march of the white man's civilization. On June 25-26, 1876, in the valley of the Little Bighorn River, several thousand Sioux and Cheyenne warriors did battle with the U.S. Army troops under the command of Lt. Col. George A. Custer. Although the Indians won this battle, killing Custer and all his men, they lost the war against the white man who brought an end to their independent, nomadic way of life. Dioramas, exhibits, and background and history programs are offered.

Big Hole Battlefield National Monument. In August 1877, a force of U.S. Army troops staged a surprise attack against a band of Nez Percé Indians led by Chief Joseph. Having refused reservation life, this nomadic tribe made a courageous though futile attempt to reach Canadian sanctuary. Audio-visual programs and displays of firearms and frontier relics are available at the vistors' center.

Bannack Monument, off US 91 near Dillon, was Montana's first territorial capital and site of the first big gold strike, on Grasshopper Creek (1862). Now a well-maintained ghost town harking back to the boom-town days.

Chief Joseph Battlefield, sixteen miles south of Chinook on a country road. The site of the final battle and surrender of Chief Joseph of the Nez Percé, which brought an end, in 1877, to Montana's Indian wars.

Indian Caves Monument, five miles southeast of Billings off US 87, 212, Indian pictographs can still be seen on the cave walls where Indians lived 4,500 years ago.

Old Fort Benton, on the riverfront near Main St. in Fort Benton. The ruins of an old trading post and blockhouse still remain from the frontier days when the town was an important commercial center.

Fort Owen Monument, off US 93 at Stevensville south of Missoula, is a restoration of Montana's first white settlement. Also here is *St. Mary's Mission,* the oldest church in the Pacific Northwest.

Missouri River Headwaters Monument, thirty-one miles northwest of Bozeman on I-90, near Three Forks. Here Lewis and Clark discovered the Jefferson, Madison, and Gallatin Rivers joining to form the Missouri.

Prehistoric fossil field, south of Fort Peck Dam in the northeastern corner of the state.

Prehistoric Indian site (Hagen), near Glendive off I-94.

Virginia City, southwest of Bozeman on Route 287. Restored early-day mining boom town and political capital.

FAMOUS LIBRARIES. *City-County Library of Missoula at Pine and Pattee Sts. has an outstanding collection of historical works on Montana and the Northwest.*

TOURS. *Glacier Park, Inc.,* offers two- to five-day tours of Glacier National Park and Waterton Lakes National Park, Canada. Tours include lodging, meals, launch cruises, and transportation via scenic coaches. Bus service is also available between hotels, and to and from depots and lakes. This is essentially a scenic tour on the park's lakes and highways. For complete information and rates write Glacier Park, Inc., East Glacier, Montana 59434.

 INDUSTRIAL TOURS. *Copper.* In Anaconda you can see the smelter, Mon. through Fri., at 9:30 a.m. and 1:15 p.m. In Butte, inquire at Chamber of Commerce about pit tour or go to viewing platform. At Great Falls, refinery and wire mill have tours 10 a.m., 2 p.m. Mon.-Fri. (10 a.m. Sat. only).

Lumber. At Bonner, east of Missoula in US 10, the US Plywood Company conducts tours explaining every phase of modern wood processing. The two-hour tours can be taken Monday through Friday. Also, at Libby, inquire about tour times of the St. Regis Paper Company, one of the largest in the Northwest. The mill is just off US 2. Wear low shoes.

Aluminum. Anaconda Aluminum Co., Columbia Falls, Mon.-Fri., 10 a.m. and 2 p.m. May-Labor Day.

Electricity. The Montana-Dakota Utilities Co., Lewis and Clark Station, two and one-half miles southeast of Sidney on State 23, generates electric power using lignite for fuel. One-hour guided tours are given Mon. to Fri. 8 a.m. to 4 p.m. Children thirteen years and under must be accompanied by an adult. Make arrangements a day in advance by calling the Plant Superintendent, or write Box 808, Sidney.

Mining: A self-guided tour around the old frontier mining town and early-day mining museum in Butte can give you a better understanding of the way life was in the early days of Montana. Further information is available by writing the Butte Chamber of Commerce.

 SPECIAL INTEREST TOURS. Buffalo, at the *National Bison Range,* at Moiese (south of Charlo and the Nine Pipe National Migratory Waterfowl Refuge), may be seen from June through Labor Day on self-guided automobile tours. There is also the possibility of seeing the majestic elk, deer, antelope, mountain goat, and bighorn sheep.

Wilderness walks into many of the remote areas of Montana designed especially for the visitor who may not have the equipment or much stamina are arranged by the Montana Wilderness Assn., 4000 4th Ave., Great Falls, Montana 59401. If you can, write ahead; if you're passing through and get the urge, call them—they may be able to work you in. These walks have informed guides and are unique.

Forest fire fighting is explained in full at the Aerial Fire Depot west of Missoula, Montana, on US 10. Special tours are held from mid-June until Labor Day. Call for times.

Ranching may be analyzed on a self-guided range tour in the Beaverhead National Forest near Dillon on I-15 in southwestern Montana. The drive takes about five hours, and signs explain modern cattle and sheep grazing techniques. Contact Supervisor of Forests, Dillon, for instructions.

Earthquake damage explained in self-guiding tour around Hebegen Lake on US 287 between Ennis and West Yellowstone.

Missouri River boat cruises, à la Lewis and Clark, are held each June depending on when water is best. They usually take three or more days, and everything's furnished. Contact State Advertising Department in Helena, or Chamber of Commerce, Fort Benton, for current information.

Big Mountain Ski Area summer chair lift operates June 15-Labor Day for a high view of the Western Rockies.

Snowmobile rides in Yellowstone from West Yellowstone in winter are a thrill. Contact Yellowstone Park Company, Yellowstone National Park, 82190.

Figure Eight Drive scenic tour of mountains and ghost towns every summer day from Helena.

Last Chance Gulch Tour around Helena on an automotive train explores the city's past and present history, including Pioneer Cabin. Built in 1865, this building has been renovated and furnished with pioneer artifacts. Tours take one and one-half hours and leave from the Montana State Historical Museum at 8:30 a.m. 10:30 a.m. 1:30 p.m., and 3:30 p.m. daily June 15 to Labor Day.

 STAGE AND REVUES. The University of Montana (Missoula) and Montana S ate University (Bozeman) are worth checking out if you are in the areas during the fall, winter, and spring. Many student and professional events take place during this time, and the prices are usually very reasonable. The hotels in major cities will be aware of any professional shows and local scheduling—such as Community Concert Series.

Summer theater is as follows: Bigfork, *Bigfork Summer Playhouse,* weekly opera beginning in June and running through August usually starts around 8 p.m. Fort Peck, *Fort Peck Summer Theater* presents shows June to August. Admission is charged. Virginia City *Players* present 19th-century drama every night June through Labor Day. Helena, the *Grand Street Theatre* offers nightly summer productions every weekend.

Kalispell, *Fort Kalispell Summer Melodrama Theater and Saloon* provides theater during the summer months. Plays range from musicals, drama, comedy, to melodrama. West Yellowstone, *Golden Garter-Old Gray Mare Theatre* gives nightly musical comedy and melodrama performances June 15 to Labor Day. *Playmill Theatre* also offers comedy and melodrama Mon. to Fri. at 8:30 p.m., Sat. at 7 and 9:15 p.m.

 MUSIC. The *Symphony Association* at Great Falls sponsors concerts during the late spring and summer. Billings and Helena both have their own symphonies, and during the summer months Helena has *municipal band concerts.*

 DRINKING LAWS. The legal drinking age in Montana is 18 years. Bars are open until 2 a.m. Monday through Saturday nights. No liquor or beer can be sold until 1 p.m. on Sundays. You can buy liquor by the bottle at state liquor stores in each town, as well as from bars. No special license is required. You may order liquor by the drink in Montana bars, and some sell bottles over the counter.

 SUMMER SPORTS. *Fishing.* Licenses are required: nonresident seasonal is $20, but you can purchase a $2 daily permit after purchasing a $1 conservation license. The fishing season usually starts in May and ends around Nov. 30. Local inquiry to the State Fish and Game Department will give you further information about laws and locations of the types of fish you want.

Some of the good fishing spots are:

Madison River Drainage. One-half mile south of Ennis on Route 287 (seventy acres); four miles south of Ennis on west side of river (27 acres); six miles south of Ennis on west shore of river (30 acres); twelve miles south of Ennis at Varney Bridges (five acres); twelve miles south of Three Forks and three miles northwest side of Norris cutoff road (604 acres); seven miles north of Ennis on northwest side of Meadow Lake (5.5 acres); Sun Ranch Road, forty miles south of Route 287 (inquire locally).

Stillwater River Drainage. Six miles south of Columbus on Stillwater River, Route

307 (four acres); at Johnson Bridge three miles south of Absarokee (two acres); Nye Bridge, three miles south of Nye (six acres); Rosebud Isle at town of Fishtail (nine acres).

Flathead River Drainage. Six miles east of Somers at New Holt Bridge (five acres).

Smith River Drainage. Eighteen miles north of White Sulphur Springs (three thousand acres).

Clark Fork Drainage. Rock Creek south of Missoula turnoff on I-90 just east of Clinton (107 acres).

Yellowstone Drainage. On Rock Creek along State 212 southwest from Billings, there are numerous areas between Red Lodge and Roberts.

For *lake* fishermen, the state provides public access at these lakes: *Sealey,* ten miles northwest of Ovando; *Sophie,* State 32 NW of Eureka; *Broadview Pond,* near Broadview; *Park Lake,* I-15 south of Helena; *Savage Lake,* near Troy; *Dailey Lake,* 22 miles south of Livingston; *Boot Jack Lake,* US 93 NW of Whitefish; *Skyles Lake,* near Whitefish, *Swain,* six miles east of Big Fork; on 209 near Eureka; *Crystal,* US 2 West of Kalipell.

A quick rundown on respected fishing locations by type of fish: *Blackfoot River,* western Montana near Bonner, rainbow and cutthroat trout, sockeye salmon in headwaters.

Big Hole River, southwestern Montana, rainbow, brown, grayling, and cutthroat trout.

Bitterroot River, near Hamilton, rainbow, brook, and brown trout with some cutthroat in lakes at headwaters.

Clark Fork River, drains west of Missoula, various trout species, with boat fishing on Cabinet Gorge Reservoir for salmon as well.

Flathead Lake. Cutthroat, rainbow, Dolly Varden, and sockeye salmon, with some bass in protected bays; salmon plentiful in fall.

Fort Peck Lake. Pike, catfish, and other warm-water species.

Gallatin River, near Bozeman, good trout, stream heading toward Yellowstone Park.

Georgetown Lake, near Anaconda. Black, spotted, rainbow, and eastern brook trout, silver salmon.

Jefferson River, above Twin Bridges, and the *Madison River* near Ennis, very good for rainbow and brown trout.

Judith River, near Lewistown, various trout species.

Kootenai River, near Libby and Troy, cutthroat and Dolly Varden.

East Mountain lakes, Stocked with warm-water species.

Marias River near Shelby and Tiber Reservoir, trout fishing in both stream and reservoir.

Milk River, Glasgow to Havre, trout near headwaters, tending to crappie and walleye pike out on plains and in Fresno Reservoir.

Missouri River, trout in the headwaters; boat fishing at Holter, Hauser, and Canyon Ferry Dams, for brown trout, rainbow, and salmon. Downstream harbors sturgeon, walleye pike, northern pike, sunfish, crappies, catfish and perch.

Musselshell River, eastern central Montana, good for brown trout.

Sun River, west of Great Falls on east slope of Rockies, good for eastern brook, rainbow, and grayling.

Yellowstone River, good from Yellowstone Park headwaters through southeastern Montana. Cutthroat high in headwaters region, then rainbow, brown and whitefish in Livingston to Columbus area, parallel to I-90. Pike, catfish, drum, and Ling take over east of Billings on the hot, dry plains where the river meanders.

Hunting. Hunting Licenses cost $225 for non-residents. Hunting regulations vary according to the game and residence status.

For full hunting details contact the Montana Fish and Game Dept., Helena 59601. Because of increased hunting pressures, the seasons tend to vary from year to year depending on the amount of kill in the previous year. There is usually an early elk and deer season in the wilder hunting areas (around the wildernesses) in September. The regular deer and elk season begins in October and generally runs until the end of November. Antelope hunting, on a drawing-quota basis only, begins one week earlier than deer and elk season and ends around the middle of November. Goat, sheep, and moose, also on the quota system, begin in mid-September and run until mid-November. Black and brown bear season opens around March 15 and runs until mid-November. Bird hunting begins in early September and runs till the end of the year for ducks and geese, November 30 for grouse and pheasant. Special quotas pertain to ducks and geese on the Central Fly Way.

Montana has more than two dozen game preserves, where many special rules apply to each species. Write for full instructions before coming to hunt.

Golfing. There are three dozen courses in Montana at most principal cities. Some are public, many private, but easy to get on if you go through your hotel or local tourist center. Your attention is especially called to three courses in beautiful vacation settings at Polson, Kalispell, and Whitefish, all public. There is a golf course at East Glacier; the nearest to Yellowstone is Bozeman. Greens fees are moderate and many of the clubs have the normal pro shop services.

Riding. See list of *Guest Ranches.* The bigger towns all have saddle clubs who can help you find riding facilities.

Rock Hunting. Montana is a rockhound's paradise. Sapphires, rubies, garnets, and moss agates are common types. The State Advertising Department has a special pamphlet for rockhounds, and agate shops are frequent on the highways.

Boating. Water-skiing and power-boating are common on the larger lakes and reservoirs. Montana boating laws, fairly standard, are available from the State Fish and Game Commission in Helena.

 WINTER SPORTS. *Skiing.* For a complete guide on skiing write Dept. of Highways, Helena, Montana 59601. Major ski areas in Montana are as follows: *Big Sky.* The late Chet Huntley's dream, some forty-three miles south of Bozeman, is one of the keystones of Western skiing. Numerous passenger gondolas, triple and double chairs span many miles of downhill and cross-country terrain. Mountain village with lodge, shops, and restaurants make this a complete resort.

Big Mountain Ski Area. Whitefish, Montana, alt. 4,774-7,000 feet. Opens around Thanksgiving, closes around May 1: lodge at area, and hotels and motels are in Whitefish; double chair lifts, vertical T-bar, pomalift, and rope tow; excellent runs for all classes; ski patrol, ski school, shops, rental equipment, a cafeteria and restaurant. Accessible by car, Amtrak, Air West.

Red Lodge Mountain, sixty-five miles southwest of Billings and six miles west of Red Lodge; alt. 7,400-9,400 ft.; season Nov. to May; hotels and motels at Red Lodge; three double chair lifts, one pomalift; twenty miles of trails and slopes from beginner to high intermediate and expert; access by train or Northwest, Frontier, or Western Airlines to Billings and from there by bus; ski patrol, ski school, rental, and chalet for meals. Summer camp for young racers.

Other Montana areas: All have some kind of lift and generate considerable local activity. *Bear Paw,* thirty miles south of Havre; *Beef Trail,* eight miles southwest of Butte; *Belmont,* twenty-five miles northwest of Helena; *Bridger Bowl,* sixteen miles northeast of Bozeman; *Deep Creek* on Wise River, forty-five miles southwest of Butte; *Lookout Pass,* eleven miles west of Saltese; *Lost Trail,* forty-five miles south of Hamilton; *Marhsall Mountain,* four miles east of Missoula; *Maverick Mountain,* west of Dillon: *Teton Pass,* twenty-three miles northwest of Choteau; *Rainy Mountain,* thirty-eight miles west of Dillon; *Termatts,* twelve miles east of Kalispell; *Turner Mountain,* twenty-one miles northwest of Libby; *Wraith Hill,* twelve miles west of Anaconda; *Z Bar T,* sixteen miles south of Butte.

WHAT TO DO WITH THE CHILDREN. The extesnsive parks and recreation areas in Montana give youngsters a chance to run free and to work off their excess energy in the clean air of the mountains, lakes, and valleys.

The opportunities to see animals in their natural habitat are unlimited, but near Ronan the *Ninepipe* and *Pablo National Wildlife Refuges* are particularly good spots to see waterfowl. Over 185 species have been observed here, including ducks, geese, grebes, bitterns, and cormorants. And at the *National Bison Range,* 300-500 head of buffalo roam over a range of 18,500 acres.

Fish, and trout in particular, of all sizes can be seen at the *Fish Hatcheries* in Great Falls and in Lewiston. And there are picnic facilities nearby.

Ghost towns and restored *frontier towns* give a sense of the frontier and mining past. Maiden, Kendall, and Gilt Edge, all near Lewiston, are ghost towns left over from the mining days of the 19th century. Helena's *Frontier Town* is a replica of a pioneer village, hewn out of solid rock and cut from giant trees. *Virginia City* is a restored gold-boom town with newspaper office, livery stable, general store, blacksmith shop and others. There is a train ride to *Nevada City* where there are authentic replicas of early mining stores, homes, and schools. The Nevada City Depot has a *railroad museum* with antique engines and cars.

At the end of a jeep railway and tram ride from Butte are *Lewis and Clark Caverns* where children can go underground into a wonderland of colorful rock formations.

 INDIANS. There are seven Indian tribes living in Montana: Blackfeet Reservation, Browning; Flathead Reservation, Confederated Salish and Kootenai Tribes, Dixon; Crow Reservation, Crow Agency; Fort Belknap Reservation, Harlem; Fort Peck Reservation, Assiniboine and Sioux Tribes, Poplar; Northern Cheyenne Reservation, Northern Cheyenne Tribe, Lame Deer; Rocky Boy Reservation, Chippewa-Cree Tribe, Box Elder. At various times during the year these reservations hold powwows, dances, celebrations, fairs, rodeos, parades, and craft and art displays. For information and schedules write to the appropriate agency headquarters.

The Crow Indian Tribe offers a special tour which includes a night on the reservation (see section on *Tours*).

 RECOMMENDED READING. A. B. Guthrie, Jr.'s novel *The Big Sky* is an excellent re-creation of the life of the early mountain men, trappers and miners in Montana. Frank Linderman's *Lige Mounts, Free Trappers,* a novel, is also set in this period. *Montana Paydirt,* by M. Wolle, deals with mining; *Ghost Towns of Montana* can also be recommended. For Montana history, read K. Ross Toole's *Montana: An Uncommon Land*; for an up-to-date look, read the same author's *20th Century Montana: A State of Extremes.*

An Official Travel Guide and Highway Map, listing points of interest, museums, campgrounds, and fishing areas, is available free from Montana Department of Highways, Helena 59601.

 HOTELS AND MOTELS. Many new representatives of the national hotel and motel chains are now in Montana, but during the prime tourist season reservations are still advisable. In fact, if you want to stay in or around Glacier or West Yellowstone parks you may well have to book reservations as much as a year in advance. Rates are lower during the off-season.

The price categories in this section, for double occupancy, will average as follows: *Deluxe* $30. *Expensive* $22, *Moderate* $16, and *Inexpensive* $12. For a more complete description of these categories, see the *Hotels & Motels* portion of THE ROCKIES & PLAINS *Facts at Your Fingertips* section at the front of this volume.

ANACONDA

Vagabond Lodge Motel. *Inexpensive.* Cafe nearby, park adjacent.

ASHLAND

Lazy FZ Motel. *Inexpensive.* 1/2mi. W. on US 212. Cafe nearby.

BAKER

Roy's Motel. *Inexpensive.* Playground, free coffee, cafe 4 blocks away, public pool nearby.

BIGFORK

Holiday Resort. *Moderate.* Cafe, sundeck, all facilities, and water sports on Flathead Lake. Open Apr. to Oct.

BIG SKY

Huntley Lodge. *Deluxe.* 40 mi. S. of Bozeman on US 191. The late Chet Huntley's ski resort in the heart of the Gallatin Canyon. Large rooms, condominiums, loft rooms, outdoor pool, and health club. Open year round.

BILLINGS

Ramada Inn. *Expensive.* Mullowney Lane and I-90. Heated pool, excellent bar and restaurant, dancing, entertainment. Free airport bus. Some suites.

War Bonnet Inn. *Expensive.* On I-90, 27th St. S. Exit. Pool, lounge, dancing, entertainment, restaurant, conference rooms. Free airport bus.

Cherry Tree Inn. *Expensive.* Near downtown, color TV, suites and apartments. Pool and playground nearby.

Holiday Inn West. *Expensive.* Some waterbeds. Indoor pool, restaurant, conference rooms. Convention area.

Imperial "400" Motel. *Expensive.* Heated pool, restaurant nearby. Friendship Inns chain. 35 rooms.

Hotel Northern. *Expensive.* Downtown near the railroad station, this is a leading hotel in southeastern Montana. Some suites available. Restaurant, coffee shop, bar, barber and beauty shops, garage. Member Best Western.

Ponderosa Inn. *Expensive.* Two heated pools, sauna, 24-hour cafe, bar, dancing, entertainment.

Dude Rancher Lodge. *Moderate.* Downtown motor hotel with distinctive Western atmosphere. Good restaurant.

Rimrock Lodge. *Moderate.* Heated pool, cafe, bar, barber and beauty shops, free airport bus. Convention facilities.

Westward Ho. *Moderate.* Many queen-size beds. Sundeck, free coffee.

Overpass. *Inexpensive.* 615 Central Ave. TV, free coffee, cafe one-half mile.

BOZEMAN

Holiday Inn. *Expensive.* 182 rooms, indoor heated pool, saunas, cafe, bar.

City Center Motel. *Moderate.* Indoor heated pool, sauna, free coffee. 24-hour cafe adjacent. Good restaurant.

Imperial "400" Motel. *Moderate.* Color TV, heated pool, free coffee, cafe nearby.

Sunset. *Inexpensive.* 24-hour cafe nearby.

BROWNING

Glacier Motel. *Inexpensive.* Small, well-kept motel.

BUTTE

Finlen Hotel and Motor Lodge. *Expensive.* A 100-room motor inn. Restaurant, bar, beauty shop, meeting rooms, free garage.

Ramada Inn. *Expensive.* 135 well-furnished units. Popular with conventions. Heated pool, 24-hour cafe, bar, entertainment, meeting rooms, free airport bus.

War Bonnet Inn. *Expensive.* Heated pool, cafe, meeting rooms.

Capri Motel. *Moderate.* Free Continental breakfast, 24-hour cafe nearby.

City Center. *Moderate.* A small establishment with pool, free coffee, 24-hour cafe four blocks.

Mile Hi Motel. *Inexpensive.* Heated pool, restaurant adjacent, free coffee.

CHINOOK

Rear Paw Court. *Inexpensive.* Free coffee, cafe nearby, some kitchenettes.

COOKE CITY

Watuck Motor Lodge. *Expensive.* Heated pool, cafe, riding, fishing, jeep tours, pack trips, snowmobiling available. (Best Western.)

DILLON

Royal Inn. *Moderate.* Heated pool, cafe. Some suites available.

Creston. *Moderate.* Free coffee, 24-hour cafe one-half mile.

ENNIS

El Western Motel. *Moderate.* Cafe nearby. On the Madison River. Hunting, fishing, float trips, guides available. Near Virginia City.

Rainbow Valley Motel. *Moderate.* Playground, cafe nearby, Float trips, hunting trips arranged.

Sportsman's Lodge. *Moderate.* Heated pool, cafe, bar. Fishing and hunting guides and float trips. Air-strip nearby.

GARDINER

Westernaire. *Moderate.* TV, cafe 3¼ mile. Closed in winter.

Mountain View. *Inexpensive.* Small motel with free coffee, cafe nearby. Patio overlooks Yellowstone River.

GLACIER NATIONAL PARK

Glacier Park Lodge. *Expensive.* Heated pool, playground, restaurant, bar, beauty shop. 9-hole golf course, pitch 'n putt, putting green, shuffleboard, volleyball, pingpong, riding, fishing. Reservations. Open June to Labor Day.

Many Glacier Lodge. *Expensive.* 12 mi. W of Babb off US 89. Restaurant, bar, barber and beauty shops, fishing, boating, riding, pack trips, volleyball. View of Swiftcurrent Lake. Reservations essential.

Prince of Wales Hotel. *Expensive.* Old World atmosphere with Scottish accent. Good food in large quantities.

Village Inn. *Expensive.* Cafe nearby, beach, fishing, boats available. Near Lake McDonald. Open late May to early Sept.

Desert Mountain Lodge. *Moderate.* A family-run lodge for hikers and cross-country skiers.

Rising Sun Motor Inn. *Moderate.* 6 mi. W of St. Mary Park entrance on Going-to-the-Sun Rd. Restaurant, playground, on lake.

Swiftcurrent Motor Inn. *Moderate.* 13 mi. W of Babb on Swiftcurrent Lake. Cafe, camp store, resort activities. Open June 15 to Sept.

Tamarack Lodge. *Inexpensive.* 8 mi. W of West Glacier on US 2. 24-hour cafe, one mile. Flathead River float trips, free RR, airport pickup.

GLASGOW

Campbell Lodge. *Moderate.* Free Continental breakfast, cafe nearby, sundeck.

Rustic Lodge. *Moderate.* Playground, free Continental breakfast, 24-hour cafe nearby, playground.

Roosevelt Hotel. *Inexpensive.* Free coffee, cafe nearby.

GLENDIVE

Holiday Lodge. *Expensive.* Indoor heated pool, sauna, cafe nearby, putting green, recreation room.

Jordan Hotel. *Inexpensive.* Pool privileges, free coffee, cafe and restaurant, beauty shop.

GREAT FALLS

Heritage Inn. *Expensive.* 185-room motor inn; indoor heated pool, cafe, bar, dancing, entertainment. Many conveniences.

Holiday Inn. *Expensive.* Elevator, heated pool, cafe, bar, dancing, entertainment. Free airport bus.

O'Haire Manor. *Expensive.* 17 7th St. Indoor heated pool, free coffee, restaurant, bar, entertainments, dancing, beauty shop.

Ponderosa Inn. *Expensive.* Rooftop heated pool, free coffee, 24-hour cafe, bar, entertainment, dancing.

Starlit. *Moderate.* Heated pool, playground, free coffee, 24-hour cafe nearby.

HAMILTON

Caprice. *Moderate.* Free coffee, cafe nearby.

HARDIN

Lariat Motel. *Moderate.* Cafe nearby.

HELENA

Colonial Inn. *Expensive.* Heated pool, sauna, cafe, bar, dancing, entertainment, barber and beauty shops. Free airport bus. Convenient. Enjoys much repeat business.

Coach House Motor Inn. *Moderate.* Sauna. Heated Pool, 24-hour cafe, bar. Free airport-bus.

Helena TraveLodge. *Moderate.* Sauna, restaurant and coffee shop, lounge, dancing, entertainment. Free airport bus.

Holiday Motel. *Moderate.* Some suites and studio rooms, cafe nearby, clean, comfortable accommodations.

Imperial "400" Motel. *Moderate.* Well furnished.

Sleeping Giant Lodge. *Moderate.* Health spa with sauna and exercise equipment, heated pool, Cedar Loft lounge, cafe. Free airport bus.

KALISPELL

Outlaw Inn. *Expensive.* An elite establishment. Attractive to conventions. Pool. Popular restaurant.

Devonshire Motor Inn. *Moderate.* Large beds, free coffee, cafe.

Four Seasons Motor Inn. *Moderate.* Highly rated. Cafe. Whirlpools.

LEWISTON

Yogo Inn Motel. *Moderate.* Heated pool, cafe, bar, picnic tables, grill.

B & B Motel. *Moderate.* With many queen-size beds. Free coffee, cafe nearby.

LIVINGSTON

Sandarosa Motor Inn. *Expensive.* 100-room, three-story motel with all amenities.

Del Mar. *Moderate.* Heated pool, playground, free coffee, 24-hour cafe in area.

MALTA

Maltana Motel. *Moderate.* Playground, free coffee, 24-hour cafe nearby.

MILES CITY

Red Rock Village. *Moderate.* Indoor heated pool, cafe, bar, dancing, entertainment. Free airport bus.

War Bonnet Inn. *Moderate.* Heated pool, free Continental breakfast.

MISSOULA

Village Motor Inn. *Expensive.* Just off Van Buren St. exit of I-90. Heated pool, therapy pool, sauna, steam baths, restaurant and lounge, beauty shop.

Executive Motor Inn. *Expensive.* 3-story, 3-star motel with heated pool, cafe.

Holiday Inn. *Expensive.* Heated pool, cafe. All the expected conveniences. Airport bus.

Red Lion Motor Inn. *Expensive.* Heated pool, 24-hour cafe. Cocktail lounge.

Forest Inn Motel. *Moderate.* 30 rooms, restaurants nearby.

Ponderosa Lodge. *Moderate.* Cafe nearby, close to town and university.

Stewart Motor Inn. *Moderate.* Heated pool, sauna, 24-hour cafe nearby.

Family Fun Motel. *Inexpensive.* Some kitchenettes.

POLSON

Queen's Court. *Moderate.* Free Continental breakfast, cafe nearby, boats, fishing, water-skiing available. On Flathead Lake.

PRAY

Chico Hot Springs Lodge. *Inexpensive.* Old resort hotel with hot pool, swimming, fishing, riding, cafe.

RED LODGE

Alpine Village Motel. *Moderate.* Large rooms. Open all year.

Bunk House Motor Lodge. *Moderate.* Free coffee, cafe nearby. Some large family units.

Yodeler Motel. *Moderate.* Free coffee, cafe nearby, playground adjacent.

SIDNEY

Park Plaza Motel. *Inexpensive.* Continental breakfast, cafe nearby, park opposite.

VIRGINIA CITY

Fairweather Inn. *Inexpensive.* Coffee house opposite, Old West decor.

Nevada City Hotel. *Inexpensive.* Cafe and music hall nearby, gold-mining camp decor. Coffee shop.

WEST YELLOWSTONE

Big Western Pine Motel. *Moderate.* Heated pool, cafe nearby, tennis, outdoor fireplaces. Open year-round.

Roundup Motel. *Moderate.* 27-room motel with heated pool, kitchenettes, near restaurant and cocktail lounge.

Thunderbird West. *Inexpensive.* 19 units, heated pool, restaurant nearby.

WHITEFISH

Alpine Glow Inn. *Deluxe.* Highly rated inn, adjacent to skiing. Dining. Cocktails.

Viking Lodge. *Expensive.* 1¼ mi. N at Whitefish Lake. Own beach, heated pool, sauna, cafe, bar, entertainment, recreation room.

Downtowner. *Moderate.* Free coffee, cafe nearby.

Mountain Holiday Motel. *Moderate.* Free coffee, cafe one mile.

WEST POINT

Big Sky Motel. *Inexpensive.* Cafe nearby, garage.

 DINING OUT. Steak, prime ribs, and lobster are big favorites in the area, and many restaurants cater to this taste. Local game, too, finds its way onto many menus and is worth eating whether it's trout, elk, deer, or buffalo. Prices are for medium-priced items on the menu.

Restaurant price categories are as follows: *Deluxe* will average $10 and up, *Expensive* $7-$9, *Moderate* $4.50-$5.50, and *Inexpensive* $3-$3.50. These prices are for *hors d'oeuvre* or soup, *entrée* and dessert. Not included are drinks, tax, and tips. For a more complete explanation of restaurant categories refer to THE ROCKIES & PLAINS *Facts at Your Fingertips* at the front of this volume.

BILLINGS

Golden Belle. *Expensive.* In the Northern Hotel. Winner of a Holiday Award for dining distinction. A Gay 90s restaurant specializing in steak and seafood.

Black Angus. *Moderate.* Steak a specialty. Children's portions.

Dude Rancher Coffee Shop. *Moderate.* Good family restaurant.

BOZEMAN

The Overland Express. *Expensive.* The leading steak restaurant in Bozeman. Cocktail lounge.

Black Angus. *Moderate.* Steak and lobster. Locally popular.

Topper. *Moderate.* Prime rib is the specialty and children's plates are available.

4 B's. *Inexpensive.* A restaurant popular locally that serves chicken, roast beef and steak. Open 24 hours.

BUTTE

Lydia's. *Expensive.* Excellent steak and Italian cuisine, or lobster, chicken. Soft candle lighting.

4 B's Restaurant. *Inexpensive.* A locally popular restaurant specializing in chicken and their own desserts. Children's plates are available.

COOKE CITY

Watuck Lodge Dining Room. *Moderate.* Aged steaks and quiet atmosphere set this restaurant off.

GLACIER NATIONAL PARK

Glacier Park Lodge. *Expensive.* On State 49. Complete dinners of prime rib, trout, steak served with their own baked goods.

Many Glacier. *Expensive.* Twelve miles west of Babb off US 89. Complete dinners of prime rib, trout, steak served with their own baked goods.

GREAT FALLS

4 B's Black Angus Steak House. *Moderate.* The motif is Bavarian and the food prime rib, lobster, and steak. A pleasant dining experience.

Freight House Restaurant and Bar. *Moderate.* In the old Milwaukee Railroad Depot. Features sandwiches, steak, lobster, and other dishes.

HAVRE

4 B's Restaurant & Supper Club. *Expensive.* One of a chain serving delicious steak, lobster, seafood. Popular family dining.

HELENA

Black Sands Supper Club. *Expensive.* Locally popular. Room for 150 people.

Colonial Dining Room. *Expensive.* Excellent steaks and prime rib. Also features chicken and seafood.

Jorgenson's. *Moderate.* This restaurant serves an assortment of good food family style.

KALISPELL

Outlaw Inn. *Moderate.* 1/4 mi. S just off US 93. Restaurant in the inn of the same name. Lounge and supper club.

MISSOULA

André's Frontier Lounge. *Expensive.* 2 mi. NW on US 10A. An intimately lit restaurant specializing in steaks and baked potatoes. Entertainment. Large capacity for dining.

Montana Mining Company. *Moderate.* A solid restaurant featuring good beef. Wine list. Relaxing atmosphere. Children's portions. Dancing nightly.

Ming's. *Moderate.* Chinese-style dinners in an Oriental atmosphere. Boneless chicken and snow peas is the specialty.

WEST YELLOWSTONE

Dude Dining Room. *Expensive.* A popular tourist restaurant that serves steak, prime ribs, and lobster. Children's portions.

Stage Coach Inn. *Moderate.* Old-fashioned ski lodge with family dining. Children's portions. Bar and lounge.

Three Bear. *Moderate.* Complete family dinners. Specialties are steak and prime rib. Own bakery.

WHITEFISH

Alpine Glow Inn. *Expensive.* A beautiful view awaits you when you come here for food after a hard day of skiing or boating. Good village location. A diverse menu including steak, lobster, crab. Salad bar.

NEBRASKA

The Good Life

by

LOWELL JOHNSON

Lowell Johnson is the editor of NEBRASKAland Magazine, *the official publication of the Nebraska Game and Parks Commission. In this capacity, he travels every corner of the state, and is familiar with its scenery, wildlife, and people. Revised by Mary Roll, native Nebraskan, educator.*

There was a time when the Nebraska Territory consisted of virtually all that was known of the western United States. It stretched from the Missouri River to the Rockies and from Kansas to the Canadian Border. Yet for all its vast expanse the state remained sparsely populated. The first territorial census in 1854 showed only 2,732 whites living within the borders.

The attraction of the real or imagined riches in the west, however, brought thousands of hopeful people pouring across Nebraska's borders on their way to easy fortunes.

A few of these recognized the potentially rich farmland in the territory and remained behind. By 1856 there were over 10,000 white settlers. But it was not until after the Civil War that the stage was truly set for Nebraska settlement. The Homestead Act of 1862 made free land available to those who would work it for five years and soldiers, at loose ends following the war, and Europeans, attracted by democracy and the lure of free land, came by the thousands.

There was nothing easy in the life of these early pioneers. The harsh climate could deliver freezing blizzards in winter and dust storms in summer, and these early settlers had to be necessarily hardy and hard working. But there were also years of milder weather when their labors were repaid with bountiful crops. More people came, attracted by the success of those already there. In 1867, they voted to join the Union and it was at this time that Nebraska was trimmed down to her present size and made the 37th state.

What we know as Nebraska today is topographically diverse. It is a plain which slowly rises from east to west changing in elevation from 824 feet to 5,340 feet. In the south and east are river-bottom farmlands which contrast with the flat wheat lands of the west, the high grasslands of the northwest and the rugged canyon country of the southwest.

The state is heavily agricultural, producing grains and livestock in particular. An extensive network of reservoirs for flood control and irrigation has been a major factor in her success.

From Desert Wasteland to Garden Spot

Where herds of buffalo formerly roamed in the millions, growing ponderous on the prairie grasses, now there are cattle. The grassy expanse of the Sand Hills, whose twenty thousand square miles of light sandy soil were once thought to be a desert wasteland, has become one of the prime cattle-producing regions of the nation. Crisscrossed by clear streams and dotted with natural lakes, the area has proven to be an unplowed garden spot.

The great number of cattle, both in the Sand Hills and on feedyards in the cropland areas, has made Omaha one of the largest livestock and meat-packing centers in the nation. With a population of 380,000, Omaha is the largest city in the state, and its location beside the Missouri River makes it a gateway in the east. Omaha, and the capital city of Lincoln just fifty miles away, are the cultural centers for the state. Two-thirds of the state's 1½ million people live in the eastern one-third of the state.

The population of the state as a whole is ethnically diverse, and the customs and culture of many of the Europeans who were attracted to the state by the promise of free land still survive. Such annual celebrations as the Czech Festivals in Wilber and Clarkson or the St. Patrick's Day festivities in O'Neill attract thousands of visitors who come to enjoy the color and gaiety.

Nebraska's earliest inhabitants also have their special observances: Indian powwows are held each year at Winnebago and Macy on the Winnebago and Omaha reservations. Lasting a week or more, these powwows feature dances in the old tradition performed in impressive ceremonial dress.

In all these respects Nebraska appears to be closely linked to the past: her primary industry remains agricultural as it was for the earliest pioneers and she has not forgotten the old traditions and customs. Yet it would be unfair to suggest that the state has failed to keep pace with modern developments. Hundreds of manufacturing firms have established main or branch plants throughout the state to take advantage of the available resources. The same dams which control flooding and provide irrigation generate electric power. The Strategic Air Command Headquarters with its sophisticated aircraft and missiles is unmistakably 20th century, with a staff of 12,000 directing this key link in the nation's defense system.

Yet in many ways the frenzy of the space age seems to have left Nebraska untouched. It is still largely free of air and water pollution. The comparative peace and serenity of rural living remains readily accessible here. To see this land as the first explorers saw it and as the early settlers saw it, one need only stroll through the picturesque openness that is Nebraska.

EXPLORING NEBRASKA

A vast array of sights awaits visitors to Nebraska, from the timbered bluffs along the Missouri River to the pine-studded buttes of the Pine Ridge country of the northwest. There are miles of perfectly level farmland interspersed with streams. There are mighty buttes and canyons in the southwest where oil derricks pump black gold from far below. There has been no extensive mining in the state, but riches are found beneath the surface in perhaps the world's largest underground reservoirs of water.

The vast Sand Hills region, unlike any other area of the world, is still of largely uncertain history. Some believe it was totally avoided by the herds of buffalo which migrated through the state in numbers estimated into the hundreds of millions, and equally avoided by the Plains Indians. Others claim it was a rich hunting ground even in the earliest times, just as it now sustains extensive cattle herds.

Nebraska has long been known as a corridor to the west, for the Mormon Trail, Oregon Trail, Lewis and Clark trail and Pony Express route all crossed through the state.

The railroad was a vital force in Nebraska's settlement and expansion, and the Union Pacific was of primary importance. It was in Omaha in 1863 that ground was broken for the eventual joining of rails to the West Coast. Headquarters for the Union Pacific are in Omaha, and a museum operated by the company houses many souvenirs from the railroad's history, including documents of Abraham Lincoln and other Civil War memorabilia.

Interstate 80's twin ribbons of concrete now carry the bulk of traffic to and through Nebraska. It closely parallels the old Oregon Trail, and modern travelers pass the guideposts which served the earlier migrations. Chimney Rock near Bayard was probably the most-mentioned land feature in pioneer journals, since it signaled the approach to the mountains. Scotts Bluff National Monument is on Rte. 92, two miles west of Gering. A museum and road to the top of the bluff are among highlights there, but many other rock formations are of nearly equal importance and interest. Indian legend says one of the formations was used by one tribe to escape another. However, once up there, they could not come down without exposing themselves, so they became prisoners. Only a daring nighttime descent by rope down the back side allowed them to escape.

A modern addition to the landscape is the "Chain of Lakes," pleasant lakes built along the interstate and open to the public.

Omaha Livestock Market, Art Centers, Other Attractions

As far as Nebraska is concerned, I-80 begins in Omaha where a number of sites should not be missed. Omaha is one of the biggest livestock markets and meat-packing centers in the world. The Joslyn Art Museum, a pink marble palace, is considered by many authorities to be the foremost center in America of early West documentation in various art forms, although it also exhibits modern art. The popular Union Pacific Historical Museum's many exhibits have to do with railroad history, including a replica of the funeral car which bore Lincoln. Father Flanagan's Boys' Town, long an institution of national fame, was founded by the kindly priest as a home and school for boys, and based on his belief that there was no such thing as a "bad boy."

Outside Omaha is the headquarters of the Strategic Air Command with its underground control center with world-wide communications and the Aerospace Museum, presently undergoing developments that will even ually entail millions of dollars.

Lincoln, fifty miles southwest of Omaha along I-80, has the state capitol, a building which should not be missed. Visible for miles, this landmark rises 400 feet. The statue at the top of the dome is Lee Lawrie's *The Sower* and the base of the dome is decorated with the symbolic Indian Thunderbird.

At the University of Nebraska at Lincoln is the State Museum, which has geology displays, fossils, natural history dioramas and the world's largest mammoth. The State Historical Society Museum has outstanding pioneer and Indian exhibits. And Sheldon Art Galleries offer permanent and traveling art exhibits.

The home of the famous orator William Jennings Bryan is here on the grounds of Bryan Memorial Hospital and contains original furnishings and memorabilia.

All across the state, towns adjacent to the interstate have links with the frontier, and have something special to offer. In North Platte, toward the western portion of the state, rodeo was born on July 4, 1882, when Buffalo Bill Cody staged his Old Glory Blowout. This was later expanded into his original Wild West Show and Congress of Rough Riders, a true western extravaganza which gained world-wide fame with tours in Europe.

Buffalo Bill's home, Scout's Rest Ranch, is now operated as a State Historical Park, with many curios and mementoes on display in the house and barn.

Pioneer Village, Other Museums and Forts

Back on I-80 one gets the feeling of the Old West at such places as Pioneer Village in Minden. One of the top attractions in the nation, the village contains over thirty thousand historic items in twenty-two buildings, including a sod house, a pioneer school, and log pony express station. There is an old steam locomotive and tender, a full-scale Indian stockade, plus artisans at work on loom and spinning wheel and in a broom factory. More than one million tourists annually visit the village, which contains one of the largest collections of antique cars, airplanes, and wagons in the nation.

A few miles south of Grand Island on US 281 is the town of Hastings, whose museum, the House of Yesterday, contains mementoes of yesteryear, dioramas, collections, a natural history section, and planetarium. Exhibits provide insights into the hardships of the courageous pioneers and demonstrate their way of life.

Head west from Lincoln on I-80 about 90 miles to Grand Island, the third largest city in the state. Its Stuhr Museum is becoming one of the most ambitious projects of its type in the world. Not only does it include a large antique vehicle collection and a beautiful, unique main building surrounded by a moat, but outlying areas are being developed into authentic sites devoted to such things as a 19th-century prairie town, a log cabin settlement, trapper's camp, and Indian village. The town is nearly complete with depot, train, early post office, and refurbished homes.

Many early military forts were established in the state, and many have been either preserved or restored, including Fort Kearny near the town of

Kearney. Located just south of the Platte River in the central part of the state, the fort was an important deterrent to Indian troubles, and provided protection for wagon trains. Fort Hartsuff near Ord is undergoing a face lifting, and Fort McPherson near Maxwell has been declared a National Cemetery. Fort Robinson, one of the major state parks, remained an active military post until after World War I. At Fort Robinson, near Crawford, the aura of the Old West survives despite the more modern facilities now there. It was here that the great Sioux chief Crazy Horse was mortally wounded. After surrendering himself and his people to the reservation life, he learned that he was about to be imprisoned and in an attempted escape was stabbed by a trooper.

Crazy Horse planned the attack on General Custer at the Battle of Little Big Horn, and he was the first to break Custer's lines there. Even now, Crazy Horse is considered to have been the greatest strategist and military genius of the Plains Indians.

The fort lies in a deep valley of the Pine Ridge with sheer cliffs rising in a long wall behind it. Trout fishing, some of the best deer, antelope, and turkey hunting in the state, trail rides and other recreation make it one of the most popular parks in the state. Only a few miles away on US 20 is Chadron whose Museum of the Fur Trade has a gun collection, Indian exhibits and relics of the fur traders who first penetrated the area. The Pine Ridge Division of the Nebraska National Forest extends north to Chadron.

Farther east on US 20, at Valentine, is still another fort, although it was never the scene of any serious conflict or confrontation. Fort Niobrara, considered rough duty for military personnel because of its isolation and weather extremes, is now a National Wildlife Refuge. Although it lies on the northern fringes of the Sand Hills, it also fronts on the scenic Niobrara River, which runs along the edge in a deep valley. During part of the year, the herd of buffalo is moved to this area, and in other seasons they roam the sandy hills to the south. An extensive herd of genuine longhorned steers and another of elk also call the refuge home.

Largest Man-Planted Forest

South of Valentine on US 83 is Thedford. West of Thedford on State 2 is Halsey and the Bessey Division of the Nebraska National Forest, the world's largest man-planted forest. In May of 1965 this was the site of a disastrous 20,000-acre fire. You can take a self-guiding tour through the Bessey Nursery and Plantation.

This loop tour through central and northwestern Nebraska has missed two regions of significant interest. Across the southern portion of the state are numerous reservoirs. Among the more noteworthy is Harlan County Reservoir at Alma. Serious floods in 1939 led to the erection of a dam across the Republican River and the formation of this 16,000-acre lake which now provides not only flood control and irrigation but also affords excellent sportsfishing for walleye, catfish and white bass. Similar measures were followed across this region of the state and Medicine Creek Reservoir near Cambridge, Red Willow Reservoir near McCook, Swanson Reservoir near Trenton, and Enders Reservoir at Enders were formed as a result. US 34 and US 6 provide easy access to these recreation areas.

Downstream from Harlan Reservoir is Red Cloud, near the Kansas Border. It was the home of Pulitzer Prize winner Willa Cather and the inspiration and setting for many of her novels, including *O Pioneers!* and *My Antonia,* and a posthumous volume of novelettes and short stories. The Willa Cather Pioneer Memorial Museum and many of the places made famous in her books can be visited in a self-guiding tour. The Childhood Home of Willa Cather has been restored and contains some of the original furnishings.

Homestead on the Range

East of Red Cloud on US 136 is Beatrice, site of the Homestead National Monument. More than 100,000 settlers came to Nebraska as a result of the Homestead Act of 1862 that provided for distribution of public lands, free of charge, to those who settled on them, cultivated and improved them, and remained for a period of five years. The Homestead Monument marks the site of one of the first homesteads: Daniel Freeman filed Application No. 1 under the Act for this land, built first a log cabin and later a brick house. A Visitor Center museum has exhibits explaining the homestead story.

Further west from Beatrice on US 136 then north on US 73, 75 leads to Nebraska City and Arbor Lodge State Historical Park. J. Sterling Morton, the founder of Arbor Day and later Secretary of Agriculture under Grover Cleveland, settled in Nebraska City in 1855 and built a house overlooking the Missouri River. Because there were no trees near his home, he planted his own—shade trees, evergreens, ornamentals, and an orchard. Eventually he became so enthused about the need for such planting that he dedicated most of his life to that pursuit, and in 1874 the state set aside a day in April as a special tree-planting day to commemorate Morton's work. Now, his former mansion is a State Historical Park, with the acres of trees open year round to visitors. Tree-planting ceremonies take place annually in the park in late April.

Also in Nebraska City is John Brown's Cave, a major station on the Underground Railroad which helped slaves to escape from captivity in the South.

This tour leaves other major points of interest unexplored. US 73 north from Nebraska City passes through the Winnebago and Omaha Indian Reservations in the Northeast corner of the state, and the John G. Neihardt Center at Bancroft. At Winnebago and Macy in July and August, the Indian tribes hold powwows and perform their traditional ceremonial dances in full tribal dress.

Whether you choose to explore Nebraska for history or recreation, the state has a great deal to offer. There are bountiful lakes and forests for camping and sports and abundant reminders in museums and historical sites of the pioneer heritage. In either case you will discover the friendliness and well-being of the people who live there.

For those who are seeking the peace and serenity of rural living, or the legacy, saga, and pageantry of the Old West, or just a picturesque and elegant jaunt in the wide-open spaces, Nebraska is the place.

PRACTICAL INFORMATION FOR NEBRASKA

FACTS AND FIGURES. Nebraska derives its name from several very similar Indian words generally accepted to have been Nibrathka, which meant "flat water." That term described the famous Platte River, and also possibly the Missouri River, both of which have been credited with being "a mile wide and a foot deep." Its nickname is the *Cornhusker State,* and the fabled football team of the University of Nebraska partially adopted the name—the "Huskers."

The state tree, formerly the American elm, is now more appropriately the cottonwood, which grows in abundance in most parts of the state. State flower is the goldenrod, the state bird the western meadowlark, and the state gemstone is the blue agate, found primarily in the northwest portion of the state. "Equality Before the Law" is the state motto. Nebraska ranks 35th among the states with a population of approximately 1,500,000. Its capital, Lincoln, has a population of 163,440.

HOW TO GET THERE. *By air:* the major airport for flights originating outside the state is Omaha which is served by North Central, United, Frontier, Braniff International, American, Eastern, and Ozark. Air Wisconsin flies into Lincoln from Minneapolis. Frontier also flies from Denver into Scottsbluff and Sidney in western Nebraska.

By train; Amtrak has passenger service into the state through Denver and Chicago.

By bus: Continental Trailways and Greyhound are the principal bus lines into Nebraska reaching Omaha from the east and Sidney or North Platte from the west.

By car: I-80 is the principal access route from the east crossing into Nebraska from Iowa near Omaha. The major highways from the west are I-80 through northeastern Colorado, US 26 and US 20 from Wyoming. I-29 reaches Omaha from the north and runs south through Iowa into Missouri. US 83 and US 81 enter from South Dakota in the north and from Kansas in the south.

HOW TO GET AROUND. *By air:* Frontier serves Sidney, Scottsbluff, Alliance, Chadron, McCook, North Platte, Kearney, Hastings, Grand Island, Columbus, Lincoln, Omaha. United has flights between Omaha and Lincoln; North Central flies between Omaha and Norfolk.

By train: Amtrak has passenger service across the state with stops at Omaha, Lincoln, Hastings, Holdrege, and McCook.

By bus: Arrow and Black Hills Stage Lines serves Lincoln, Omaha, Fremont, West Point, Norfolk, Wayne, O'Neill, Ainsworth, Valentine, Gordon, and Chadron. Star Bus Line stops at many towns between Chadron and Kimball, and Kimball and Omaha. Wade Bus Lines runs between Ogallala and Scottsbluff with several stops in between. Continental stops at Sidney, North Platte, Lincoln and Omaha. Greyhound has service to many towns between Kimball and Omaha.

By car: the major east-west routes across the state are I-80 from Omaha through Lincoln, Grand Island and North Platte and US 20 from South Sioux City through O'Neill, Valentine and Chadron. Highways running north-south include US 385 through Sidney, Bridgeport, Alliance and Chadron; US 83 through McCook; North Platte and Valentine; US 281 through Red Cloud, Hastings, Grand Island and O'Neill; and US 81 through Columbus and Norfolk.

TOURIST INFORMATION For information about touring the state, events, or about convention facilities and business opportunities, contact Dept. of Economic Development, 381 Centennial Mall South, Lincoln 68509, phone 402-471-3111. Specific information about outdoor recreation activities is available from Nebraska Game and Parks Commission, 2200 N 33rd St., Lincoln 68503, phone 402-464-0641. The Commission publishes a monthly magazine, NEBRASKAland, available by subscription. Metro and outstate tourist information is available at the Omaha Convention and Visitors Council, 1620 Dodge St., Omaha 68102, phone 402-341-1234. During June, July, and August guides are posted at all rest stops on I-80 to give assistance.

SEASONAL EVENTS. *January and February:* Big Eight Basketball, University of Nebraska at Lincoln. *March:* Pari-mutuel horse racing opens at Grand Island. State basketball tournament, Lincoln. St. Patrick's Day celebration, O'Neill. *April:* Horse racing continues at Grand Island. National Arbor Day celebration in Nebraska City. Activities include tree-planting ceremonies at Arbor Lodge State Historical Park. *May:* Horse racing moves to Ak-Sar-Ben in Omaha, continues into July. There are German Heritage Days festivities at McCook and a Danish festival at Blair. Brownville has a Spring Festival to open the Historical Tours season. *June:* Horse racing at Omaha. Omaha hosts the NCAA Baseball World Series. For a week at mid-month is NEBRASKAland Days at North Platte, when entertainment typical of Nebraska's pioneer days and western heritage includes rodeos, barbecues, ceremonial Indian dances, frontier musicals, and western art exhibits. *July:* Horse racing continues in Omaha until late in month, when the sport moves to the State Fair grounds at Lincoln. The Winnebago tribal powwows are on the reservation at Winnebago. *August:* Horse racing at Lincoln. Nebraska's Big Rodeo takes place at mid-month in Burwell. The Czech Festival is held in Wilber. The Omaha Indian powwow is at Macy. *September:* Horse racing at Columbus. The Nebraska State Fair takes place at the Fairgrounds in Lincoln during the first week. In Omaha is the Livestock Show and Rodeo during the last week. At Lincoln the University of Nebraska begins the Big Eight football season, which continues through the fall. *October:* Horse racing moves to South Sioux City. There is a Czech Hobby Show at Wilber. *November:* Horse racing season closes at South Sioux City. Omaha hosts the Holiday on Ice Show. *December.* Minden offers the Annual Light of the World Pageant.

NATIONAL FORESTS. The *Nebraska National Forest* is located in three areas of north central and north western Nebraska. The Forest covers over 300,000 acres of lake and river country. State 97 south from Nenzel leads to the Samuel R. McKelvie National Forest (formerly Niobrara Division). The Bessey Division, 15 mi. E of Thedford on State 2, then 2 mi. S on an unnumbered road, was the site of a disastrous 20,000-acre fire in 1965 and is now the largest man-planted forest in the world. It offers hunting, camping, hiking, picnicking, pool and lookout tower. The Pine Ridge Division lies 8 mi. S of Crawford on State 2 and has picnicking, hunting, fishing and camping.

Valentine National Wildlife Refuge, 17 mi. S of Valentine on US 83, then 13 mi. W on State 16B, consists of several lakes. These are closed to fishing during waterfowl hunting season, but the area also offers nature study, birdwatching, picnicking, upland game bird and deer hunting. Free.

STATE PARKS. *Indian Cave* is the newest of the Nebraska state parks. It borders the Missouri River and includes some of the finest of that scenic territory. Rich in wildlife and native plants this park is one of the most varied in the state because of the relatively high rainfall and diverse habitats. The park is accessible from the main county road just north of Shubert on State 67. Facilities include hiking, fishing, hunting, picnicking, drinking water, and primitive camping.

Fort Robinson, 3 mi. W of Crawford on US 20, surrounds the fort established in 1874 in the midst of Indian fighting. Crazy Horse, the Sioux Indian chief, was killed here. Today this 11,000-acre park offers hiking, fishing, picnicking, horseback riding, non-power boating, and trailer, camping, and sanitary facilities. There are also a lodge, restaurant, rides and museums.

Chadron, 9 mi. S of Chadron on US 385, is a modern recreation complex amidst streams and ponderosa pine. Hiking, fishing, picnicking, power boating, horseback riding, camping, trailer, and sanitary facilities are all available.

Ponca, 2 mi. N of Ponca on State 12, overlooks the Missouri River Valley. Here campgrounds include paved pads for trailers with electrical hookups and sewage dump facilities. Hiking, fishing, river boating, a pool for swimming, and complete camping and sanitary facilities are available.

Niobrara, 1 mi. W of Niobrara on State 12, includes a portion of the Lewis and Clark Trail through hardwood forests and across sandy bottoms. The park offers hiking, fishing, picknicking, camping, boating, swimming pool, and trailer and sanitary facilities.

CAMPING OUT. Nebraska has more than fifty recreation areas in addition to other special use and wayside sites. Camping is generally limited to only two days in wayside areas and to fourteen days in state-run recreation areas. The following are some of the larger campgrounds. "Complete facilities" as used here means sanitary facilities, drinking water, picnic tables, fireplaces, hiking, fishing, and hunting.

Bridgeport, in Bridgeport, offers complete facilities (except hunting) and boating and swimming.

Branched Oak Lake, 3 mi. N of Malcolm or 4 mi. W of Raymond, is the largest lake in the Salt Valley complex. The recreation area offers complete facilities and boating, swimming, and shelter houses.

Fremont Lakes, 3 mi. W of Fremont, has complete facilities (except hunting) plus boating, swimming, showers, and trailer sanitary hookups.

Lake McConaughy, northwest of Ogallala, has five campgrounds with complete or nearly complete facilities plus boating and swimming.

Lewis and Clark, 15 mi. N of Crofton, has several campgrounds with complete facilities along with boating and swimming. Most have shelter houses.

Medicine Creek, 2 mi. W and 7 mi. N of Cambridge, has complete facilities and shelters, boating and swimming.

TRAILER TIPS. In addition to the state parks and recreation areas already mentioned, Nebraska has a number of county or civic trailer sites. Those listed below are among the more complete.

Sutherland Reservoir Park, 1½ mi. S of US 80 at Sutherland, has water and electric hookups and sanitary station.

Fairgrounds Trailer Park, on the S side of US 30, 1-½ mi. W of Sidney, has water and electric hookups and sanitary dump facilities. It is open all year and there is no minimum fee.

Crystal Springs Park, in Fairbury, has water and electric hookups and sanitary dump facilities. Open all year; there is no fee.

Mormon Island, south of Grand Island, jct. US 281 and I-80, has water and electric hookups. Sanitary facilities. Fee.

FARM VACATIONS AND GUEST RANCHES. *Johnson's Three Eagles Guest Ranch* is a new facility in the Valley of the Three Eagles near O'Neill. Emphasis is on the riding school for young and old. Other activities include swimming, hiking, archery, volleyball and stagecoach rides. Casual western atmosphere prevails. Contact Gordon Johnson, O'Neill 68763.

Pine Hills Ranch is in the scenic pine country of northwestern Nebraska. This is a cattle ranch which also grows wheat and alfalfa. You may join in the ranch activities, hunt rocks and Indian artifacts, or tour the Black Hills. Up to 10 can be accommodated. Contact Alan and Kathy Harris, Rte. 1, Box 30, Rushville 69360.

Rimrock Recreation Ranch is an 800-acre cattle ranch near scenic Pine Ridge. It adjoins the state's largest park and recreation area. Housekeeping cabins are available. Guests may enjoy ranch activities, plus hunting, fishing, horseback riding, and jeep trips through Butte country, or to the Black Hills and Ft. Robinson. Indian artifacts and fossils abound. Contact Glen and Patty Houser, Crawford 69339.

MUSEUMS AND ART GALLERIES. The *Stuhr Museum of the Prairie Pioneer,* located on the outskirts of Grand Island $3\frac{1}{2}$ mi. N of the Grand Island Interchange at the intersection of US 281 and 34, consists of a building on an island in a man-made lake, an outdoor museum, and a collection of farm machinery. Designed by Edward Durell Stone, the main building houses displays and historical exhibits relating to pioneer life in Nebraska including agricultural implements, Harness Shop and Blacksmith. There are also facilities for displaying art work. The outdoor museum is a late 19th-century railroad town with log cabins, school house, railroad station and many others. Most of the farm machinery exhibited is in running condition including many steam engines.

The *Museum of the Fur Trade,* $3\frac{1}{2}$ mi. E of Chadron on US 20, traces American fur trading. Frontier weapons, trade goods, Indian exhibits and relics of the frontier past are displayed. There is also a restored trading post.

The *Hastings Museum,* at 1330 N. Burlington at 14th St. on US 34, 281 in Hastings, has wildlife, Indian, and natural history exhibits and pioneer displays including an extensive Smith and Wesson gun collection.

Joslyn Art Museum, 2200 Dodge St. in Omaha, is a magnificent marble structure which houses collections of art from ancient to modern times. Particularly impressive are the paintings and documents from Prince Maximilian's 1833-34 Upper Missouri River Expedition. Concerts, lectures, and classes are offered.

Also in Omaha are the *Union Pacific Historical Museum* at 1416 Dodge St. where there are thousands of interesting artifacts from the railroad's past including a replica of Lincoln's funeral car. The *Strategic Aerospace Museum,* 12 mi. S of Omaha on US 73, 75 near Bellevue displays bombers, fighters, and missiles used by the Strategic Air Command.

On the campus of the University of Nebraska at Lincoln are several significant museums including the *University of Nebraska State Museum* at 14th and U Sts. in Morrill Hall. Displays include geology and wildlife of the Great Plains and the world's largest mammoth. Also on campus, the *State Historical Museum* at 15th and R Sts. summarizes Nebraska history with exhibits covering the early days of the pioneers and Indians. The *Sheldon Memorial Art Gallery and Sculpture Garden,* at 12th and R Sts. houses over 1,100 paintings and offers rotating exhibits.

Harold Warp Pioneer Village, on US 6, 34, State 10 in Minden, re-creates the country's pioneer heritage with original buildings, including a sod house, pony express station, and more than 30,000 historic and antique items.

Willa Cather Pioneer Memorial and Museum, 38 mi. S of Hastings on US 281 on Webster St. in Red Cloud, contains her letters, first editions of her books, and family memorabilia. Also here is her *Childhood Home* which has been restored and contains some of the original furnishings.

The *State Capitol Building* in Lincoln has long been recognized as one of the world's architectural masterpieces. Designed by Bertram Grosvenor Goodhue, the building combines sculpture, paintings, mosaics and inscriptions. Atop the dome is a bronze statue, The Sower, symbolically sowing the seeds of good will. Around the dome are symbolic Indian Thunderbirds. Inside are murals and paintings, carved doors and mosaic floors.

The *Meriwether Lewis,* the large river boat of 19th century vintage, is being given a permanent berth at Brownsville. When restoration is completed, it will be the State Historical River Museum with authentic relics of river trade and travel.

HISTORIC SITES. *Scotts Bluff National Monument,* 2 mi. W of Gering on State 92, is a massive promontory rising 800 feet above the valley floor. It served as a major landmark on the Oregon and Mormon Trails. Exhibits at the Oregon Trail

Museum in the visitor's center tell the story of this westward migration, and paintings by William Henry Jackson, the famous pioneer photographer and artist who followed the trail in 1866, are also on display.

Homestead National Monument, 4 mi. NW of Beatrice, just off State 4, is on the site of the claim of Daniel Freeman, one of the first applicants to file for land under the Homestead Act. Signed in 1862, this act permitted every citizen or anyone who declared his intention to become a citizen, to file claim to 160 acres of unappropriated Government land. The visitor's center near the monument entrance exhibits historical objects of pioneer days and presents graphic accounts of life during settlement of the public domain. There is a 1½-mi. self-guiding tour of the area.

Chimney Rock National Historical Site, 16 mi. W of Bridgeport off US 26, State 92, is a landmark of the Oregon Trail, marking the end of the prairies. The cone-shaped mound narrows to a 150-foot column rising 500 feet above the North Platte River.

Agate Fossil Beds National Monument, 9 mi. NW of Scottsbluff on US 26 to Mitchell, then 34 mi. N on State 29, is an area where the fossils of animals alive 20 million years ago are concentrated. The site is still under development but offers a self-guiding nature trail and temporary visitors' center whose exhibits explain the story of the fossils found here and of the animals which once roamed this region.

John Brown's Cave on State 2 near 20th St. in Nebraska City. This was a major station of the famed "Underground Railroad" which helped slaves to escape from captivity in the South. It was run by John Brown, the Great Abolitionist who later became famous at Harpers Ferry, W. Va.

Arbor Lodge State Historical Park, 1 mi. NW of Nebraska City on US 73, is Nebraska's oldest state historical park. Once the home of J. Sterling Morton, founder of Arbor Day, Arbor Lodge is a 52-room mansion furnished with period decor. An arboretum with hundreds of varieties of trees surrounds the home. The park is open all year.

Fort Kearny State Historical Park, 8 mi. SE of Kearney on State 10, recreates the frontier outpost as it was a century ago. The fort, originally in Nebraska City, was moved here in 1848 to protect the Oregon Trail. The stockade has been reconstructed as well as a replica of the sod blacksmith-carpenter shop.

Buffalo Bill Ranch State Historical Park, at North Platte, 1½ mi. N on Buffalo Bill Ave., was William F. Cody's ranch and winter quarters.

Fort Hartsuff State Historical Park, 2½ mi. NW of Elyria on State 11, is still under development. Fort Hartsuff was established to protect pioneers in the Loup Valley from the Sioux. It is still being restored.

Champion Mill State Historical Park at Champion and *Ash Hollow State Historical Park,* 2½ mi. S of Lewellen on US 26, are being developed. Champion Mill is the last working water-powered mill in Nebraska. Ash Hollow still shows evidence of the passage of the Conestogas. Ruts, chiseled by the wheels of the prairie schooners over 100 years ago, are visible yet today.

 TOURS. The *Belle of Brownville,* the largest excursion boat on the Missouri River, offers scenic cruises on the river during June, July, and Aug.

Stardust River Cruises leave from the Marina Inn at 4th and B Sts. in South Sioux City from July to Labor Day.

Free guided tours of the *State Capitol Building* in Lincoln are given every day of the week.

 INDUSTRIAL TOURS. The *Good Year Tire and Rubber Company* at 4021 N. 56th St. in Lincoln has tours of their plant operations. A minimum 1 day's advance notice is required for these tours. For safety reasons children under 12 are not allowed. Contact the office, 466-2311.

The Control Data Corporation, 11615 T St., Omaha, manufacturer of computer components, has daily tours by appointment. No cameras or sketches are permitted. Contact Ralph Johnson, (402) 333-0850.

SPECIAL INTEREST TOURS. *Boys Town,* 10 mi. W of Omaha on Dodge St., US 6. Father Edward J. Flanagan founded this institution for homeless and underprivileged boys in 1917. The facility offers opportunities and training for several hundred boys between the ages of 10 and 18. The administration of the government in this community is in the hands of those who live there, including the management of the post office, library, and bank. A map with an outlined tour is available at the entrance.

The *U.S.S. Hazard,* which ran antisubmarine patrol sweeps during World War II, is now permanently berthed in the N.P. Dodge Park at 11000 N. River Dr. in Omaha. Virtually intact, the ship has most systems in operating condition.

STAGE AND REVUES. From July to mid-Aug. the Nebraska Wesleyan University students give theatrical performances in the Village Theatre in Brownville. Reservations advised, phone 825-4121. A variety of theater is offered in Omaha through dinner theaters, a classic repertory company, and a community playhouse.

A number of Nebraska towns have theaters where touring companies give performances and several have community theaters which draw on local talent.

Lincoln has a *Children's Theatre* which gives performances and puppet shows of special interest to children.

MUSIC. In Omaha, the Orpheum is home of the symphony orchestra, opera company, and ballet, which provide fine musical fare throughout the season. Lincoln also has a symphony orchestra. A number of Nebraska towns host touring symphonies and operas.

DRINKING LAWS. Liquor is sold by the drink or the bottle from 6 a.m. to 1 a.m. Sun. no package liquor sales may be made except beer. Liquor sale is subject to local option. The minimum drinking age is 19.

SUMMER SPORTS. *Fishing.* Game fish are so abundant in Nebraska that a fisherman may indulge himself all year and catch black bass, trout, crappie, northern pike, walleye, catfish and sauger. There are 2,300 lakes and some 11,000 miles of streams which provide ample opportunity for sports fishing. The state stocks many of these lakes.

Hunting. The ring-necked pheasant is the prime target in Nebraska. In addition there are seasons on rabbits, geese, ducks, squirrels, grouse, quail, and prairie chickens. For bow and arrow hunters there are seasons for turkey, deer, and antelope. The State Game and Parks Commission in Lincoln has information regarding seasons and licenses.

Boating, swimming, and *water-skiing.* Dams associated with conservation projects have backed up such rivers as the Missouri, Platte, Loup, Republican, and Frenchman and formed large lakes well-suited to water sports. Power boats are not permitted on some of the smaller lakes in the state so check first to avoid disappointment.

WINTER SPORTS. *Ice skating* and *ice boating.* When weather conditions permit, many of the same lakes that serve summer sports enthusiasts can provide activity for the winter months.

SPECTATOR SPORTS. *Rodeo.* These events take place all over Nebraska during the summer and fall. The largest event is the rodeo at Burwell around mid-Aug.

Horse Racing. Pari-mutuel thoroughbred racing starts in Grand Island in March, moves to Ak-Sar-Ben in Omaha in May, then to the state fairgrounds at Lincoln in July and August, followed by Columbus in September, and the season ends in South Sioux City in October and November.

Football, basketball, baseball. The University of Nebraska competes in Big Eight football and basketball in the fall and winter. The NCAA World Series of Baseball is held in Omaha in June.

WHAT TO DO WITH THE CHILDREN. In Omaha, children may visit Peony Park, an amusement center, or spend hours at the Henry Doorly Zoo.

The Children's Theatre in Lincoln has performances and puppet shows of special interest.

At Front Street in Ogallala children can take a stagecoach ride and also tour a free cowboy museum.

There are guest ranches operating specially for children in various parts of the state. One of the well-known guest ranches is the Ponda Rosa Western Ranch SE of Nebraska City. Boys and girls, ages 8-15, are accommodated. Activities include swimming, archery, hiking, horseback riding, and fishing. Contact Bill Stites, Nebraska City 68410.

INDIANS. Nebraska has three Indian reservations: The Santee Reservation in the north bordering Lewis and Clark Lake and the adjacent Winnebago and Omaha Reservations just below South Sioux City. The annual Winnebago Indian Powwow at Winnebago in July and the Omaha Indian Powwow at Macy in August are major events on the Nebraska calendar and feature the traditional ceremonial dances of these tribes.

RECOMMENDED READING. Mari Sandoz is considered the chronicler of pioneer history on the Plains with such works as *Hostiles and Friendlies, Old Jutes,* and *Crazy Horse: The Strange Man of the Oglalas.* There are also the writings of Willa Cather. *The World of Willa Cather* by Mildred R. Bennett is a good introduction to this famous writer. John G. Neihardt, Nebraska's Poet Laureate, whose office in Bancroft is open to visitors, has written about the Indians of the state in *A Cycle of the West* and *Dreams are Wiser Than Men.*

HOTELS AND MOTELS. Omaha and Lincoln offer a good selection of hotels and motor inns. Elsewhere in the state, motels are usually chosen for their proximity to tourist sites. There are definite summer and winter seasons so rates may be slightly higher or lower in or out of season. Listings are in order of price category.

The price categories in this section, for double occupancy, will average as follows: *Deluxe* above $28. *Expensive* $25 to $28, *Moderate* $18 to $25. *Inexpensive* below $18. For a more complete description of these categories see the *Hotels & Motels* part of THE ROCKIES & PLAINS *Facts at Your Fingertips* at the front of this volume.

BEATRICE

Best Western Holiday House. *Moderate.* Opposite airport. Comfortable rooms, heated pool, restaurant and lounge.

CHADRON

Grand Motel, Friendship Inn. *Inexpensive.* Well-maintained, comfortable, small motel. Cafe adjacent.

GRAND ISLAND

Holiday Inn I-80. *Expensive.* Heated pool, wading pool. Cafe. Bar.

Ramada Inn. *Expensive.* First class motel. Bridal suite with private pool. Heated pool, sauna. Cafe. Bar. Entertainment, dancing. Units for handicapped.

Holiday Inn-Midtown. *Moderate.* Heated pool. Cafe. Bar. Entertainment. Free airport bus.

Yancey Hotel. *Moderate.* Completely renovated commercial hotel; convenient, well-run. Restaurant, cocktail lounge.

Best Western Island Inn. *Inexpensive.* Convenient location. Cafe nearby. Airport bus available.

Grand Island Travelodge. *Inexpensive.* Comfortable, commercial, downtown motel. Heated pool. Restaurant nearby.

HASTINGS

Holiday Inn. *Expensive.* New chain member. Spacious rooms. Lobby fun center—heated pool, sauna, games. The Gardens cafe, lounge connected.

Clarke Hotel. *Moderate.* Large, comfortable, pleasant older hotel; recently renovated. Restaurant, lounge, barber and beauty shops. Civic and social groups frequently use the meeting facilities.

Midlands Lodge. *Moderate.* Modern, handsomely furnished motel with heated pool, playground. Chinese-American restaurant, lounge adj.

KEARNEY

Best Western Tel-Star. *Expensive.* Medium-size motel. Heated pool, playground, sundeck, restaurant.

Ft. Kearny Inn. *Expensive.* Large motel, has heated pool, restaurant, lounge. Horses can be boarded. Stocked pond available for fishing.

Holiday Inn I-80. *Expensive.* This large member of the chain has heated pool, sauna, playground. Restaurant, lounge, live entertainment, dancing. Wheelchairs accommodated.

Ramada Inn. *Expensive.* Superior motel. Sundome recreation area with heated pool, saunas. Restaurant, lounge. Entertainment.

Best Western-Western Inn. *Moderate.* Small pleasant motel with heated pool, cafe, lounge.

Friendship Inn International. *Moderate.* Attractive, spacious grounds. Indoor pool, saunas, playground. Cafe, lounge.

LINCOLN

Hilton Hotel. *Expensive.* 9th and P Sts. Impressive commercial downtown hotel. Glass-enclosed pool, cafe, bar. Entertainment, dancing. Free airport bus. Special rooms for handicapped.

Villager. *Expensive.* 5200 O St. This large motel has heated pool, 24-hour cafe, lounge, dancing, entertainment, putting green.

Best Western-Airport Inn. *Moderate.* NW Twelfth St. at W Bond St. Modern inn with pool, restaurant, lounge, entertainment.

Best Western-Sleepy Hollow. *Moderate.* 4848 O St. One of the older motels in this area which has been kept up-to-date. Heated pool. Restaurant nearby.

Buffalo Friendship Inn. *Moderate.* 347 N 48 St. Medium-size motel, has heated pool, playground. Cafe nearby.

Clayton House. *Moderate.* 10th and O Sts. Modern, commercial, downtown motel. Rooftop pool, sundeck. Restaurant, lounge. Convenient location.

Holiday Inn-Airport. *Moderate.* 1101 W. Bond St., 3 mi. W at I-80, airport exit. Heated pool. Cafe, lounge. Live entertainment, dancing.

Holiday Inn-Northeast. *Moderate.* 5250 Cornhusker Hwy. A large member of the chain with indoor heated pool, sauna, recreation room, putting green. Restaurant, lounge.

Radisson Cornhusker. *Moderate.* 13th & M Sts. A full service hotel with barber shop, beauty salon, gift shop, travel agent, drug store, catering. Restaurant, lounge. All rooms recently renovated. Family plan. Free parking.

Ramada Inn. *Moderate.* 3 mi. W at I-80, airport exit. Heated pool. Cafe, bar, entertainment. Free airport bus.

Motel 6. *Inexpensive.* 3001 NW 12th St. at I-80, airport exit. Comfortable rooms. Heated pool. Restaurant adj.

McCOOK

Chief. *Moderate.* Medium-size motel located downtown but the pleasant grounds give it a country atmosphere. Family units. Restaurant. Free passes to city pool.

Cedar. *Inexpensive.* A delightful small motel with a stream running through its back yard. Rooms are nicely furnished. Family units.

NORTH PLATTE

Best Western Circle C South. *Expensive.* A fine, large motel with indoor-outdoor heated pools, sauna. Cafe, bar. Miniature golf. Free airport bus. Buffalo Bill's Ranch State Park nearby.

Holiday Inn. *Expensive.* Large member of chain featuring solardome, indoor heated pool, putting green, games, saunas. Cafe, bar, entertainment, dancing.

Howard Johnson's Motor Lodge. *Expensive.* First class motel, 1½ mi. from downtown. Heated pool. Cafe, bar.

Ramada Inn. *Expensive.* A large two-story motel. Has heated pool, playground, restaurant, bar, entertainment, dancing. Free airport bus.

Sands. *Moderate.* A two-story motel, heated pool, restaurant, lounge. Free airport bus.

OGALLALA

Holiday Inn. *Expensive.* Large, two-story motel with heated pool, cafe, bar, entertainment, dancing.

Ramada Inn. *Expensive.* Motel has variety of accommodations. Heated pool, playground. Cafe, bar, entertainment.

I-80 Inn. *Moderate.* Small, comfortable. Heated pool, Cafe adj.

OMAHA

Granada Royale Hometel. *Deluxe.* 7270 Cedar St., 2 mi. N of I-70, 72nd St. exit. Every unit is a spacious suite with outdoor and poolside views. Kitchen facilities. Good for families. Indoor heated pool, sauna. Attractive lobby. Free continental breakfast and free cocktail hours. Free airport bus.

Hilton Inn. *Deluxe.* 16th & Dodge Sts. A large, contemporary style hotel in the heart of the downtown business district. Luxurious guest rooms. Several restaurants and bars, including the rooftop Beef Baron with carousel lounge. Enclosed pool. Barber and beauty shops. Free parking.

Best Western New Tower Courts. *Expensive.* 78th and Dodge Sts. Very modern facilities. A large, crystal Skydome covers pool and whirlpool bath. Ornate dining room. Coffee shop. Lounge.

Holiday Inn I-80. *Expensive.* 3321 S. 72nd St., I-80 at 72nd St. 6 mi. from downtown, half mile from Ak-Sar-Ben race track. Restaurants, lounges, live entertainment. Indoor, outdoor pools. Saunas. Putting green.

Holiday Inn Northwest. *Expensive.* 655 N 108 St., 3 blks. W of I-680. Dodge St. exit. Indoor heated pool, sauna. Cafe, bar, entertainment, dancing. Recreation room. Miniature golf.

Ramada Inn. *Expensive.* 7007 Grover St., 7 mi. SW of I-80, 72nd St. exit.

Ramada Inn. Airport. *Expensive.* 2 mi. NE, I-480, Eppley Airfield exit.

Ramada Inn-South. *Expensive.* 1811 Hillcrest Rd. 8 mi. SE on Nebr. 370.

Ramada Inn-West. *Expensive.* 909 S. 107 Ave. 10 mi. W at I-680, Pacific St. exit.

All Ramada Inns are first class with indoor heated pools, saunas, cafes, bars, entertainment, dancing.

Guest House. *Moderate.* 24th St. at Dodge. A moderately large downtown motor inn. Restaurant, lounge. Barber shop. Airport bus available.

Howard Johnson's. *Moderate.* 72nd St. & Grover. A large member of the chain with indoor heated pool, sauna, barber shop. Restaurant, lounge. Rooms for handicapped.

Sheraton Inn-Southwest. *Moderate.* 4888 S 118 St., 12 mi. SW on US 275, 1 blk W of I-70, L St. exit. Near Ak-Sar-Ben race track. Indoor heated pool, sauna. Cafe, lounge, entertainment.

Motel 6. *Inexpensive.* 10708 M St., 11 mi. SW on US 275. Cafe adj. Playground, picnic tables, grill. Wheelchair accommodations.

Sandman. *Inexpensive.* 105 S. Ft. Crook Rd., Bellevue. A small motel set back from the highway on a hill. Restaurant nearby.

O'NEILL

Best Western Town House Inn. *Moderate.* A small, nicely furnished motel. Hea ed pool, restaurant, lounge. Free airport bus.

Town House Inn. *Moderate.* A small nicely furnished motel with heated pool, restaurant, cocktail lounge. Free airport bus.

SCOTTSBLUFF

Best Western Lamplighter. *Moderate.* Popular, modern, well-designed motel, Indoor heated pool, sauna. Restaurant, lounge.

Candlelight Inn. *Moderate.* Heated pool. Playground. Cafe opp., bar, dancing. Free airport bus.

Lamplighter. *Moderate.* This modern, well-designed motel is very popular, indoor heated pool, sauna, restaurant, cocktail lounge.

Park. *Inexpensive.* Conveniently located near shopping center and restaurants. A medium-sized facility with comfortable rooms.

SOUTH SIOUX CITY

Best Western Marina Inn. *Expensive.* This large motel has year-round heated pool, sauna, restaurant, lounge, dancing. Beauty shop. On the Missouri River with marina, boat ramp, dock.

Marina Inn. *Expensive.* This large motel offers year-round heated pool, sauna, restaurant, cocktail lounge, dancing, beauty shop. On the Missouri River with marina, boat ramp, dock.

Park Plaza Friendship Inn. *Moderate.* Comfortable motel near city park. Restaurant, lounge. Playground.

Ramada Inn. *Moderate.* A very fine motel with attractive accommodations. Pool, restaurant, cocktail lounge. Exercise room, sauna.

South Sioux City TraveLodge. *Moderate.* This chain member is quite attractive and has a restaurant and cocktail lounge, heated pool.

Travelodge. *Moderate.* This chain member is quite attractive. Restaurant, lounge, heated pool. Wheelchair accommodations available.

VALENTINE

Best Western Trade Winds Lodge. *Moderate.* Near city center. Pool, playground. Restaurant nearby.

Valentine Motel. *Inexpensive.* Small, well-equipped motel. Playground. 24-hr. cafe nearby. Camper-trailer facilities.

 DINING OUT in Nebraska usually means eating at a restaurant connected or adjacent to a hotel or motel. Distances are great in this state, and there are few good, independent restaurants outside the two major cities, Omaha and Lincoln. There are plenty of bus stop cafes and gas station diners though, and most are clean and pleasant and serve good, wholesome food. A few of the state's outstanding establishments are listed below.

Restaurant price categories are as follows: *Deluxe* over $12, *Expensive* $7.50 to $12, *Moderate* $3.50 to $7.50, *Inexpensive* below $3.50. These prices are for *hors d'oeuvre* or soup, *entrée* and dessert. Not included are drinks, tax and tips. For a more complete explanation of restaurant categories, refer to THE ROCKIES & PLAINS *Facts at Your Fingertips* at the front of this volume.

GRAND ISLAND

Dreisbach's. *Moderate.* An attractive restaurant that serves really hearty portions. Great steaks and seafood. Family style dinners are available for four or more.

KEARNEY

Cattleman's Mining Co. *Moderate.* Has a wide reputation for fine food. Specialties: prime rib, steaks seafood. Salad bar. Wines. Western decor.

Grandpa's Steak House. *Moderate.* This is a cozy place, red tapestry wallpaper gives it an elegant touch, but it is very much a family spot. Steaks, seafood, and chicken are specialties.

LINCOLN

Tony & Luigi's. *Moderate.* 5140 O St. A locally popular restaurant featuring steak and Italian dishes. Dinner music and entertainment add to your enjoyment.

Bishop Buffet. *Inexpensive.* 61st & O St. in Gateway Shopping Center. Large selection of entrees, salads, desserts. Special children's menu. Own baking. Trays carried. Pleasant atmosphere with background music, fireplace.

Miller & Paine Tea Room. *Inexpensive.* 13th & O St. Nebraska beef and chicken pot pie are the specialties here. They make their own pastries. Located on the 5th floor. Also at Gateway Center, 61st & O St. on US 6, 34.

NORFOLK

Prenger's. *Moderate.* Steak, prime ribs and seafood. Background organ music enhances this pleasant atmosphere.

NORTH PLATTE

Tucker's. *Moderate.* Good steaks, chicken and seafood. Bar. Western atmosphere.

OMAHA

French Cafe. *Expensive.* 1017 Howard St. An unusual dining experience in the Old Market area. Charmingly decorated with antiques, murals, and a magnificent Tiffany window. Langoustine thermidor, escargot, sweetbreads in lemon sauce are suggestions from the varied menu. Own pastries. Lounge, entertainment. Reservations suggested.

The House of Genji. *Expensive.* 8809 W. Dodge. Rd. Atmosphere, decor, and food authentic Japanese. Food is attractively prepared at tables. Specialities include Teppan Yaki, abalone, chiri-chiri beef. Cocktails. Reservations suggested.

Bohemian Cafe. *Moderate.* 1406 S. 13th St. This cafe has authentic Czechoslovakian specialties such as beef in dill gravy, kidney stew, goulash, and hasenpfeffer. Their dumplings are popular. Cocktails. Simple provincial decor.

The Golden Apple. *Moderate.* 8901 W Dodge Rd. Charming atmosphere. Continental cuisine. Famous for their Brittany crepes, fondues, baked French onion soup and roast duckling Montmorency. Cocktails. Live entertainment.

Hilltop House. *Moderate.* 4911 Dodge St. Pleasant family restaurant. Specialities include beef stroganoff and chicken paprika. Homemade pastries. Cocktails. Reservations essential.

Ross' Steakhouse. *Moderate.* 909 S. 72nd St. A very popular long-established cafe, family-owned and operated. Steaks, prime rib, seafood, and Italian dishes are featured. Two lounges, entertainment, piano bar. Reservations recommended.

Bishop Buffet. *Inexpensive.* 7 mi. W on US 6, 30A in Westroads Shopping Center, I-680 Dodge exit. A cafeteria with a large selection of salads, pastries. Special children's portions are available.

NORTH DAKOTA

The Polychromed Prairies

by

JOHN R. MILTON

John R. Milton teaches literature and writing at the University of South Dakota and has recently published books on Oscar Howe and Crazy Horse. He has lived in both North and South Dakota.

Because of its position just south of the Lake Winnipeg, Canada, fur country, North Dakota was first explored by the French and British. Between 1738 and 1800 this area was visited by Pierre de la Verendrye, Jonathan Carver, David Thompson, Charles Chaboillez, and Alexander Henry, all noted exploreres or fur traders. The first non-Indian child to be born in the state, however, was the daughter of Pierre Bonza and his wife, Negroes, at Henry's Pembina trading post in 1802. Two years later, Lewis and Clark, accompanied by Sacajawea (spelled "Sakakawea" in North Dakota), crossed the state, spending the winter with Mandan Indians, fighting the cold but also commenting on the delightful sunshine. Extensive fur-trapping operations followed immediately. The way was opened for early tourists when, in 1832, "The Yellowstone" made the first steamboat trip up the Missouri River to Fort Union. Among the passengers during the first years were George Catlin, Prince Maximilian, and John James Audubon. With them came Protestant and Catholic missionaries, but the first permanent settlement was at Pembina in 1851.

Just after the organization of Dakota Territory, in 1861, refugees from the Sioux massacre in Minnesota fled to North Dakota for safety. Ironically, they were shortly followed by the Sioux themselves as the army chased Little Crow and his band out of Minnesota. Scattered battles were fought west of the Red River, but they were not serious enough to deter the homesteaders. Greatly increased migration to the northern plains coincided with the building of the Northern Pacific Railroad. Because the railroad went temporarily bankrupt before it spanned the state, impetus was given to migration by the sale of eleven million acres of the railroad's land grant. Speculators came from Minnesota, Iowa, Illinois, Ohio and elsewhere to buy pieces of land ranging up to 75,000 acres. Not pioneers, they came to get rich quickly. The soil was excellent, and although the growing season was short it featured long and sunny days.

The railroad then advertised widely, using the success of the bonanza farms to lure people from Norway, Germany, Poland, Iceland, and Russia, in addition to states east of North Dakota. Most of the advertisements emphasized the "choice prairie, the hardwood-timbered lands, the natural meadows, the healthful climate," and of course the convenience of the railroad. The timber was actually in neighboring Minnesota; otherwise the advertising was fairly accurate. Wheat quickly became the major crop, especially spring wheat and the hardy durum used to make macaroni. But the bonanza farmer did not diversify his crops, nor did he always live on his property and take part in community affairs. As a result, he lasted only twenty years, with a few exceptions. As the population grew and the number of smaller farms increased, the land dried out. In their haste to make a profit from the rich soil, the farmers had overworked it. By the time of the big winds in the 1930's, the land was ready to be blown away.

Meanwhile Custer and his troops had been annihilated by the Sioux, the Indians had been punished and put on reservations, higher education was inaugurated in Jamestown College and the University of North Dakota, and Theodore Roosevelt had come to the state for his health. After all this, in 1889, North Dakota was admitted to statehood. President Harrison signed the proclamation for North and South Dakota at the same time, covering the names so that he would not know which of the two states had been admitted first. Today North Dakota is given alphabetical precedence.

Dakota for Dakotans

At the time North Dakota became a state, the Republican Party was in control. It has retained control ever since, more or less, although state politics have been stormy. Behind many of the controversies of the past seventy-five years has been a feeling of resentment by North Dakotans over their dependence on St. Paul, Minneapolis, and the East. In the early days the railroad, with headquarters in St. Paul, wielded both economic and political influence. Today, Minneapolis is the financial center of the northern prairie region. But North Dakotans are extremely independent, when they can be, and are reluctant to admit competition from outside the state. With the help of A. C. Townley and the Nonpartisan League formed in 1915, they established a state mill and elevator association, a state bank, and a state hail insurance program. These come under occasional criticism, but they still operate and testify to the state's fear of exploitation by outside corporations. For many years most official communications within the state bore the legend, "Buy Dakota Maid Flour" (made at state mills). Later the imprint was changed to "Buy North Dakota Products."

The tension between outstate big business and instate socialism had made

North Dakota unique in local politics. Lynn Frazier, the state's first Nonpartisan governor, was removed from office after a recall measure had been passed by the legislature in 1920; however, two years later he was elected to the U.S. Senate. William Langer, the third Nonpartisan governor, was disqualified from office in 1932 and then elected again in 1936. Thomas Moodie, a Democrat, was elected in 1935 and immediately declared ineligible.

The general image of the state is just as confused. Strangers from afar view North Dakota as a Siberian wasteland or a hot dust bowl. It is true that this state holds the western hemisphere record for absolute range in temperature—from 121 degrees above zero to 60 below in the same year. It is true that writers have emphasized the drought in the 1930's because the dust storms were North Dakota's major crisis in modern times. But those days are gone. Crop rotation, irrigation, and conservation methods have stabilized the land, and each year seems to bring a bumper crop. Although industry has not really penetrated the state as yet, the building of the Garrison Dam on the Missouri River has at least made available a vast potential of power for new development. Upstream from the dam lies the largest man-made lake, 609 square miles, and boats now speed back and forth where dust once blew.

North Dakota is a state of contrasts: monotony and beauty, freedom and loneliness, courage and defeat, heat and cold (although dry air moderates both). One can be frightened by the immensity of the land and sky even while experiencing a tremendous exhilaration. It is the tension between these extremes that is exciting and stimulating, if you watch the people closely enough to notice it. Yet, Theodore Roosevelt once said that he could not have become president except for what he learned in North Dakota. One can indeed learn a great deal. A man out in the open is on his own, and he is likely to be independent and self-sufficient in whatever he does.

EXPLORING NORTH DAKOTA

Except for the northern fur traders, Fargo has always been the main entry to North Dakota. It is the state's largest city, with a population of 50,000, and it wants to be Eastern and cultured. In this endeavor it has help from its Minnesota neighbor, Moorhead, just across the river, which has two colleges. The Fargo-Moorhead area has been designated a standard metropolitan area with a population of over 100,000.

The Northern Pacific Railroad brought life to this area in 1871 as fortune seekers dashed up and down the Red River of the North trying to guess where the railroad would cross. Once the tracks reached Moorhead, a settlement called "Fargo in the Timber" sprang up on the west side of the river, with a post office called first Centralia then Fargo, after the head of the Wells-Fargo Express.

The rich soil of the Red River Valley is the result of glacial action which formed Lake Agassiz centuries ago. The people of the area recognize their reliance upon agriculture. More than three thousand farms are located within a 50-mile radius. Major crops are grains, potatoes, and sugar beets. In northwest Fargo, the North Dakota State University conducts agricultural research, maintains grain and animal experimentation farms, and through its Institute for Regional Studies stimulates research into the resources of the region. The interest in culture lags behind that in agriculture, but the arts are being encouraged. Poets and publishers of little magazines work back and forth between Fargo and Moorhead to give the area significant literary activity.

Fargo keeps its eye on Minneapolis but goes ahead with projects to modernize and beautify the city. When a slum area was replaced by a new Civic Center costing ten million dollars, Fargo was designated an All-American city. A newer project is called "Main Avenue Urban Renewal" and involves six blocks along both sides of Main Avenue, parallel to the Northern Pacific tracks.

In contrast to the city's concern for the future is the Forsberg House collection of historical objects and paintings; but for a more serious look into the past, one must drive to Fort Abercrombie, about an hour to the south on US 81. Partially restored, this was the first federal fort in North Dakota, established in 1857. It was subjected to a long-term attack by the Sioux Indians during the 1862 uprising in nearby Minnesota. The grounds now contain a stockade, blockhouses, and museum.

Just a few miles south of Abercrombie, the North Dakota State School of Science and the Indian School are located in Wahpeton. A recent teacher at this Indian School was Mrs. Robert Horne, a great great granddaughter of Sacajawea, the Indian girl who helped guide the Lewis and Clark expedition as far as Idaho in 1805.

Side Trip to Grand Forks

The border between North Dakota and Minnesota is mainly comprised of the Red River of the North. This unusual river flows northward, emptying into Lake Winnipeg. To drive north from Fargo on I-29 is to cross some of the flattest land to be seen. Paradoxically, the tallest structure in the state rises from the prairie—the tower for Fargo's Station KTHI-TV (2,063 feet) south of Mayville on State 18. At the end of a 77-mile stretch lies Grand Forks, with a large air force base and the University of North Dakota. Here, in the center of the nation, a new program in education is proceeding successfully while at the same time scholars are interpreting the past. The old and the new exist together, the union symbolized not long ago when a spacecraft flew high above an ox-cart train celebrating an anniversary. North of Grand Forks, in the northeast corner of the state lies Pembina, site of the first two settlements in North Dakota, now a state park. The first, in 1797, was for fur traders. These men later resented the Scottish immigrants brought by the Earl of Selkirk in 1812.

Westward Through Flatlands

Although the early fur traders came in from the North, and Lewis and Clark came in from the South, the main entry to modern North Dakota is Fargo. The 19th-century trail which ambled west from here is now a four-lane highway which gently winds its way across the flat and broad prairie. Where tall grass once grew, and buffalo bones were scattered over the earth, wheat now waves in the brisk winds. The land appears crude and monotonous, yet Holger Cahill found here a mystic quality which he wrote about in his novel, *The Shadow of My Hand*. The horizon seems too far away to reach, even in a speeding automobile. Sky is everywhere, and one must look down occasionally at the ducks swimming in sloughs and ditch-pools to realize that one is not in an airplane. The first real break in the flatness is the Sheyenne River Valley. Here in Valley City is the oldest of the state teachers colleges. North of the city, Lake Ashtabula is a 27-mile recreational area formed by the damming of the Sheyenne River. The entire valley is a refreshing oasis on the plains, with fishing, boating, swimming, and camping.

The landscape changes little as we proceed west, except that slightly rolling hills, low ridges, shallow coulees, and a few small lakes indicate the western end of glacial Lake Agassiz, the huge lake formed by the glacier that ten thousand years ago flattened eastern North Dakota. The glacier probably ended at the Missouri River, and at that time the Missouri probably flowed in what is now the James River Valley. Here the highway passes Jamestown, said to be the prettiest city in the state because of its two rivers, the valley which curves like a crescent, the parks and trees, and the wide streets. In 1872, Jamestown was the site of Fort Seward, built to protect the railroad workers and the travelers who crossed the river at this point. From where the fort stood, a little north of town and above the valley, one can look down at the river and a good portion of the valley in which Jamestown stands. Almost immediately below is the nationally famous Crippled Children's School, directed by Dr. Ann Carlson. Across the valley, on the opposite bluff, stands Jamestown College, one of North Dakota's two private liberal arts colleges (Presbyterian). On another hill nearby, a pioneer town and a large buffalo statue are new landmarks.

Up the river one mile, the Jamestown Dam Recreation Area is a 14-mile lake behind a large earthen dam. This is the most popular swimming, boating, fishing, and picnicking area for many miles around. Upstream thirty miles, the Arrowwood National Wildlife Refuge is a nesting and feeding ground for migratory birds and various kinds of wildlife. Twice a year the skies over Jamestown are almost blackened by millions of migrating ducks and geese. Because there is no longer an unlimited number of ducks for hunting, a one-million dollar Northern Prairie Wildlife Research Center has been built in Jamestown. At the Center's I. G. Bue Laboratory, research is carried on to try to maintain the kind of hunting conditions which have existed in the past. Adding to Jamestown's reputation as a wildlife center, Carl E. Strutz recently discovered an Aleutian Goose, long thought to be extinct. Strutz is a resident of Jamestown and is associated with the International Wild Waterfowl Association.

Art in Jamestown tends to be imitative, especially of the Western past, although a variety of paintings may often be seen on exhibit in local restaurants. J. A. Kirkpatrick maintains a studio at 412 Seventh Avenue Northwest, and a large mural and several paintings of his may be seen at the Hawkins Clinic Drugstore. Kirkpatrick reproduces scenes of the Old West, somewhat in the manner of Frederic Remington and Charles Russell. His details, though authentic, are given an aura of romanticism. A different kind of reproduction of the Old West stands high on the western bluff, visible from the town below and the highway beyond. Hailed as the world's largest buffalo, it is a statue of an American bison, forty-six feet long by twenty-six feet high and weighing sixty tons. Its bones are eight-inch steel beams; its flesh is steel rods and wire mesh; and its skin is sprayed concrete. Some early accounts tell of buffalo herds ranging up to ten thousand animals, and a

Great Plains total of one million. To the Indians, the buffalo was life itself. It provided them with food, clothing, and shelter. And so the statue is not merely a tourist gimmick but a serious memorial to a way of life now past. Near the statue, reminiscent of early days, is Frontier Village, with railroad depot, land office, fire hall, newspaper shop, jail, old-fashioned restaurant, drug store, barber shop, prairie school, and other facilities.

Whitestone Battlefield

One of the state's more interesting battlefields is an hour's drive south of Jamestown on US 281 and then west from either Monango or Ellendale. Whitestone Battlefield has a museum and picnic grounds. On this spot a battle was fought in 1863 between troops under General Sully and the Sioux Indians.

To continue south on 281 would take you into South Dakota; a longer tour follows US 281 north through Devils Lake and on to Canada. Devils Lake was named by the Indians "Bad Spirit Lake" for its turbulence during storms and for its undrinkable water, much like ocean water. For years, visitors to this area were bothered by the city's drinking water, but recently installed facilities have changed that situation and provide good water now. Yet, among the more than one thousand Sioux Indians living on Fort Totten Reservation, bordering the lake on the south, there are still tales and legends which give a mysterious atmosphere to the lake. One tells of an Indian brave sitting on the shore who stuck his knife into a log. The log slid into the lake and turned out to be a sea monster which is said to still live in a hole at the bottom of the lake. Another story concerns a party of Sioux returning from a successful battle against the Chippewa: As they crossed the lake they were swallowed up. During certain weather conditions the lake sends off a vapor which tends to magnify birds swimming on the water, and this has led to talk about phantom ships. Or were they really birds after all? In recent years the waters of Devils Lake have risen and sweetened and now are a center for fishing and water sports.

The Indians now living here are descendants of three separate Siouan tribes—the Wahpeton, the Sisseton, and the Yanktonai. Their subagency is at Fort Totten, across the lake from the town of Devils Lake. At one time the fort was the last outpost for three hundred miles of unprotected prairie. Its Cavalry Square, the only one of its type remaining, has been preserved. Its original (1870) design and condition remain nearly intact. Some of the buildings are open to the public, and there is a display of frontier objects in the old hospital building. The surrounding countryside was once very bleak, and posed a survival problem for the early settlers. Wallace Stegner has described those problems in his fine novel, *The Big Rock Candy Mountain.* Summer turned to winter—without an intervening eastern autumn. The land turned brown and gray, and alternating rains and freezes made huge ruts in the roads, and the landscape more desolate. The wind blew all the time and made people tense. The land is not quite so desolate now, but wind still blows, and it affects the people in at least two ways: those who cannot endure it are made irritable; others learn to live with it and seem somehow more stable and calm for it. It can work either way.

In any case, the visitor will be less impressed by the wind than by the scenic drive along the shores of Devils Lake, the fort, and Sully's Hill

National Game Preserve with heavy woods, numerous wild birds, elk, deer, bison, and picnic grounds with play areas. Here the wind does not matter as it does out on the open plains. Continuing north, US 281 shortly arrives at the second of North Dakota's four Indian reservations. The land area of the Turtle Mountain Reservation is the smallest of the four, but the enrollment is the largest. Over nine thousand Indians are registered here, mostly Chippewa, although only half of them live in the county. Only part of the group is socially recognized as Indians, the others are of mixed blood, or *Metis*. These people are descended from an earlier Minnesota Chippewa tribe which was pushed out of the eastern Great Lakes region by the Iroquois and in turn (because they had Eastern firearms) drove the Sioux from the Minnesota woods onto the plains of the Dakotas. Once the Sioux adapted themselves to their new environment, they became a proud people who looked down on the Chippewa. Today there is no real animosity, although the Chippewa are largely confined to this area near the Canadian border, while the Sioux have three reservations of considerable size.

Indians Bearing Jewels

Rolla, just east of the Turtle Mountain Reservation, is a small farming town which paradoxically boasts the largest jewel bearing factory in the United States. Operated by the Bulova Watch Company for the Federal Government, this plant produces tiny jewels from synthetic sapphires for defense weapons and time-pieces. At Belcourt, within the reservation but still on the main highway, is the reservation headquarters. A few miles west an Indian-owned company makes and sells Chippewa gift items.

At Dunseith, the highway turns north again for a short run to the Canadian border. This area is perhaps the only one in North Dakota which looks a little like Minnesota, or Wisconsin, or Ohio, for there are trees, lakes, and hills. In some respects the more attractive drives and campgrounds are on the Canadian side, but they are reached with no fuss and no formalities. The International Peace Garden is really a series of gardens on both sides of the border. These are laid out in a formal and classic arrangement and are surrounded by two thousand acres of landscaped park. The gardens serve as a reminder that Canada and the U.S. have always been at peace and that there is no need to guard the border. It is merely marked at intervals. Near the Peace Garden is another wooded lake area, Lake Metigoshe State Park, reached from Bottineau. Although this border area is possibly the most beautiful part of the state, and North Dakota license plates bear the name "Peace Garden State," few state residents spend much time there. The one local attraction is the International Music Camp held each summer, with concerts and an art exhibit, on the U.S. side of the gardens.

Quite by coincidence, the geographical center of North America is only a half-hour's drive to the south, at Rugby on State 3. A monument designates the exact spot determined by the 1931 U.S. Geological Survey.

Through Cleveland to the West

Since we began this northern tour at Jamestown, we might mention that whether you stay on the east-west Interstate 94 or go north to the Peace Garden, the next destination is Bismarck, the capital city. Between Jamestown and Bismarck is the major flyway to Canada for ducks and geese. Obviously, it is a favorite place for hunters and makes North Dakota one of the most rewarding duck-hunting areas in the United States. The land has many hillocks and sloughs. It is here that most of the German-Russians settled after the railroad advertising lured them from South Russia. They spoke little English, and they were slow in adopting conservational methods of farming so that they lost most of their valuable topsoil during the dust bowls of the 1930's. Their story is included in Lois Phillips Hudson's excellent novel, *The Bones of Plenty*. Mrs. Hudson now lives in Washington, but she grew up near Cleveland, thirty miles west of Jamestown. To see the exact location of most of her story, drive only four or five miles south of Cleveland on a gravel road.

If you take the northern tour when you leave Rugby, drive west on US 2 to Minot. Once a railroad town made up mostly of tents, Minot is now one of the largest cities in North Dakota. It is just getting over its growing pains, having been fairly successful in getting rid of those elements which once made it a rather wide-open town. It is a relatively rich town, the center of a large agricultural district and of a field of lignite coal that amounts to billions of tons. Oil was discovered in this area, from Minot past Williston, and will bring in a great royalty in the future. Adding to the economy is Minot Air Force Base, a dozen miles north of the city. Because North Dakota guards the northern circle route between Russia and the Midwest, it has become an important defense center. Environmental protection is also important. Two wild life refuges extend away from the city, one of them having facilities for picnics and fishing.

Garrison Dam

South on US 83 about forty miles is Garrison, which gave its name to one of the largest earthen dams in the world. Part of the Missouri River Basin project, this dam is also one of the most important structures along the entire river. It is over two miles long, or wide, and also serves as the roadbed for State 200. Recreation areas have been constructed along the lake upriver from the dam, denying the fact that North Dakota is known as a water-less prairie. The dam's statistics are impressive, but its real importance is seen in flood control, recreation, and expanded possibilities for irrigation and cheaper electric power. For the water to back up some two hundred miles, three towns had to be eliminated. A new town was built for the displaced people and was called, appropriately, New Town. Most of the land covered by the lake is, or was, part of the Fort Berthold Indian Reservation, which lies on both sides of the river. About 2,500 Hidatsa (Gros Ventres), Arikara, and Mandan Indians are enrolled at the agency in New Town. However, in 1952, only 1,700 of these people were actually living on the reservation and there will be fewer each year because of the flooding of the Missouri Valley.

Bismarck and the West

Facing each other across the Missouri River, Bismarck and Mandan are still associated with cavalry and Indians. It is at this point, too, that the West begins. In some years the grass will be green on the east side of the river and brown on the west. Increasing aridity is one of the signs of going west. The peculiar mark of Bismarck is the state capitol, a white limestone and black granite skyscraper shooting up eighteen stories from the prairie. Many people have thought it ridiculous that in a land of wide expanses there should be a need for a skyscraper. However, it might be noted that North Dakota's flatland is dotted with grain elevators—white cylinders sticking up into the sky—and the capitol is at least a symbol of these important structures. Along with the ever-present hawks and geese, the capitol may also represent ''a looking up'' which has become part of the character of North Dakotans. The ''looking-back'' in Bismarck may be accomplished at the fine State Historical Museum, or the Camp Hancock Museum, or even at the memorial statue of Sacajawea, the Shoshone girl who gave much help to Lewis and Clark. Bismarck was the nearest settlement when Lt. Col. Custer (he was no longer a general, having lost his brevet commission) was preparing to go after Sitting Bull and Crazy Horse. It was to Bismarck that Custer's troop flocked for their off-duty entertainment, and it was to Bismarck that news first came of Custer's death. The people here still talk about Custer and debate his decisions and actions.

But the past, vivid as it still is, does not keep the people of Bismarck from going forward. Their city is as crisp, clean, and modern as any in the state. Bismarck sponsors the largest state-wide art show, usually in November. Because the city is more isolated than those in the eastern part of the state, the people are more ready to do things for themselves. As a result, the visitor is likely to feel that curious and wonderful Western combination of energy and relaxation which carries a city forward even while it remains immensely proud of its frontier past.

Fort Abraham Lincoln

Across the river, Mandan has some of the appearances of a frontier town and western clothing becomes even more evident. About five miles to the south is the site of Fort Abraham Lincoln, perhaps the historical and spiritual center of the state. Standing in one of the reconstructed blockhouses of Fort McKeen at the top of the hill, one sees a vast panorama of river, bluffs, coulees, Indian lodges, and Custer's old campground. It is almost possible to hear the bugles over the wind, and to see the troops riding up the draw to the west on their way to battle. It is an easy walk around the ruins of the old cavalry post, where troops, far from their eastern homes, led a crude life before they went out to chase Sitting Bull, many of them never coming back. Grouped loosely around a parade ground now in grass, the stone foundations are marked, and it is not difficult to imagine the incidents of 1875. An excellent museum nearby has exhibits showing details of that year and inexpensive books which explain the post, the Indians, and the cavalry.

Behind the museum once stood a Slant Indian village. Although Lewis and Clark spent the winter of 1804-05 a little farther upriver, it is likely that they also stopped here to visit the Indians. Several of the earth-lodges have been authentically restored, and the largest one may be entered as the Indians themselves once entered it. Below the village is a park on the shore of the river with camping and picnicking. Downriver is the site of Fort Rice, also prominent during the Indian wars. Farther south, about seventy miles from Bismarck, is the Indian community of Fort Yates. The older Standing Rock Sioux frequently sit in front of the grocery store at Fort Yates, reminiscing and telling their legends to eager visitors. It was at Fort Yates that Sitting Bull, mighty chief of the Sioux, was buried. His grave was opened one night in 1953 by South Dakota Indains who felt that the chief did not belong in North Dakota. They claim to have found Sitting Bull's bones, which they then reburied near Mobridge, South Dakota, However, North Dakotans say that the chief was originally buried in lime, so that there could be no bones. In any case, both states now claim to have the well-known chief, while almost a century ago no one wanted him. Meanwhile, in a fine Indian school at Fort Yates, the children of the chief's grandchildren are taught to forget Sioux and speak English. And the town attracts tourists to the lake formed by damming the Missouri River in South Dakota.

Roosevelt National Park

From Mandan west the interstate highway follows for a while the route taken by Custer when he set out after Sitting Bull. One hundred miles to the west lies the most spectacular part of North Dakota. The Badlands are now a part of Custer National Forest and also include Theodore Roosevelt National Memorial Park, the only national memorial park in the nation. Here one can see wild horses, or perhaps the bighorn sheep, as well as buffalo, deer, and antelope. Amusing prairie dogs have built several large towns and sit straight and alert by their holes. Coyotes, porcupines, bobcats, rabbits, beaver, and other small animals live within the park, while overhead soar hawks and an occasional eagle. The landscape has a strange and wild beauty, both in topography and in color. Hillocks, buttes, domes, cones, pyramids, and ridges are piled up along the Little Missouri River valley. Stripes of brown, red, gray, and yellow run across the buttes. Lignite veins stand out in black. Old fires of underground coal have burned pinks and reds into the clay. The vegetation has its colors too: blue-gray and silver of sage, light green of the rather scarce grass, dark green of the cedars, and the various colors of fruit from small trees and bushes. In addition to common flowers, the white gumbo lily grows here, and the purple and white Mariposa, as well as the lemon-yellow prickly pear cactus. Altogether, the Badlands are an exciting place.

Famous men have lived here. Theodore Roosevelt came to hunt in 1883 and returned to take part in the open range cattle industry. His first ranch was established seven miles south of Medora, and the second about thirty-five miles north. Because he was an easterner and wore thick glasses, he was labeled a "four-eyed dude," a name which was softly changed to "Old Four-eyes" after he subdued a local bully. The Marquis de Mores, a young, rich, handsome Frenchman, came west on a hunting trip at about the same time and decided to build a packing plant in the Badlands so that cattlemen need not ship east. Although his 1883 venture failed, de Mores left behind him a number of buildings, an impression not yet forgotten, and the town of Medora, which he founded and named after his wife. More recently, but still in the image of the West, Tom Mix, the early cowboy star of the screen, lived in Medora for a short time.

There are two major units in the Roosevelt Memorial park. The South Unit borders I-94. The North Unit is a half-hour drive to the north on US 85. Both units are reached from Belfield. Visitors should probably go first to Park Headquarters inside the Medora entrance to the South Unit. Here information can be obtained conerning the roads in the Badlands, places to see, campgrounds, trails, evening entertainment, and trailer space. Remember that a large segment of the Badlands is still wild, and the "eastern dudes" are not encouraged to go off alone without full information or advice from the rangers.

The De Mores Historic Site is immediately southwest of Medora and features the 26-room chateau, with many of the original furnishings, and the ruins of the packing plant. Nearby is the Medora Zoo with birds and animals native to the region in their natural surroundings. The town itself has a museum of fur trade, Indian, and wildlife collections, and one may see restored historic buildings within Medora.

PRACTICAL INFORMATION FOR NORTH DAKOTA

FACTS AND FIGURES. *Dakota* means "allies" in the Sioux language. The state's nicknames are *Flickertail State* and *Peace Garden State*. The state flower is the wild prairie rose; the state tree, the American elm; the state bird, the western meadow lark. "Liberty and Union, Now and Forever, One and Inseparable" is the state motto. "North Dakota Hymn" is the state song.

Bismarck is the state capital. The state population was 617,761 at the last census.

Lake Sakakawea, formed when the Garrison Dam was erected across the Missouri River, is the largest man-made fresh-water lake in the United States; 609 sq. mi. with 1,340 miles of shoreline.

The world's largest buffalo, a steel and concrete replica of those that once roamed freely across the prairies stands on a hill overlooking Jamestown.

The geographical center of the U.S., as determined by the Geological Survey, lies ½ mi. S of Rugby, N.D.

North Dakota is the only state that operates a state bank, Bismarck; and mill elevator, Grand Forks.

HOW TO GET THERE. *By air:* Northwest, North Central, and Frontier airlines fly into North Dakota principally from Minneapolis-St. Paul, Rapid City, and Billings.

By train: Amtrak passenger service is available from Minneapolis in the east and from Billings and Havre in the west stopping at Fargo, Bismarck, Williston and Grand Forks.

By bus: Greyhound, Continental and Interstate Transportation Co. are the major interstate carriers in North Dakota.

By car: I-94 and US 2 provide access to the state from Minnesota in the east and from Montana in the west. US 85, 83, 281, and 81 reach the state from South Dakota in the south and run through to Canada in the north.

HOW TO GET AROUND. *By air:* Frontier flies to Williston, Minot, and Bismarck. Northwest provides service among Bismarck, Fargo, and Jamestown and between Fargo and Grand Forks. North Central lands in Devils Lake, Grand Forks, Fargo, Bismarck, and Minot.

By train: Amtrak has two branch lines, one through Fargo, Grand Forks, Devils Lake, Minot and Williston, the other through Fargo, Jamestown, Bismarck and Dickinson.

By bus: in addition to the service provided by Greyhound, Continental, and Interstate Transporation Co., Star Bus Lines serves Grand Forks, Devils Lake and Minot and other local carriers connect the smaller cities.

By car: I-94 is the major east-west route across the southern portion of the state and US 2 across the northern. US 81, 281, 83 and 85 run north-south. US 52 extends in a rough diagonal from Fargo and Jamestown in the southwest to Minot, Kenmare, and Portal in the northwest.

TOURIST INFORMATION. The *Roughrider Guide to North Dakota* is a particularly useful summary of the principal attractions, parks, campgrounds, museums, and events in North Dakota. This brochure and other information are available from North Dakota Highway Dept., State Capitol Grounds, Bismarck 58501.

The Greater North Dakota Assn., Box 1781, Fargo 58102 also provides useful information.

SEASONAL EVENTS. *February:* The *Winterfest* in Minot at mid-month features curling and hockey competition, Festival of Ethnic Foods, snowmobile races, which include the Regina Minot Itasca International 250 Race, a beard-growing contest, and other exciting events.

March: At Valley City, early in the month, is the *North Dakota Winter Show,* the largest agricultural exposition in the northwest, which includes a livestock show and three-day rodeo. At the Winter Show Building, The *National Curling Finals* are held at Grand Forks.

May; Fishing Derby, Fort Totten: competitive fishing on Devils Lake. *Stock car racing* begins mid-month at Grand Forks Speedway. Beginning in late-month, the Fort Totten Reservation holds *powwow, horse and chariot races* Sun. afternoons through Sept. at Fort Totten.

June: Beginning in June for 8 wks. the *International Festival of the Arts* takes place in the International Peace Garden. A cultural festival, this features special activities in each area of the arts including dance, drama, music, fine art, sculpture, and crafts and performances by the International Music Camp participants. The *State Championship Horse Show* takes place mid-month at Rugby. On the Turtle Mountain Reservation at Belcourt there are *Sun Dance* and *Grass Dance* in early June. Late in the month there are the *Upper Missouri Valley Fair* at Williston and the *Centennial Celebration* at Grand Forks. The *Lewis and Clark Pageant,* at the Ft. Mandan Historic Site in Washburn, depicts the early explorers' era.

July: Dickinson hosts the *Roughriders Festival.* The *North Dakota State Fair* at Minot highlights fair activities with a midway, rodeo and entertainment. At mid-month, Bottineau hosts a *Water-Ski Carnival* at Lake Metigoshe. *Buffalo Days* at Jamestown offers several attractions including the Stutsman County Fair and State Dairy Show, historic trail rides between Ft. Ranson and Ft. Lincoln, and parades and rodeos. The *Red River Valley Fair* and the *State Machinery Show* are at Fargo.

August: Champions Ride Rodeo, at Home on the Range for Boys in Sentinel Butte, features the top rodeo riders and calf ropers in the world of rodeo. The *All-Indian Rodeo and Powwow* on the Fort Berthold Reservation at New Town.

September: The World Championship, All-American Indian Activities Association, Powwow and Rodeo Finals is a major Indian event in North Dakota. Held in early September on the Standing Rock Reservation at Fort Yates, it attracts Indians from all over the nation. The *Badlands Trail Ride* draws horseback riders from across the state for a six-day ride through the badlands area around Killdeer and Medora. *Annual Threshing Bee* at Edgeley consists of threshing on the grounds with steam and gas engines, large display of pioneer tools, rope making demonstrations, parades, and antique cars and trucks. In Fargo, the *Imagination Art Festival* focuses on the multiple arts available in the area including workshops, displays, demonstrations, and performaces in the visual, performing and popular arts. *Pioneer Days,* held in Bonanzaville, U.S.A., in West Fargo, demonstrate pioneer methods in action.

October: New Leipzig hosts the *Annual Sauerkraut Day, Wishek,* and the *October Fest* in community celebrations tied closely to the German population of the region.

December: Ski season begins.

NATIONAL PARKS. The *Theodore Roosevelt National Memorial Park* in western North Dakota is the nation's only national memorial park and a memorial to the 26th President who, in addition to his other vigorous pursuits, was a champion of conservation and natural resources.

Set in the area the Indians called *mako sica*—bad lands to cross—the Park displays the harsh natural beauty of canyons and valleys, of buttes and cliffs, shaped and molded by centuries of wind, water, and fire.

There are two major units to the Park: the South unit whose attractions include prairie dog towns, nature trails, burning coal veins, columnar junipers and a variety of wildlife; and the North Unit, 65 mi. N on US 85, which offers a majestic view of a more rugged section of the badlands. A third unit, Teddy Roosevelt's Elkhorn Ranch site on the Little Missouri River north of Medora, is accessible only over rough dirt roads. Consult Park Headquarters in Medora before setting out.

The rebuilt *Old West cowtown of Medora* is located at the entrance to the South Unit. Theodore Roosevelt and the Marquis de Mores made history here. The park headquarters has a visitor center and museum, open 8 to 8 in the summer and 8 to 5 in winter. Theodore Roosevelt's original Maltese Cross cabin stands nearby.

STATE PARKS. *Beaver Lake State Park,* 2 mi. N & 1 mi. E of Burnstad, offers swimming, fishing, picnicking, camping, and trailer space. *Fort Lincoln State Park,* 4 mi. S of Mandan on Rte. 1806, is on the Missouri River. It was from here that Custer set out on the disastrous Little Bighorn Expedition. Besides camping and picnicking, visitors can see the original fort site, restored blockhouses, Indian mounds and a museum. *Icelandic State Park* is 5 mi. W. at Cavalier, Rte. 5. Swimming, fishing and boating are available. Camping and trailers are permitted. *Lake Metigoshe State Park* is 13 mi. NE of Bottineau and is near the *International Peace Garden.* A variety of wildlife is found here, and deciduous forests, rolling glacial moraine and beautiful lakes make this one of the most attractive areas in the state where visitors can enjoy fishing, water sports, picnicking and camping. *Turtle River State Park,* 22 mi. W on Rte. 2, Grand Forks, in the forests of the fertile Red River Valley, has water sports, fishing, cabins, ski chalet, camping and winter facilities for summer and winter fun. *Lake Sakakawea State Park,* 1 mi. N of Pick City, has facilities for camping, boating, fishing, and swimming, picnicking and water-skiing on Lake Sakakawea. *Little Missouri Bay State Park* is 18 mi. N of Killdeer on Rte. 22. Located in some of the state's most rugged badlands terrain, this park offers camping, picnicking, canoeing, hiking, and horseback riding. There are no roads in the interior of the park. *Doyle Memorial State Park,* 7 mi. SE of Wishek, has primitive camping, picnicking, swimming and fishing. *Sully Creek State Park,* 2½ mi. S of Medora on the East River Rd., is an ideal area for horseback riders and offers primitive campgrounds, horse corral, and picnic area.

Entry fees at state parks are $1 per vehicle per day or $4 per vehicle for an annual permit. A fee of 50¢ per vehicle is charged for groups of ten or more traveling together. In addition, a $2 per night, $10 per week, or $15 annual camping fee is charged. North Dakota has approximately 200 camping areas. For a complete list and map write to the North Dakota State Travel Divison, Bismarck.

FARM VACATIONS AND GUEST RANCHES. *Joe J. Hansel Farm.* A working farm with cattle, ponies, pigs, chickens, geese. Riding and fishing. Serves one meal a day. Seven children. Meets all nearby transit. Rte. 1, Box 80, Langdon 58249.

CAMPING OUT. For a complete list of campgrounds and their facilities contact the North Dakota State Travel Division in Bismarck. Given below is a brief list of campgrounds at or near the major cities or tourist attractions.

Theodore Roosevelt National Memorial Park: in the South Unit, Cottonwood Campground has fishing, fireplaces, picnic tables, drinking water and flush toilets; North Unit, Squaw Creek Campground has playground, fireplaces, picnic tables, drinking water and flush toilets. There is no charge for use of the picnic or camp grounds and there are evening campfire programs in summer. Normally, the South Unit is more crowded than the North Unit.

Lake Sakakawea: Totten Trail Park, E of US 83 and S of Garrison jct., has swimming, fishing, boating, fireplaces, picnic tables, drinking water and pit toilets.

Devils Lake: Lakewood Park, 5 mi. SW of city, has swimming, fishing, boating, playground, fireplaces, picnic tables, drinking water and flush toilets.

Bismarck: General Sibley Campground, 4 mi. S on Washington St., has fishing, boating, playground, fireplaces, picnic tables, showers, drinking water, and flush toilets.

Fargo: Lindenwood Park, 5th St. and 7th Ave. S., has fishing, boating, playground, fireplaces, picnic tables, showers, drinking water and flush toilets.

Jamestown: Jamestown Reservoir-George's Landing, 7 mi. N on US 281 then 2 mi. E, has swimming, fishing, boating, playground, fireplaces, picnic tables, showers, drinking water and flush toilets.

Williston: Lewis and Clark Recreation Area, 18 mi. E on Rte. 1804 then 3 mi. S at Lake Sakakawea, has swimming, fishing, boating, drinking water, and flush toilets.

 TRAILER TIPS. Mobile home and camper trailer regulations are: length not more than 70 feet, width not over 8 feet, height not over 12½ feet. Wider mobile homes and trailers require special permits and are not allowed to travel at night, or on Saturday p.m., Sunday and holidays. Speed limit for all mobile homes is 50 mph.

In addition to the facilities already listed under *Camping Out,* the following areas also have trailer facilities.

Theodore Roosevelt National Memorial Park: in the South Unit, Cottonwood Campground has 53 trailer sites; Squaw Creek has 18 sites.

Lake Sakakawea: Totten Trail Park has large areas devoted to trailer sites; Fort Stevenson Recreation Area, 3 mi. S and 1/2mi. W of Garrison, has a large area devoted to trailer sites, sewage disposal and hookup, and 10 electrical connections in addition to complete campground facilities.

Devil's Lake: Lakewood Park has 30 trailer sites with electrical hookups.

Bismarck: General Sibley Campground has 120 trailer sites, 95 electrical hookups, and sewage disposal.

Fargo: Lindenwood Park has 40 trailer sites with 30 electrical hookups.

Jamestown: Jamestown Reservoir has 50 sites with 39 electrical hookups.

Williston: Lewis and Clark has 50 sites with electrical hookups and sewage disposal.

 MUSEUMS AND GALLERIES. Historical: *Bismarck: Historical Society Museum,* on the Capitol Grounds. The state collection of 19th-century Indian and pioneer artifacts can be seen Mon. through Fri. Another collection is at the *Camp Hancock Museum,* open mid-May to mid-Sept. *Devils Lake: Pioneer Museum,* at Fort Totten. Open June to Labor Day.

Art: *Grand Forks: University Art Gallery,* U of North Dakota. Features work of artists in and around North Dakota; regional grass roots art. Closed University holidays. *Medora: Western Gallery.* Pioneer quiltwork displays and sculpture and paintings by western artists. May to Oct.

Special Interest: *Abercrombie: Fort Abercrombie State Park Museum* features a rare Red River ox cart from the early fur trade, Indian artifacts, pioneer and military exhibits. *Fargo: Herbarium & County Museum,* in Minard Hall on University campus. *Grand Forks: University of North Dakota Zoology Museum. Jamestown: Fort Seward Historical Society, Inc.* General collection. June to Sept., *Stutsman County Memorial Museum,* Indian artifacts, medical, military and musical exhibits. June to Oct., Wed., *Mandan: Fort Abraham Lincoln State Park Museum.* Mandan Indian artifacts; 7th Cavalry and Custer. *Medora: Doll House Museum,* 18th-, 19th- & 20th-century dolls and toys. May to Oct. *Fur Trade, Wild Life, and Indian Museum,* May to Oct., *Wahpeton: Richland County Historical Museum,* housed in an old schoolhouse. *West Fargo: Bonanzaville, USA,* museum furnished with many artifacts telling the story of the early settlement days in North Dakota, located in the Cass County Fair Grounds. May to Labor Day.

HISTORIC SITES. Many sites and remnants of forts remain from the Indian wars. Perhaps the ones remembered best were associated with those two archfoes, Lt. Col. George A. Custer and Sitting Bull. Custer is often referred to as a "general," but he lost his brevet commission because of a number of "mistakes." Sitting Bull is known as the chief of the Sioux, but, in reality, he was the peace chief, or civil chief.

Custer commanded the 7th Cavalry at *Fort Lincoln:* from here he took his men to Montana where he and approximately 200 of his unit were killed. The fort is gone, but many of the foundations of the original building may be seen around the parade ground, about 5 mi. S of Mandan. The site of Custer's home is marked in Officers Row across the road. Up on the hill, in 1875, stood an infantry post, Fort McKeen. Three blockhouses have been rebuilt there. An excellent museum tells the story of Custer's fame and misfortune. The museum is open May through October. Near the museum stand reconstructed Indian earth lodges at a spot visited by Lewis and Clark in 1804.

Sitting Bull fled to Canada after Custer's death, but returned in 1881 to surrender at *Fort Buford,* 5 mi. W of Williston on US 2 and then 17 mi. SW following the signs. On the Missouri, the stone powder magazine and the officers' headquarters still stand. A military cemetery is nearby. Museum, open June 15 to September 15.

Medora, west end of the state on US 10, was the scene of many fascinating events involving Theodore Roosevelt and the Marquis de Mores. The Rough Riders Hotel gave its name to Roosevelt's regiment in the Spanish-American War. The Joe Ferris Store was visited often by Roosevelt. St. Mary's Catholic Church was built by the Marquis. All of these buildings date back to about 1885.

Just west of Medora, and ½ mile S of US 10, are the ruins of the De Mores packing plant and the intact 26-room chateau in which he lived. Admission charged, 8 a.m. to 5 p.m. Guided tours only. Closed when weather is bad.

The *Fort Mandan Historic Site,* 4 mi. W of Washburn, overlooks the site of the Lewis and Clark winter camp near the Mandan Indians. A pageant depicting the Lewis and Clark era is held annually in June.

Pembina Historic Site and Museum, 50 mi. NE of Grafton via US 81, I-29 in Pembina. This is the site of the first settlement in North Dakota established in 1812. The museum is open May 15 to Sept. 15.

Twenty-eight mi. NW of Ellendale is the *Whitestone Battlefield Historic Site.* This is the site of the largest major battle between whites and Sioux Indians east of the Missouri River.

The best preserved military post of the Indian Wars period in the Trans-Mississippi West is located at the *Fort Totten Historic Site* at Fort Totten. Fifteen original buildings remain with a museum and summer theater located on the site.

Fort Union National Historic Site, 5 mi. W of Williston on US 2, then SW on an unnumbered road. Fort Union was constructed as a fur trading post in 1828 at the confluence of the Yellowstone and Missouri Rivers. It was built and operated by the American Fur Company. The first steamboat, the "Yellowstone," owned by the Fur

Company, navigated the Missouri to Fort Union in 1832. Guided tours of the site are provided by National Park Service during summer months. (This Historic Site is shared with Montana.)

 FAMOUS LIBRARIES. The *Chester Fritz Library* on the campus of the University of North Dakota in Grand Forks has a display of Oriental tapestries and other art works. Open Mon. to Fri. 8 a.m. to 4:30 p.m.

 GARDENS. The *International Peace Garden,* with over 2,300 acres on both sides of the Canadian border, is 13 mi. N of Dunseith. Dedicated as a monument to the peaceful coexistence the United States and Canada have enjoyed for 200 years, the Garden forms a tranquil setting with flowers, trees, pools and walks. An all-faiths Peace Chapel with quotations from men of peace throughout history is an impressive sight. Camping, picnicking, and cabins are available. The Garden is open year-round, but the best time to visit is from May through September.

 MUSIC. The *International Music Camp,* held each summer at the International Peace Garden, has become recognized as one of the leading summer schools of fine arts in both the US and Canada. This unique cultural center includes instruction, performances and exhibits in all areas of the fine arts. On alternative years, a select group of 140 music students serve as "musical ambassadors" from the U.S. and Canada and present a series of good-will concerts throughout England, Western Europe, and North America. These tour bands and choirs have won top honors at three international youth music contests and festivals in Europe.

Through June and July, the International Music Camp gives Sun. afternoon concerts in the International Peace Garden led by internationally known guest conductors.

 STAGE AND REVUES. *Fort Totten Little Theatre,* in Old Cavalry Sq. of the Fort Totten Historic Site, offers summer musicals produced by the Devils Lake Community Theatre. Performances take place from July to mid-Aug. on Thurs., Sat., and Sun. at 8 p.m.

Sosondawah Amphitheatre, on the Dickinson State College campus, has summer melodrama productions from late June to July, Wed. to Sun. at 8:30 p.m.

Medora Musical, in the Gold Seal Amphitheatre 1 mi. SW of Medora. This stage production in an open-air theatre that overlooks the Medora countryside presents early Dakota territory history in a blend of comedy, music and special acts as a tribute to Theodore Roosevelt, the 26th Pres., who ranched in Medora as a young man. Performances nightly July 1 to Labor Day.

 DRINKING LAWS. Liquor can be purchased by the drink at bars and by the bottle at stores from 8 a.m. to 1 a.m. No liquor is sold on Sunday, after 6 p.m. on Christmas Eve and all Christmas Day, election day, and Memorial Day. Legal drinking age is 21.

 TOURS. *Theodore Roosevelt National Park,* located in the western North Dakota badlands, has a 28-mile circle scenic drive through the badlands. Wild animals abound. The earth formations are multicolored, and flowers bloom in odd places in the summer. For an unusual night scene, see the burning coal vein in the South Unit. For further ideas, talk to the rangers inside the Medora entrance to the park.

The *Lewis and Clark Trail,* which follows the scenic Missouri River through the heart of North Dakota, also parallels Lewis and Clark's famous Missouri River Expedition. Boat launching facilities, historic sites and recreation areas are located at several locations on the trail. The *Garrison Dam,* one of the largest rolled earth dams in the nation, and the 200-mile-long man-made lake, Lake Sakakawea, are part of the immense river system.

INDUSTRIAL TOURS. The *William Langer Jewel Bearing Plant* in Rolla offers tours to those who make appointments. Operated by the Bulova Watch Company for the federal government, this plant produces tiny jewels from synthetic sapphires for defense weapons and time-pieces. It is the largest jewel-bearing factory in the U.S.

Westgo Industries in West Fargo is a manufacturer of truck bodies, rock pickers and auger elevators as well as an installer of truck equipment and related items.

Rugby Creamery Company offers tours of their installation at 209 W. Dewey St. in Rugby which include a look at the making of cheese, butter, ice cream and at milk bottling.

SPECIAL INTEREST TOURS. *Sully Hill National Game Preserve,* 12 mi. SW of Devils Lake on State 57, has a self-guided auto tour through this scenic acreage where bison, elk, and deer can be observed in a near natural habitat. There are also flocks of ducks, geese and swans. Open May to Oct., daily 8 a.m. to sunset. The *Aububon National Wildlife Refuge* at Garrison Dam has a short auto tour for wildlife observation. Open daily during daylight hours.

The *Old Danish Mill* in Kenmare is one of six such mills in the nation. Built over 70 years ago, it could grind 200 bushels of grain a day. The millstones weigh 1,800 lbs., the wooden gears are hand hewn, and its mechanism still operates.

Bonanzaville, USA, restored in the tradition of the bonanza farm days, is located in West Fargo. A vintage church, school, barbershop, general store, theater and other historic buildings have been restored and furnished as they were in the early days of North Dakota statehood. A museum in the village helps tell the historic tale.

Frontier Village, on I-94 in SE Jamestown, is a reconstructed authentic frontier village with railroad depot, land office, fire hall, newspaper-print shop, jail, knick-knack shops, restaurant, drug store, barbershop, church, school, and log cabin. Towering above the village is the world's largest buffalo. This landmark, 46 ft. long and 26 ft. high, made of 60 tons of steel reinforced concrete, is a memorial to the vast herds of buffalo that once thundered across these prairies. Open Memorial Day to Labor Day.

SPORTS. *Fishing.* Major sport, particularly since completion of Missouri River dam. Small lakes included in 128 acres. All-year angling fine for perch, crappies, blue gills, catfish, and bullheads. Best winter fishing in well-stocked Garrison Reservoir. Game fishing great except March 27 to May 7, northern pike, muskellunge, walleye, sauger, trout, and bass. Non-resident license: week, $2; season, $6. "Whopper Club" membership (Game and Fish Department) for large catfish and pike. *Hunting.* Extremely popular. Whitetail deer throughout state; mule deer in west; antelope in southwest. Birds galore. One of the best duck areas in the United States. Pheasants in southern third of the state, geese coming down flyway from Canada enticing. Partridge; three kinds of grouse. Write Game and Fish Department, 2121 Lovett Avenue, Bismarck, North Dakota 58501 for further information. *Golf.* Eastern section best. Fargo boasts four courses. One of Grand Forks' two links, Lincoln Park, borders Red River. Wahpeton's Bois de Sioux course has elaborate 1966 clubhouse; Chahinkapa Park, next door, offers excellent swimming

pool. Sand greens found west of Valley City. The Travel Division has a complete list.
Swimming. In state parks and reservoirs. Along Missouri, water sports at Garrison,
Riverdale, New Town, Williston. Jamestown Reservoir and Ashtabula Reservoir (20
mi. N of Valley City) have complete aquatic facilities. Most towns over 10,000
population have pools. *Horseback riding.* Horse rentals and guided trail rides available at Rhame. Turtle River State Park at Arvilla, Medora. Peaceful Valley Ranch in
Theodore Roosevelt National Park and the Little Missouri Bay State Recreation Area
north of Killdeer. *Canoeing.* The water level is best in late May and early June but in
some cases canoeing on the rivers is possible into late fall. Some parts of the Missouri
River are recommended for experienced canoers only. For those unfamiliar with the
territory, county maps are available from the Maps Sales Division of the State
Highway Dept.

Skiing. There are six ski areas located at Devils Lake, Bottineau, Rolla, Endin-
burg, Arvilla and Fort Ranson. Cross-country skiing is becoming increasingly popular and the North Dakota countryside lends itself well to this sport. *Snowmobiling.*
Theodore Roosevelt National Park and all the state parks have snowmobiling trails.

SPECTATOR SPORTS. *Rodeo* is a big event in North
Dakota and nearly every town of any size sponsors one or
more throughout the year. Among the major events are North
Dakota State Fair at Minot and Roughrider Festival at
Dickinson. *Hockey:* the University of North Dakota Fighting Sioux in Grand Forks
competes in the Western Collegiate Hockey Association. The Canadian Estevan
Bruins, a semi-pro hockey team, thrills fans in Bismarck. *Curling:* The National
Curling Finals are held annually in Grand Forks and several other competitions take
place locally, particularly in the eastern and northern portions of the state. The
colleges offer *basketball* and *football* action. *Auto racing.* Stock car racing takes
place at the Grand Forks Speedway from mid-May to mid-Sept. on Fri. and hols.

WHAT TO DO WITH THE CHILDREN. Playground
facilities and parks are available at many towns in North
Dakota. A few areas have amusement centers and zoos. In
Bismarck, the Riverside Sertoma Park is located near the
Missouri River. It includes a playground. Next to the Park is the Dakota Zoo with over
100 species of native animals. The zoo is open mid-May through September. A
miniature train ride takes visitors through the zoo. The playground at *Devils Lake* is in
the Sullys Hill Game Preserve 14 mi. S of town. *Jamestown* features the world's
largest buffalo and Frontier Fort for the children. In *Minot,* the Roosevelt Park and
Zoo includes not only many animals but also a children's amusement park with a
swimming and wading pool.

In *Wahpeton,* children enjoy the zoo and birds at Chahinkapa Park on the Red
River while mom strolls through the gardens and dad plays golf (half in North Dakota
and half in Minnesota). An Old West adventure can be enjoyed at the restored
cowtown. *Medora.* Special features include: feeding of the elk and buffalo, the
Medora Zoo, Dollhouse Museum, art gallery, Medora Museum, and the Medora
Musical.

Williston's Spring Lake Park has wild animal collections, swimming, playgrounds
and hiking trails.

The *Fish Hatchery* at Garrison Dam produces northern pike, walleye, smallmouth
bass and rainbow trout for waters in the area. There is an aquarium where children can
get a close look at these different types of fish.

INDIANS. North Dakota has four American Indian Reserva-
tion locations across the state which are inhabited by the
Sioux, Mandan, Hidatsa, Arikara and Chippewa Tribes. A
South Dakota reservation known as the Lake Traverse Indian
Reservation extends a little into the southeastern corner of North Dakota.

The *Turtle Mountain Indian Reservation,* located about ten miles east of the International Peace Gardens and ten miles south of the Canadian border, is the home of the Turtle Mountain Band of Chippewa. Although the smallest in area (only two townships), this reservation has the largest population of the four. The tribal headquarters is located in the community of Belcourt. Area powwows are usually held in July.

The *Fort Totten Indian Reservation,* located just south of the city of Devils Lake, is the home of the Sisseton-Wahpeton Sioux Tribe, better known as the Devils Lake Sioux. A well-preserved Cavalry Post stands on this reservation land. The tribal headquarters is located in the community of Fort Totten. A number of rodeos and powwows are conducted from spring to early fall.

The *Fort Berthold Indian Reservation,* located near the center of the western half of North Dakota, is the home of the Three Affiliated Tribes (Mandan, Hidatsa, Arickara). This reservation is divided into five segments which surround beautiful Lake Sakakawea. A forty-unit motel is owned and operated by the tribes on the Four Bears Recreation Complex. The tribal council office is located in the community of New Town. Rodeos and powwows are held throughout the summer months.

The *Standing Rock Indian Reservation,* located on the west bank of Oahe Reservoir (Missouri River), also extends into South Dakota. The North Dakota portion includes all of Sioux County. The tribal council headquarters is located in the community of *Fort Yates.* Chief Sitting Bull was buried at Fort Yates. Also at Fort Yates is a statue of the Indian woman who turned to stone when she looked around, this incident giving its name "Standing Rock" to the area. Powwows and rodeos are held at various communities throughout the summer months.

All of the above reservation locations offer an abundance of recreational activity. Your visit will be quite welcomed at any one of these areas.

RECOMMENDED READING. *The History of North Dakota* by Elwyn B. Robinson is a good general history of the state. Two other excellent books deal with specific periods: *Nothing but Prairie and Sky: Life on the Dakota Range in the Early Days* by Walker D. Wyman and *The Day of the Bonanza* by Hiram Drache.

HOTELS AND MOTELS. in North Dakota are mostly geared to family travelers and, although the summers are short, the frequent heated swimming pools can be used for several marginal months of the year. Rates are lower here than most other states.

The price categories in this section, for double occupancy, will average as follows: *Deluxe* $24, *Expensive* $20, *Moderate* $16, and *Inexpensive* $12. For a more complete description of these categories, see the *Hotels & Motels* section of THE ROCKIES & PLAINS *Facts at Your Fingertips* at the front of this volume.

BISMARCK

Holiday Inn. *Expensive.* A large member of this well-known chain. Family rates. Inroom coffee, restaurant, cocktail lounge, room service. Spacious nicely furnished rooms. Indoor heated pool, recreation area, playground. Kennels for pets.

Seven Seas Inn. *Expensive.* Overlooking Bismarck and Mandan, this large motel is within minutes of the State Capitol. Children under twelve, free. Lounge and dining room with nautical atmosphere. Indoor pool, whirlpool, elevator and meeting facilities.

Town House Motor Inn. *Expensive.* Located just north of the State Capitol grounds. Offers indoor heated pool, sauna, putting green. Lounge and dining room. Family rates.

Bismarck Motor Hotel. *Moderate.* Partly two-story, this medium-sized motel has family rates. Recreation area. Restaurant next door.

Fleck House Motel. *Moderate.* Two-story medium-size downtown motel with large attractive, air-conditioned rooms. Family rates. Pool. 24-hour restaurant nearby.

CARRINGTON

Chieftain Motor Lodge. *Inexpensive.* A medium-size motel. Family rates and connecting units. Restaurant, cocktail lounge, coffee shop. Tastefully decorated. Complete meeting facilities. Private collection of Indian artifacts and antique gems.

Del Clair. *Inexpensive.* Large rooms and family rates. Pool privileges. Restaurant adjacent.

DEVILS LAKE

Artclare. *Moderate.* Besides connecting units, there are two-room units and efficiencies. Recreation area. Lounge and restaurant. Indoor heated pool.

Davis Motel. *Inexpensive.* Located in an area of good hunting and fishing, this small motel offers air-conditioned comfort. Several drive-ins and restaurant nearby.

DICKINSON

Nodak. *Moderate.* A small motel but with a variety of accommodations including connecting units, two-room units, four kitchenettes, and two housekeeping apartments. Heated pool, recreation area. Restaurant nearby.

FARGO

Fargo-Biltmore. *Expensive.* An attractive and excellent large two-level motel with everything the modern traveler wants. Good restaurant, cocktail lounge. Spacious rooms. Heated pool, children's area.

Kahler Motel. *Expensive.* On nicely landscaped grounds with spacious, tastefully decorated rooms. Inroom coffee, restaurant, cocktail lounge. Heated pool and playground. Meeting facilities.

Motel 6. *Inexpensive.* Heated pool. 24-hour cafe adjacent.

GRAND FORKS

North Star Inn. *Moderate.* A medium-size, very attractive motel with excellent restaurant. Lounge, indoor pool and recreation area. Family rates. Meeting facilities.

Plainsman Motel. *Moderate.* Medium-size motel with gift shop. Weekly rates available. Babysitting service offered at small hourly cost. Restaurants and shopping areas nearby.

Westward Ho. *Moderate.* There is a variety of things to do for the family at this medium-size motor hotel, including lawn games, miniature golf, a putting green, model Western village, and pool. Family rates. The motel has well-decorated rooms. Chuck House Ranch is an excellent restaurant with entertainment in lounge. Pets. A good place to stop.

JAMESTOWN

Tumbleweed. *Moderate.* Up the hill from Ranch House. Indoor heated pool. Restaurant and lounge. Family rates. Spacious paneled rooms.

Jamestown. *Inexpensive.* This medium-size motel has 24-hour cafe nearby. Free airport bus.

MEDORA

Bad Lands Motel. *Moderate.* All rooms in this large motel have two double beds. Pool. Pets welcome. Dining facilities in *Rough Riders Hotel.*

Rough Riders Motel. *Moderate.* All rooms have one double bed and air-conditioning. Pool privileges. Dining facilities in *East Room* and *Chuck Wagon Cafeteria.*

MINOT

Ramada Inn. *Expensive.* Restaurant, coffee shop, cocktail lounge with entertainment, room service. Indoor heated pool. Meeting and banquet facilities. Airport courtesy car.

Sandman. *Moderate.* A medium-size motel with well-furnished rooms. Restaurant, room service, recreation room. Heated pool. Meeting facilities.

Thunderbird Motel. *Moderate.* Located across from State Fairgrounds. A small motel with restaurant adjacent.

WAHPETON

Valley Motel. *Inexpensive.* Back from highway. On expansive grounds. Family rates and connecting units. Indoor pool, open year round. *Kelly's Restaurant, Bar and Lounge* next to motel.

WILLISTON

El Rancho. *Moderate.* This medium-size motor hotel offers varied accommodations, including larger new rooms, some with kitchens. Restaurant, cocktail lounge. Heated pool, recreation area.

Dandy Motel. *Inexpensive.* Very clean, old and small motel. Nine units with kitchenettes. Restaurant and stores nearby. Pets allowed. Weekly rates available.

 DINING OUT. North Dakotans like good food, but they lean heavily to steaks and other staples. One does not often find exotic foods (even at high prices) in the state. When these people go out to have a special treat, they do not expect fancy trimmings, just good food. The listing below categorizes each restaurant according to the medium-priced items on its menu.

Restaurant price categories are as follows: *Deluxe* $8.50 and up, *Expensive* $6-$8, *Moderate* $3.50-$5.50, and *Inexpensive* $2-$3.50. These prices are for *hors d'oeuvre* or soup, *entrée,* and dessert. Not included are drinks, tax and tips. For a more complete explanation of restaurant categories refer to THE ROCKIES & PLAINS *Facts at Your Fingertips* at the beginning of this volume.

BISMARCK

Gourmet House. *Moderate.* W of the Missouri River Bridge. A reliable, charming restaurant specializing in steak, lamb, and lobster at lunch and dinner. Cocktail lounge.

Jerry's Supper Club. *Moderate.* A steak and seafood restaurant with a lot of local clientele. Children's plates.

DEVILS LAKE

The Ranch. *Moderate.* Rustic Western decor in a remodeled barn. Steak is the specialty. Cocktails, children's plates.

DICKINSON

Esquire Steak House. *Moderate.* Watch your steak or other specialty being broiled at this locally popular restaurant. Also serves seafood, chicken, and spaghetti. Cocktails.

FARGO

Black Angus. *Expensive.* Offers daily luncheon buffet. Steaks and seafood served during the evening. Nightly entertainment in the *Red Ram Lounge.*

Tale of the Whale. *Expensive.* Located in the Fargo-Biltmore Motor Hotel, this restaurant features steaks, seafood, and several gourmet dinners for two. Each dinner is complete with salad bar, homemade breads.

GRAND FORKS

Palace Dining Room. *Expensive.* Located in the Westward Ho Motel, this restaurant offers such specialties as Chateaubriand and lobster thermidor.

The Bronze Boot. *Moderate.* Features steaks broiled over an open charcoal pit, and chops, Chinese food. Lunch is chuck-wagon style. Cocktails.

JAMESTOWN

Mac's. *Moderate.* A well-recommended family restaurant, not large, but very pleasant. Ham, beef, chops are served.

MINOT

Gordon's Holiday Spot. *Moderate.* Fine beef and chicken specialties but with a general menu. Cocktails.

RUGBY

Andrew's Steak House. *Moderate.* Popular in the area, this restaurant serves seafood and chicken as well as steak. Children's plates. Bar and lounge.

VALLEY CITY

Howard's. *Moderate.* Next to Flickertail Inn. Popular in a rather wide area. Specialties are steak and ribs. Cocktails.

SOUTH DAKOTA

Black Hills and Badlands

by

JOHN R. MILTON

John R. Milton teaches literature and writing at the University of South Dakota and has recently published books on Oscar Howe and Crazy Horse. He has lived in both North and South Dakota.

If the traveler could get high enough above the state and look down, he would see South Dakota has four major physical features: the eastern prairie, the Missouri River, the western plains, and the Badlands and Black Hills. Of these, the river is most important. It enters from the north, bisects the state as it flows south, and then turns to become the southeast boundary for 150 miles. The two parts of the state, separated by the river, are often known locally as East-river and West-river, leading to occasional rivalry in politics, economics, and sports. East of the river are the major colleges and universities, all but one of the population centers, gently rolling farm lands, and pheasants to attract hunters from all over the world. West of the river are the Black Hills, most of the state's Indian reservations, and millions of acres of wide-open cattle country. The climate at the eastern edge of the state is much like that in Minnesota and Iowa, while at the western end the air is drier and the wind blows more often.

Physically, then, South Dakota has all the variety of a transition region. From the climate and elevation (965 feet) of the Midwest, it climbs to high plains (3,500 feet) and Harney Peak (7,242 feet), and comes to resemble the West. Again, the Missouri River is the rough line which divides the two quite different regions.

It was up the Missouri that Lewis and Clark boated and portaged on their historic journey of exploration from St. Louis to the Pacific Ocean. They were not, however, the first white men to enter what is now South Dakota. Chevalier de la Verendrye, French explorer, reached the center of the state in 1743, near today's Pierre, the state capital. The first known "settler" was Pierre Dorion, who married a Sioux woman and lived on the lower James River in 1775. Dorion later served as a guide for Lewis and Clark; their trip out in 1804 and back in 1806 opened the immense northwest country to commerce, particularly fur trading. Their journals mark the beginning of the literature of South Dakota.

Not until half a century later did Dakota become much more than a wilderness which fur traders had to cross in going from St. Louis to the richer fur trapping regions of the Northwest. The establishment of Dakota Territory in 1861 and the Homestead Act of 1862 brought in the first long-term settlers, although half of them left the territory during the 1862 Sioux uprising in nearby Minnesota. A larger wave of homesteaders arrived with the railroads in the 1870's, and men of adventure were lured across the territory by the promise of gold in the Black Hills. Lt. Colonel George A. Custer's expedition discovered gold in 1874, perhaps the most important incident in South Dakota history. A year earlier, much of the nation had gone into bankruptcy, and finding of gold helped both financially and psychologically to bring recovery from panic. On the other side of the ledger, the discovery brought about a series of Indian wars with the Sioux who resented this invasion of their holy land. Custer's famous defeat at Little Bighorn brought a call for reprisal and led to even further bloodshed throughout the territory.

By the time South Dakota was admitted as a state in 1889, four groups inhabited the area within its borders—farmers in the eastern section, miners in the Black Hills, and cattlemen and Indians in between. Later, Hamlin Garland and Ole Rölvaag were to write about the stark life of the farmers, while a host of novelists exploited the romance and myth of the other groups. For a century, South Dakota has had this double image.

Today the cowboy still rides his horse, and there remain large herds of buffalo in the western part of the state, but jeeps and light airplanes are also used to round up both cows and buffalo. Despite disastrous blizzards in 1873, 1880-81, and 1888, the cattle industry which began shortly after the Civil War still flourishes. Some farming operations have penetrated the range land. More gold is still produced in the Black Hills than anywhere else in the nation, and silver and twenty-seven other minerals are mined in commercial quantity. The Indian population has grown a little, with about 32,000 currently living in the state. More than 27,000 of them are on the nine reservations.

Men of the Soil

So although the marks of the Old West remain in South Dakota, the major industry is agriculture, including crops and livestock. The dust bowl of the 1930's was a major tragedy still vividly remembered, but South Dakotans come from hardy stock (including Swedish, Norwegian, German, Dutch, and German-Russian) and have recovered nicely. Even the absence of defense plants during World War II did not seriously injure the economy of the state. South Dakota is one of the few debt-free states in the nation. Its people have been accustomed to saving money. They do not launch out into building and expansion until there is an absolute need for it. The early residents were men of the soil—strong, enduring, and not inclined toward frivolity or luxury. Yet, the very first influx of settlers came not from Europe but from the neighboring states of Iowa, Wisconsin, Minnesota, and Illinois, and these were people who had come into contact with the cultures of the eastern United States. This has meant that South Dakotans have been basically conservative and religious, but there is an element which is cultured, well-educated, inclined toward liberalism, and often dissatisfied with the slowness and the "leave-things-as-they-are" attitude of its fellow citizens. Even this group, however, has been influenced by the land and the sky and generally chooses to remain in South Dakota in order to enjoy the freedom and open spaces of a region as yet relatively unpopulated.

The population of South Dakota has doubled in the last seventy years but remains low at around 665,000. The state is 55 per cent rural. Of its people who are engaged in manufacturing, 36 per cent live in one city—Sioux Falls. There is room to move around in, which the residents of the state appreciate. The population does not increase at the same pace as the birth rate, which suggests that the young people often leave the state to find better opportunities for employment, more money, and a more diversified social and cultural life. Those who stay are a curious mixture of the pioneer-cowboy and the sophisticated modern. Close proximity to Minneapolis, Denver, and Omaha, and easy driving without the congestion found on eastern and coastal highways, means frequent participation in city life. The word "conservative" in South Dakota really means "independent." The people want to be individuals; they fear big government and large and lonely cities.

However, they are uneasy, because the old way of life does not buy the many things which modern life seems to require; such as bigger schools, wider highways, and increased luxury. Interstate highway construction has proceeded rapidly, but only because it need not deal with metropolitan difficulties. Books and paintings are not quite considered luxuries, but neither are they easily available. South Dakota, in effect, is still a pioneer state in many ways, just beginning to feel the pressures of complex society. Its people are friendly and easy-going, not taking well to formality and artificiality. They would like to remain that way, even while meeting the problems of the modern world.

EXPLORING SOUTH DAKOTA

Like its sister state to the north, South Dakota has been known throughout the rest of the country for its summer droughts and winter blizzards because writers such as Hamlin Garland and Ole Rölvaag gave this impression half a century ago. While the state's weather and terrain do vary markedly at times, the overall picture is not discouraging. An increasing number of visitors annually discover that South Dakota is both exciting and comfortable at almost any time of the year. Because it is big and has relatively few people (16th in size and 44th in population), points of interest are often far apart by Eastern standards; yet, it is possible to drive across the state in either direction in one day at moderate speeds. The two largest cities, Sioux Falls and Rapid City, are situated at opposite ends of the state along the same major highway, I-90. A north-south highway (I-29) is complete from State 28 to the southern tip.

Where Iowa, Minnesota, and South Dakota come together, just a little east of Sioux Falls, is the center of a region called "Siouxland" by most of the people, by the newspapers, and by the television stations. The name was first applied by novelist Frederick Manfred, who is claimed by all three states.

Indians of Sioux Falls

Sioux Falls itself has been closely associated with the Sioux Indians. First established at the falls of the Big Sioux River, the town was abandoned in 1862 when the Indians went on a rampage in what is now referred to as the Sioux Uprising. The town remained deserted until May 1865, when a fort was built and the settlers returned to stay and found the present city. As for the Indians, the Pettigrew Museum, Eighth Street and Duluth Avenue, has an excellent collection of their arts and crafts, including a cowhide Blackfoot tipi and a large gun collection. In marked contrast to its stormy past, Sioux Falls now boasts the first nuclear equipment in a commercial plant to be used for super-heating steam. The Pathfinder Atomic Power Plant, seven miles northeast on Brandon Road (County 140), is open to visitors almost every day of the year. Add a third fact: the Sioux Falls Stock Yards are at or near the national top in activity. This, then, is a good picture of modern-day South Dakota: Indian lore, agriculture, and splitting atoms.

Animals—Alive and Kicking

Sioux Falls is a bustling city of 77,000 with fine stores, elegant residential areas, parks, and two colleges, Augustana and Sioux Falls. As the city expands and new highways are built, the residents fully expect that Sioux Falls will be the important crossroads of the northern region. Some of the more impressive commercial concerns are several first-class printing companies. In terms of volume, however, the leading industries are the stock-yards and packing companies.

Sioux Falls has live animals, too. Its Great Plains Zoo near the west edge of town, just off US 16 in Sherman Park, is one of the finest small zoos in the country. In addition to those animals and birds which are found on the Plains, the zoo exhibits llamas and lions, and others. Adjoining the zoo is a children's park with a jet plane, army tank, fire engine, and other items which may be climbed on and played in. Four blocks away, in the same park, see a 1,600-year-old Indian burial mound.

Because, in a sense, the heart of the nation is its livestock industry, visitors may take a two-hour tour of the Morrell Meatpacking Plant at 1400 North Weber Avenue and the Sioux Falls Stock Yards. Approximately 100 beef, 200 sheep, and 750 hogs are processed at Morrell's every hour. Needless to say, it is not difficult to get an unusually good meal in Sioux Falls—featuring beef on the plate. Beef on the hoof is a common sight on every farm in the surrounding area, and you will see the herds as you leave Sioux Falls and drive north on US 77. At Dell Rapids the Sioux River has cut a gorge through the red quartzite, forming the Dells. For a close look, leave the car and walk on the top of the cliffs. Then, continue north on I-29 to

Brookings, home of South Dakota State University. Coughlin Campanile is 165 feet high and has been named "The Singing Silo" by students. In the South Dakota Memorial Art Center there is a collection of paintings by Harvey Dunn, many of which were used as national magazine cover illustrations. Tours may be made of the 960-acre farm run by the Agriculture Experimental Station.

The northeast corner of the state, above Brookings, is lake country. Watertown, on US 81, has a large lake with recreation areas. The Mellette House, 421 Fifth Avenue Northwest, which has been restored and furnished in the style of the 1880's, was the home of the first governor of South Dakota. At Milbank, on US 77, a monument marks the birthplace of American Legion Junior Baseball. Here also are the world's largest mahogany granite quarry, the only granite bowling lanes, and a windmill (near railroad depot) built in 1885. The agency for the Sisseton-Wahpeton reservation is located in Sisseton, north again on US 81. Turn west twenty miles to Lake City for excellent fishing. This is where Inkpaduta, a renegade Indian, held white women as hostages during the Indian wars. One of the best-preserved forts of that time is seven miles west of Lake City and about the same distance south. Fort Sisseton was built in 1864 at a cost of two million dollars, with bricks being hauled in from St. Cloud, Minnesota, supplies from St. Paul, and many stones from as far away as Wahpeton, North Dakota. During the 1880's, the fort was the social center of the eastern half of Dakota Territory.

Webster, south on State 23, has one of the five salt-water conversion plants in the U.S. A guided tour is available. The plant is used to make fresh water from brackish water. Aberdeen, west of Webster on US 12, is a railroad town and farm shipping center which was settled largely by German-Russian immigrants. Two authors lived here, L. Frank Baum who wrote the *Wizard of Oz* stories, and Hamlin Garland whose homestead is near Ordway.

US 281 runs straight and fast south from Aberdeen. For almost one hundred miles, to Huron, there is little to see except fields. But, this is the world-famous pheasant country. The problem is often not one of finding pheasants, but avoiding them. At certain times of the year they literally swarm across the highway at intervals, and the motorist must slow down and keep a careful watch. The bird has been memorialized in Huron, on US 14 near Memorial Park, with a steel and fiberglass statue, forty feet high, billed as the world's largest pheasant. Huron seems to like big things: the high school auditorium seats 8,000. The town itself, however is small and pleasant. Huron College is on Illinois Avenue. Huron is the hometown of former Vice-President Hubert H. Humphrey. The pharmacy in which he worked his way through college is still owned by the family who employed him and still in business.

From Huron it is only an hour's drive south on State 37 to the Mitchell Corn Palace. This huge building looks more Oriental than Midwest with turrets and spired domes that soar into the South Dakota sky and flags and pennants that wave in the breeze. Each year the outside of the building is decorated in murals made of colored corn and cereal grasses. Two to three thousand bushels of corn are needed to make the designs. Late in September an elaborate festival is held here, at Main and Sixth streets. Near the campus of Dakota Wesleyan University is a museum sponsored by a unique organization, The Friends of the Middle Border. Among the people who began this venture were Hamlin Garland, John Dewey, and James Adams. The Middle Border Museum of Pioneer Life maintains six buildings not far from I-90 and State 37. A full day could easily be spent here.

If you take time to talk with the small-town people in the eastern half of South Dakota, you will find them friendly, genuine, and perhaps a bit homey or unsophisticated. Some are reserved, but all are willing to help a stranger. They are Norwegian, German, Czech, Dutch, Swedish, and Danish in background, although in some towns (especially those with the colleges) there is a more diverse population. Withal, the most exciting place in this half of the state is Gavins Point, near Yankton. From Mitchell take State 37 south to State 50, then east to Yankton. As you reach the edge of town, you will see the beautiful Gothic buildings of Mount Marty College and Sacred Heart Hospital. Turn right (west) on State 52 for approximately four miles. Stop first at the Federal Fish Hatchery and Aquarium, where you can see rainbow trout, catfish, bass, northern pike, and other fish. In the hatchery building there are hatching jars which hold up to forty million eggs. The aquarium has thirteen display tanks, each fitted realistically with rocks, tree trunks, and gravel. The huge catfish and sturgeon vie for attention, but the most fascinating fish is a prehistoric carryover, the paddle fish. He has a long flat paddle instead of a nose, and is found in only two places in the world: the Missouri River and the Yangtze River in China.

Fishing in Lewis and Clark Lake

Just above the hatchery turn left and drive across the mile-long earthen dam which backs up the Missouri to form Lewis and Clark Lake. The power plant, located on the Nebraska side of the river, is open to visitors. A new visitors center is perched higher on the bluffs. The Missouri River was one of the mightiest in the world until partially tamed by six dams in South Dakota, North Dakota, and Montana. The dams have altered the land, changed the psychology of the people, and provided immense potential in irrigation and electric power. The lakes created range from forty to more than two hundred miles long. They currently provide some of the best fishing in the nation. As you watch speedboats and fishermen, remember Lewis and Clark came up this fearsome river in keelboats propelled by hand. Nearby, up the bluff, they made camp and held their first formal council with the Sioux Indian nation. This was the site of the main camp of the Yankton tribe of Sioux, and one occasionally finds arrowheads, beads and pieces of pottery along the lake shore, washed up by the river which swallowed the old Indian villages.

Back on the South Dakota side of the river many attractions await your pleasure. At the marina there are boats available for fishing or sightseeing. For almost forty miles up the river (take State 52 and be prepared to turn off on the side road of your choice) there are many areas for picnicking, camping, or exploring. Near the dam and marina is Fort Dakota, built recently to resemble an authentic frontier city inside stockade walls. Meals and refreshments are available here, and a small train takes passengers on a mile-long trip around the grounds. The stockade includes a schoolroom, a jail, a newspaper office, a chapel, a soda parlor, and a saloon, all done in frontier style.

It would be easy to spend several days on Lewis and Clark Lake, but for accommodations it is necessary to return to Yankton. This is a small, unassuming city, which was perhaps the scene of more historical events than any other place in the state. Its many 19th-century houses give it an air of dignity, and much of its tradition has been set by Yankton College, the first in Dakota Territory. Yankton was the territorial capital before South Dakota became a separate state, and the first legislature met in the home of William Tripp. The house has been restored as a museum in Waterworks Park overlooking the river. When the Indians rebelled in 1862, a stockade was erected at Third and Broadway to protect residents of both Yankton and Sioux Falls. The oldest daily newspaper in the state is still being published on Walnut Street. Its first issue appeared during the Black Hills gold rush of 1875, and a year later it carried the story of Custer's death under these angry and biased headlines: "Telegraphic: Death. Custer and His Entire Command Swept out of Existence by the Wards of the Nation and the Special Pets of Eastern Orators." To the settlers who lived in the midst of a clear danger the Indian was simply a menace. Modern South Dakotans have also been slow in changing that early opinion, so that Indians must still fight hard for recognition. Nevertheless, the state has been represented by a Sioux Congressman.

Wild Bill Hickok's Killer

As in most Western towns, the old and the new blend nicely. A marker shows where Jack McCall was hanged for the murder of Wild Bill Hickok, and a sign explains somewhat apologetically that his was the last hanging in South Dakota, 1877. At Second and Capital streets, the Gurney Seed and Nursery Company is one of the largest of its kind, doing mail order business throughout the United States. Do not leave Yankton without enjoying a steak at *The Black Steer,* 300 East Third, an outstanding steakhouse in a region which prides itself on good beef. Continue east on State 50 to Vermillion, the last stop on our tour of the eastern half of the state.

Because of the constant threat of flooding by the Missouri, Vermillion is a river town which had to be relocated on higher ground. Lewis and Clark stopped here, getting out of their keelboats and walking a few miles north to Spirit Mound (now on State 19), held sacred by the Indians. Thirty years later, the American Fur Company built a fort on the river, and in 1843 John James Audubon, the famous naturalist and wildlife painter, visited the fort and walked through the present city. Vermillion is a typical sleepy town except for the University of South Dakota which gives it a cosmopolitan atmosphere and keeps it growing. The story is told that when Yankton was being considered as the capital for the new state, Sioux Falls was given first choice of state institutions; Vermillion had second choice. Sioux Falls took what to them seemed a sure thing, the state penitentiary, and has regretted the decision ever since. Vermillion chose the state university. Its first president (and lone faculty member) was Dr. Ephriam Epstein, a Russian Jew who had become a Baptist clergyman only to organize a secular university.

Cultural Center

Vermillion is the cultural center of the state, because of the activities of the University. It has a collection of old documents and historic newspapers in the library, and it has the excellent but crowded W. H. Over Dakota Museum on East Clark Street. Here are Indian relics, firearms, stones, fossils, a Pioneer Room, an Indian panorama, and the Arne B. Larson collection of old musical instruments, one of the largest anywhere. The museum also has a widely known collection of pioneer and military photographs which are often used to illustrate books about the Old West. A number of Indian activities are associated with the museum and with specific Indian organizations on campus.

Carrying the past into the present, Oscar Howe, a Sioux Indian who is artist-in-residence at the university, paints with the symbols of his ancestors but gives them contemporary designs and meaning. Winner of many national competitions, Mr. Howe finds his paintings in great demand. His studio and gallery are in the museum. Also working in contemporary techniques but basing his themes on regional history is Dr. Robert Marek, musical composer. The *South Dakota Review,* emphasizing Western American literature and regional writing, is published at the University. Frederick Manfred is writer-in-residence. The university radio and television stations, under the current direction of Martin Busch, are leaders in their field, producing programs of a regional emphasis which appear on educational channels throughout the Midwest. The university is active in many other areas which affect the state as a whole, including research centers in social work, psychology, speech and hearing, government, and geology.

A fast, pleasant drive back to Sioux Falls (I-29) completes the tour of Eastern South Dakota.

The western half of South Dakota is in some ways a different country altogether, with greater aridity, fewer trees and people, wider and more open spaces, and drier air which is easier to breathe. There are more Indians, and, until you get to the Black Hills, everything is farther apart. This means that the traveler must decide whether to head straight for the Hills or to devote at least several days to seeing many fort sites or Indian reservations. The Missouri River flows southward across the state, and is the dividing line between the two halves of the state. It is crossed by five major highways, four of which go to the Black Hills, and by two state roads.

US 12 crosses at Mobridge, in the north. The municipal auditorium at Mobridge has several murals by Oscar Howe depicting the ceremonies and historical events of his Indian people. The Land of the Sioux Museum, at the north end of Main Street, has Indian relics. Again you are in the middle of Sioux country. Sitting Bull was born and was slain not far from Mobridge. A monument to his memory stands on a hill with an exceptional view of the Missouri and its valley, three miles west on US 12 and two miles south on an unnumbered road. Whether the old chief really rests beneath his monument is a matter of debate: South Dakotans say yes, he does, and North Dakotans say no, it is impossible. Wakpala, north about ten miles on US 12 and then east at Sherwood's Corners (saloon and filling station) on a dirt road, is the location of St. Elizabeth's School for Indians. The director of the school from 1958 to 1961 was William McK. Chapman, former editor for *Time, Sports Illustrated,* and *House and Garden.* In 1965 Chapman published a book devoted entirely to his experiences at Wakpala. *Remember the Wind: A Prairie Memoir,* destined to make Wakapala a good deal more famous than it had been, is both humorous and tragic in its presentation of the Sioux Indians.

To the south again, Highway 212 crosses the river west of Gettysburg and then goes through the center of the Cheyenne River Indian Reservation. This is lonely country. South once more, US 14 passes through Pierre at the river. Pronounced "peer" by the natives, this is the capital city of South Dakota. Rich in history, it has not yet become a modern or impressive city. Early fur trade centered around the fort which was across the river, and the current economy is based on government almost as mush as on cattle and crops. The state legislature is highly conservative and boasts of keeping the state out of debt. In fact, the state has a surplus in its treasury, a condition almost unbelievable in this day of deficit spending. However, it has meant that the state school system lags in building, in staffing, and in salaries. One source of new potential is the Oahe Dam with its power plants six miles north on State 514. This is the largest of the six Missouri dams and the largest rolled earth dam in the world.

At the south end of the state, US 18 crosses the river on top of Fort Randall Dam. Remains of the old fort may be seen on the south shore just below the dam. Abandoned in 1892, the parade ground is still visible, as well as excavations of several buildings, and the ruins of the chapel. If you like ruins, this is one of the best until you get to Fort Laramie, Wyoming. West is cattle country, and Winner was the scene of an old-style cross-country cattle drive only a few years ago. The cowboys are still rugged, even though they bunk in motels. At Mission you are well into the Rosebud Indian Reservation. Six miles west of town turn left on an unnumbered road and drive eleven miles to the reservation headquarters and seven miles more to the St. Francis Indian Museum. A few hours to the west, again on US 18, lies one of the most famous (or infamous) battlefields in the West. Nine miles past Denby, turn north for six miles on another of those unnumbered roads so common in the West. This is Wounded Knee. A Nevada Paiute Indian who claimed to have seen a vision following an eclipse of the sun in 1889 convinced many Indians that they were invincible and that they should drive the white man off the face of the earth. The confusion and terror which followed have been referred to as the Messiah Craze. Ghost shirt rituals reached their height, and after Sitting Bull was killed his followers gathered near Wounded Knee Creek. The U.S. Seventh Cavalry searched the band for weapons. A shot, presumably accidental, set off a fight in which sixty-two women and children were among the Indian dead. The public was aroused by this slaughter. Some people suggested that cattlemen had encouraged a war-scare to keep homesteaders out of the newly opened range. The proud Sioux, after this last conflict with the U.S. Army, did not take well to farming so they remained poor for a long time. Today they engage successfully in arts and crafts, which may be seen at Pine Ridge.

Another route to the Rosebud and Pine Ridge Reservations takes you across the new (1966) Francis Case Bridge on State 44 west of Platte. This is the longest bridge between the Mississippi and the Pacific, spanning a mile-wide channel.

The Badlands

The Missouri may be crossed at Chamberlain, on the main route (I-90) from Sioux Falls to Rapid City; or, north on State 47 and back down on 47W takes you across Big Bend Dam and circles a small area where many forts and trading posts once stood. It will also take you through another Indian reservation. Crow Creek is on one side of the river and Lower Brule on the other side. On the way now to the Badlands and Black Hills, you may wish to see the Pioneer Auto Museum and the well-run Indian Museum in Murdo, an old cowtown. At Kadoka the Badlands Petrified Gardens have on display many of the petrified woods, fossils, and minerals to be found in the Badlands. The Badlands themselves are reached by turning south on Alternate US 16, just eighteen miles west of Kadoka. The headquarters are at Cedar Pass, another nine miles, where exhibits and audio-visual programs illustrate this fantastic area of wind- and water-eroded rocks. Millions of years ago this jagged and desolate area was a flat grassland and the home of prehistoric beasts such as the sabertoothed tiger and the titanosaur. Then the earth's crust rose and volcanic ash drifted down. Rivers carved gorges and the winds of thousands of centuries slowly wore away the softer rock and left sharp spires, rounded cones and grotesque designs. The Badlands are a rich fossil bed, but it is illegal to remove specimens. Picture-taking, however, will provide a thrill almost equal to the finding of a tiger bone. Subtle colors, especially striking in early morning and late afternoon, are difficult to capture but are worth many hours of trying. As for the fossils, see them under plexiglass along the fossil trail, exactly where they were found.

As you come back to the main highway again, at Wall, stop to see the wildest drugstore in the West. From the time it began offering free ice water, in 1936, the store has prospered and grown into an incredible establishment housing many small stores, dining rooms, exhibits, and the ice water well. At Wasta, the Sioux Indians have built an authentic Indian camp where the Old West comes to life again.

The fabled Black Hills are entered from Rapid City, a fast-growing community which depends primarily upon ranching, farming, and tourism. Growth was stimulated during the war years by an air base. But there is no doubt that its economy and its people are deeply affected by the Black Hills, which begin to rise on the edge of the city. There is probably more sightseeing to be done within ten miles of Rapid City than in hundreds of miles elsewhere in the state. The South Dakota School of Mines on St. Joseph Street has an outstanding geological museum. A federal Indian museum in Halley Park has dioramas and other displays of Sioux life. Five miles southwest of Rapid City, the Stave Church, a replica of an 800-year-old church in Norway, has become one of the most popular attractions in the area. For the children, a fairy tale playground is located on Story Book Island, two miles southwest on State 40; and lifesize models of dinosaurs, which once romped around rather heavily in this very spot, stand on a hill by Skyline Drive. South on US 16 are the reptile gardens (five miles) where the children may ride a giant tortoise, a horseless carriage museum (ten miles) where Dad can reminisce, and Rockerville (twelve miles) where a placer mining town has been re-created.

The Black Hills are really green, of course, close up. From a distance they look black, as they did to the Indians who considered them to be a holy place. The white man invaded the Hills almost overnight, and most of the towns and villages which you see now are still mining for gold—the tourist's gold. Tourism is the big business, although the Homestake Mine in Lead (pronounced Leed), after 100 years of profitable operation, produces more gold than any mine in the Western Hemisphere. Tours are conducted here, but only on the surface.

For an exciting underground tour, go to the Broken Boot gold mine in Deadwood, one mile west of town on US 14A. It no longer produces gold, but that hardly matters to the visitors who venture into the tunnels. Deadwood is also the place where Wild Bill Hickok and Calamity Jane are buried (in Mount Moriah Cemetery look for signs downtown). Deadwood is a one-street town; its main thoroughfare runs down the narrow Deadwood Gulch and the side streets are little more than alleys up the mountain. A highway is being built on top of Deadwood Creek, because there is no other level place for it. At Hill City (on US 16) you can go up the mountain in a small steam train. Or drive up the mountain from Hill City (south on US 16 and State 87) to Sylvan Lake, the prettiest spot in the Hills and a popular resort area. If you want to go still higher, take an exciting jeep ride up Harney Peak—way up.

Everything in the Hills seems dramatic, from the natural heights and curving roads to the elements which man has introduced. Mount Rushmore, about twenty-five miles southwest of Rapid City on US 16A, is impressive enough as a mountain, but man has added to nature here. Carved into the granite face of the mountain are the amazingly detailed likenesses of Washington, Jefferson, Lincoln, and Theodore Roosevelt. Blasted with dynamite and carved under the supervision of Gutzon Borglum, each face is almost seventy feet high. This is the one place no one misses on his first trip to the Hills. Signs will direct you to the best places for taking pictures of the faces on the mountain.

A thrill for children is Bedrock City, on the west edge of Custer, where the Flintstones stand in concrete amid a prehistoric atmosphere. Flintstone movies are shown in the theatre, and there is a playground and a camping area.

Five miles north of Custer on US 16 an even larger memorial is being slowly carved out of the mountains. When Crazy Horse and his horse are completed they will be over five hundred feet tall and over six hundred feet long. The sculptor, Korczak Ziolkowski, welcomes visitors to his home, studio and gallery. Drama in a different fashion is found in Custer State Park, where, from the Game Lodge, the visitor may take a jeep ride out to one of the largest buffalo herds in the country. The trip is a far cry from automobile travel on four-lane highways, for the jeeps cross rough terrain, go up small mountainsides, cross dry creek beds, and head out onto open prairie to take you inside a buffalo herd. Don't forget the camera this time, because you may be staring a ferocious-looking bull right in the eyes before the day is over. It's perfectly safe, but a thrill nevertheless.

Drama on stage is found at the Black Hills Playhouse, which has been in operation for more than 30 years. Ten miles east of Custer, go north on State 87 and watch the signs. The playhouse operates as part of the summer session of the University of South Dakota, but its actors come from all over the country. Plays are presented six nights a week during the summer, both legitimate theater and melodrama. One of the most popular performances is the historical fantasy, *The Legend of Devil's Gulch.* Farther north, at Spearfish, the *Black Hills Passion Play* is in its forty-sixth season in the U.S. after originating in Germany. Incidents in the life of Christ are presented by a cast of hundreds in a natural mountain amphitheatre.

Spearfish is the logical place of departure from the Black Hills if you are going north or west. If you are going south from here, Hot Springs makes a good last stop. But first visit the caves about ten miles north of town. Wind Cave National Park takes its name from curious air currents which blow in and out of the cave. Park rangers conduct safe tours underground. Above ground there are herds of buffalo, deer, and antelope, and visitors should not get out of their cars in the presence of these wild animals. Before leaving the state, plunge into the largest indoor natural warm-water pool in the world, Evans Plunge, 1145 North River Street in Hot Springs.

PRACTICAL INFORMATION FOR SOUTH DAKOTA

 FACTS AND FIGURES. In Sioux Indian, *Dakota* means "allies." The state's nicknames are *Coyote State* and *Sunshine State*. The pasqueflower is the state flower; the black hills spruce, the state tree; the ring-necked pheasant, the state bird. "Under God the People Rule" is the state motto. "Hail, South Dakota" is the state song.

Pierre is the state capital. The state population was 683,291 at the most recent census.

The broad Missouri River runs from north to south through the center of the state, separating the lake-dotted prairies of the east from the rolling uplands of the west. In the southwest are the strange eroded formations of the Badlands, the most spectacular bit of landscape of its kind in the world. In the west is the somber beauty of the forested Black Hills, site of Mt. Rushmore. South Dakota is a state of big, highly merchanized farms, and cattle and grain are the chief sources of income. Mining, centered in the Black Hills, is not so important, but South Dakota is the nation's leading producer of gold. There is little industry. The climate is variable, with hot summers and cold winters in the west, and high humidity in the east.

 HOW TO GET THERE. *By air:* North Central, Western, Frontier and Ozark Airlines provide service principally into Sioux Falls, Aberdeen and Rapid City.

By bus: Greyhound, Continental Trailways, Jack Rabbit Lines, and Midwest Coaches provide the bulk of the passenger service into the state serving Sioux Falls, Aberdeen, Rapid City and Pierre.

By car: I-90 enters South Dakota from Minnesota in the east and from Wyoming in the west. I-29 is the principal access from Nebraska in the south and US 281 from North Dakota in the north.

 HOW TO GET AROUND. *By air:* North Central and Western provide service between cities in South Dakota. One or both land at airports in Sioux Falls, Brookings, Watertown, Aberdeen, Huron, Mitchell, Pierre, and Rapid City.

By bus: Jack Rabbit Lines offers extensive service within the state serving all of the major cities and many smaller ones. Sedalia-Marshall-Boonville Stage Line provides transportation to Sioux City, Yankton, Mitchell, Rapid City, Huron, Pierre, and Aberdeen.

By car: the principal east-west routes are I-90 across the lower half of the state and US 212 across the upper half. The major cities served by I-90 are Spearfish, Sturgis, Rapid City, Wall, Kadoka, Murdo, Kennebeck, Chamberlain, Mitchell, and Sioux Falls. US 81, 281, and 83 run north-south, and I-29 runs north-south through Brookings, Sioux Falls, Beresford and Vermillion.

TOURIST INFORMATION. A free brochure, *South Dakota Vacation Guide*, as well as information and other leaflets are available from Travel Director, Dept. of Highways, Pierre 57501.

SEASONAL EVENTS. *January:* Pierre hosts a *Winter Carnival* early in the month.

February: The Black Hills Stock Show takes place in Rapid City during the first week. Deadwood is the site of *Annual Winter Wonderland* the third week.

March: Sioux Empire Arts Festival runs all month in Sioux Falls. The *Little International Livestock Show* in Brookings is South Dakota State University's agricultural and home economics show. Patterned after the Chicago International Exposition, it takes place during the third week. Among the ethnic festivals is Freeman's *Schmeckfest* during the last few days of the month.

April: Brookings opens the month with a *Fine Arts Festival* and Rapid City holds an *Arts and Crafts Fair* at mid-month. At Sioux Falls near the end of the month is the *Sioux Empire Gem & Mineral Show.*

May: The *Jackrabbit Stampede,* which includes a rodeo, takes place on the South Dakota State University north campus at Brookings early in the month. At mid-month is the *South Dakota Gem & Mineral Show* at Watertown.

June: The *Black Hills Passion Play* opens the month and is performed Sun., Tues., and Thurs. at Spearfish into Sept. Among this month's ethnic festivals are *Danish Days Celebration* at Viborg and *Annual Czech Days* at Tabor. DeSmet is the site of *Old Settlers' Days* during the second week and of *Pioneer Acres Gas and Steam Show* the third week. The *Crystal Springs Rodeo* at Clear Lake closes out the month.

July: The month opens with Mobridge's *Sitting Bull Stampede,* a parade and rodeo around the 4th of July. Other Independence Day celebrations include the *Annual Black Hills Roundup* at Belle Bourche, the century-and-a-half-old *4th of July Celebration and Rodeo* at Ft. Pierre, and *Sunfish Sailboat Regatta* at Lake Madison. At mid-month is the *Corn Palace Stampede* at Mitchell. During the last week is *Gold Discovery Days* at Custer which includes a Pageant of the Gold Rush, Custer's war with the Sioux, and Indian raids. A rodeo and carnival are also part of the festivities. Closing the month are the *Dakota Wagon Train* from Faith to Deadwood and the *Annual Black Hills Trail Ride* at Rapid City.

August: During the second week, the *Black Hills Motorcycle Classic* at Sturgis includes AMA sanctioned Gypsy Tour and motorcycle racing. *Oahe Days* at Pierre and *Sioux Empire Fair* at Sioux Falls both have rodeos as part of their events. Country and western entertainment and livestock exhibits make up the *Day County Fair* at Webster and Lake Madison is the scene of the *South Dakota Sunfish Championship Regatta.* The third week Rapid City hosts the *Central States Fair* with a Wild West rodeo, carnival, and Indian dances. The *Antique Festival and Steam Threshing Jamboree* at Prairie Village outside Madison displays antique farm machinery and has parades, arts and crafts shows, rides, and steam railroad. The *Rosebud Sioux Rodeo and Pow Wow* in Rosebud includes dances, Indian arts and crafts displays, and a traditional buffalo dinner. Late in the month, the *South Dakota State Fair* takes place at Huron.

September: Late in the month are the *Black Hills Steam & Gas Threshing Bee* at Sturgis, the *Corn Palace Festival* at Mitchell, and the *Vanishing Trails Expedition* at Wall.

October: Pheasant hunting season opens about the third week.

November: Black Hills *deer hunting season* opens Nov. 1.

December: Deadwood hosts the *Annual Black Hills Snowmobile Classic* and *ski season* begins.

NATIONAL PARKS. *Wind Cave National Park,* is located in the Black Hills north of Hot Springs. Wind Cave, one of many in the Black Hills, was named for the wind currents that blow in or out depending on atmospheric pressure. The whistling sound of the air coming out led to its discovery in 1881. The 28,000 acres of park which surround the cave are covered with prairie grasslands and forests. On a wildlife preserve are bison, elk, deer, and prairie dogs. Tours, nature trails, and camping and picnicking facilities are available.

Jewel Cave National Monument, in the Black Hills west of Custer, is a nearly 1,300-acre area covered with ponderosa pine and wildflowers. It surrounds Jewel Cave, a series of subterranean chambers and limestone galleries whose jewel-like calcite crystals produce unusual effects. Guided tours and picnicking facilities are available.

Badlands National Monument, 62 mi. E. of Rapid City via I-90, US 14, 16, 16A, is one of the most impressive pieces of natural sculpting in the world. Over millions of years, layer upon layer of mud, sand, and gravel along with skeletons of the animals of the period—dinosaurs, saber-tooth tigers, bison and tinier water and marsh creatures—were built up to a depth of over 600 feet. Probably during the great land upheaval which formed the Rocky Mountains, the earth's crust rose and the action of wind and water began to form the cones, spires and jagged peaks, the banded gullies and canyons which now make up this colorful region. This is a simple but striking demonstration of geologic processes. A Visitor Center is open year round, accommodations and meals are available during the summer, and there is camping nearby at Cedar Pass and Sage Creek.

The *Black Hills National Forest,* nearly 1¼ million acres, encompasses almost all of the Black Hills. Formed when wind and water eroded the softer limestone and sandstone surrounding the granite core (or, if you prefer, by the tears of Paul Bunyan upon the death of his blue ox, Babe), the area is now one of towering spires, magnificent forests and mountain scenery. Named by the Indians for the dark, appearance given by the thick pine covering, these mountains were considered sacred ground. Harney Peak, at 7,242 feet, is the highest mountain in the Black Hills.

A variety of recreational activities are possible throughout the year including camping, picnicking, hiking, swimming, boating, fishing, hunting, and skiing. The visitor center at Pactola Lake has information and exhibits on the forest and wildlife.

Custer National Forest. Part of this 2½-million-acre forest lies in northwestern South Dakota. Mostly rolling hills and grassland, it offers camping and picnicking facilities and hiking trails.

STATE PARKS. *Custer State Park,* 3 mi. E of Custer on US 16A, is one of the largest state parks in the U.S. Over 72,000 acres are given over to this park in the rugged Black Hills. On the park's wildlife refuge are herds of bison, deer, and bighorn sheep and other native animals. Four lakes and many streams offer excellent fishing and swimming. The park also has a zoo, museum, and theatre and facilities for camping, picnicking, boating, horseback riding, and hiking.

Fort Sisseton State Park, 12 mi. N of Webster on State 25, then 10 mi. N on an unnumbered road, was built in 1864 during the Sioux Indian uprising and is an excellent example of a stone frontier fort. The visitors center has historic exhibits and picnic facilities are available.

Bear Butte State Park, 6 mi. NE of Sturgis on State 79, is the site of a huge volcanic bubble which rises 1,400 feet above the level of the surrounding plains. Indians still regard it as a religious shrine. The Cheyenne Indian Shrine is at the visitor center. Camping, picnicking, boating, swimming, and fishing facilities are available.

Fisher Grove State Park, 7 mi. E of Redfield on US 212, covers 306 acres and offers camping, electrical hookups, picnicking, hiking, boating, fishing, and golf.

Hartford Beach State Park, 15 mi. NW of Milbank on State 15, offers camping, picnicking, boating, swimming, fishing, flush toilets, and electrical hookups.

Newton Hills State Park, 7 mi. S of Canton off Us 18, offers complete camping, picnicking, boating, swimming and recreation facilities.

Union County State Park, 11 mi. S of Beresford off I-90, offers camping, picnicking, and hiking.

Palisades State Park, 10 mi. E of Sioux Falls on I-90, then 14 mi. N on State 11, has camping, picnicking, fishing, and hiking.

Oakwood Lake State Park, 10 mi. N of Volga off US 14, offers complete camping, picnicking, boating, swimming and recreation facilities.

Lake Herman State Park, 2 mi.1W of Madison off State 34, offers camping, electrical hookups, picnicking, boating, swimming, and fishing.

Roy Lake State Park, 3 mi. W of Lake City off State 10, offers camping, electrical hookups, picnicking, boating, fishing, swimming, and hiking.

Lake Hiddenwood State Park, 4 mi. NE from Selby off US 212 and US 83, offers camping, electrical hookups, picnicking, boating, and swimming.

Sica Hollow State Park, 15 mi. NW of Sisseton off State 10, offers picnicking, horseback riding, and hiking.

CAMPING OUT. From May to Sept. a carload permit is required, good for use at all state parks and recreation areas. A five-day camping limit applies in many areas.

In addition to the state parks, camping facilities are available at most recreation areas. The larger ones are listed below.

Angostura. 10 mi. SE of Hot Spring off US 18, offers sixty-four sites. Facilities include fishing, boating, swimming, and pit toilets.

Farm Island, 3 mi. E of Pierre off State 34, offers seventy-two sites. Facilities include boating, swimming, fishing, electrical hookups and flush toilets.

Gavins Point, 6 mi. W of Yankton on State 52, has sixty sites. Facilities include boating, swimming, fishing, electrical hookups and flush toilets.

Pickerel Lake, 10 mi. N of Waubay on US 212, has sixty-seven sites. Facilities include boating, fishing, swimming, electrical hookups and pit toilets.

Yankton, 5 mi. W of Yankton on State 52, has fifty-five sites. Facilities include boating, swimming, fishing, electrical hookups and flush toilets.

TRAILER TIPS. In addition to the state parks and recreation areas already covered, there are a number of city, county and civic campgrounds with trailer facilities.

Huron Memorial Park Campground, in Huron, 1 mi. E of State 37, has trailer sites with water, sewer, and electric hookups and air conditioning and sanitary dump. The season runs from Apr. to Sept.

Burke City Park, 300 ft. off the side of US 18 and 47, is open all year and has water, sewer, and electric hookups and a sewage disposal station. Spaces are limited.

Groton City Park, on Main St. 2 blks. S of US 12 on the north side of Groton, has water and electric hookups and sewage disposal station. It is open from May to Oct.

Maxwell Park, on the north side of US 14 in Arlington, has water and electric hookups and a sewage disposal station is nearby. The season runs from Memorial Day to mid-Sept. Reservations are accepted.

FARM VACATIONS AND GUEST RANCHES. Dude ranches and vacation farms, a popular form of vacationing in other states, are becoming increasingly popular in South Dakota. The following is a sampling of what is available.

4T Guest Ranch, located approximately in the center of the Black Hills. Horseback riding, pack trips, fishing and many kinds of western ranch excitement. Contact 4T Guest Ranch, Nemo 57759.

Guy's Vacation Ranch, located in the LaCoteau Hills of northeastern S.D. Both children and adults enjoy the routine farm life. Horseback riding, hunting, fishing, and cookouts are available. Swimming, sunbathing and water-skiing during the summer. Winter season, sledding, skiing and skating. Write Hurshall Guy, RR 3, Veblen 57270.

Hutchinson Ranch, located in southcentral S.D. Ranch living for a day, week, or month. Can accommodate a family of six or fewer, or couples. Also camping facilities. Transportation facilities, horseback riding, swimming, rock hunting, fishing, hiking or just relaxation. Larry A. Hutchinson, White River 57579.

Medicine Creek Ranch, located 4 mi. from the Big Bend Reservoir, on the Lower Brule Sioux Indian Reservation. Live a real ranch life. An offer for young people 9 to 14 years of age to spend a vacation on one of Dakota's large ranches under supervision. Medicine Creek Grazing Assn. Inc., Reliance 57569.

  MUSEUMS AND GALLERIES. The *Museum of Geology,* in O'Harra Memorial Building on the campus of the South Dakota School of Mines and Technology in Rapid City, has excellent exhibits of rocks and minerals from the Black Hills and fossils from the Badlands.

Sioux Indian Museum and Crafts Center, at 1002 St. Joseph St. in Rapid City, exhibits historic and contemporary Sioux clothing, weapons, pictures, and arts and offers for sale authentic Sioux craft items.

Horseless Carriage Museum, 10 mi. S of Rapid City on US 16, displays antique cars and 10,000 other artifacts of automotive and general history including firearms, musical instruments, clothing, drugstore items, and doctor and dentist equipment. Open May to Oct.

South Dakota State Historical Society, in the Soldiers' and Sailors' War Memorial opposite the State Capitol in Pierre, has pioneer, Indian and historic exhibits including a lead plate buried by the first known white men in South Dakota.

Pioneer Auto Museum and Antique Town, at the junction of I-90 and US 83 in Murdo, has a collection of over 200 antique cars, many still in running condition. There are also antique farm machinery, horse-drawn carriages and wagons, a blacksmith shop, other antiques and exhibits.

Way Park Museum, in Way City Park on Mt. Rushmore Rd. in Custer, is an 1875 log cabin which houses historical and mineral exhibits. Open June to Aug.

How the West Was Won Memorial Museum, at 624 Crook St. Frontier in Custer, is another log building and houses guns, photographs, and other memorabilia from westward expansion. Also here is the *Black Hills Museum of Mining and Minerals* which displays early mining equipment and ores and minerals from the region. Both museums are open May to Oct.

Adams Memorial Museum, at Sherman and Deadwood Sts. in Deadwood, has exhibits of pioneer days in the Black Hills.

Dakota Territorial Museum, on Summit Ave. in Yankton's Westside Park, is housed in the restored Dakota Territorial Legislative Assembly Building and offers historical exhibits from early pioneer days. Open Memorial Day to Aug.

Because this is Indian country, almost every museum in the state has a few Indian artifacts. Two special museums are only one hour apart. In Sioux Falls, the *Pettigrew Museum,* at 141 N. Duluth Ave., combines Indian exhibits with other historical subjects and natural history. In Vermillion, the *W. H. Over Museum* is on the University campus, on Clark Street. Some exhibits here change from time to time, but Indian materials are excellent because the University is a state center of Indian studies. There are also old guns, equipment, uniforms, bones of prehistoric animals, stuffed animals, an extensive rock and agate collection, and special collections of art and musical instruments.

 HISTORIC SITES. *Mount Rushmore National Memorial.* Here the faces of four great American Presidents—Washington, Jefferson, Lincoln and Theodore Roosevelt—have been carved and blasted out of the granite of a 6,000-ft. mountain in the Black Hills. These 60-ft.-high heads are the dream of Gutzon Borglum who began the work in 1927. Fourteen years later, in March 1941, he died without having completed it; his son, Lincoln Borglum, took over, finishing in October of that year. Today, more than 2 million visitors each year come to marvel at this massive work.

The memorial is open all year, but snow in the hills can make driving difficult in winter. Located 22 mi. S of Rapid City off US 16A.

What will be the largest statue in the world is being carved out of solid granite atop Thunderhead Mountain, 5 mi. N of Custer off US 16, 385. Korczak Ziolkowski, who assisted Gutzon Borglum on Mt. Rushmore, has undertaken singlehandedly to depict Crazy Horse, the Sioux chief who defeated Lt. Col. Custer, astride an enormous horse. This *Crazy Horse Memorial* will be 641 feet long and 563 feet high, and is intended to honor not only the great Indian chief but also the unconquerable spirit of man. Ziolkowski's 57-room home displays a scale model of the statue.

The *Sitting Bull Monument,* on a hill overlooking the Missouri River, marks the burial site of another famous Indian. The bust for this monument was also the work of Korczak Ziolkowski. Located 3 mi. W of Mobridge on US 12, then 4 mi. S on an unnumbered road.

The *Battleship U.S.S. South Dakota Memorial,* at W. 12th St. and Kiwanis Ave. in Sioux Falls, commemorates the famous World War II battleship. The outline of the memorial is the same dimension as the South Dakota. A museum exhibts relics and mementoes of the ship. Open Memorial Day to Labor Day.

Nine mi. E of Pine Ridge on US 18 and then 7 mi. N on an unnumbered road is the *Wounded Knee Battlefield* where the last major confrontation between the Sioux and the U.S. Army took place. A monument marks the mass grave site of the many Indians, including women and children, who where shot during and following this battle.

Buried in *Mt. Moriah Cemetery* in Deadwood are such Wild West characters as Wild Bill Hickok, Calamity Jane, and Preacher Smith.

TOURS. *Gray Line* offers a varied program of tours of the Black Hills and Badlands which can include the Passion Play. Free pickup and return to hotels and motels. Write Gray Line of the Black Hills, P. O. Box 1106, Rapid City 57701.

Rushmore Coach Lines has the closest guided tours to Mt. Rushmore and the Southern Black Hills. Daytime tours to points of interest in the Black Hills and an evening schedule to the lighting program at Mt. Rushmore. Free pickup and delivery in the Keystone area. Write Box 253, Keystone, 57751.

The *Needles Highway Scenic Drive,* NE from Custer on State 87, passes tall, granite spires which give the highway its name. This is the most scenic route to many of the other Black Hills attractions.

INDUSTRIAL TOURS. The *Sioux Falls Stockyards Co.,* in the Livestock Exchange Building at Rice St. and Cliff Ave. in Sioux Falls, offers daily tours of the entire stockyard operation from receiving through selling and shipment. Tours are given 24 hours a day.

Homestake Forest Products Co., on W. Oliver St. in Spearfish, gives one-hour guided tours of its lumber production facilities.

Black Hills Jewelry Manufacturing Co., at 700 Jackson Blvd. in Rapid City, shows how it produces gold jewelry. Contact Milt Shaver, 343-0157.

Homestake Mine, on Lead's Main St. between Mill St. and the city limits, offers 1½-hour tours of its surface workings and information about gold production.

SPECIAL INTEREST TOURS. The *Black Hills Central Railroad* offers a 2½-hour, round-trip tour between Custer and Hill City in an 1880 steam train with open and closed cars. The train passes through the magnificent scenery of the Black Hills and near Crazy Horse Memorial. From mid-June to Aug. there are three trips daily (phone 574-2222 for schedule and prices). Also, out of Hill City is a 96-mile trip to Deadwood over Nahant Pass. Excursions take place Sat. only. Reservations required.

Tours of the *Missouri River Dams* are given regularly, seven days a week, from May 27 to Labor Day. Big Bend Dam at Fort Thompson has tours from 8 a.m. to 4:30 p.m.; Ft. Randall Dam at Pickstown, from 9 a.m. to noon and 1 to 5 p.m.; Oahe Dam at Pierre, 9:30 a.m. to 6 p.m.; and Gavins Point Dam at Yankton, from 10 a.m. to 6 p.m.

The *Corn Palace,* at 604 N. Main St. in Mitchell, while especially interesting for its unusual mixture of architectural styles and its exterior mosaic murals of colored corn, grain and sudan grass, is also open for inspection inside during the summer months. African Trophy Display, art exhibits, souvenirs, free tours and information booth are all accessible from 8 a.m. to 9 p.m. daily, June 1 to Labor Day.

 STAGE AND REVUES. The *Black Hills Passion Play,* in the amphitheatre at 421 Meier Ave. in Spearfish, is a famous annual dramatization of the last seven days in the life of Christ. Performances take place June to Aug., Sun., Tues. and Thurs. For details write Box 469 or phone 642-2646.

The *Crazy Horse Pageant,* which portrays the life of the Sioux warrior, is given every summer, mid-June to late Aug. in the amphitheatre, 5 mi. SE of Hot Springs on US 18, 385. For details phone 745-4140.

Rockerville Meller Drammer Theatre, in the Rockerville Ghost Town near Keystone, offers melodrama and vaudeville from early-June to Labor Day, nightly. Phone 348-1991.

The Black Hills Playhouse in Custer State Park performs contemporary plays in conjunction with the University of South Dakota. On Mon. evenings is ''The Legend of Devil's Gulch,'' the story of the gold rush and arrival of the white man in the Black Hills. Presented mid-June to late Aug., Mon., Wed. to Sun. For information phone 255-4141.

On 8th St. in Custer is the melodrama, ''*The Hangin' of Flyspeck Billy,* '' the tale of a Custer City lynching in 1881. Performances at mid-June to Aug., Mon. to Thurs.

 DRINKING LAWS. Liquor may be purchased both by the bottle (in stores) and by the drink. Liquor may be sold in stores from Mon. to Sat., 7 a.m. to midnight; by the drink to 2 a.m.; Sun. 1 to 10 p.m.; subject to local option. Legal drinking age is 18 for 3.2 beer; 21 for all other alcoholic beverages.

 SUMMER SPORTS. *Fishing.* The four huge lakes created by damming the Missouri River have made South Dakota one of the finest sportfishing areas for walleye and northern pike. The reservoirs and streams of the Black Hills offer excellent trout fishing and there are many largemouth bass in stockponds across the state. Nonresident license fees are $15 for a full year or $8 for a five-day permit. *Hunting.* Many consider South Dakota the Pheasant Capital of the world, and grouse, prairie chicken, quail and partridge are also plentiful. There are also seasons for duck and geese. Nonresidents may hunt deer with rifles, or deer and antelope with bow and arrow. Nonresident waterfowl licenses cost $30, small game, $30, and large game $30. Nonresidents must purchase a general hunting license ($2) before they can obtain any other hunting license. *Boating* and *water-skiing.* The same four reservoirs on the Missouri which offer exciting fishing provide ample space for boating and skiing. *Swimming.* In addition to the lakes and reservoirs, there is Evans Plunge, the largest, indoor warm-water pool in the world at Hot Springs. *Golf.* There are numerous courses, although most are 9-hole. Brookings, Canton, Chamberlain, Clark, Milbank, Mitchell, Pierre, Sioux Falls, Vermillion, Watertown, Webster, Pickstown, Yanktown, Belle Fourche, Deadwood, Lead, Rapid City, Spearfish, and Sturgis all have one or more courses.

SOUTH DAKOTA

WINTER SPORTS. *Skiing.* There are five ski areas in operation in South Dakota. Best known is Terry peak in the Black Hills whose 1,200-foot vertical drop from over 7,000 feet makes it the highest ski area east of the Rockies. Facilities include both chair and poma lifts and cross-country trails. The other areas are Great Bear Ski Valley near Sioux Falls, La Coteau near Sisseton, Deer Mountain Ski Area near Lead, and Inkpa-du-ta near Big Stone City. Ski season generally runs from Thanksgiving to April. *Snowmobiling.* Miles of Forest Service trails in the Black Hills are open to snowmobiles, and shoreline trails in the Northeast Lakes region are cold but extensive. Some of the rolling ranch land of Central South Dakota is open with permission of the owners.

SPECTATOR SPORTS. *Horse racing.* Park Jefferson in Jefferson offers pari-mutuel racing from June to Sept. *Greyhound racing.* The Black Hills Track at Rapid City and Sodrac Park in N. Sioux City have races from June to Sept.

SHOPPING. Authentic Indian items are available throughout the state but the *Sioux Indian Museum and Crafts Center* in Rapid City and at the *Arts and Crafts Center* in Rosebud on the Rosebud Indian Reservation near Mission have particularly interesting displays.

WHAT TO DO WITH THE CHILDREN. Sioux Falls is a good place to bring children because the small but excellent *Great Plains Zoo* (at Kiwanis Ave. and 18th St.) is next to *Dennis the Menace Park.* In the zoo, the children may roam freely and safely. In the park, they may play on a jet plane, a fire engine, and an army tank. A short drive leads to *Terrace Park* (Menlo Ave. and W. Madison St.) where children may fish in a stocked lake. In Rapid City, *Dinosaur Park* on Skyline Dr. has life-size models of prehistoric dinosaurs; eons ago these beasts romped on this spot. Gift shop; soft drinks. See also *Bedrock City,* home of the Flintstones, on the west edge of Custer.

At *Reptile Gardens,* 6 mi. S of Rapid City in US 16, children may view an extensive reptile collection which includes an underground snake den. There are performing animals and children may ride giant tortoises. *Marine Life Aquarium,* 3 mi. S of Rapid City on US 16, has native and tropical fish and performing seals and porpoises. *Story Book Island* is a fairyland park in Rapid City where nursery rhymes come to life. Animals are erected in gigantic living color especially for children's enjoyment. Open all year, the park is free.

INDIANS. Approximately five percent of South Dakota's population is Sioux Indian. Once a woods people, the *Sioux* were driven from Minnesota by the Chippewa, who had obtained firearms from the white man to the east. The Sioux adapted themselves readily to life on the plains, becoming essentially nomadic in peace and adept horsemen in war. The horse provided transportation, and the buffalo gave them almost everything else. A proud and mighty people, they have not fared well on the reservation during the past century. Their name, "Sioux," is an abbreviated French corruption of a name given to them by their traditional enemies, the Chippewa, "Nadowe-siw-eg," meaning "enemies" or "the snake-like ones." But he Indians have always called themselves "Dakota," which means "allied" or "friends." Because the Dakota Nation is made up of many tribal groups, this name is fitting, and it has become in turn the name of two states.

South Dakota has eight reservations. Three of them are no longer marked on highway maps—*Sisseton* in the northeast corner, *Yankton* in the southeast, and *Standing Rock* on the Missouri River at the North Dakota border. In effect, these lands have been fully passed over in rental or sale. *Cheyenne River,* west of the Missouri between Pierre and Mobridge, is near the place where Sitting Bull was killed. *Crow Creek,* east of the Missouri between Chamberlain and Pierre, is the home of the Yanktonnais Tribe, and right across the river to the west are the Teton Sioux of *Lower Brule.* A few fort sites and Big Bend Dam are worth looking at here. Of major interest are the two southern reservations. *Rosebud* has the *Sioux Indian Museum* at St. Francis. *Pine Ridge* is the site of the *Battle of Wounded Knee,* west and north of Denby.

The two kinds of *dances* performed by the Indians may be seen at the town of Pine Ridge in the summer. Inquire at the Agency for times and places. Arts and crafts may be purchased here, and summer activities also include rodeos. See also the Indian church, decorated in Sioux symbols. *Our Lady of the Sioux Catholic Church* has Indian murals on the walls, a peace pipe above the altar, and a Christus which looks very much like an Indian.

The only rules for visitors to the reservations are those of common courtesy. No special permission is needed to bring cameras.

RECOMMENDED READING. Herbert Schell's *History of South Dakota* is the most recent state history. *Black Elk Speaks* is the story of one of the state's most famous Indians, as told by Black Elk himself to John Neihardt. Doane Robinson's *History of the Sioux Indian* is the most comprehensive account of the state's earliest people.

HOTELS AND MOTELS in South Dakota, because they are generally smaller than those in the east or west, offer the tourist a homelike atmosphere and friendly good will. Rates out of season may be lower than the in-season categories we quote.

The price categories in this section, for double occupancy, will average as follows: *Deluxe* $24, *Expensive* $20, *Moderate* $16, and *Inexpensive* $12. For a more complete description of these categories see the *Hotels & Motels* section of THE ROCKIES & PLAINS *Facts at Your Fingertips* at the front of this volume.

ABERDEEN

Sheraton Motor Inn. *Deluxe.* Restaurant, pool, saunas, adjacent to 18-hole golf course.

Holiday Inn. *Moderate.* Indoor heated pool, restaurant, lounge, playground, recreation room.

BELLE FOURCHE

Kings Inn. *Moderate.* Heated pool, restaurant and lounge. Bowling alley, beauty salon and laundromat adjacent.

BROOKINGS

Staurolite Inn. *Expensive.* 1½ mi. from South Dakota State University. Heated pool, sauna, coffee shop and dining room, bar and lounge, meeting rooms. Courtesy car service is available.

Brookings Downtown. *Inexpensive.* An appealing motel with heated pool. Well-furnished rooms. Family rates and units. Restaurant nearby.

CHAMBERLAIN

Lake Shore. *Inexpensive.* Nice view of Missouri River. Small quiet motel with comfortable rooms. Restaurant nearby.

CUSTER

Hi-Ho Best Western. *Deluxe.* Located next to Flintstone village, this motel has playground, pool, restaurant.

State Game Lodge Resort. *Deluxe.* Located in the center of beautiful Custer State Park, this lodge was the Summer White House for two US Presidents. Conveniently located for hiking and fishing. Restaurant.

Bavarian Inn. *Expensive.* Brand new, surrounded by the natural forest. Has heated pool, playground, picnic area, restaurant.

Rocket Motel. *Moderate.* Newly remodeled. Restaurant nearby. Closed Dec. to Apr. 14.

Sylvan Lake Resort. *Moderate.* In Custer State Park. Has a variety of hotel rooms and cabins, with kitchens in some. The emphasis is on outdoor living. Restaurant areas, boats, fishing, riding. In the Black Hills overlooking the lake.

DEADWOOD

Western Motor Inn. *Moderate.* Restaurant, attractive rooms.

HURON

HIckory House Motor Inn. *Expensive.* Restaurant, pool, banquet and meeting facilities.

Plains. *Expensive.* Heated pool. Extra-large rooms tastefully furnished. Restaurant and cocktail lounge. Family rates.

Traveler. *Inexpensive.* Small and comfortable. Nicely landscaped grounds with picnic area and playground. Cafe nearby.

KADOKA

H & H El Centro. *Moderate.* Large, well-furnished rooms. On spacious grounds with heated pool, wading pool, recreation area. Restaurant. Meeting facilities.

MITCHELL

Anthony. *Expensive.* Has cheerful rooms with phones, and air-conditioning. Recreation and picnic area. Restaurant next door.

MOBRIDGE

Wrangler. *Moderate.* A small, two-story motel overlooking Lake Oahe. Spacious and well-furnished rooms. Recreation area. Restaurant 1 blk. Main thing here is the view and the convenience to the dam.

MURDO

Graham Motor Lodge. *Moderate.* Inviting and attractive. This medium-size, nicely decorated motel offers heated pool, playground. Cafe nearby. Pioneer Auto Museum nearby. Family rates.

PIERRE

Holiday Inn. *Expensive.* Heated pool, restaurant, bar, dancing, entertainment. Family plan.

State. *Moderate.* While quite small, this motel has very pleasant rooms with air-conditioning. Restaurant nearby.

RAPID CITY

Alex Johnson Hotel. *Deluxe.* Newly remodeled, located in the center of downtown. Free parking, limousine service available to airport.

Gill's Sun Inn. *Deluxe.* This medium-size motel has a wide variety of well-maintained and attractive units, including studios and suites. Heated pool, restaurant, bar. Baby sitters, house physician and dentist.

Holiday Inn. *Deluxe.* A large, two-story chain member with nicely furnished rooms. Heated pool, playground, restaurant and cocktail lounge. Meeting facilities. Airport courtesy car. Family rates.

Howard Johnson Motor Lodge. *Deluxe.* Indoor-outdoor pool, sauna and whirlpool, restaurant.

Sands of the Black Hills. *Deluxe.* All pool-side rooms. Efficiency rooms available.

Town 'N Country. *Deluxe.* Handsome, medium-size motel of one and two stories set back from the highway. Very charming and spacious rooms, many newly built. 2 heated pools, playground, rock and gem shop. Tour arrangements.

Imperial "400" Motel. *Expensive.* A two-story, downtown motel with colorful rooms, heated pool, sauna, restaurant, lounge, coffee shop. Meeting, banquet and convention facilities.

Tip Top. *Moderate.* A medium-size motel with well-furnished rooms plus a few kitchen units. Heated pool, sundeck, Coffee shop and cocktail lounge. Family rates.

Dakota Motel. *Inexpensive.* Some kitchenettes. Restaurant adjacent. Tours arranged.

SIOUX FALLS

Holiday Inn Airport. *Expensive.* Heated pool, whirlpool bath, sauna. Recreation room. Putting green. Restaurant, bar, dancing, entertainment. Free airport bus.

Lindendale Motel. *Moderate.* A small motel, large rooms. Spacious grounds with shade trees, heated pool, children's play area. Restaurant and shopping area a few blocks away.

Ramada Inn. *Moderate.* Heated pool, restaurant, lounge, dancing, entertainment. Close to airport, shopping. Great Plains Zoo. Airport courtesy car.

Town House. *Moderate.* The convenience of downtown location near restaurants and shops. Nicely furnished, this medium-sized motel offers heated pool, restaurant, bar.

Train-Motel. *Inexpensive.* A small motel with heated pool, playground. 24-hour cafe nearby. Horseshoes. Camp and trailer sites, picnic tables.

SPEARFISH

Royal Rest. *Moderate.* A small motel located near the amphitheatre where the Passion Play is performed in summer. Good selection of accommodations and rates, including family. Restaurant across the street.

McColley. *Inexpensive.* Small downtown motel set around a shaded courtyard. Has nice well-furnished rooms and a few family units with kitchens. Heated pool. Restaurants nearby.

VERMILLION

Lamplighter. *Moderate.* Very nice accommodations. Heated pool, restaurant next door. Near University of South Dakota campus.

WATERTOWN

Plateau Inn. *Moderate.* Extremely nice two-story motel with handsome rooms and oversize beds. Heated pool, playground, Wedding Chapel, dining room, coffee shop, cocktail lounge. Bowling. Family rates.

YANKTON

Kochi Motel. *Expensive.* Medium-size, two-story motel with large rooms, all with balconies. Heated pool, children's pool, bowling. Coffee shop and supper club, bar, dancing. Set back from highway on impressive grounds.

Skyline. *Inexpensive.* A small, well-run motel with delightful accommodations, heated pool, sundeck, play area. Restaurant and coffee shop, lounge, dancing. Family rates.

 DINING OUT. The number of tourists visiting South Dakota has increased dramatically in recent years, and as a result many of the newer restaurants have been built in conjunction with the motels intended to accommodate this influx of visitors. But there remain a number of restaurants, not associated with any lodging establishment, which serve good food, usually at moderate prices.

Restaurant price categories are as follows: *Deluxe* will average $8.50 and up, *Expensive* $5-$7.50, *Moderate* $3-$5, and *Inexpensive* $1.75-$3. These prices are for *hors d'oeuvre* or soup, *entrée,* and dessert. Not included are drinks, tax and tips. For a more complete explanation of restaurant categories refer to THE ROCKIES & PLAINS *Facts at Your Fingertips* at the front of this volume.

CUSTER

Skyway Cafe. *Moderate.* Rushmore Rd. Serves steaks, seafood and other well-prepared foods and baked foods in pleasant modern surroundings. Cocktail lounge.

State Game Lodge. *Moderate.* Features an excellent salad bar, buffalo steaks, roasts, and burgers. Located in the beautiful Custer State Park.

HILL CITY

Chute Roosters. *Moderate.* Housed in a barn converted to dining use. The cuisine is western with a cowboy flair. Specialties include Son-of-a-Gun Stew. Outdoor corral picnic area. Dancing in the hay loft.

KEYSTONE

Buffalo Room. *Moderate.* View the Mount Rushmore Memorial in the Black Hills. Cafeteria style service featuring salad bar, homemade pastries and rolls. Snack bar and gift shop.

MITCHELL

Chef Louie's Steak House. *Expensive.* Mitchell's leading steak house and cocktail lounge. Friendly atmosphere. Specialties include pheasant with wild rice, as well as a fine variety of steaks.

MURDO

Star Restaurant. *Moderate.* Serves wholesome food, with steak the specialty. Children's plates.

PIERRE

Falcon. *Moderate.* Features prime rib and charbroiled steaks. Good general menu.

Kings Inn. *Moderate.* Walleye is a house speciality. Very pleasant atmosphere and good menu.

RAPID CITY

The Embers. *Expensive.* Its cozy atmosphere is just right for grilled specialties and the late evening entertainment or dancing. Cocktails. Polynesian and American menu.

The Landmark. *Expensive.* Located in the Alex Johnson Hotel. Newly remodeled, one of the best places in Rapid City to eat out.

The Chuck Wagon. *Moderate.* Western decor includes waitresses in costume. Fun for the children. Chuck Wagon buffet daily, fish fry on Friday. Children's portion available.

Taylor's. *Moderate.* Locally popular, this restaurant serves basic fare in an early American decor.

Vern's Steak House. *Moderate.* Excellent service, atmosphere and steaks. Not a place to miss.

Westwood. *Moderate.* An attractive modern setting for a variety of popular beef specialties. Children's plates.

SIOUX FALLS

Depot. *Expensive.* Located in a remodeled train depot, the salad bar is unsurpassed, the service noteworthy. An excellent place to take the family or just go for a quiet evening.

Wilson's Town 'N Country Restaurant. *Moderate.* Serves a variety of home-cooked food including their own pastries and breads.

Lemonds' Finer Foods. *Inexpensive.* Steak is the specialty but sandwiches and salads are also served. A good restaurant for families. Does its own baking.

VERMILLION

The Prairie. *Moderate.* Coffee shop and dining room, serving steak but with a broad, general menu. Cocktails and bowling on premises also.

YANKTON

Castle Coombe. *Expensive.* Run by two English ladies, the restaurant serves only one or two dishes each day. The food is excellent, and the atmosphere relaxing.

Happy Jack's. *Expensive.* A very good supper club specializing in steaks and excellent service.

The Black Steer. *Moderate.* Rated highly by people in this corner of the state. Pleasant atmosphere for the charcoal-broiled steaks, chicken. Children's plates. Cocktails.

Kochi Lounge and Supper Club. *Moderate.* In an impressive Oriental decor, this restaurant features prime steaks and a weekly special. Children's servings. Cocktails.

Russo's. *Moderate.* Enjoy Italian atmosphere and fine Italian cuisine at this small restaurant specializing in pasta dishes. Also serves pizza and sandwiches.

UTAH

The Outdoor Amphitheater

by

HARRY E. FULLER, JR.

Harry Fuller has lived in Salt Lake City for fifteen years, where he is an editorial writer for the Salt Lake Tribune.

There is a sort of topographical symmetry to Utah. Almost 85,000 square miles in area, this 45th of the 50 states, squatting in the Rocky Mountain Great Basin, is divided down the middle by a huge, jutting spine—the Wasatch Range, looming to rugged peaks between 9,000 and 12,000 feet high. On either side a wrinkled, mostly arid landscape slopes away to the lower elevations. The western flank is almost completely wrapped in desert, picturesque at dawn or dusk, but hostile and harsh in the sun's punishing glare. The state's eastern shoulder is at least relieved by powerful waterways, principal among them the Green and Colorado Rivers. But even these alternately cascading and drifting waters pass through occasionally barren desolation.

Prominent landmarks of water distinguish the state's northern and southern extremes as well. Not much more than thirty miles below the Idaho border is the familiar natural wonder, Great Salt Lake. The ghostly remnant of an even greater inland sea—Lake Bonneville—Great Salt Lake is still approximately thirty miles wide by seventy-five miles long. It is hospitable to sailing, a buoyant brand of swimming and, at the Bear River drainage, duck hunting.

More to the north and east, Bear Lake, fresh water and a favorite of boaters, dips its southern two-thirds from Idaho into Utah at Rich County.

On Utah's southern rim, man has created new and immense Lake Powell,

180 miles long, deepening and reaching out behind Glen Canyon dam astride the Colorado River.

Utah is as varied as it is large—parched desert and snow-capped mountains; hard-rock plateaus and green-carpeted valleys; dry gullies and roaring-water gorges; sand dune windrows and rippling expanses of cooling lakes. Through reclamation and cultivation much has been artificaly enhanced, even while being exploited.

Exploitation of the land has been an absolute necessity for Utah to support permanent communities. At that, growth has been slow and often hesitating. The state is littered with shards of abandoned town sites. In 1972, Stephen L. Carr compiled a book that listed and described over 150 ghost towns languishing throughout Utah. It confirms a considerable background of pioneer trial and error. Steadily, however, Utah has developed into a single, elongated urban center embracing Salt Lake City, surrounded by thinly populated areas with residents depending for livelihoods on agriculture, mining, light manufacturing, oil production or an accelerating tourist trade.

It's not always love at first sight between Utah and its newer arrivals. The state lacks a cultural profusion found in older, more heavily populated regions of the U.S. Beyond that, community life in Utah manifests a definite insular quality. The power and presence of the Mormon Church, with few exceptions, strongly influences politics, government and social standing. This, quite naturally, affects non-Mormons in ways ranging from mild amusement to angry resentment. To get the feel for Utah "atmosphere," it's essential to understand some of the state's quite unique history.

Out of the Mainstream of American History

Utah is, not by original plan but rather by consequence of violent events, headquarters and sacred home of the Church of Jesus Christ of Latter-day Saints. The church, a Christian denomination, blossomed 155 years ago in New York, the gospel revelations announced by a prayerful young man named Joseph Smith, Jr. With a loyal following, he first moved west, settling in Kirtland, Ohio. The next move was to Jackson County, Missouri, and finally to a place called Nauvoo, Illinois. Surmounting constant difficulty, Smith managed to build a thriving community at Nauvoo, but at the expense of so much local enmity that a mob murdered him in a jail where he and other church leaders were being held. Smith's life ended prematurely, but his vision survived to inspire yet another migration, this one the most successful and significant.

Led by a colonizing genius, Brigham Young, the Latter-day Saints packed what they could into wagons and escaped their tormentors, seeking a haven isolated from those not of their creed. This turned out to be the Great Salt Lake Valley, at the foot of the Wasatch Mountain Range. In 1846, the time of their advance party's arrival, the area was actually Mexican land. Through man-fashioned irrigation, effective organization, backbreaking toil and unshakable faith, the pioneers, as they have since been reverently titled, made the harsh surroundings livable.

Descendants of those original settlers, and there are thousands, consider the memory of the dedication and sacrifice of their forebears to be a consecreated legacy. Utahns aren't always alert to the tangible remains of pioneer times. Irreplaceable hundred-year-old church buildings have been blithely razed. It's more the spirit of devoted perseverance that is lodged firmly in the Mormon heart. This helps account for a particular brand of conservatism or provincialism.

Modern Mormonism

Actually, modern Utah has abundant reason to be, for its small population, uncommonly cosmopolitan, even sophisticated. Its education level per capita is a national leader. From the beginning, Utah was a melting pot. Brigham Young dispatched missionaries throughout likely places in Europe as well as the U.S. to spread the glad news of a blessed Zion in the American West. And scores answered. Immigrating across the seas they eagerly joined homegrown converts. To this day the church maintains a foreign language capability at its Salt Lake City offices that surely rivals the United Nations'.

Most good church members are well traveled beyond the average. As young people, they are called to the missionary field, spending at least two years tending church business, preaching the gospel somewhere other than Utah, as often in England, Germany, Scandinavia, France and Italy as along the Eastern or Western seaboard or among the Polynesian or Japanese islands. Yet with all these eye-opening influences, Utah's Mormon majority can still identify with views formulated in the nineteenth century.

This includes adherence to the concept that life is a literal struggle between divinity and evil; that while God leads the truly devout, Satan guides the footsteps of the wrong-doer. Also, individual dependence on public assistance deprives the individual of the opportunity to choose, as a matter of judgment, a correct or mistaken path. Church policy condemns abortion as it does murder and all ordinary crime. It stresses self-reliance, although from Brigham Young's day, it has also operated a church welfare program as an interim help for the unfortunate.

As an article of faith, practicing church members abjure liquor and tobacco. Among the bitterest battles waged statewide during recent years were those over to what degree Utah would permit liquor to be sold publicly. A referendum held in 1968, asking whether mixed drinks could be sold in licensed outlets, went down to crushing defeat after a campaign that nearly polarized the entire state population.

Does this mean Utah is a collection of close-minded, parochial bluenoses? Not at all. In the first place, approximately 40 percent of the state is non-Mormon. Beyond that, however, while most adherents to the state's principal institution abide strictly by doctrine bequeathed from their elders, they can also be disarmingly tolerant. LDS thinking is neither slavish nor monolithic. Church members are united behind established precepts, but that doesn't prevent them from differing among themselves on politics, economics, social theory or even theology.

Stodginess is not a principal Utah characteristic. Rather an active interest in entertainment has produced the likes of the late jazz great Red Nichols, the Osmond Brothers, along with actresses Maude Adams, Laraine Day and Fay Dunaway. Sports are almost an obsession, especially basketball, which the Mormon Church encourages with a competitive program organized in full LDS thoroughness. National caliber athletes have come from Utah, including former boxing champion Gene Fullmer, world record co-holder in the discus, L. Jay Sylvester, and professional football players Golden Richards,

Marv Bateman and Ron Rydalch. Enthusiasm for dancing since pioneer days provided instrumentalists a pay day in Utah long after America's big band era ended.

Other pioneer preoccupations are shared today by most Utahns Mormon and non-Mormon. One is transforming drab desert into grassy vale. Water originally diverted from highland streams for nurturing crops now pours onto surburban lawns so every growing season will adorn yards in emerald green framed by flourishing flower beds.

A Modern Theocracy

Still, the difference between being Mormon and non-Latter-day Saint, or Gentile, in Utah is, if sometimes only subtle, always basic. In his 1957 Frederick William Reynolds lecture at the University of Utah, English Professor William Mulder, himself a Utah Mormon, explained: "Utah was a land where the Mormons at last could be the original settlers, keeping the outsider in the decided minority. . . . It was a Bible commonwealth, making no distinction between temporal and spiritual affairs under the strong central direction of the great colonizer as President of the Church and for ten years as Governor of the Territory (Brigham Young)."

And Leonard J. Arrington, recently named LDS Church historian, wrote in his 1958 book, *Great Basin Kingdom,* that: "The establishment of God's Kingdom on earth, according to Mormon belief, required great attention to the temporal and spiritual needs of man. . . . Economics, and secular policy in general, were thus placed on a par with—or incorporated in—religion. . . . Of the 112 revelations announced by Joseph Smith, 88 dealt partly or entirely with matters . . . economic in nature. . . . There is no doubt of the Mormon teaching that religion was concerned with the everyday duties and realities of life, and that church leaders were expected to minister not only to the spiritual wants of people, but to their social, economic and political wants as well."

These scholars were writing about early Mormon history. But while attitudes and policy have altered considerably with conditions, the pervasive effects of that deep-down Mormon belief has not disappeared in Utah.

Through its banking affiliate, Zion's First National, the church stays deeply in the state's economic mainstream. It retained control of Utah-Idaho Sugar Company after the Federal Trade Commission forced Henry Havemeyer to break up the American Sugar Refining Company in 1914. In the seventy years after 1900, the church helped promote and finance insurance companies, textile mills, hotels, an airline, hospitals, radio and television stations, aggregating an investment said to total well over $200 million by the '60s.

Non-Mormons have had successful political careers in Utah. But not many. They include but two governors, Simon Bamberger, 1917-21, who was Jewish, and J. Bracken Lee, 1949-57, from a Protestant background. No member in Utah's congressional delegation during modern times has been anything but a nominal or devout LDS member. The State Legislature, with 29 senators and 75 representatives, is considered 90 percent Mormon. Generally, it's considered extremely difficult for a Gentile to win statewide, and many district-wide, offices in Utah elections.

Political competition is brisk between traditional Republican and Democratic parties. The Democrats hold a registration edge, which may seem anomalous in a fundamentally conservative state, but Utah brand Democratic persuasion isn't the orthodox liberalism the party represents elsewhere.

In 1972, a Democrat, Calvin L. Rampton, shattered Utah political tradition by winning re-election to the governor's office for a third consecutive term. Until then, several men had served two straight terms as governor, but none three. Many observers argued Utah voters considered the two term limitation, although not a law, fundamental custom. Governor Rampton proved them wrong. Personality—not charisma, but the individual characteristics displayed—counts for a great deal in Utah elections.

Utah voters pride themselves on going to the polls, but are also apt to say, "I vote for the man, not the party." This has resulted, recently, in a Democratic governor and Republican control over one and sometimes both chambers of the state legislature.

Utah needs effective representation in Washington, D.C., because the state's land area is over 60 percent federally owned. A large portion is uninhabitable or used for grazing, but under the circumstances, Utah's development and growth have been ever more impressive.

One hundred and twenty-five years after the first Mormon settlers camped in the Great Salt Lake Valley, Utah the state has become a prosperous, forward-looking enterprise. Residents don't yet number much more than 1 million, and over half cluster in a narrow urban corridor running about forty miles north and south of Salt Lake City. Few pockets of chronic poverty exist and confidence in the future seldom lags. Economic fluctuations experienced in the past have been evened out by a diversifying industry. Mining and agriculture are increasingly complemented by light manufacturing, service trades of every description and a technological capacity germinated by participation in America's space and missile development. Tourism recently became the state's second ranked income producer.

An Outdoor Paradise

An old-timer, making conversation while riding the Germania chair lift at Alta's famed ski resort, pointed to the headwall looming high above "Ballroom" run and said: "One day we skied here in early morning, went back to Salt Lake City (only twelve miles below in the valley) and played several sets of tennis. That afternoon we played eighteen holes of golf and that night we camped in Provo Canyon after doing some fly-fishing in the evening along the Provo River." It was a triumphant account of some rather unusual exertion, but it was not unbelievable.

That versatile day outdoors is quite credible. It reflects, without exhausting, Utah's vast recreational inventory. The man in the chair lift could have added that his group ate lunch while sailing on Great Salt Lake. Or he could have said the next day they struck camp and drove north out of Provo Canyon on US 189 for daybreak horseback riding near Park City and later indulged in some water-skiing at Rockport reservoir fifteen more miles north.

Still, such travels would not have included the state's five spectacular national parks, two national recreation areas, seven national monuments, five national historic landmarks or one high mountain wilderness area. It would, however, have touched two of the state's nine national forests, one of forty-four state parks, one of fourteen ski areas and two of seventeen major reservoirs or lakes. Utah, from end to end, is a sportsman's smorgasbord.

Tennis courts dot each public park, municipal golf courses regularly decorate the landscape, including one state course at Wasatch State Park near Midway in Summit County. Mountain streams feed river systems famous for angling or white water boat floating.

Amazingly, 150 years after the mountain men stalked its northern slopes and 125 years after Mormon settlers started founding permanent communities, Utah is still being "discovered," by its own residents as well as by its visitors.

EXPLORING UTAH

Salt Lake City serves three essential purposes. First, and eternally foremost, it is the headquarters—the Mecca, the Vatican, the Jerusalem—of an international religion: the 4-million member Church of Jesus Christ of Latter-day Saints. Next, but not necessarily in that order, it is Utah's economic drive wheel. Finally it is the state's capital city. From any direction, the setting is impressive.

Approached from the west, Salt Lake City is seen as an urban ribbon, expanding gently and steadily up the jagged mountains that loom over the puny buildings below. From the north, there's the impression of a brick, steel and concrete wave washing into a protective cove formed by high, rocky headwalls. From the south the same suggestion of a gigantic, unbreachable wall is perceived, but it seems, this time, to be protecting a vast settlement, rolling beyond the northern horizon.

The view from the east is what most early pioneers encountered in their first introduction to a home in Utah, or as they knew it, the Territory of Deseret. The sight is much more spectacular today. The scene is a valley, hemmed on the opposite side by another ridge of low mountains—the Oquirrhs—running southward, interrupted on the north by the glinting Great Salt Lake. In the immediate foreground are gathered homes, churches, schools and shopping centers of a thriving metropolis. Farther to the right, on a prominent hill, stands the Christopher Wren-style state capitol building and, just below it, downtown Salt Lake City. Rising like a single, white-ribbed column is the sparkling new Mormon Church Building, the fourth "skyscraper" built recently at the head of State and Main Streets. The other three, University Club, the Kennecott Building and ZCMI center, have, along with the 30-floor church office building, given the city a high-rise skyline it previously lacked. They have also sharpened a local debate over developments that are drastically altering the city's former unique appearance.

The Pioneers' Progress

When the first Mormon refugees from midwestern persecution emerged from the mouth of Emigration Canyon, they glimpsed a valley stark and intimidating. Few trees shaded the land, the sun beat down unchallenged on the earth. Indeed, the ground was too hard for growing ample crops. Yet, these indomitable folk stayed. They constructed aqueducts and diverted water from the mountain streams. They organized the toil that lay ahead, they heeded commands issued by their leader, Brigham Young, they trusted

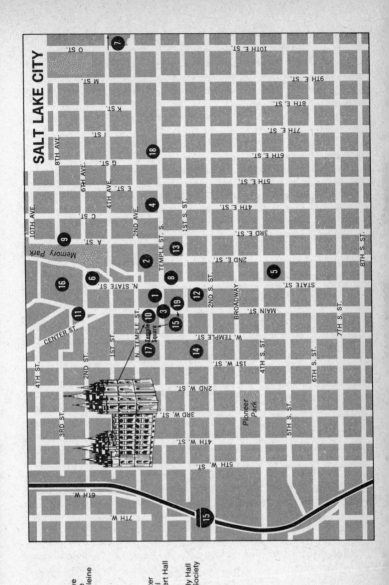

SALT LAKE CITY

Points of Interest

1) Beehive House
2) Brigham Young's Grave
3) Brigham Young Statue
4) Cathedral of the Madeleine
5) City County Building
6) Council Hall
7) Fine Arts Museum
8) Hansen Planetarium
9) Memory Grove
10) Mormon Temple
11) Pioneer Museum
12) Promised Valley Theater
13) Saint Mark's Cathedral
14) Salt Palace and Concert Hall
15) Seagull Monument
16) State Capitol
17) Tabernacle & Assembly Hall
18) Utah State Historical Society
19) Wax Museum

the Lord's word as revealed to them by their martyred prophet, Joseph Smith, Jr., and they prevailed.

Salt Lake City proper has, in the past decade, lost population, but in the manner of other U.S. urban centers: people have moved to new, outer residential areas. The metropolitan area has constantly grown until it numbers more than a half-million.

In 1847, Brigham Young and his followers laid out their city by plotting a four-square grid oriented east-west and north-south. They made the streets 132 feet wide with 20-foot sidewalks, and 10-acre blocks about 650 feet to the side. Then they lined the residential streets with trees and irrigated the pavement by streams of clear water flowing in the gutters. The spaciousness has been preserved and recently enhanced when the city government required all downtown commercial signs to be flush against their buildings. This was the first step in a comprehensive downtown redevelopment project called "The Second Century Plan" which also led to three blocks on Main St. being improved with wider sidewalks featuring fountains, trees and other decorative plantings. Salt Lake City depends on the airiness of its wide streets along with accelerated renovation and new construction for a persistent sense of dynamism.

The newer residential neighborhoods are scattered along the series of "bench land" terraces several hundred feet above the city. Almost every lot has a view and the danger is that too much slope will be converted to home sites, preventing natural absorption needed for flash flood rain storms. Salt Lake City's normal weather pattern is seasonal in the familiar fashion. Temperatures can rise into the hundreds during summer months and plunge to near zero during winter. But conditions can also turn perverse, with sudden showers dropping several inches of rain in a few hours. Dan Valentine, humor columnist for the daily *Salt Lake Tribune,* once wrote: "Utah has two seasons: winter and August." The exaggeration was apt enough. Some years, wet, cool springs can last through June, when it suddenly turns uncomfortably hot. And fall has been known to return, accompanied by snow, in early September. But the quirky and extreme weather seldom lasts. Fall is usually beautiful, with warm days and cool nights. A normal spring is about the same, but clothed in blossoms bursting from bushes and fruit trees. Summer's heat is at least "dry," with little relative humidity. Brisk canyon winds can, however, make the dryness a discomfort rather than a relief.

The Temple Square

Salt Lake City's greatest single attraction for visitors is the Temple Square area. This is the sacred ground of Mormonism. Here, on two ten-acre blocks flanking Main Street, in the middle of town, are the central religious shrines of Latter-day Saint worship. The Temple block, on the west, is surrounded by a 15-foot-high adobe wall. On the grounds stand the Temple, Museum, Tabernacle, Assembly Hall and Visitors Center. Parking around the square is reserved for tourists from out of state.

Guided tours are offered on the Temple grounds every half-hour. On the itinerary is the Tabernacle, which houses the famous Temple Square pipe organ and from where Sunday Tabernacle Choir concerts are broadcast. This is an elongated structure with rounded ends that resembles a grounded dirigible. It is actually 250 feet long and 150 feet wide. Its vaulted self-supporting roof is 70 feet from the floor. Completed in 1867, the building can seat over 5,000 and is used for the church's biannual conferences. It also served many years as a cultural center, where the Utah Symphony presented its season and visiting concert artists performed. Those programs are now presented in the city's new concert hall at the Salt Palace complex.

As an auditorium, the Tabernacle is known for its remarkable acoustics, although you can get an argument from different performers about whether the sound-carrying qualities are really helpful. In any case, no listener misses much. The choir, 375 mixed voices, was organized in the early 1850's and can be heard during its Thursday evening rehearsals as well as on Sundays, when the formal program is presented in its entirety.

South of the Tabernacle is Assembly Hall, a gray, granite structure seating 2,000, which also doubles as a lecture hall and place of worship. Facing the hall's east entrance is the Sea-gull Monument, said to be America's only historic monument to birds. It commemorates "The Miracle of the Gulls." In 1848 swarms of crickets descended from the mountain slopes to devour the pioneers' crop, the food that would protect them from famine the following winter. All eradication methods were insufficient and after the Mormons turned to prayer, flocks of sea-gulls appeared from the west, gorging themselves on crickets and rescuing the situation from certain disaster. Sea-gulls instantly earned an honored place in Mormon tradition.

Temple Square also holds monuments to the martyred Joseph Smith, the prophet, and his brother Hyrum, and the Three Witnesses Monument, with bronze bas-relief of the trio who testified that an angel showed them the golden plates from which the Book of Mormon was translated. A pedestaled statue of Brigham Young stands outside the Temple Square, at its southeast corner, in the intersection of Main St. and South Temple St.

Overawing all else in Temple Square is the Temple itself. Although there are six other LDS temples in Utah, the Salt Lake City version has a majesty and singularity about it denied the others. Its architectural style is imprecise. Some have called it "Mormon Gothic," and the appearance is not dissimilar from Europe's Middle Ages cathedrals. And yet it departs from that design, too. In any case, the building was dedicated in 1893, exactly forty years to a day after ground was broken for the foundation. Granite for its 167-foot-high walls was quarried from the nearby mountains and first dragged by oxen and mules to the building site. Later, rails were used for transportation. At each end of the 163-foot-long, 100-foot-wide edifice rise three spire-tipped towers, the highest, 204 feet in the air, centered above the east façade. Balanced on that point is a gilded statue of the angel Moroni, heralding toward the east with a long-stemmed trumpet. According to Joseph Smith, it was Moroni, pronounced Mo-rown-eye, who led him to the golden plates engraved with hieroglyphics described as "Reformed Egyptian." Smith testified that with heavenly aid he was allowed to translate the record into English. Two years of laborious writing became the Book of Mormon. By 1830, Smith had six followers and the beginning of the Church of Jesus Christ, which eventually lengthened into the Church of Jesus Christ of Latter-day Saints.

Mormon History

The Book of Mormon is a facinating work, purporting to be a history of Israelite wayfarers who reached the American continent about 600 B.C. They are supposed to have multiplied and moved into North, Central and South America. War developed between two nations, the Nephytes and Lamanites, until the latter completely destroyed the former about 400 A.D. The surviving Lamanites are considered by LDS members to be ancestors of present-day American Indians. Mormon was the Nephyte prophet who abridged and summarized the historic account divinely revealed to Joseph Smith.

Latter-day Saints belief isn't grounded exclusively in the Book of Mormon. They accept the Bible as the Word of God, as far as it has been "correctly interpreted." Mormon theology is outlined in 13 Articles of Faith and much of their moral teaching is found in the supplemental Word of Wisdom and Pearl of Great Price. The Doctrine and Covenants also contains Prophet Smith's later revelations. From the Word of Wisdom Mormons take their instruction against alcohol, tobacco, coffee, tea and other strong stimulants. Some argue it has become too central a dogma with the church, out of proportion with the Prophet's intention; that such counsel was meant only as sound advice on moderation. In this connection, it's often pointed out that Joseph Smith took wine just prior to his martyrdom in an Illinois jail. But stout Mormon adherents denounce a tippler as vigorously as they might an apostate. Simply put, the LDS people stress personal cleanliness, inside and out; that the body should be spared the ravages of excessive smoking and too much alcohol. Medical science doesn't refute the concept.

While all other buildings on Temple Square are open to the public, particularly the new Visitor Center at the northwest corner, the Temple is not. It is consecrated to Mormons in good standing only, where sacred rites, such as marriages, and other devotional work are performed. Mormons don't attend communal worship services in their Temples. These take place in neighborhood Ward and Stake Houses, which, in Salt Lake City, seem to dot every fourth or fifth street corner.

At the corner of South Temple and State Street are two buildings which originally served as office and residence for the church's second prophet, Brigham Young. They are the Lion House, his headquarters, and the Beehive House, appropriately named for the quarters he shared with his 26 wives and 56 children, at least some of them. Polygamy, of course, was the stigma that caused early Mormons their deepest trouble. It wasn't practiced by every LDS male, but, nonetheless, it had the first prophet's blessing, who said God willed that men take more than one wife. The indulgence had its practical value in the early days when husbands often died on the difficult way west and widows arrived in Utah without immediate prospects of support for themselves or their children. Still, America couldn't accept polygamy, even if—or perhaps especially if—it was approved by a Christian denomination. Congress denied Utah statehood until polygamy was purged and in late 1890, Church President Wilford Woodruff issued a manifesto removing plural marriages from Mormon sanction. Statehood followed, but along with perpetual prosecution of polygamous elders who could not or would not accept the prophet's word. A splinter group still practices plural marriage in and around Utah. One investigator claimed during the 1960's there were 30,000 polygamists in Utah. What the figure may be now is only a guess. One thing is certain, plural marriage is enough to earn instant excommunication from the central LDS Church.

Brigham Young had other homes in Salt Lake City. One is preserved at the city's largest public park—Liberty Park, a grassy, tree-filled greensward that features a small amusement park and Tracy Aviary, a colorful collection of birds and some animal life. The park also has its complement of tennis courts.

Salt Lake City has other parks. Pioneer Park, initially a gathering place for new arrivals, has a vintage steam engine donated by the Union Pacific. And Jordan Park is the location of the International Peace Garden, which has known times of neglect.

Capitol Hill

Salt Lake City is the state's capital city and Capitol Hill is worth a visit. It is reached on State Street, moving under restored Eagle Gate, marking the original entrance to Brigham Young's northside estate. On the hill, city dwellers used to gather wood from the prophet's grounds. Now forty acres are carefully landscaped around the granite and marble statehouse and office building. Completed in 1914, the copper-domed Capitol was designed for largely ceremonial uses, although it contained chambers for two houses of the bicameral legislature, the five-member State Supreme Court and the governor's office. Extensive interior remodeling has made space for administrative agencies. Expanding state government also led to construction in the late 1950's of an office building, north, across a plaza, from the older structure. The capitol first-floor hallway is lined with showcases exhibiting the qualities of every Utah county, mostly by region. Though sometimes slightly outdated, the displays are accurate enough to be edifying.

A favorite attraction is the original Mormon Meteor, the piston-driven car in which Ab Jenkins set endurance records at the Bonneville Speedway some thirty years ago. The speedway is about 120 miles west of Salt Lake City and in the Great Salt Lake Desert. It still hosts drivers and their crews attempting to set every imaginable land speed mark, in rocket cars, stock engine vehicles and motorcycles. The activity grows brisk toward summer's end, when the salt flats have dried to a table-top firmness, and continues until weather conditions force a halt, usually by November.

Skiing Around Salt Lake City

A central exhibit in the Capitol display consists of a large relief map of the state, shaped by the U.S. Forest Service. The mountain terrain around Salt Lake City stands out conspicuously, indicating why, in 1962, the city was selected as this country's nominee for the 1964 winter Olympics. Skiing is the area's chief winter pastime. East from the city, up two adjacent canyons are four ski areas that rival any in the U.S. for snow depth and consistency. Big Cottonwood Canyon leads to Solitude and Brighton. Little Cottonwood Canyon, a few miles farther south, trails up the mountain side to Snowbird and famed Alta. All operate a complex of chair lifts, but Snowbird features an aerial tramway that ferries skiers and sightseers to the top of 11,000-foot-high Hidden Peak. The trip takes about six minutes, and each of two cars carries 125 passengers in warm, dry enclosures. Snowbird is a year-round resort, with a village consisting of hotel, restaurant and condominium accommodations. It hosts conventions throughout most of the year.

On the east side of the mountains, Salt Lake City residents have been skiing at Park City for more than a decade. Originally a mining town, Park City made a comeback from "ghost" status when its recreational potential was discovered. Developers have since filled vacant property with new condominium groupings, close to skiing in winter and golf courses and tennis courts in summer. Downtown Park City has retained much of its old mining character. As a "Gentile" town, Park City differs markedly from other Utah communities. Its streets are two-lane, it has more former saloons on the Main Street and its past is charred by horrendous fires that repeatedly leveled homes, stores, bars, churches and schools. Most of the mine owners, who took their riches from hills around Park City, lived in Salt Lake City. Today, remaining homes built by these mineral kings can be seen lining South Temple Street east of Brigham Street. One, belonging to the Thomas Kearns family, was eventually deeded to the state and served as the governor's mansion. In the 1950's it was transferred to the Utah Historical Society for use as an office and a library when a new governor's residence was built. In 1977, the State Legislature authorized the governor's family to move back into the old Kearns mansion following its renovation.

"This is the Place"

South Temple is a good street to follow east from downtown. It leads to the University of Utah, laid out on a fine vantage point from which to view the city below. The campus, 482 acres large, was animated by a massive building program during the 1960's. New structures and landscaping created a particularly engaging combination at the institution's southern half, which embraces pleasant walkways and fountains. The north half is older, the original campus, but well cared-for and a portal to nostalgia. It also contains a highly regarded Museum of Natural History, housed in the university's former library. Guided tours are available. The school of architecture maintains a Fine Arts Museum and, year round, the school's various theaters and auditoriums produce drama, ballet, popular music festivals and classical recitals. Ballet West, a professional troupe supported by the intermountain region, was home-based at the university until it obtained new facilities in downtown Salt Lake City. On the campus edge, the Art Barn provides new showings of contemporary paintings, drawings, photography, sculptures and industrial art about every three weeks. The university's teaching hospital is nationally acclaimed, the only one between Denver and the West Coast. Its researchers have excelled in bone, blood and organ transplant work. Experiments with creating an artificial heart have attracted considerable scientific attention to the university's medical research program, and federal funding. The University Hospital and Medical Center is almost ninety percent federally financed. The campus has always been aware of the U.S. Government. At its back is the 9,000-acre Fort Douglas Military Reservation, complete with barracks, officers quarters and parade grounds. Much was declared surplus by the Pentagon and deeded to the state, to serve the university and other purposes. One of the other uses will be to enlarge Pioneer Monument State Park, which is south of the university and approximately at the spot where Brigham Young is supposed to have uttered his famous line, "This is the place," after emerging from Emigration Canyon overlooking Salt Lake Valley.

More precise historians quote Brigham as actually saying: "It is enough.

This is the right place. Drive on!" And he knew exactly where he was going. That had been decided after advanced parties reported back about the prospects near the Great Salt Lake. In any case, the park has a "This is the Place Monument," a stone shaft and flanking extensions decorated by bronze figures of such early area explorers as Jim Bridger, Father Escalante and General John Fremont. The State Parks & Recreation Division is developing a Pioneer Village on the park area grounds. Nearby stands a visitors center with murals telling the story of the Mormon migrations. Opposite the monument is Salt Lake City's Hogle Zoological Gardens, a well-stocked, neatly kept zoo.

Below the zoo, south on Wasatch Boulevard, is a shopping center fairly typical of many that dot neighborhoods in the Salt Lake Valley. At least five are indoor "shopping malls," the most unique located at 7th East and 5th Sought. It is called Trolley Square because it is in converted bus line barns dating back to 1908. Tastefully modeled for functional purposes, this shopping mall boasts more than fifty tenants, ranging from specialty stores, snack bars and a farmers market to restaurants and craft shops. Six small, but comfortable theaters operate in the adjacent building. The location is marked by a gold-painted and iron-ornamented water tower. Light bulb trimming gives the tank and its embellishments a special night-time appearance. Trolley Square is an extraordinary example of commercial recycling.

America's First Department Store

The newest enclosed shopping complex is downtown Salt Lake City's ZCMI Center. The initials stand for Zion's Cooperative Mercantile Institution, which means more in history than in the present. It was Brigham Young's answer to storekeepers who seemed to be profiteering among the early, struggling Mormon settlement in Salt Lake Valley. He simply put the Church in the retailing business and neutralized the competition. As it evolved, ZCMI is claimed by some to be America's first department store. Whatever the fact on that score, ZCMI is Utah's leading department store today and its new downtown building devoured the old structure, which was actually a collection of stores at the corner of Main Street and South Temple. Retained, however, as part of the new building's façade, is the cast-iron front that decorated ZCMI's Main Street entrances for decades. Another compromise between old and new can be seen on 1st South Between Main and West Temple Streets. This short block was "renovated" in 1970, given new sidewalks, a median strip planted with seedling trees and stone benches at the corners. Yet the street lighting shines from vintage candelabra lamp posts, deliberately installed to retain a dated, but ageless, ingredient. This street leads to the new Salt Lake County civic auditorium, called the Salt Palace. It seats 14,000 in the main area and has smaller meeting and exhibition rooms, as well as a little theater. A separate concert hall stands north of the main building.

Advent of the Salt Palace has transformed the city's downtown west side. A restaurant and specialty shop compound, entitled Arrow Press Square, blossomed in aged, rejuvenated brick buildings opposite the Salt Palace on West Temple. Three new hotels were constructed in the immediate vicinity. All in all, the effect has been a wholesome one. A minor league hockey team, the Golden Eagles, uses the arena through the winter season, a member of the Central Hockey League. The building's versatility accommodates circuses, track meets, concerts and rodeos. It has become the modern home of the Pioneer Days rodeo.

Pioneer Day

July 24 is Pioneer Day, a state holiday in Utah. It commemorates the day in 1847 when the first Mormon pioneers reached their promised land, and in Salt Lake City it is preceded by a full week of activity. On the 24th, an enormous parade, featuring floats, marching bands, men's and women's horse brigades, clowns and dignitaries galore, files down Main Street, then to Liberty Park. In 1970, President Nixon attended the rodeo that July 24th. The city has recurrently hosted U.S. Presidents, almost steadily since World War II.

It may be, as some have suggested, that a national politician knows the value of paying a courtesy call on the favored city of a three million-member organization. And in fewer places is there more ingrained respect for the U.S. presidency, no matter who holds it. Joseph Smith taught that America's constitutional form of government was divinely inspired. Beyond this, nevertheless, few cities rise above the nationwide urban monotony and represent a distinctive personality quite the way Salt Lake City does. People, whether President or plain traveler, need no other reason than their curiosity for inspecting this "City of the Saints" firsthand.

The Lake Itself

Two landscape imprints indelibly associated with Salt Lake City and Utah deserve special mention. One, of course, is Great Salt Lake. The other, Kennecott Copper Corp.'s mammoth open pit mine.

Great Salt Lake is indeed a natural wonder. Approximately 1,500 square miles in area, it is the nation's largest inland sea. Twenty-five percent saline, the lake is five times saltier than any ocean. Utah's relationship with the lake has changed through the years, just as the waterline has fluctuated.

Except for a species of tiny shrimp, no fish live in Great Salt Lake, so it had little practical value to the pioneers. Eventually, wood-hauling stern-wheelers plied its waters. Some were converted to early-day cruise ships. Lakeside resorts, dance halls and amusement parks have been operated around Great Salt Lake's eastern and southern shores through the years, but all have either burned or been abandoned. The last, giant Saltair, with its Arabian Nights-inspired pavilion, disappeared in flames during 1972. It had been closed since the mid-'50s.

The state created a park on Antelope Island in Great Salt Lake, east of Layton on State 127, but it has few improvements. The easiest public access to Great Salt Lake beaches is west of Salt Lake City on US 40. The area is also owned and operated by the state. If a pungent odor fills the air, it is not from sewage or industrial waste, it is the smell of dead brine shrimp washed up on the nearby shore. It's true, swimmers can bob on the lake surface "like a cork," without any effort. But some bathers suddenly discover they are allergic to salt in such concentrated solution. The reaction is a stinging sensation over that part of the skin immersed in the water. By all means shower under available fresh-water tanks after leaving the lake water.

Minerals Around Great Salt Lake

For years sodium chloride, common table salt, has been taken from the lake. Lately, other minerals, long known to be suspended through Great Salt Lake in measurable but elusive quantities, are being extracted. And the bed is being explored for oil.

In any case, Great Salt Lake is always a magnificent sight at sundown when clouds are also hugging the western horizon.

Kennecott's copper mine lies up Bingham Canyon. But it is visible from miles away as a tan and gray terracing on the face of the Oquirrh Mountains, sloping to Salt Lake Valley's western floor. Mining and its associate industries, smelting and refining, have, off and on for at least one hundred years, been a key factor in Utah's economy. Which is ironic because Brigham Young disdained the activity as too transitory and a magnet to unsavory types. He wanted his settlements snug to the ground, engaged in farming and farm-related industry. But it was too easy to find mineral deposits in such mountainous surroundings and a Mormon-baiting U.S. Army officer, Colonel Patrick E. Connor, commanding federal troops in Salt Lake City during the early 1860's, encouraged his men to conduct prospecting expeditions. They found gold and silver, which produced other discoveries of zinc, silver-lead, coal, and copper. Ore from Bingham Canyon was taken to Colonel Connor by an apostate Mormon, George Ogilvie. The colonel's assayer confirmed a rich lead and silver content, putting Bingham Canyon firmly in the nation's mining history. Low-grade copper, scattered finely through the ground, was eventually dug from the canyon; but not until the turn of the century, when mining engineer Daniel C. Jackling developed an economical metallurgical process, did the metal become a significant state resource. Since then, it has been Utah's most consistently important mineral product. Approximately $130 million worth of copper has been extracted annually from the Kennecott pit. The deepening, stair-step excavation can be viewed from an enclosed overlook, which features an amplified recorded message about the mine's past, present and future.

Jedediah Smith's Trail

In 1826, Jedediah Strong Smith, a mountain man known more for exploration than fur-trapping, hiked what is now Utah from north to south. He hugged the western flank of the Wasatch, searching for better beaver-snaring territory. Smith and his party had a desperate time of it—they nearly starved. Today, travelers following an equivalent route not only eat well, they linger at countless restful, scenic and thought-provoking intervals.

Jed Smith entered Utah through Cache Valley in the northeast corner. That probably would be done now on US 91 or 89, both rolling south from Pocatello. Or on US 30, which becomes State Route 30, from Rock Springs, Wyoming, on the east. Except for extensive cultivation, the country retains much of the naturalness encountered by fur-tracking wanderers over 150 years ago.

US 89, east of Logan, carries motorists through highland beauty in the Cache National Forest, Logan Canyon is particularly facinating, with two glacial lakes—Tony Grove and White Pine—both reached by paved road or foot-path. The Jardine Juniper, said to be the oldest tree in Utah—over three thousand years withstanding wind, cold and sun—is also in Logan Canyon. US 89 nudges alongside Bear Lake, enjoyably frequented by water-skiers, sailing craft, fishermen and scuba divers. Bear Lake is acquiring an increasing assortment of condominium resort developments. It has had for years a state park on the western shore and the principal adjacent town is hundred-year-old Garden City.

Logan, at the junction of US 91 and 89, is the commercial hub of northeastern Utah. It is the location of Utah State University, originally limited to agricultural and forestry studies, which currently offers other courses as well as recurrently nationally ranked football and basketball teams. Logan also has one of Utah's four Mormon temples, a stone-hewn structure, finely landscaped and flower decorated during summer months.

Nine miles south and sixteen miles east of Logan, through Hyrum on State 101, a rare encounter is staged every winter. The Utah Wildlife Division has established, at a place called Hardware Ranch, an elk feeding station. The animals, mostly cows and an occasional lame bull, congregate in the snow to survive on daily alfalfa handouts. Visitors are transported into the midst of the herd by horse-drawn sleighs. It's a singular experience, mingling with five hundred seldom-seen creatures, approachable only because of their hunger.

Another entry to Utah known by the mountain men is along the present Interstate 80. It leads, after a junction at Echo, forty-three miles beyond Wyoming, to either Ogden or Salt Lake City. The I-80N branch traverses stunning Weber Canyon on its way to Ogden. Near Morgan, the super highway gives travelers an opportunity to view Devil's Slide, two parallel slabs of limestone twenty feet apart and forty feet high sticking to the mountain side. It helped conjure many Indian legends.

The Coming of the Railroad

Ogden, thirty-three miles north of Salt Lake City, is Utah's second largest city with 126,000 residents. It was also planned by Brigham Young, but, after the arrival of transcontinental rails in 1868, Ogden gained the reputation as a railroad town. It was, during those track-laying days, a brawling, free-for-all hot spot, causing the Mormon population considerable unease.

Now, the city is a quieter commercial and industrial center, beneficiary of a new church temple and home of Weber State College, a four-year vocational and liberal arts school. With the help of an active industrial development program and several federal installations—Hill Air Force Base and an Internal Revenue Service computer center and Regional Forest Service office—Ogden continues growing. The Browning brothers, inventors of automatic weapons, were from Ogden. The John M. Browning Armory and Firearms Museum displays eighty-six original and production models of Browning rifles, pistols and machine guns.

On I-15, northwest from Ogden, in an especially tranquil setting, is Brigham City, given a space-age boost by missile industry firms located nearby. Via Brigham City, on State 83, motorists can visit one of Utah's latest National Historic Sites—the Golden Spike site at Promontory. It features a tourist center and replicas of two engines used during the driving of the last spike which completed America's first transnation railroad. During summer months the 1869 ceremony is reenacted at the Golden Spike

National Historic Site as the finale to a film, narration and tour of the museum.

The Northern Tier

Doubling back, through Brigham City toward Ogden, travelers can encounter a collection of bird management areas around bays on the east-central portion of Great Salt Lake. At Willard Bay State Park, summer regattas for both power and sail boats are held annually.

Utah's northern tier fluctuates dramatically, from the Great Salt Lake Desert on the western hand and the High Unitas Wilderness Area on the east. This magnificent slab of the Uinta Mountains, the only continental range running east and west, contains Utah's loftiest point—Kings Peak, 13,528 feet high. It is also preferred terminal for backpackers and campers. Mirror Lake resort touches the wilderness area at its eastern extremity and can be reached on U-150 as soon as the road is cleared of snow, sometime in late spring. Uinta mountain lakes and streams are a hardy fisherman's challenge.

Fishing in northeastern Utah can be successful without being strenuous, especially at Flaming Gorge Reservoir in the Flaming Gorge Dam. This is a delightful outdoor offering tucked into the northern and most eastern corner of Utah, approximately seventy-five miles due north from Vernal. Previously a hunter and fisherman rendezvous, Vernal has lately become the center for oil field development. The area has another distinction—prehistoric fossil remains at Dinosaur National Monument, twenty miles east of Vernal, where visitors can actually watch workmen patiently unearth bones of long-extinct giant reptiles. At Vernal, the state maintains the Field House of Natural Science, an exhibit of local geological features, prominent Utah scenes—not always up to date—and ancient Indian artifacts. This is Indian country.

The main highway between Vernal and Salt Lake City is US 40, which passes through the Uintah and Ouray Indian Reservation. The principal towns along this stretch are Roosevelt and Duchesne, but about seven miles east of Roosevelt is a modest experiment in contemporary Indian self-sufficiency. The Bottle Hollow Resort, a motel complex built alongside a 450-acre reservoir, is owned and operated by the Ute Indian Tribe. It derives its name from a previous custom of locals pitching empty liquor bottles into a natural depression in the brush dotted landscape between settlements at Roosevelt and Ft. Duchesne. The resort advertises ceremonial Indian performances and has a trading post dealing in native artwork and craft specialties.

On farther, closer to Salt Lake City, US 40 passes two more large fishing holes, Starvation and then Strawberry Reservoir, impounded sources of irrigation water also stocked with trout. Beyond, at Heber City, a left turn off US 40 leads to Provo along US 189. A right turn, staying with 40 to I-80, leads to Salt Lake City. Delaying at Heber City isn't a bad idea.

Heber is a familiar Mormon name, but the place could have easily been called Basel or Tavaness, anything from the Swiss foothills, as this is what the Heber Valley resembles. And it did to the Mormon converts from Switzerland who settled there. Directly west lies 22,000-acre Wasatch Mountain State Park, a hiking, camping and picnicking wayside that includes a 27-hole golf course nestled in a crisp Alpine setting.

Railroad Run

During summer months, a steam engine recalled from railroading's smoke-puffing past hauls a four-car coach-load from Heber City to Bridal Veil Falls in Provo Canyon. The round trip meanders through meadowland, along streams and reservoirs while penetrating a mountain pass. It's a quaint way to sightsee.

Bridal Veil Falls is a double cataract that splashes in steep descent down Provo Canyon's sheer mountain walls. It's viewable from alongside US 189, if that's the route selected out of Heber City. Provo Canyon is one of the principal passes slicing through the Wasatch Range and, most of the way, it follows Provo River, a premier trout stream. Also off US 189 in Provo Canyon is Sundance Resort, a development led by film actor Robert Redford. It features skiing during the winter and camping or horseback riding through the other seasons.

US 189 is an old, narrow road, but preferred by conservationists attempting to prevent a planned widening and straightening project. Whatever the outcome, the highway will still lead to Provo, Utah's second largest city.

Provo and BYU

Located at the foot of 11,000-foot-high Provo Peak, the city is typically Mormon, with clean, wide streets and well-tended landscaping. It is a combination farming, education and industrial center. The Mormon Church's biggest and best college campus graces Provo—Brigham Young University. Handsome and sprawling after a massive 1960's construction program, BYU, or "The BY," as it is colloquially called by many Utah admirers, attracts a 25,000-member student body from LDS families throughout the U.S. and foreign countries. Its rigid, and obeyed, code of conduct rivals its nationally ranked basketball teams for far-flung recognition. BYU administrators make a point of avoiding federal financing.

A U.S. Government decision to scatter basic industry during World War II gave the area around Provo a steel mill. Now owned and operated by the Columbia-Geneva Division of the U.S. Steel Corp., the mill has provided steady employment for over thirty years, also persistent air pollution. Protecting air and water has been a problem in this area.

Utah Lake, twenty-three miles long north to south and ten miles wide, ripples just west of Provo. It is Utah's largest fresh-water lake. And while much is fit for boating, fishing and water-skiing, parts are termed a health hazard by state officials. The culprit is sewage, being treated, but not under full control before it finds the lake. A wise swimmer looks first for posted warnings. The situation hasn't discouraged Saratoga, a lakeside amusement park that attracts sizable crowds all summer long.

Just south of Provo, on US 89, lies Springville, also called Art City. The honorary title goes with Springville's Art museum, which contains an acclaimed collection of paintings and sculpture. In April, the permanent display is enhanced with an annual exhibit by nationally known artists.

To the north, near Lehi, is Timpanogos Cave National Monument. Located in American Fork Canyon, the cleverly lighted caves were formed by a now-vanished underground river. The monument visifor center is open from May to October and the setting is spectacular. The cave is at the head of a long, uphill walk not recommended for the aging or infirm.

Gateway to Southern Utah

Provo could be considered the gateway to Southern Utah, the point from which the state gradually changes, becoming less populated, not as arable, with but a few exceptions, nonindustrialized, and cross-cut by geologic extremes.

Brigham Young intended for the Mormons to be fully self-sufficient so that never again could they be easily uprooted and driven from their land. To this end he regularly sent immigrant groups streaming downstate with instructions to farm and create industry wherever possible. His expectations weren't always fulfilled, but the strength of his resolve is reflected in two early temples built in southern Utah. Provo only recently acquired a temple. Manti, 176 miles south of Salt Lake City, has had one since the late 1800's. It's said Brigham Young was particularly concerned about the region around Manti because an Indian chief had asked him to send white men bearing the Christian teaching. Be that as it may, settlements waxed and waned through the area during the pioneering era. To an extent that Fillmore, opposite Manti, on the west side of the Valley Mountains and farther south, was at one point competing with Salt Lake City for designation as state capital. It still retains the old territorial statehouse as a museum. Fillmore, named after the 13th President of the U.S., had a population numbering slightly under 2,500 in 1970. The largest city in south-central Utah is Richfield, about 4,400 strong on US 89, surrounded by sections of the Fishlake National Forest. It's also a jumping-off place for Capitol Reef National Park. The eighty-mile drive on State 24 provides a sudden and startling introduction to Utah's Colorado River canyon country. Crossing open, wind-weathered Awapa Plateau to a height of 8,410 feet, the highway drops into an attractive valley at the head of east-flowing Fremont River. Then, beyond Torrey, the descending roadway enters an arid land of rocks, buttes, mesas, and gorges striped with brilliant colors. On the left is Waterpocket Fold, a 150-mile line of red, yellow and brown cliffs, several hundred feet high, capped by pinnacles and white capitol-like domes.

Colorado River Canyon Country

Sixty-one square miles in area, Capitol Reef National Park includes twenty-mile stretches of the cliff. The road moves along the base, encountering spurs and graded trails leading to impressive Grand and Capitol Gorges, Chimney Rock, Hickman Natural Bridge, petrified forests and Indian petroglyphs engraved on stone 1,200 years ago.

The Capitol Reef escarpment marks the southern boundary of Wayne Wonderland, a desert region of canyons, basins and sheer cliffs, the most awesome work produced by natural upheaval and erosion. Here stand Cathedral Valley, Walls of Jericho, Hoodoo Arch and the surrealistic Valley of the Goblins. Ask about road conditions before exploring these sites in standard model cars.

After departing the park, State 24 winds to Hanksville, the now-renowned Robbers Roost headquarters, made famous by the film "Butch Cassidy and the Sundance Kid." Yes, they were actual early-day Utah outlaws and this was their hideaway country. It is, today, a well-traveled way toward Lake Powell and the Glen Canyon National Recreation Area. Southwest from

Hanksville, State 95 drops to a junction with State 276, which finally reaches Bullfrog Basin at lakeside. There are marinas and overnight facilities at the basin.

An alternate course follows State 95 to a river crossing at Hite. As long as the road is passable, this way leads to Natural Bridges National Monument, three gigantic rock spans and cliff ruins in tranquil high desert, dotted by piñon and juniper growth. East and north lies a section of the Manti-La Sal National Forest, and directly east a fork in State 95 leads to either Blanding, north, or Bluff, south. Blanding is larger, 2,250 people, and closer to Monticello, which is the actual center of the region's tourist activity. But Bluff is the more interesting, a tiny community with a dramatic past. It is the first white settlement in southeastern Utah, an oasis reached in 1879 by a Mormon party after an epic winter trek across the canyon harshness. From Bluff it's possible to boat through whitewater rapids of the San Juan River to Mexican Hat, named for a nearby sombrero-shaped rock. Also north on State 261 outside Mexican Hat, the nine-mile sidetrip to an overlook above the Goosenecks of the San Juan is worth taking. The river has carved a narrow canyon, 1,200 feet deep, in a sequence of horseshoe bends. Water must flow six miles to proceed one.

East of Bluff are the widely scattered prehistoric ruins of Hovenweep National Monument. South from Mexican Hat, on US 163, travelers enter the northern rim of the 25,000-square-mile Navajo Indian Reservation, largest in the U.S. Here, on the Utah-Arizona border, is awesome, incredible Monument Valley. Mile after mile, the pavement passes huge red sandstone buttes, pillars, columns and needles soaring more than one thousand feet above the wide desert floor. The unforgettable shapes have been given such names as Totem Pole, Castle, Stagecoach, Brigham's Tomb and Mitten Buttes. Indians still spend summers amid these wonders, living much as their ancestors did centuries ago. The Navajos have created Monument Valley Tribal Park, taking in 96,000 acres. It offers an observation building, Indian crafts center, campgrounds, fourteen miles of passable roads and trips to remoter sections in special big-wheeled vehicles.

Returning through Monticello, US 163 meets Moab, another tourist base camp. The Old Testament name is misleading these days. Moab bustles, often with Hollywood film companies, shooting outdoor scenes on location. They headquarter in Moab and search surrounding terrain for likely background to go with westerns, desert dramas and, yes, Biblical enactments. Scenes from "The Greatest Story Ever Told" were shot outside Moab. The desired "authenticity" isn't difficult to find.

In the 1950's, Moab enjoyed a different kind of drama. Uranium was discovered nearby and, while it lasted, the mining and prospecting was frenetic. Located above the confluence of the Green and Colorado Rivers on the Colorado, Moab makes the most of its river country. Various boat tours are available at the landings, including a night ride that takes sublime advantage of shapes formed on gorge walls with high-powered flood lights.

Arches and Towers

Crossing the Colorado, US 163 passes Arches National Park, featuring a fifty-three-square-mile area with rock spires, pinnacles and narrow fins pierced by 88 naturally formed openings. One is a 291-foot bridge, the largest known natural arch. Paved roads reach the finest specimens, but some walking is necessary to see rock-formed skyscrapers of Park Avenue, Landscape Arch, The Devil's Garden and whimsical Delicate Arch. Called Schoolmarm's Britches by local cowhands, the last is the most beautiful and remarkable of the bunch. Rising more than one hundred feet high, it stands alone and unsupported in a setting of slickrock domes, with the gorge of the Colorado River and the 12,000- to-13,000-foot peaks of the La Sal Mountains in the distance.

Castleton Towers and Fisher Towers are two other areas of unique rock formations northeast from Moab. They can be visited by a black-topped road through the multi-hued Colorado River gorge.

Canyonlands National Park envelops the confluence of the Colorado and Green Rivers and exhibits the greatest variety of rock sculpture found anywhere on earth. Elevations range from 3,700 feet in the depths of Catarac Canyon to over 6,000 feet on the plateau rims. Between both a half-billion years of the planet's life is apparent in countless folds, warps, shifts and tilts. Canyonlands, established as a national park in 1964, is still fairly untamed. The more intrepid visitors can explore it satisfactorily on Jeep roads, but other autos are advised to proceed with advance knowledge about conditions ahead. Local pilots have offered sightseeing flights over the area and information on such possibilities is available at the Arches Visitor Center.

For a less expensive bird's-eye view of the Canyonlands region, a black-topped county road leads west from US 163, north of Moab, to Dead Horse Point State Park, a magnificent overlook on the Colorado gorge. Also, a graded road veers away from the Dead Horse Point approach southwest across the plateau to appropriately titled Island in the Sky, ending at Grand View Point. This jutting promontory provides a giddy, 2,500-foot-high view of the merging Colorado and Green Rivers.

US 163 continues north to I-70, built through country never before crossed by road or trail. Scenery this opened up is typical of the entire area. The 235-mile trip from here to Salt Lake City is usually made on US 50-6, branching north from I-70, through Green River and Price. At Green River, the annual Friendship Cruise is annually launched in late May. Power boats of every description, conveying groups that vary from sightseers to fishermen to outdoors enthusiasts to purely revelers, compose the armada. Their destination is Moab, which is usually reached the second day out, total elapsed time depending on the boatman's skill.

Price and Helper are centers of Utah's coal-mining industry. Most Utah miners came from non-Mormon stock and the coal communities are no exception. They evidence a firm individuality verging on truculence toward the predominantly LDS settlements. In the past, Price was known to openly defy state laws restricting liquor sold in bars. A former mayor, J. Bracken Lee, who subsequently became a two-term Utah governor and then mayor of Salt Lake City, once arrested state liquor control officers in Price, claiming they had no jurisdiction interfering with municipal matters. Price is also the home of Eastern Utah College, formerly Carbon College, a two-year state institution.

Further South

Southern Utah is, for its population, particularly blessed with state colleges. Others include Snow College at Ephraim and Southern Utah College at Cedar City. The Cedar City campus has developed as a center for arts instruction. This extends through painting, metal work and drama. Utah's summer Shakespearean Festival is held on the college campus every year in July.

Cedar City, on I-15, 260 miles south of Salt Lake City, is also a recreation and tourist center. It reclines on the western edge of the Dixie National Forest and is within eighteen miles of Cedar Breaks National Monument. Farther east, on State 14, then north on US 89, Bryce Canyon National Park drops away in a multi-hued extravaganza. One of Utah's newest ski resorts, Brian Head, is less than a two-hour drive, depending on road conditions, from Cedar City. The facility, with chair lifts rising above 10,000-foot elevations, is a favorite with skiers from Nevada, Arizona and even California.

Zion National Park is located directly south of Cedar City, off I-15 and then along state routes that take motorists through small prim Mormon settlements named Toquerville, LaVerkin and Virgin. A tranquil, wooded camping site east of Cedar City off State 14 is Navajo Lake. The lake is cold enough for good trout fishing and big enough for boating. The area around it is being "found," and fast acquiring vacation cabin sites. Another rediscovery is taking place at St. George in southern Utah.

St. George has Dixie State College and was a favorite wintering retreat for Brigham Young. His two-story house, an echo from New England, has been restored as a Utah State Park museum. Lately, condominium developers have done well at St. George, with accommodations for retirees, weekend recreation seekers and tourists traveling at a leisurely and stylish pace. The permanent community, 8,000 at the latest census, started with a cotton mission sent to the Virgin River Valley by Brigham Young in 1861. The pioneers endured considerable hardship, but managed to succeed. Utah's first Mormon temple, white stucco surrounded by desert palms, was erected at St. George in 1871. Early vineyards once produced quality Utah wine around St. George until a burst of abstinence wiped the industry out.

North of town rise the cool, forested Pine Valley Mountains, topped by 10,325-foot-high Signal Point. Five miles west from St. George is Dixie State Park at Santa Clara, featuring the formidable rock-fortress home built in 1862 by Jacob Hamblin, an outstanding Mormon explorer and missionary to the Indians. No one was more familiar with the obscure trails of southern Utah. Hamblin devoted almost half a century to keeping the peace between Indian tribes and white settlers. He died in 1886 while on the run from officers arresting polygamists. Southwest from Santa Clara, the highway passes through the Shivwits Indian Reservation, winding over the Beaver Dam Mountains as high as 4,800 feet.

An eastward route from St. George leads past Zion National Park on State 15 to a junction with US 89 on its way south to Kanab. Kanab has been called "Hollywood's backyard" because of the countless outdoor films photographed in its vicinity. The credits run from the early "Drums Along the Mohawk," to the more recent "Planet of the Apes." Parry Lodge in Kanab was made famous by the interviews with movie stars conducted there. Scenery around Kanab is literally "too magnificent to be real." The Moqui Indian caverns are located five miles north of town, displaying the largest fluorescent mineral exhibit in the United States. Immediately south of Kanab, the small Kaibab Indian Reservation hugs the state line in Arizona.

The settlement, accessible from US 89 after that highway exits Utah, is exactly 305 miles beyond Salt Lake City and 71 miles away from the north rim of Grand Canyon.

PRACTICAL INFORMATION FOR UTAH

UTAH FACTS AND FIGURES. Utah is named for the Ute Indians, and means "hill dwellers." Its nickname is *Beehive State.* The sego lily is the state flower; the blue spruce, the state tree; the California gull, the state bird and the elk, the state animal. "Industry" is the state motto. "Utah, We Love Thee" is the state song.

Salt Lake City is the state capital. By the most recent figures population is 1,059,273.

The promised land of the Mormons is a country of rugged mountains, salt deserts, fertile valleys, eroded rock and rich mineral wealth. Mountains cover much of the eastern and central portions of the state, and in the southeast is the dramatic landscape of the Colorado Plateau—cut by canyons, gorges, mesas and buttes. In the west, beyond the Great Salt Lake, are the mud and salt flats of the Great Salt Lake Desert. Mining and light manufacturing lead the state's economic activities. Agriculture is important as well, while tourism has lately become the second best income producer. Utah's climate is dry, with hot summers and cold winters, except in the southwestern corner, where temperatures usually remain moderate in winter. Heavy mountain snowfalls supply spring, summer and fall water needs.

HOW TO GET THERE. *By car:* I-80, probably the most heavily traveled transcontinental highway, passes through Salt Lake City. From the north I-80N runs southeast through Salt Lake from Portland, Oregon. I-15 comes from the Los Angeles area through Cedar City, Utah, and up to Salt Lake.

By air: Salt Lake City is the major terminal. Among the long-distance carriers serving it are United, American, Frontier, Texas International, and Hughes Airwest.

By train: Amtrak's *Rio Grande Zephyr* runs from Denver to Ogden, Utah, about 30 mi. north of Salt Lake City. Amtrak's Pioneer connects Salt Lake City with Seattle, through Ogden and Boise.

By bus: Trailways and Greyhound are the major carriers to Utah (Salt Lake City is the busiest terminal) but the region is also served by numerous other lines including Crown Transit, Linea Azul, Sun Valley and Bremerton-Tacoma.

HOW TO GET AROUND. *By car:* The Interstates (I-70 and I-80 eastwest, and I-15 north-south) are the primary means of communication where there are long distances between towns. State roads crisscross the rest of the state except in truly desolate areas like the Great Salt Like Desert to the west of Salt Lake City.

By air: From Salt Lake City, Hughes Airwest flies to Cedar City, in the southwest part of the state; and Frontier flies to Vernal in the northeast. There is also charter service from Salt Lake City to local airports near Zion, Bryce and Canyonlands National Park.

By train: Ogden and Salt Lake City are on the Amtrak line.

By bus: All the major cities and towns in Utah have good bus service. Trailways, Greyhound, Sun Valley and Mid-Continental are some of the carriers.

TOURIST INFORMATION. Detailed information about anything in the state may be obtained from the Utah Travel Council, Council Hall, Capitol Hill, Salt Lake City 84114. Tel. (801) 328-5681.

SEASONAL EVENTS. Utah keeps busy year round with entertainment, cultural, sporting and festival events. As with most states, winter month attractions are mostly indoor, of a cultural nature and not quite as plentiful as spring, summer and fall activities. The more urban the setting, the more versatile the annual events calendar.

January: In Salt Lake City, the drama season is still in full swing, with productions at *Promised Valley Playhouse, Theatre 138* and the *Glass Factory.* Auditorium events are held year round in Salt Lake City's municipal coliseum, *The Salt Palace.* It is home for the Central Hockey League, Salt Lake. At Park City, the *Silver Wheel Theatre* presents old-fashioned melodrama. Winter resort specials include the *Color Country Winter Classic* at Brian Head ski area and the *Snow Cup Race* at Alta. Tremonton usually schedules the *Bear River Cutter Races*—horses pulling chariots on ice runners—during January.

February: Kingsbury and Babcock Theatres at the University of Utah usually present drama and music performances during the month. These will probably include a Ballet West performance. Park City's ski resort will hold the *Canada-American-Lowell Thomas Classic* and the *Dave Novelle Memorial Dual Slalom.* Both are ski races. Pro hockey will continue in Salt Lake City.

March: Special events centers at University of Utah in Salt Lake City, Utah State University, at Logan, Weber State University, Ogden, and Brigham Young University, Provo, usually hold public programs varying from concerts to pop artists. The *Mormon Festival of Art* is usually conducted at Brigham Young University. Hockey near season's end in Salt Lake City.

April: Springville Museum of Art, Springville, holds its annual national art exhibit. *Utah Symphony* and *Ballet West* spring gala at Utah State University. The annual *jeep safari* rendezvous in Moab—bring your own jeep. Brian Head Ski Resort holds its spring fiesta. The *Dixie College Rodeo* is held at St. George.

May: Golden Spike Celebration at Brigham City; *Smithfield Health Days,* Smithfield; *Black and White Days,* Richmond; *Cache Dairy Festival,* Logan; annual *Ute Indian tribal bear dances* at Whiterocks; *Green River Friendship Cruise,* 180 miles from Green River to Moab.

June: The Lagoon amusement park opens for the summer season near Farmington. The Salt Lake City municipal band starts its Sunday concerts in Liberty Park. At Moab, the *Canyonlands Festival and Rodeo* is presented, while at Bluff an annual *Indian Days* festival is held. Rodeos at Price, Lehi and Pleasant Grove are usually produced during June. As is the *Dinosaurland Art Festival* at Vernal. *Saratoga Amusement park,* near Lehi, opens for the summer.

July: Annual celebrations are in high gear. *Bridger Days* at Hyrum; *Freedom Festival,* Provo; *Mormon Miracle Pageant,* Manti; *Old Capital Days,* Fillmore; *Ute Stampede,* Nephi; *Annual Utah Shakespearean Festival,* Southern Utah College at Cedar City; *Days of '47 parades statewide; Ute Indian tribal sun dances,* Whiterocks.

August: County fairs are prevalent, in Heber City, St. George, Salt Lake City, Logan, Tremonton, Nephi, Parowan, Farmington, Manti. Park City usually holds its annual art festival and speed trials get underway at the Bonneville Salt Flats. Swiss Days, Heber City, which can also be scheduled for the first week of September, usually cap August.

September: Park City stages an outstanding Labor Day program including mining skill contests and rugby matches. Later in the month a *Rugby Challenge Cup* tournament is played at Park City. *Peach Days Art Festival* at Brigham City and the *Cache Valley Threshing Bee,* featuring old-fashioned steam-driven machinery, is held at College Ward, Salt Lake Public Library holds a fine arts festival.

October: Golden Eagles hockey starts another season. The *Hansen Planetarium* in Salt Lake City also launches a new season. Annual ram sale and harvest festival is held at Spanish Fork.

November: Golden Spike livestock show, Ogden; Christmas parades in Cedar City and Ogden. College and university football games conclude at University of Utah, Utah State University, Weber State College and Brigham Young University.

December: An international *Christmas celebration* is held at Ogden's municipal gardens, *Utah Symphony* and *Ballet West* launch season in Salt Lake City. The Salt Lake Oratorio Society's annual performance of "The Messiah" is performed in the Salt Lake City Tabernacle. On Saturdays, cutter races are held at Tremonton.

 NATIONAL PARKS. The five national parks in the state of Utah offer much in the way of outdoor living for hardy travelers who enjoy roughing it. *Bryce Canyon National Park* is located in the southwest part of the state. Its multicolored layers of limestone and clay produce a quilted effect that is enhanced by the rays of the sun. Bryce Canyon itself is particularly impressive, as are Yellow Creek, Willis Point and Rainbow Point. There are 20 miles of roads in the park, but some sections are accessible only on a mule or horse. For those without cars, the park provides transportation at a nominal charge. The Rim Road trip will cover most points of interest. In addition to a hotel and lodge the park has improved camp sites. Camping time is limited. Bryce Canyon also has a well-organized museum with lectures and illustrations explaining the origins of its outstanding features.

At *Zion National Park,* the emphasis is also on natural beauty. But while at Bryce most of the viewing is down, at Zion it is up. At the entrance visitors pass between two enormous colored monoliths, indicating what is to come. After entering the "gate," visible in the distance is the famous Bridge Mountain, so named because of a natural rock bridge high on the crest. Past this is a succession of rainbow-hued rock formations including Streaked Wall and the Mountain of the Sun. Driving north to the road's end leads to the Great White Throne and The Organ. The green, wooded canyon and murmuring river combine with majestic temples and towers to make this a magnificent showcase of natural splendor. Hiking trails lead to such places as Emerald Pool and the Hidden Cave. Swimming in the Virgin River is an unforgettable experience. A hotel, cabins and campsites offer accommodations for extended stays. Many Jeep camp tours are available for a good, close look at Utah's newest National Park— *Canyonlands.* They can be engaged at Moab, Blanding or Monticello. This park is divided roughly into the Needles Section at the southern end and the Island in the Sky at the northern end. Between the two are fascinating formations in The Maze, Land of Standing Rocks, Doll House, Salt Creek, Horseshoe Canyon and White Rim. In the south lies Chesler Park, a secluded valley completely ringed by fingers of rock jutting skyward.

Arches National Park, north of Moab, has five distinct sections, all unique in geology and scenery. The Windows Section is centrally located. Courthouse Towers is in the southern end, Klondike Bluffs at the northernmost point and Devils Garden and Delicate Arch fill the rest of the northern section. The park gets its name from the 89 erosion-formed natural arches scattered around its interior.

Stone portals and bridges are found in *Capitol Reef National Park,* a slender stretch of sightseeing country about midway between Bryce and Canyonlands. It also contains petrified forests and artifacts left by pre-Columbian Indians of the Fremont culture. It is named for the gigantic, domed formations, capped with white sandstone and resembling the nation's capitol. They are part of the Waterpocket Fold, a 100-mile-long bulge in the earth's surface that contains depressions eroded in the rock and capable of holding thousands of gallons of rain water. In the north end, on cliffs behind the peach orchards at Fruita, are petroglyphs carved by ancient Indians. Outlaws, including the infamous Butch Cassidy, knew the area as a perfect hideout.

In addition to the national parks, Utah has seven national monuments. On State Route 14, near Cedar City, is *Cedar Breaks National Monument,* red and white colored rock country decorated with a profusion of wild flowers in season. Near Point Supreme are full service camp facilities, an information center and a museum explaining the various natural surroundings.

Dinosaur National Monument is particularly fascinating. East of Vernal in northeastern Utah, the area has supplied the largest collection of prehistoric vertebrates in the U.S. Entire skeletons have been excavated intact by several archeological institutions. Some are kept at a small museum in the monument for visitors to inspect. Many canyons remain unexplored, but it's possible to ride big rubber rafts on safe guided trips through such perilous-sounding places as Split Mountain Canyon and Whirlpool. Cave dwellers have left crude pictures in the monument caves.

Natural Bridges National Monument takes its name from three rock bridges visible from White Canyon. In cave dwellings, open to the public, a fine, sweeping view of the area is possible. This monument is in southeastern Utah, approachable on U-95 or U-261 off U.S. 163.

On the Navajo Indian Reservation is *Rainbow Bridge National Monument.* It features a fantastic natural bridge which is now only a quarter mile away from the rising waters of Lake Powell. Eventually, as the reservoir water reaches maximum levels, boats will be able to move even closer.

Timpanogos Cave National Monument, in north-central Utah, east of Lehi in American Fork Canyon, features sidewall scenes of white and pink crystals enclosing stalagmites and stalactites shimmering in artificial lighting. The caves are open from May to October. Picnic facilities lie nearby, along with a convenient grocery store.

Newly established *Golden Spike National Historic Site,* at Promontory in Northern Utah, marks the completion point of America's first transcontinental railroad. It includes replicas of the two steam engines that met nose to nose in 1869 when driving the final "golden" rail spike was celebrated. A museum at the site also tells the country's cross-nation railroad story.

 STATE PARKS. There are 44 state parks in Utah, the largest are Snow Canyon, Dead Horse Point and Wasatch Point.

Snow Canyon (5,688 acres), near St. George in the southwest corner of the state, is formed by a large gorge cut out of multi-colored sandstone. There are facilities for both recreational vehicles and tents. Open all year.

Dead Horse Point (4,627 acres) is an area of deep gorges and mesas. Dead Horse Point itself rises about 2,000 feet above the Colorado. Located southwest of the town of Moab. There are tent and recreational vehicle spaces and flush toilets. Open all year.

Wasatch Mountain (22,000 acres), near Heber City southeast of Salt Lake City, has trailer hookups, tent spaces, fishing and hunting. There is a golf course nearby. In Heber City is the Wasatch Mountain Railway which chugs along a 3-hour trip through Heber Valley, Provo Canyon and Bridal Veil Falls.

 FARM VACATIONS AND GUEST RANCHES. There are not as many guest ranches in Utah as in some of the other "Old West" states, but the ones here have some of the most spectacular scenery in the country. *Triple R Farms* in Payson, about 50 miles south of Salt Lake City, has all the ranch activities and animals. This and most guest ranches are great places for children.

Bottle Hollow at Fort Duchesne is owned and operated by Ute Indians. You can take it easy around the modern lodge and pool or take guided trips into the Green River Wilderness.

On the Navajo Reservation in the Monument Valley area is *Gouldings Trading Post and Lodge.* You can take guided jeep tours through this almost unbelievable country of towering mesas and pinnacles and precipitous gorges.

  MUSEUMS AND GALLERIES. *Paiute Indian Museum,* Public School Administration Building, Cedar City, has a collection of many items reflecting the life of the Paiute Indians. *Southern Utah Museum of Natural History,* College of Southern Utah, is open daily and features collections and exhibits of Utah's relationship with studies in such fields as anthropology, biology and geology. *Worthens Store of Ten Thousand Stones,* Fremont, has an excellent geological collection from around the world. *Man and His Bread Museum,* Logan, in the library of the Utah State University, traces the history of agriculture from origin of man to the present. Closed Sunday, *Pioneer Museum,* Provo, contains a particularly extensive assortment of pioneer utensils, tools and weapons used in the early West. No charge, closed weekends. *Golden Spike Monument* museum at Promontory tells the story of America's first transcontinental railway. *Utah Field House of Natural History.* Vernal, features displays telling the state's geologic and human history, from prehistoric to modern times. Open afternoons all summer. No admission charge.

Art exhibits may be seen at the *Salt Lake Art Center,* near the University of Utah Campus, Salt Lake City, Closed Mondays and holidays. *Fairbanks Gallery of Sculpture,* Fairview, is open during the summer. Admission free. The *Springville Museum of Art,* Springville, Utah County, is Utah's most well-known art center. Outdoor art festivals are held annually at many of Utah's resort areas. Park City closes its Main Street for such an occasion, usually sometime in August.

HISTORIC SITES. Utah is a perpetual history lesson, with special locations to underline the text. St. George has the first Mormon temple built in Utah as well as Brigham Young's winter home, now a state park museum. Other pioneer homesteads are preserved in the area, particularly the *Jacob Hamblin Home* at Santa Clara.

The oldest House, the *Miles Goodyear Cabin,* is on display in Ogden. Built around 1841, the log-hewn house was used by the first white family settling permanently in what became Utah.

The town of Fillmore is the original Territorial Capital and retains the 1855 building that accommodated the state's first legislative sessions. It's now a museum.

Salt Lake City is packed with historic reminders. Prominent among them are *Lion House,* Brigham Young's office, and *Beehive House,* right next door, which was one of his homes. Also, there's "This is the Place" monument, the *Daughters of the Utah Pioneers Museum* and *Council Hall.* The last two are on Capitol Hill. The *Salt Lake City and County Building,* on Washington Square, is an original and still used for local government purposes. The inside has been extensively remodeled, the second-floor walls are lined with vintage photographs and blueprints. The outside walls are being completely reconditioned. a job that is expected to take 20 years.

Ghost town prowling has become a popular Utah pastime, principally because there are so many abandoned settlements throughout the state and because it's another enjoyable way to see the countryside. Stephen L. Carr, in a 1972 publication, listed 150 ghost towns marking Utah's landscape. A good many are deserted mining camps, but some are former agricultural centers. Among the more interesting are Mercur and Ophir in Tooele County; Rockport, Summit County, Blacks Fork, Summit County; Rainbow, Uintah County; Scofield, Carbon County; Latuda, Carbon County; Eureka, Juab County; Mamoth, Juab County; Spring City, Sanpete County; Frisco, Beaver County; Cove Fort, Millard County; Osiris, Garfield County; Silver Reef, Washington County. In Pine Valley, Washington County, due north of St. George, stands a dignified old two-story church, a magnificent example of meeting house construction common a century ago. But standing as it does, isolated, yet still useful, it is one of rural Utah's most poignant sights.

TOURS. Few tours are confined to the state itself. But many companies that conduct tours of the region include trips into Utah. Those services operating within the state generally restrict themselves to particular areas and cover certain attractions rather than the full locale.

Gray Line Motor Tours conducts many short trips in and around Salt Lake City. These are perfect for seeing a great deal in a short time. The company also runs shuttles to Alta and Snowbird ski resorts up Little Cottonwood Canyon out of Salt Lake City. Gray Lines offers tours to Bryce Canyon National Park, Zion National Park and Cedar Breaks National Monument, as well as a Canyonland tour.

Continental Trailways schedules three-day tours from Salt Lake City to Zion National Park, Bryce Canyon National Park and Cedar Breaks National Monument, Also, a five-day tour including Grand Canyon, to the north rim. These tours are available from June 1 to Sept. 1.

With the construction of two high dams, one in Utah, the other just below the border in Arizona, more lake water is provided for several boat tours. Such trips are offered on Flaming Gorge Reservoir behind Flaming Gorge Dam by Hatch River Expeditions. Similar outings are available at Lake Powell behind Glen Canyon Dam, at Page in Arizona.

For the intrepid, white-water river running on the Green and Colorado Rivers is conducted by *Hatch Expeditions* in Vernal and *Tag-a-Long Tours* in Moab.

Silver Sands Beach, on Great Salt Lake, offers a boat cruise on the lake, including a dinner ride in the evenings.

INDUSTRIAL TOURS. Although famed for its natural beauty, Utah accommodates considerable industry. Many plants are open to visitors. While most of the following firms are pleased to welcome tourists, it is suggested they be notified before a planned arrival.

Several food processing places are open to public view. *Winder Dairy,* Salt Lake City, offers tours to those over six years old. These include milk, cheese and bread production, not animal herds. *Hi Land Dairy* of Salt Lake provides a milk processing tour. *Snelgrove Ice Cream Co.,* Salt Lake City, offers tours of an ice cream plant and the *Salt Lake Donut Co.* permits public inspection of its product in the making, any weekday before 4 p.m. *The Macaroni and Noodle Co.* in Kearns, Salt Lake County, is an LDS Church operation, using volunteer workers, and welcomes visitors.

Anyone interested in building material manufacture is invited to tour the *Otto Buehner Co.,* or *Buehner Block,* in Salt Lake City.

Utility tours are limited to those conducted by *Utah Power and Light Co.* at Castle Gate, Carbon County; *Orem,* Utah County; and the *Gadsby Plant* in Salt Lake City. *Young Electric Sign Co.* demonstrates methods of cutting, assembling and sewing wearing apparel on Thursdays only. Saturday, at noon, *Wells Tannery,* Salt Lake City, conducts tours of the leather processing plant.

The Doll Hospital, Salt Lake City, has a fine display of dolls, varying in age, size and life-like appearance.

MUSIC. The Tabernacle on Temple Square in Salt Lake City is home of the world-famous *Mormon Tabernacle Choir.* The Choir can be heard on Thursday evening rehearsals or on Sundays for the formal performance. The Tabernacle was host to visiting symphonies and home of the *Utah Symphony.* However, such performances will now be conducted in the new Bicentennial Concert Hall built on the grounds of the Salt Palace.

DRINKING LAWS. Utah's liquor control laws beg the visitor's indulgence. Beer is the only alcoholic beverage served in all public bars. And it is the 3.2 variety. Certain licensed restaurants also serve 2-ounce "mini-bottles" of the most commonly preferred cocktail or highball liquor. But they can only be ordered with food. That applies to wine as well. Private clubs, however, can serve mini-bottle mixed drinks whether food is also served or not. Some private clubs aren't overly careful in verifying the membership of their customers and all have liberal guest privileges. The difficulty is finding these oases without a local resident as guide. Almost all public eating and drinking establishments permit customers to carry their own liquor to the table or bar. This has earned collective state restrictions on the subject the title of "brown bag laws." And remember, in public restaurants, waiters and waitresses aren't permitted to fetch, open or mix mini-bottles. That all must be done by the customer. Mix will be served, however, and most good restaurants will chill wine brought to the establishment. Retail liquor is only sold in state stores, or package agencies. The legal age is 21 and, for the most part, strictly enforced.

 SUMMER SPORTS. Utah is a wonderland for outdoor recreation, a land of wide-open spaces, magnificent scenic variety and matchless natural wonders. Tennis and golf courses seem to be everywhere and for hardy individualists, possibilities for fishing, hunting, camping, hiking, horseback riding, swimming, water-skiing and boating abound.

Generally, Utah's *fishing* season starts the Saturday closest to June 1 and runs through November. However, some 200 waters are open year round. The state's most popular and regularly caught fish is the rainbow trout. Frequently taken from many waters are brook, native cutthroat, brown, Kokanee salmon, Mackinaw or lake trout, grayling, largemouth and white bass, channel catfish and walleyed pike.

Two large man-made lakes furnish spectacular opportunities for anglers—Flaming Gorge in northeastern Utah and Lake Powell in south-central Utah. The state has other reservoirs and several streams, running through high mountain country and down along valley floors, joining sizable rivers, and all are sport for fishermen. These include the Provo, Weber and Logan Rivers; streams in Big Cottonwood Canyon, the High Uintah Mountains and most of the state's national forests. Non-resident licenses good for a year cost $25. A five-day adult tourist license is $7.50, a one-day tourist license, $2. Non-residents under 12 may fish without a license provided they are accompanied by a licensed angler and their catch is counted in the adult's daily limit.

Limits are: trout, salmon, 8 fish, except in some counties a bonus of 6 cutthroat and/or brook trout; grayling, 8 fish; Bonneville cisco, 50 fish, Bear Lake only; black bass, 10 fish; white bass, no limit; crappie, 10 fish, but in Lake Powell, no limit; walleyed pike, 6 fish except in Provo River, where the limit is 2; whitefish, 10 fish; channel cat, 4, except in Utah Lake and Willard Bay, where it is 16 fish. All other species, no limit.

Trails are excellent for *hiking* in Utah's national forests for short trips or several weeks backpacking. Long pack trips are advised to use guide services on the Colorado Plateau and High Uintahs Wilderness Area. An especially memorable hike is the 20-mile walk through Zion National Park's Virgin Narrows. This can be done in a day, but is better appreciated if planned for an overnight camp in the deep crevice of a canyon. Most of the walk is through the Virgin River water, which seldom reaches above waist height on an average adult. The hike starts several miles below Navajo Lake in the Dixie National Forest and concludes at the bottom of a foot path in Zion National Park. Guide information at the park is available for this spectacular hike.

River running is a fast growing lure in Utah. These trips, in large unsinkable rubber rafts, carry thrill enthusiasts through rough water on the San Juan, Green and Colorado Rivers. Charter arrangements can be made at Moab, Green River, Bluff and Mexican Hat. Boating, both water-skiing and sailing, can be enjoyed on Utah's several man-made reservoirs and lakes. In addition to Flaming Gorge, Lake Powell, Great Salt Lake, Bear Lake and Utah lake, there are Strawberry, Pineview, Scofield, Deer Creek, Rockport, East Canyon, Otter Creek, Steinaker and Bottle Hollow Reservoirs.

There are 45 public *golf courses* in operation around Utah. Many are nestled in unique mountain or desert settings. The state maintains one, at Wasatch Mountain State Park, near Midway in Wasatch County.

Hunting is widely practiced in Utah, whether for deer, elk, antelope, jack rabbits, badgers, woodchucks and gophers or quail, pheasant, chukar partridge, ducks and geese. The large mule deer has been stocked around the state wherever browse and competition for the range allows. For years the annual harvest, attracting hunters from throughout the west, has averaged 100,000 deer. A non-resident big game license costs $75 for one deer, either sex.

Quail is best hunted in Washington County and the Uintah Basin while ringnecked pheasants can be found throughout central Utah during a short season in early November. Marshes along lakes and rivers are usual ambush sites for ducks and geese. Non-resident waterfowl and game bird licenses cost $20. Minimum age for hunting big game is 16, for waterfowl and game birds, it's 12.

 WINTER SPORTS. Utah's mountain winters are long, snowcovered and, though cold, often sunny for extended periods. The official state guide book lists 14 *ski resorts* in Utah, but not all excel. Those most likely to have ample, skiable snow on open slopes suitable for beginner as well as expert are Alta, Brighton, Solitude, and Snowbird near Salt Lake City; Park City and Park City West, in Summit County; Beaver Mountain, 27 miles east of Logan; Nordič Valley, 17 miles east of Ogden; Snow Basin, 19 miles east of Ogden; and Brian Head, 29 miles east of Cedar City. Overnight accommodations range from non-existent, at Snow Basin, to modest, at Brian Head, to limited, at Brighton, to adequate and comfortable, at Alta, to new and plush, Snowbird, to village size, Park City. Snowmobiling is catching on in Utah's snow country. It is allowed in certain areas of local canyons. One of the state's finest public ice-skating rinks is at Salt Lake County's Salt Palace arena in downtown Salt Lake City.

 SPECTATOR SPORTS. The Minor Central Hockey League team, Golden Eagles, plays at the Salt Lake City Salt Palace through the late fall, winter and early spring. The University of Utah in Salt Lake City, Brigham Young in Provo and Weber State in Ogden have full athletic schedules, and the California Angels' farm team, the Salt Lake Gulls, plays in the Pacific Coast League at Dirks Field in Salt Lake City.

 HOTELS AND MOTELS in Utah are relatively inexpensive. Their highest rates will be in effect for the "in-season" period which, according to the locale, is either ski time (November through April) or the summer months that bring tourists to the National Parks and forest lands. These are the rates we have used to compile our categories.

Based on double occupancy, the rate categories for Utah are: *Deluxe* over $27, *Expensive* $22-27, *Moderate* $16-22 and *Inexpensive* under $16.

For a more complete explanation of hotel and motel categories, refer to ROCKIES AND PLAINS *Facts at Your Fingertips* at the front of this volume.

ALTA

Alta Lodge. *Deluxe.* This ski resort has a variety of accommodations and prices—call for rates or package plans. Meals are served in the cafe and dining room and there is a package store. After skiing enjoy a game of pingpong, pool, sit by the fireplace or read in the library.

Rustler Lodge. *Expensive.* Offering everything from dormitory-style rooms to suites as well as family rates and ski package plans, this ski lodge has a cafe, bar, and package store; also saunas and a recreation room.

BEAVER

Beaver TraveLodge. *Moderate.* Within a block you'll find a coin laundry and a cafe open 24 hours. Rooms have dressing areas.

Paice. *Moderate.* Attractively landscaped with a heated pool. A cafe open until midnight, and a coin laundry are nearby.

Sleepy Lagoon. *Moderate.* The small pond helps create the restful atmosphere suggested by the motel's name. Inside you will find attractive rooms and dressing areas. The motel also offers a heated pool while a cafe and laundromat are within a half mile.

BLANDING

Cliff Palace. *Inexpensive.* Large, comfortable rooms and convenient at-door parking. The cafe one and a half blocks away is open until 10 p.m. and a coin laundry is also nearby.

Gateway. *Inexpensive.* The local cafe is directly opposite and the coin laundry is just down the street. Some rooms are better than others. Pets are allowed.

BLUFF

Mokee. *Inexpensive.* Although the rooms are not of uniform quality, you will enjoy the calm atmosphere and the beautiful cliff view. There is an adjacent cafe.

Recapture Lodge. *Inexpensive.* If you are interested in exploring, geologist-guided trips and river trips are available here. Closer to home, use the heated pool or the shaded grounds for lawn games. A cafe and launderette are nearby.

BRIGHAM CITY

Red Baron. *Moderate.* They have a heated pool, will allow some pets. Their cafe opens 6 a.m.; it's 10 blocks to a laundromat.

Best Western Motel. Adjacent to city park.

Sweetwater Park and Resort. *Moderate to Expensive.* Complete resort complex with condominium-type rooms. Includes lake, and pool swimming, restaurant, lounge, horse riding, tennis and golf. Sailboats available for rental.

BRYCE CANYON

Bryce Canyon Pines. *Moderate.* The rooms are furnished in a rustic, early American style but are uneven in quality.

Pink Cliffs. *Moderate.* Besides cafe, coin laundry, and beauty shop, Pink Cliffs also has a trailer park. If you are flying, use the free airport bus.

Ruby's Inn. *Moderate.* Ruby's has a cafe, laundromat, and a pool table. Some rooms are off central halls and are quiet and comfortable.

CEDAR CITY

Astro. *Moderate.* For relaxation the Astro provides a heated pool, sauna. The rooms have queen-size beds. Cafe and coin laundry are close by.

Cedar City Travelodge. *Moderate.* Provides swimming pool, king and queen sized beds.

Cedar Crest. *Moderate.* Golfers will appreciate the putting green and 9-hole course and there is a playground for children. A cafe open 24 hours and a coin laundry are within 2 blocks.

El Rey. *Moderate.* After a long drive, the El Rey's therapy pool and sauna may be just what you're looking for. There is also a heated pool.

Friendship Inn Village Motel. *Moderate.* Features a recreation area, convention facilities, a swimming pool and washing machines.

Imperial 400 Motel. *Moderate.* In a convenient location, the Imperial has a pool.

Knell. *Moderate.* Unusually attractive rooms. Some pets are allowed.

Town and Country Inn and Restaurant. *Moderate.* Some say this hostelry serves the best food in town. It has convention facilities and comfortable rooms.

Zion's. *Moderate.* Zion's offers somewhat lower rates from November to March. They allow some pets. A cafe and launderette are within easy walking distance.

COALVILLE

Moore. *Moderate.* For $2 extra you get a kitchen with your room. Or, you can eat at the cafe half a block away. A playground is on the premises and a public pool and coin laundry in the next block.

DUCHESNE

Gateway. *Moderate.* For those who want to stay awhile, the Gateway has weekly rates in its older rooms. A deposit is required; you get large beds; a cafe and a nearby laundromat.

Ells. *Inexpensive.* If you're traveling in the summer you may appreciate the refrigerator available with some rooms. A cafe open until 10 p.m. and a laundromat are within easy reach.

FILLMORE

Fillmore. *Moderate.* Across the street is a 24-hour cafe and less than a mile down the road is a coin laundry.

Paradise Inn. *Moderate.* The rooms fulfill the promise of the motel's name with their decor, dressing areas, and oversize beds. Heated swimming pool. The cafe is open from 6 a.m. to 10 p.m.; a coin laundry is a mile distant.

GARDEN CITY

Bear Lake Motor Lodge. *Moderate.* This motel features rooms you can feel at home in and a cafe. If you are down to your last clean shirt, a laundromat is 3 miles away.

Baugh. *Moderate.* If you're on a honeymoon, ask for the bridal suite. Enjoy the heated pool, sundeck, and spacious grounds. Some rooms have a fireplace and dressing rooms.

Sherwood Hills. *Moderate.* A somewhat secluded resort-type facility. Fine for the family. Features all-season activities. Two outdoor pools and winter ski rentals. Comfortable rooms are complemented by restaurant serving ample meals.

GREEN RIVER

Green River. *Expensive.* Your children and pets can amuse themselves in the playground while you swim in the pool. Afterwards, drop your laundry into the coin machines two blocks away and then proceed to the nearby cafe, open until 10 p.m.

Overniter Motor Inn. *Moderate.* Comfortable accommodations. Pool.

Sleepy Hollow. *Inexpensive.* Guests at Sleepy Hollow can be energetic by playing tennis in the adjacent city park. The motel is also near a cafe and a coin laundry.

HEBER CITY

Green Acres Lodge. *Moderate.* For those arriving late, or getting up early, there is a 24-hour cafe nearby. Ten blocks away you'll find a coin laundry and the lodge itself has a playground and heated pool.

Homestead. *Moderate.* Reservations are necessary to stay at this resort-type motel which has 2 heated spring-fed pools, pony rides, tennis, a putting green, horseback riding, and bicycles. You may also play volleyball and ping-pong or just enjoy the lovely grounds and duck ponds.

Wasatch. *Inexpensive.* Since this motel's heated pool is open to the public, you have a chance to meet some of the town's residents. Volleyball and picnicking are available too, as well as ping-pong. You'll find a cafe a block away and a coin laundry a little further on.

Bar-M. *Inexpensive.* Bar-M welcomes children and pets and has a playground for them plus a heated pool for adults. A cafe is across the street, a launderette just down the block.

KANAB

Parry Lodge. *Moderate.* Until 10 p.m., room service provides liquor, wine, and beer. In the summer don't miss the melodramas performed on the covered patio or shady lawn. Other features are a heated pool, coin laundry, and specially arranged tours.

Red Hills. *Moderate.* You can get a tan at Red Hills by using the sundeck and heated pool. In the shade, sip a soda in the nearby cafe. Coin laundry 4$^1/_2$ blocks away.

Four Seasons. *Moderate.* The rooms here are especially spacious and well-appointed. After a swim in the heated pool, stop in at the cafe only a block away.

K. *Inexpensive.* The K is a small motel with trailer facilities and boat parking. The owners keep a sitter list and provide a playground and pool.

Coral Sands. *Inexpensive.* If your children prefer not to sightsee, the motel provides a babysitter list. The rooms are large and a cafe and laundromat are conveniently near.

LOGAN

Alta. *Moderate.* Here you'll find a playground for children and a cafe and coin laundry nearby. But more important, you won't have any trouble getting to sleep because this motel rates as more than usually quiet.

MEXICAN HAT

Canyonlands. *Inexpensive.* Large families (5 to 7) get a good rate here. Pets are allowed and a cafe and coin laundry are near by.

San Juan Trading Post. *Inexpensive.* Did you forget your toothpaste or razor-blades? Befitting its name, the Trading Post sells sundries. The cafe serves until 9:30.

MOAB

Green Well. *Expensive.* Maybe it's just the color of the upholstery, but some motels have an indefinable aura of quality. This is one. It offers a heated pool, a cafe, and a launderette 10 minutes away.

Inca Inn. *Moderate.* If a Spanish motif is your preference, this is worth a try. Pool, sundeck, and cafe nearby.

Moab TraveLodge. *Moderate.* Not only is the cafe open until 10 p.m. but liquor is available after 4 p.m. The rooms are appealing to a weary traveler. Heated pool.

Ramada Inn. *Moderate.* A full service motel, with pool, restaurant, car rentals, and access to Colorado River tour reservations.

Apache. *Inexpensive.* Since some of the local scenic tours might be too rugged for small children, the Apache provides a list of babysitters. It also has parking for self-contained trailers and a heated pool.

Canyonland. *Inexpensive.* It's always handy to be located in a motel with a cafe and coin laundry nearby. The cafe is open from 6 a.m. to 10 p.m. and the laundry is only a 6-block roundtrip.

MONTICELLO

Canyonlands Motor Lodge. *Moderate.* Here's a marvelous setting for a quiet game of croquet or an old-fashioned barbecue. Children will delight in the playground, pool.

Navajo Trail. *Moderate.* Playground for the kids. The cafe, a block away, is closed on Sunday.

Wayside. *Inexpensive.* There aren't many "extras" here, but you'll be comfortable and get a good night's sleep. The cafe ½ block away opens at 6 a.m. The ever-important coin laundry is 3½ blocks from the Wayside.

NEPHI

El Tonya. *Moderate.* This is a small motel that allows pets, has a playground, a cafe nearby and is 2 blocks from a coin laundry.

Safari. *Moderate.* Besides the playground there's a wading pool for small children.

Adults may swim in the heated pool, play ping-pong or watch others from under a shade tree. A convenient feature of the rooms is that they have both front and rear doors.

Starlite. *Moderate.* If you've been hiking hear the Anasazi Indian ruins you may want to hike 4 more blocks to the coin laundry. If not, head for a relaxing swim in the heated pool.

OGDEN

Holiday Inn. *Expensive.* Not only is there a heated pool, but poolside service of food and, after 4 p.m. setups and 3.2 beer. Another out-of-the-ordinary service is the kennel. Also at your disposal are a sitter list, cafe, room service, and free airport bus.

Circle R. *Moderate.* Anyone who has driven late into the night can really appreciate a 24-hour-cafe—there's one just 2 blocks from the Circle R. If you have time for relaxation, let the kids discover the playground.

Weston's Lamplighter Motel. *Moderate.* Beauty shop, sundries counter are among the features here along with heated pool and early-opening cafe.

Ogden TraveLodge. *Moderate.* The restaurant next door is open late and there's a rec room for indoor fun. Heated pool, launderette nearby.

Imperial 400 Motel. *Moderate.* Newer accommodations, with water beds as well as the king and queen variety. Has kitchenette units.

Millstream. *Inexpensive.* An unexpected delight is the stream running across the well-cared-for lawn in back and the picnic tables and playground. There is a cafe on the premises and space for truck and trailer parking.

ORDERVILLE

Orderville. *Inexpensive.* Opens its seven attractively appointed rooms April through December. There are restaurant and launderette across the street.

PANGUITCH

New Western. *Moderate.* Convenient to Bryce Canyon, this little motel caters to travelers with swimming pool, some in-room refrigerators and thrifty family rates. Laundromat and restaurant are close.

Bryce Way. *Moderate.* Their cafe, open Mon.-Sat., serves until 10 at night. The rooms are comfortable, most with large beds. There's also a heated swimming pool.

Blue Pine. *Inexpensive.* Just the essentials: bed, sitter list. But the price is right and you don't have to check out 'til 2 p.m. Convenient to restaurant and laundromat.

PARK CITY

Park City Resort. *Deluxe.* Offers a variety of condominium living. Everything is nearby for outdoor activity—golf and tennis in summer, and skiing and snowmobiling in winter.

Treasure Mountain Inn. *Deluxe.* Convenient to the slopes, this facility has kitchen apartments, so, if you want to cook, there is an opportunity to economize. Some rooms have private terraces and the mountain views are a treat. Rec room and heated pool provide fun when you're not skiing.

Silver King Lodge. *Deluxe.* This mid-sized inn is near the Ski Area and has pool, rec room where a roaring fire can be so welcome on frosty evenings. They have pool and sauna plus a private club selling drinks.

Chateau Apres. *Moderate.* Rustic, but comfortable. Near ski slopes, golf course and downtown. Restaurant and all-weather swimming pool.

PRICE

Green Well. *Expensive.* Unlike most Utah accommodations, those in Price cost the most in summer. The explanation is the nearby Manti-La Sal National Forest. The nicely decorated rooms, swimming pool and on-premises lounge and cafe add up to a pleasant stay here.

Crest. *Moderate.* Their restaurant can give you breakfast at 5 a.m. The rooms are neat, the beds are large. It's two blks. to a launderette.

El Rancho Siesta. *Inespensive.* You won't get much more than a siesta at this very basic motel, but it will be peaceful. Adjacent cafe cooks 6 a.m. to 10 p.m.

PROVO

Holiday Inn. *Expensive.* This typical chain motel is opposite a golf course and has pools for wading as well as swimming. They do their best with the liquor laws; set-ups and light beer. The rooms are spacious and there is one specially for handicapped guests.

Columbian. *Moderate.* There's a heated pool, coil for brewing the morning coffee and a sitter list. Laundromat is 5 blks. away, a restaurant awaits, 6 a.m.-10 p.m. across the street.

Rodeway Inn. *Moderate.* Thrifty family rates prevail but the only pets that do are small 'uns—leashed. Light beer and set-ups may be purchased and the cafe never closes. There's a golf course across the road and you can tee off early; inn check-out isn't til 2.

Royal Inn. *Moderate.* Probably the poshest place to stay in Provo, this handsome hostelry has a health spa with saunas and a whirlpool bath. There are lavish suites, two with their own refrigerators. Several rooms have private patios. The inn houses a popular local restaurant and is near the Brigham Young campus.

Uptown. *Inexpensive.* Some kitchen units and agreeable family rates distinguish this small but serviceable motel. All pets are welcome. A block to a cafe, 5 to a launderette.

RICHFIELD

Holiday Host. *Moderate.* Largest motel in town, so a good place to begin if you wheel into town *sans* reservations. There's a heated pool, and a restaurant across the street. Pets are welcome.

Rodeway Inn. *Moderate.* Children under 12 stay free, as is true in most motels in the eastern states but not too often around Utah. Heated pool. The inn's dining room is a locally popular steak house.

ROOSEVELT

Bottle Hollow Resort. *Moderate.* This motel, actually in Fort Duchesne, is Ute Indian-owned and has water sports available and is one of the few lodgings in the state to offer entertainment. Very attractively designed.

Friendship Inn, Western Hills. *Moderate.* Welcome resting place after long drive. Restaurant. Pool.

Frontier. *Inexpensive.* They've just added 20 new rooms here and charge only $1 per day extra for a kitchen unit. Pets are welcome; cafe operates 5 a.m.-10 p.m.

SALT LAKE CITY

Little America. *Deluxe.* 500 S. Main. A combination motel and high rise, with different rates for each. Highrise tower features indoor and outdoor swimming pools, sauna, and exercise room. Entertainment in lounge. Coffee shop open 24 hours.

Ramada Inn. *Deluxe.* 999 S. Main. A rambling, comfortable motel. Bus service to ski slopes in winter. Outdoor swimming pool. Restaurant, 24-hour coffee shop, liquor store, barber, and beauty shop. Pets allowed in rooms.

Salt Lake Hillton. *Deluxe.* 150 West 5th South. Pleasant hotel-motel complex suited for conventions as well as tourists. Four restaurants, top floor lounge featuring seafood and fine city views. Services include barber, beauty shops, package liquor store, sauna, whirlpool and swimming pool.

Utah. *Expensive.* South Temple at Main St. You can swim at a nearby pool and the hotel has a barber shop and beauty salon. Free bus to the airport is available.

Hilton Inn. *Expensive.* 154 West 6th South (near I-15). Two-level motel with three restaurants, one lounge and 24-hour coffee shop. Allows pets. Short walk from laundromat. Three blocks south of Salt Palace.

Royal Inn. *Expensive.* 206 S. West Temple St. Conveniently situated opposite the Salt Palace—one of its popular crowd-pullers is pro-hockey—this inn tries to keep you happy: sauna, therapy pool, swimming pool . . . and a dance combo. Many of the sumptuous suites include a bar. Coffee shop never closes but the package store does.

Tri-Arc Travelodge. *Expensive.* 161 West 6th South (near I-15). High rise hotel-motel with two restaurants and two lounges. 13th floor lounge has magnificent view of Salt Lake Valley. Enclosed pool is only play area for children. Barber and beauty shops, and package liquor store.

Desert Inn. *Moderate.* 50 W. 5 South St. There's a pool and adjacent sundeck for fresh-air relaxation. Suites are available and a third of the rooms have extra-large beds. You can get room service until 9 p.m.

Imperial "400" Temple Square. *Moderate.* 476 S. State St. (US 89A, 91A). Again, you can be next door to the Salt Palace and opposite a park. The cafe next door stays open late and the motel itself offers you a swim.

Temple Square Hotel. *Moderate.* 75 West South Temple. An older hotel, recently remodeled. Conveniently located downtown, opposite famed Temple Square and the Salt Palace. Coffee shop. Tour arrangements made for visitors.

Covered Wagon. *Expensive.* 230 W. North Temple. It's close to I-80 and the rates are truly modest. Across the street is an all-night restaurant.

Colonial Village. *Inexpensive.* 1530 S. Main St. They have a pool and are right next door to a popular German restaurant. A coin laundry is 3 blks. distant.

Scenic. *Inexpensive.* 1345 Foothill Dr. (US 40, 3½ blks. SE of midtown). Opposite the shopping center, next door to a cafe, this motel is good for a quick overnight stop when you don't want to start off the day in mid-city.

SNOWBIRD

Snowbird Lodges. *Deluxe.* This complex has three condominiums and one hotel. Complete mountain setting, with accommodations for summer and winter vacations. Skiing, tennis, hiking, swimming pool. Some units have kitchens, fireplaces, open balconies, and saunas. Restaurants close by. Shops, lounges with live entertainment.

ST. GEORGE

Four Seasons Motor Inn. *Expensive.* Caters for family comfort. Restaurant, games room, lounge, pool, putting green. Coffee shop, liquor store and in-room steam bath.

Coral Hills. *Moderate.* Has saunas, therapy and swimming pools. Nearby restaurant.

St. George Travelodge Downtown. *Moderate.* Saunas, swimming and therapy pools. Space for parking boats and campers. Restaurant. Baby-sitting arranged.

Travelodge East. *Moderate.* Swimming pool, baby-sitting. Nearby cafe.

VERNAL

Dinosaur. *Moderate.* Basketball is on top of the activities list here. The restaurant's one of the best in town and the rooms are clean and comfortable.

Echo Park Lodge. *Moderate.* You can park at the door and there are picnic tables on the grounds. Restaurant and laundromat are just across the road.

Ute. *Inexpensive.* The town park, with museum and sports opportunities, is across the way. Motel cafe opens 5 a.m.

WENDOVER

Wend-over. *Moderate.* The heated pool beckons, but so do the gambling tables and machines, just over the state line in Nevada.

ZION NATIONAL PARK

Pioneer Lodge. *Moderate.* There's a heated pool, restaurant, and the rooms are tastefully appointed.

Bumbleberry Inn. *Moderate.* Plenty to do right here: sauna, therapy pool, swimming pool and various lawn games. There's a sundry counter and lots of nice rooms in quiet side halls.

Zion Lodge. *Inexpensive.* The Interior Dept. runs this thrifty *pied-à-terre* in the beautiful park. Some games and Saturday night dances complement the offerings of nature all around. Dozens of cabins have fireplaces.

 DINING OUT. There is nothing different or unique about Mormon cooking. Statewide restaurant quality has improved considerably since tourism developed into such a big, booming business. It's possible to discover an especially tasty cuisine in out-of-the-way locations, but don't count on it. Salt Lake City, however, is beginning to acquire a kitchen. The going is slow because liquor laws discourage heavy investment in grand cafes or exclusive type restaurants. But specialty places, offering French, Spanish and German dishes, are increasing. Seafood, believe it or not, is found fresh and well prepared in several Salt Lake City dining rooms. Some of the best menus will be found up nearby canyons or south of the city.

Restaurant price categories are as follows: *Deluxe* $10 up; *Expensive* $5.50-$9. *Moderate* $3.50-$5.50 and *Inexpensive* $2-$3.50. For a more detailed explanation of restaurant categories see THE ROCKIES & PLAINS *Facts at Your Fingertips* at the front of this volume.

ALTA

Alta Lodge. *Expensive.* Specialties are fondue and scampi. Lunch is a bargain.

Rustler's Lodge. *Expensive.* At the Rustler Lodge Resort. A varied American-Continental menu in pleasant surroundings.

BRIGHAM CITY

Idle Isle. *Inexpensive.* 24 S. Main St. Prime rib and seafood here, but the kids will probably be most interested in their candy factory.

Red Baron. *Inexpensive.* Good food for the family. Open for breakfast, lunch and dinner.

CEDAR CITY

Sugar Loaf Cafe. *Moderate.* Specialties include broasted chicken, steak.

GREEN RIVER

Oasis Cafe. *Moderate.* Seafood, chicken, steaks and a variety of short orders.

HEBER CITY

The Hub. *Inexpensive.* Open 24 hours for the weary traveler. Children's portions.

KANAB

Chef's Palace. *Expensive.* Specialties are chicken and char-broiled steak.

LOGAN

The Bluebird. *Moderate.* A locally popular restaurant that makes its own candy and ice cream.

Country Kitchen. *Moderate.* Good food family style.

The Loft House. *Moderate.* Steaks, chicken and shrimp are featured on the menu. There is also a coffee shop.

MOAB

Bob & Olive's Sundowner. *Moderate.* Steak and chicken here, liquor also available.

Golden Spike Restaurant. *Moderate.* Steaks, sandwiches and salads are specialties of the house.

OGDEN

Hermitage Inn. *Expensive.* Scenic canyon setting. Menu varies, but usually includes fish, chicken and beef dishes.

Warehouse. *Expensive.* Fine food in a tastefully renovated warehouse. Specialties include steak and prime rib.

Bamboo and Noodle Parlor. *Moderate.* Tasty oriental and American entrees.

Bratten's Grotto. *Moderate.* Seafood in a nautical atmosphere.

Olde Country Bar. *Moderate.* Old-fashioned American food served family style.

Rigo's. *Moderate.* 2788 Washington Blvd. A large restaurant serving Italian cuisine.

PARK CITY

Adolph's White Haus. *Expensive.* Swiss atmosphere and specialties. Reservations recommended.

Car 19. *Expensive.* 438 Main St. Mostly steaks served in an old railroad car.

Das Gasthaus. *Expensive.* Features German cuisine and a hunt breakfast in summer months.

Treasure Mountain Inn. *Moderate.* Fine family dining at this resort hotel. They have a hunt breakfast on Sunday.

PRICE

Husky Highway House. *Moderate.* The best in home cooking.

Jean Selmes' Fine Foods. *Inexpensive.* Steak and seafood at good prices.

PROVO

Golden Spike Restaurant. *Moderate.* Steaks, sandwiches and salad for the entire family.

Royal Inn. *Moderate.* Good steaks and home baking at this large restaurant near Brigham Young Univ.

RICHFIELD

The Wood Platter. *Moderate.* Steaks, chicken and—if you're tired of those—pizza.

BJ's Family Restaurant. *Inexpensive.* Special children's menu featuring steak, chicken and trout.

Slice-em Thins Restaurant. *Inexpensive.* An Old West setting for their specialty of prime rib.

ROOSEVELT

Frontier Grill. *Moderate.* A variety of home-style cooking.

SNOWBIRD

Forklift. *Expensive.* Set in most impressive mountain resort surroundings. Breakfast, lunch and dinner. Menu features stuffed mountain trout, Cornish game hen and prime rib.

Steak Pit. *Moderate.* Lower level restaurant, informal but proper. Hot artichokes a specialty. Entrees run from steak to crab and teriyaki chicken.

ST. GEORGE

Chez Maggy. *Expensive.* Gourmet French food in a renovated home. Small and intimate. Reservations recommended.

Atkin's Sugar Loaf Cafe. *Moderate.* The specialties here are broasted chicken and steak.

Dick's Cafe. *Moderate.* Western-style cooking with seafood, steaks and chicken the feature.

SALT LAKE CITY

EDITORS' CHOICES

Rating restaurants is, at best, a subjective business, and obviously a matter of personal taste. It is, therefore, difficult to call a restaurant "the best" and hope to get unanimous agreement. The restaurants listed below are our choices of the best eating places in Salt Lake City, and the places we would choose if we were visiting the city.

TRI ARC 13TH FLOOR   Western American
Soup is served in individual tureens, and loaves of hot bread accompany every meal. There's also a great view of the entire Salt Lake Valley. Steaks and prime ribs are the staples of the menu. West Temple at 6th South. *Expensive.*

LA FLEUR DE LYS   French Cuisine
Serious diners choose this establishment. Sweetbreads, roast pheasant, and live lobsters cooked to order are part of the appeal. The rest is the posh atmosphere and fine service. *Deluxe.* 338 South State St.

RISTORANTE DELLA FONTANA   Italian Cuisine
Actually, there are representative dishes from many Mediterranean countries, and the normal dinner runs to a full seven courses. The dining room is in an old church, complete with fountain and ornate carved interior. A real local favorite. 336 South East. *Moderate.*

QUAIL RUN   American Cuisine
The kind of country atmosphere that only the wealthy can produce, with fires often

burning brightly in the huge fireplaces. Local residents regularly make the drive out of the city to enjoy the home baking, fresh flowers, and candlelit atmosphere. *Expensive.* Open on Friday and Saturday evenings only. 9564 Wasatch Blvd.

THE ROOF.   French Cuisine
Formerly called the Sky Room, this dining experience in elegant but subdued surroundings, atop Hotel Utah, affords a magnificent view of Temple Square. Live piano accompaniment completes the setting for superb dining. *Expensive.* South Temple and Main St.

Other recommended restaurants:

Balsam Embers. *Expensive.* 2350 Foothill Dr. (US Alt. 40). Specialties include stuffed breast of chicken and medallions of veal.

Log Haven. *Expensive.* Millcreek Canyon. Variety menu with a mountain setting overlooking a lake. They bake their own breads. Reservations required.

Paprika. *Expensive.* 2302 Parleys Way (US Alt. 40), German and American cooking. Specialties are beef Stroganoff and sauerbraten.

Athenian. *Moderate.* 247 E. 2nd St. Authentic Greek food and the whole family is welcome.

Hawaiian. *Inexpensive.* 2928 Highland Dr., 4 mi. SE on State 152. Chinese and Polynesian food is accompanied by the sound of a Hawaiian thunderstorm.

La Morena. *Inexpensive.* 346 W. 1st Ave. Good, authentic Mexican food.

Spaghetti Factory. *Inexpensive.* 189 Trolley Sq. Great family dining in a fun setting.

The Royal Palace. *Expensive.* 249 S. 4th East. One of the city's more unusual dining interiors, converted from a former Jewish temple. Plush and formal with side enclosures off main dining room. One "courtyard" room includes a tiled fountain. Musical background of piano and violin. Haute cuisine, ranging from French to Persian.

VERNAL

The Skillet. *Expensive.* 251 E. Main St. (US 40). Steaks, chicken, lobster and shish kebab. They do their own baking.

Diamond Lils Cafe. *Moderate.* 248 Main St. They are justly proud of their steak and prime rib.

WYOMING

The Cowboys Still Ride

by

BRUCE HAMBY, ROY PECK, LEAVITT F. MORRIS and CURTIS CASEWIT

Bruce Hamby has worked for the Denver Post *for many years, and is now its travel editor.*

Roy Peck is co-publisher of the Riverton Wyoming Ranger.

Leavitt F. Morris, former travel editor of the Christian Science Monitor *and still a frequent contributor to the publication, contributed most of the Exploring section on Wyoming.*

Curtis Casewit is a Denver-based freelance writer.

Wyoming is a vast, majestic land of contrasts—rolling plains, high plateaus, rivers, lakes and snowcapped mountains; rich farmlands, grass- and sagebrush-covered prairies, sudden red and purple-striped badlands; fiery, steam-belching geysers and hot springs; cowboys and Indians, oilmen and miners, ranchers and farmers, professors and artists; and buffalo, wild horses, elk, deer, antelope, moose, bear, mountain sheep, trout, sage chickens, wild turkeys, pheasant, and an abundance of cattle and sheep.

Wyoming is one of the last frontiers of the fifty states; a land inhabited by real cowboys and Indians and rich in natural resources and exceptional mountain scenery; a progressive 20th-century state still living its 19th-century history. Though modern highways crisscross the state, and rail, air, and tourist facilities dot Wyoming's 97,914 square miles (it is our ninth largest state), the forested mountain ranges, the lush high mountain valleys, and the grass-covered prairies which first drew fur trappers, cattlemen, and miners remain much as they were one hundred years ago.

Crumbling remains of isolated forts offer visual evidence of the bitter battles between U.S. Troopers and marauding Indians. Still visible ruts make it possible to follow the tortuous paths of wagon trains that inched their way west across the rugged terrain.

Today's traveler can still see, alongside modern four-lane highways, herds of antelope gracefully bounding across the plains. Majestic elk graze peacefully in protected mountain valleys.

Highway signposts and historical markers recall places and people still very real to Wyoming residents, not to mention millions of Americans whose sole relationship with the pioneer West is in the roll call of television "westerns"—places like Fort Laramie, Medicine Bow, Cheyenne, Fort Bridger, and names such as Buffalo Bill Cody, Jim Bridger, and William Sublette.

The oil fields, mining operations, and 20th century missile bases are swallowed up in Wyoming's expanse. The state remains a proud outdoor land of huge cattle and sheep ranches, some of which, measured in thousands of acres, are large enough to contain many an Eastern metropolis.

Much of Wyoming's scenic grandeur remains untouched and unspoiled in national parks and forests. Yellowstone and Grand Teton National Parks, joined together by the new John D. Rockefeller Parkway in the northwest corner of the state, annually attract more than six million visitors.

Colter's Hell

Wyoming is a young state. It celebrated its 75th anniversary in 1965, and oldtimers noted that the observance differed but little from that of July 10, 1890, when fireworks left over from a pioneer Fourth of July fete were used to celebrate the advent of statehood.

The first white men to visit Wyoming were probably French-Canadian fur trappers who ventured south from Canada in the 1730s. Records show that the Lewis and Clark expedition, going up the Missouri on its historic trek west, met fur traders coming down the river with loads of pelts.

Modern Wyoming history, however, dates back to 1807, the year John Colter, an enlisted man with the Lewis and Clark party, left the group to head south into what we now know as Yellowstone Park. He became the first U.S. citizen to lay eyes on the marvels of the area, but when he returned east his tales of steam-heated pools and spouting geysers drew scoffs from unbelieving listeners. They called it Colter's Hell.

But even though Colter's tales drew laughs, his accounts of the rich, primitive areas abundant in game proved irresistible, and many headed west to seek valuable fur-bearing animals.

For twenty years mountain men and trappers roamed the northern part of Wyoming. Tales of these courageous and foolhardy men, of their exploits and daring, survive in legend.

There were David Jackson, the Sublette brothers (William and Milton), Jedediah Smith, Kit Carson, Jacques LaRamie, and Jim "Old Gabe" Bridger. The wily old scout's fort and trading post was an important stop on the Oregon Trail, a place where the weary pioneers in the wagon trains could rest and obtain supplies for the final push to their destination, whether it be the Mormon capital at Salt Lake City, the wilderness lands of the Pacific Northwest, or the gold fields of California. At one point conflicts between Bridger and the Mormons led to violence, and the Mormons burned Fort

Bridger; it was rebuilt by the U.S. Army. Married three times to Indian girls, Bridger was the most colorful of the characters who wrote their names big on the pages of Wyoming history.

David Jackson, pioneer trapper, was one of the first men to explore what is now Jackson Hole just south of Grand Teton National Park. Jacques LaRamie's name, with a slight change in spelling, now tags the Laramie River and the city of Laramie.

Then there were the bad guys, the rustlers who hustled other men's cattle off the range, rebranded them, and sold them as their own. Most colorful was Cattle Kate and her bartender boy friend. Kate, it is said, used her feminine wiles to convince the cowboys to present her with gifts, a steer or two, and in due time amassed a respectable herd. Her career as a cattle queen was pulled up short when the ranchers dangled her from the end of a rope.

While these and other equally resourceful and colorful men played a major role in early Wyoming history, it was a different breed that laid the foundation for settlement and eventual statehood.

For Wyoming was on the direct route of the mass migration west which followed the Depression of 1837. By the 1840s word of fabled lands west of the Rocky Mountains—the Oregon Country stretching to the shores of the Pacific—had trickled east, and thousands of fortune-hunting individuals and families began to trek toward California. Wagon trains rolled across southern Wyoming heading for the only access route through the formidable Rockies, the South Pass near the headwaters of the Sweetwater River.

Beset by Indians and sickness, the wagons stopped for supplies and rest at the trading posts first established in trapping days. Forts the mountain men had built became headquarters for U.S. troops sent out to guard the long and lonesome trail.

Shortly after the Civil War two more developments helped move Wyoming toward statehood: the railroad and cattle drives.

The Coming of the Railroad

The railroad, following to a large extent the trail blazed by wagon trains and the Pony Express, came in the 1860s after Congress granted a subsidy to the Union and Central Pacific lines for a transcontinental route west to the Pacific. Within five years of the Congressional action, wood-burning locomotives roared through the southern Wyoming prairies. Soon new communities began to sprout up along the line—Cheyenne, Laramie, Rawlins, Green River, and Rock Springs. Today's traveler driving cross-country in air conditioned luxury, will find that the route of the Union Pacific varies little if any from that original roadbed.

While the rails were pushed west, cattlemen from Texas began to push north through Wyoming, driving huge herds of cattle to summer pasture lands in Montana and Canada.

The rails and cattle were a natural combination. Cattlemen found in Wyoming plenty of free land covered with nutritious prairie grass. The railroad furnished a convenient way to send the critters to market.

Riding herd on steers was hard work, on the horses especially, so the Texas cowboy who came up to Wyoming invariably had anywhere from two to six extra horses with him, many of which eventually became strays and later formed the foundation for extensive wild horse herds.

Still another animal entered the scene—and much blood was shed before the Wyoming cattlemen reconciled themselves to the fact that sheep were there to stay. At first the intrusion of the sheepherders was bitterly resisted, principally because the cattlebreeders claimed sheep cropped grass so close to the ground that nothing was left for the cattle. Homesteaders meanwhile fought with them over the right to fence open ranges. The homesteaders won the last battle, in court, and the big cattle spreads were reduced and fenced off.

Wyoming is still the cowboy state, however, and cattle is still a mainstay of the economy, along with sheep, sugar beets, and the raising of hay. But all these important agricultural products are overshadowed by the vast and growing minerals industry, for Wyoming is one of the nation's energy capitals with extensive reserves of oil and gas, coal, uranium, and oil shale. The world's largest open pit uranium mine is located in the Gas Hills of Fremont County. Wyoming has nearly 140 billion tons of producible coal, and her reserves are conservatively estimated at 545 billion tons.

Coming up fast in the economic picture right behind agriculture and minerals are tourism and recreation. All the wonders of nature are on display to the visitor. Year-round recreation abounds—fishing, hunting, hiking, mountain-climbing, trail riding, snowmobiling, camping, skiing, river floating, historical sightseeing, and camping.

Wyoming has become a blending of the people who explored, trapped, fought and died here—French trappers, Irish and Chinese rail workers, Texas and British families who founded the first large cattle ranches, miners who dug for gold and iron, homesteaders. They form what must be the most independent roster of citizens to be found on the continent.

For example, in its territorial constitution, Wyoming pioneered in giving women the vote, an action preserved in the state constitution. Wyoming is called the Equality State. It had the first woman justice of the peace, Esther Hobart Morris, and elected the first woman governor in America, Nellie Taylor Ross. It was one of the states to ratify the Equal Rights Amendment in 1973. Very early Wyoming granted women rights to own property. Wyoming has been progressive with the working man, a leader in legislating the eight-hour working day and workman's compensation. Wyoming people are fiercely independent. Rugged individualism and free enterprise are prominent in the state's political philosophy and account for its consistently conservative Republican trends.

While few storeowners observe an old law requiring them to provide hitching posts for horses, today's visitor to Wyoming can still get an authentic picture of Western living. Pass any ranch, you'll see the cattlemen and working cowpokes in action; or in the summer months you can rub shoulders with the men at county fairs and rodeos.

Many of the big working ranches also accept guests; here the Western dude can play-act at cowpunching amidst some of the most magnificent scenery in the world, shouting, "Powder River, let 'er buck." Which is another story for another time.

EXPLORING WYOMING

Any avid watcher of TV westerns can tell you that Buffalo Bill, Jim Bridger, and Laramie are synonymous with the State of Wyoming, part of the roaring Wild West of nearly a century ago. The exploits of these daring and brave men are a constant source of inspiration for television.

Today Wyoming is a peaceful state; its citizens are gracious hosts to the thousands of visitors who come from all over the country to see its varied attractions and to participate in its many recreational opportunities.

Motorists glide smoothly and swiftly over the Lincoln Highway, US 30, I-80, modern-day counterpart of the Overland Trail where the cumbersome prairie schooners headed for the California gold fields once rumbled and swayed.

Wyoming sits in the lap of the broadest part of the Rocky Mountains. Rectangular in shape, its boundaries follow the meridians of longitude and parallels of latitude. To the north lies Montana; to the east, South Dakota and Nebraska; to the south, Colorado and Utah; and to the west, Idaho and Utah.

The state occupies a lofty plateau, four to seven thousand feet above sea level. The mountain ranges average 11,500 feet and many exceed 13,000, thus Wyoming is at a higher average altitude than any other state.

While the two national parks, Yellowstone and the Grand Teton, are the principal attractions for most visitors to Wyoming, many other worthwhile spots of interest can easily be taken in by making "loop" tours with off-the-beaten-path side trips.

The big loop tour can start at Newcastle, where US 16 runs into Wyoming from South Dakota's Black Hills. Newcastle is a trading center for the surrounding ranches and thus provides an early sense of the Old West. Cowboys in their high-heel boots, some with guns on their hips, clomp along the streets, battered Stetsons shading their eyes from the sun.

Follow US 16 northwest out of Newcastle, passing through the small communities of Osage, and Upton, an important oil-producing center, then pick up US 14 at Moorcroft for the 33-mile side trip to Devils Tower National Monument, a stump-shaped cluster of volcanic rock columns 1,000 feet across at the bottom and 275 feet at the top. Looming over the Belle Fourche River some 1,280 feet, and 865 feet above its wooded base, Devils Tower is the core of an extinct volcano. In 1906 it was proclaimed the first National Monument in the United States.

Exhibits in the visitors' center (about three miles from the monument's east entrance) explain the geology, history, and natural environment of the tower.

The best views of the tower are from the self-guiding nature trail. A nature trail leaflet is available either at the visitors' center or from a box at the beginning of the trail. The trip around the tower is about a mile, or an hour's walk. Campsites with fireplace and table facilities and adaptable to both trailer and tents are provided on a first-come, first-served basis. The monument is open the year-round.

Retrace US 14 to Moorcroft to US 16 and join I-90 for the trip through Gillette, a modern oil boom town, and on to Buffalo, a historic town near the Red Fork of the Powder River, where the power of the Indians in Wyoming was broken. The embattled Indians, under Chief Dull Knife, fell before the onslaught of a blue-coated U.S. Cavalry troop. Buffalo is at the entrance to the 9,000-foot-high Power River Pass, which, despite its height, is open the year-round.

At Buffalo take a "detour" to the Bradford Brinton Memorial Ranch, about twelve miles south on State 1703 leading southwest through Big Horn.

The memorial is open daily to visitors without charge. Interesting things to see include the spacious 20-room main ranch house; an outstanding collection of western paintings; an extensive display of Indian arts and crafts; a collection of trophies from hunting trips; and the buildings which comprise a "working ranch"—stables, carriage barns, blacksmith shop, saddle houses, bunkhouse and servant quarters, and a large horse barn.

Returning to Buffalo, take US 87, I-90 to Sheridan, the largest city in northern Wyoming.

Indian Days at Sheridan

When the All-American Indian Days celebration is held in Sheridan—usually the last weekend of July and the first two days of August—the frontier spirit of the Old West comes to life. Of special interest are the Indians. In addition to exhibiting their arts and crafts, they compete with each other in athletics, and delight the visitors with their native dances. Tribes from forty states gather here for the fun.

During the third week each July the Sheridan-Wyo. Rodeo, one of the oldest in the country, takes place. Sheridan is the headquarters for the Bighorn National Forest, covering 1,113,597 acres. There are sixty camp-sites and many picnic spots in the forest. Fishing and hunting expeditions can be arranged, as can saddle and pack pleasure trips deep into the wilderness area.

In order not to retrace your route, drive on to Dayton, via I-90 and US 14, and take a look at one of the finest cattle and horse regions of the West. Genuine western hospitality reigns in Dayton, where the locals like to use first names as soon as you're introduced and want you to reciprocate. Here in Dayton is America's oldest dude ranch, and the Fourth of July celebration features a Bar BQ, with all visitors welcome.

Buffalo Bill Land

From Dayton drive over the summit of the Big Horn Mountains along US 14 to Greybull, where US 20 and 16 join for the journey to Yellowstone National Park, the first and the largest in the U.S. park system. En route the town of Cody, at 5,016-foot elevation, can be visited. Check in at a working or dude ranch for a few days of rest and unhurried sightseeing amid awesome scenery. An equestrian statue of the great scout, "Buffalo Bill" Cody, looks down the main street of the town that has taken his name. Mementoes of the famed Westerner are on exhibit in the Buffalo Bill Historic Center, which includes Cody's boyhood home, and a replica of the old Cody ranch. The Center adds up to 4 museums. Cody was born in LeClaire, Iowa, and his house was knocked down and re-erected here. During the summer months, visitors flock to the area for an exciting rodeo. The Whitney Gallery and Buffalo Bill Museum contain one of America's greatest collections of western art.

From Cody to Yellowstone National Park is fifty-three miles via US 14, 16, and 20, known collectively as the "Buffalo Bill Scenic Hiway to Yellowstone." Open from May 1 until Nov. 1, this hard-paved road snakes west through the Shoshone Canyon, tunnels its way beneath Rattlesnake Mountain, and affords sweeping panoramic views of the Buffalo Bill dam and canyon. There are spacious parking places where stops can safely be made to better appreciate the view and to take pictures.

The highway passes lush western ranch country through the Shoshone Valley, plunges into the Shoshone National Forest, then twists through the Absaroka mountains where such strange and colorful rock formations as the Chinese Wall, Laughing Pig Rock, and Devil's Elbow, the Camel, the Palisades, Chimney Rock, and Holy City are found in the area known as the Playgrounds of the Gods. Finally, you enter Yellowstone Park, past Lake Eleanor, Sylvan Lake, to reach Yellowstone Lake, the largest high-altitude lake in the United States.

So vast is Yellowstone National Park—about 3,472 square miles—that weeks on end are needed to explore all of its scenic and varied attractions. No other national park embraces so many of nature's masterpieces. Most outstanding among the park's many natural wonders are the world's largest geyser basins and the thundering falls and canyon of the Yellowstone River.

Nowhere else in the world is there so large a wildlife sanctuary. Powerful binoculars are useful for looking closely at bear, elk, buffalo, moose, deer, and antelope. It's also the safest way, for although the black bear may appear amiable, they are extremely dangerous, and it is strictly against park regulations to feed or walk near them.

An excellent highway system swings close to many of the prominent sights, but accommodations within the park, including campgrounds, are far from adequate during the height of the summer season. Early reservations at the hotels, lodges, and inns are advised.

There are five entrances to Yellowstone National Park. From the north, by way of Livingston, and Gardiner, Montana, I-90, US 10 and 89; from the northeast, by way of Billings and Cooke City, Montana, I-90, US 10 and 212; from the east by way of Cody, Wyoming, US 14, 16 and 20; from the south by way of Jackson, Wyoming, and Grand Teton National Park, US 26, 89, 187, 189, and 287; and from the west by way of West Yellowstone, Montana, US 20 and 191.

From the east entrance the highway passes Yellowstone Lake, whose sparkling blue waters invite a tour of its 110-mile shoreline. Scenic cruisers operate daily during the summer, and from their decks the wildlife and waterfowl can be observed in a truly natural setting virtually unchanged since fur trappers discovered the lake more than a hundred years ago.

On past the lake, the road leads to Fishing Bridge Junction, where anglers attempt to lure the large trout that abound there. Rustic cabin accommodations are available 2 miles south of the lake.

Scenic Treasures of Yellowstone

Starting out from Fishing Bridge, go north on the road leading to Canyon Village at Canyon Junction. This circle tour offers a close look at some of the park's outstanding scenery and passes near several areas offering good accommodations.

At Canyon Junction is one of the park's most spectacular sights, the magnificent Grand Canyon of the Yellowstone. This 24-mile-long, 1,200-foot-deep gorge is a visual delight. The countless shades of red and yellow within the canyon are enhanced by the emerald green of the surrounding forest. There are also two waterfalls, of splendid beauty and size, that will thrill you. While the canyon and the falls may be viewed and photographed from several angles, Inspiration Point on the north rim and Artist Point across the gorge are perhaps the best vantage points.

Mt. Washburn, rising 10,317 feet, is on your right as you drive the nineteen miles from Canyon Village to Tower Junction. The road slips through Dunraven Pass at an elevation of 8,859 feet before dropping a couple of thousand feet to Tower Fall, where the Roosevelt Lodge provides excellent rustic accommodations. Pause here to enjoy steak cookouts and to allow the children the fun of riding on a stagecoach.

Mammoth Hot Springs, at the north entrance, is just about eighteen miles from Tower Junction and is but one more scenic spectacular in a region literally filled with them. The impressive travertine terraces of these fabled springs are sometimes vividly colored, sometimes snow white. If you want to spend some time here, there are accommodations at the Mammoth Hot Springs Hotel Motor Inn and Cabins.

Having reached the top of the loop at Mammoth Hot Springs, the route swings down twenty-one miles to Norris Junction, then fourteen miles to Madison Junction, and finally sixteen miles to Old Faithful.

Old Faithful

Nowhere in the world can match Yellowstone for the variety of geysers. Some erupt in rage and fury spewing thousands of gallons of water over one hundred feet in the air, others merely splash up a few inches.

And most beloved of them all is Old Faithful.

Old Faithful is one of the gathering points for all visitors to the park, and no one leaves until he has seen this geyser shoot its thousands of gallons of steaming water high into the air. It "blows" on the average of every 66 minutes and has not missed a performance in over eighty years. In the Old Faithful Visitor Center is a geyser diagram which explains in detail just what goes on beneath the ground to cause this phenomenon. Old Faithful Inn is hard pressed to take care of the demands for accommodations, and reservations must be made in advance.

If you have an appetite for more geysers you can walk around the Old Faithful area and see others, like "Grotto." Leaving Old Faithful southbound, take the 17-mile drive from Old Faithful to West Thumb Junction, where the Grant Village Campground offers camping facilities.

From West Thumb to Bridge Lake and the start of this loop is a distance of twenty-one miles. In Bridge Lake there are two worthwhile points of interest: the Bridge Bay Marina, capable of handling two hundred boats, and the Lake Hotel, with every facility, including a hospital.

Visitors to the park interested in seeing its remotest areas can do so by either hiking or on horseback. There're some 900 miles of trails in the Park, including some short ones. You will need a pair of sturdy, comfortable hiking boots, and it's best to break them in before arriving at the park.

For the experienced horseback rider there are more than nine hundred miles of paths. Horses may be rented, but all horseback trips into the wilderness areas must be accompanied by a guide.

You can visit Yellowstone all year-round, and there are always accommodations open in the communities that surround the Park. In winter highways are open through the Gardiner Gate into Park headquarters, but most other roads are closed. From the south entrance access is possible by snow coach or snowmobile, and this winter trip into the Park is spectacular.

Grand Teton National Park, 485 square miles packed with some of this country's best mountain, valley, and lake scenery, can be easily reached over a 22-mile stretch of smooth highway, US 89 & 287. Even though the area is compact the traveler here can spend several weeks, with each day revealing something new in scenic views and recreational offerings.

Scattered throughout Teton National Park are a variety of facilities and campgrounds. You can spread your bedroll on the ground, pitch your tent, find a simple tent village with the tents already pitched for you, utilize the marina on Jackson Lake, or enjoy the more comfortable surroundings at one of the lodges.

Rustic Luxury at Colter Bay and Signal Mountain

Set in the natural, wooded area on the shores of Jackson Lake are the Colter Bay Cabins. Many cabins are equipped with cooking facilities, heated with electricity, and have bathrooms and showers.

The Colter Marinas are fully equipped, including boat launching ramps and boat rentals. There is great fishing in Jackson Lake and a cruise that brings the mountain grandeur of the Tetons into your lap.

In the evenings there are programs about the area offered in an amphitheater, and a museum and information center are close by.

The magnificent scenery of the Grand Teton National Park extends continuously from the lakes and valleys skyward to 13,000-foot mountain peaks. Snowcapped and glacier covered, the towering mountains are a backdrop to the placid, emerald lakes, to craggy canyons and pristine forests.

Blinding Glaciers

By the way, be sure to pack sunglasses, for the brilliance of the sun on the snowfields and glaciers can be blinding. Perhaps nowhere else is there a greater variety of glaciated canyons than in the Tetons.

One of the most interesting and varied ways of touring the park is to hedge-hop from one accommodation to another. After Colter Bay Village it is a short move on to Jackson Lake Lodge. Here you have a choice of 385 luxurious rooms spread in the lodge itself and in adjacent cottages. In the Lodge's main lounge a ceiling-to-floor picture window frames the lake and the Grand Teton Range. Dining facilities include coffee shop dining room and room service. A few steps from the main lodge and cabins is the Olympic-sized pool. There is a teepee snackbar at poolside.

Moving on from Jackson Lake Lodge be sure and take the Teton Park Road to Jenny Lake Lodge, one of the most luxurious accommodations in the park. There are campgrounds here, too, and excellent fishing sites; most of the trails through the mountains start at this location.

At Colter Bay or Jackson Lake Lodge, saddle up and jog along astride a gentle mare through the piney woods and breathe in the sweet, clean air of early morning. The long ride (over three hours) ends with a bountiful breakfast of bacon and eggs to sate the big appetite you've worked up.

A beautiful lodge, dining room and lounge, and new rustic motel units have been built at Signal Mountain Lodge. The Lodge is famous for its western menu. Grocery store, gift shop, and filling station serve the visitor. Fishing guides for Jackson Lake are available from the marina. The Lodge operates its own river float trips.

You should also remember that one of the most important items you should pack for a visit to Grand Teton National Park is a pair of sturdy, comfortable hiking boots. Be sure to break them in before leaving on your trip.

Motor through the park first to familiarize yourself with the various areas so you can revisit and spend more time at those you find especially appealing. Then park your car and take to the trails, either on foot or on horseback, for intimate and uninterrupted views of the natural beauty of the region.

Each of the six major routes traversing the park offers an entirely different set of attractions. You might find that some trails are too long and arduous to be followed on foot, so rent one of the docile, sure-footed horses and settle back on the creaky leather for a relaxing ride through the dramatic scenery that characterizes Grand Teton. Other trails, shorter and less rugged, can be appreciated on foot. And, for the truly adventurous, there are combination horseback-and-foot trails that end at the dizzying height of 11,000 feet on the Static Peak Divide. Many a mountain climber has been lured to the summit.

If the lowlands are your ticket, try the Lakes Trail, which hugs the lakes at the bottom of Teton range. Branching out from this point, three other routes cut deeply into the canyon territory. Slicing into the mountains, Death Canyon, Cascade Canyon, and Indian Paintbrush Canyon, with incredibly steep walls and myriads of wildflowers are thrilling to behold. If you are lucky, you may catch a glimpse of one of the large and small wild animals that inhabit the region.

Skyline Trail and Teton Glacier Trail into the highlands are unforgettable visual experiences, but you should not attempt them alone or before mid-June or after mid-September. Before starting out, check in with officials. If you have had no experience but would like to give it a try, mountain climbing is taught in the Park at a fee.

If water is your element, float trips down the Snake River are available at the Lake or from Jackson. These exciting trips take either a half or a full day. Along the route the majestic Bald Eagle may be seen high in the trees in one of his few remaining natural habitats. You travel past the historic Menor's Ferry at Moose.

You may visit the Grand Teton National Park all year long with facilities open at Signal Mountain Lodge.

Gateway to the Tetons and the National Parks is Jackson, just eight miles from Moose, on a straight new highway through the majestic Teton Mountains. Located at the southern entrance to the parks, Jackson is headquarters for the Teton National Forest, an area of 1,701,000 acres of wilderness land bordering on both Grand Teton and Yellowstone National Parks. This resort community offers year-round recreational opportunities. The town and nearby countryside abound with dude ranches, motels and entertainment centers, good fishing and hunting, and three exceptional ski slopes, Snow King, Teton, and Targhee. A Robert Trent Jones championship 18-hole golf course is also available. There is a modern airport with transportation service to the hotels and motels in Jackson, Teton Village, and Jackson Lake Lodge.

For those whose interests are culture and history Jackson offers both. On the one hand it remains entirely Western, and on the other boasts fifteen art galleries, a summer Fine Arts Festival, summer symphony, and summer stock theater.

Arts Festival in the Mountains

With camera in tow, summer or winter, board the chair lift at Jackson and ride to the crest of Snow King Mountain some two thousand feet above. Or look out the 50-foot-high lobby windows of the Ramada Snow King Inn and watch the skiers slaloming down Kelley's Alley.

Another scenic aerial tramway ride leaves from Teton Village, part of the Jackson Hole Ski area just twelve miles west of Jackson on the Wilson-Moose road. Teton Village consists of chalets, lodges, and condominiums. The Ski Tram here rises 4,100 feet in an almost vertical ascent to Rendez-vous Peak. The ride takes less than fifteen minutes and offers a panoramic view of the Teton Range.

Or travel over scenic Teton Pass west of Jackson to the newest ski area in Wyoming, Grand Targhee Village. Targhee has some of the finest, earliest, and latest snow in the West. Unless you're delayed by blizzards, it takes forty-five minutes to get there from Jackson.

For the non-skier, Jackson Hole Country has week-end recreational opportunities which include cutter racing down the main street. These races usually are held during January and February, with the All-American Cutter Race finals held on the weekend of George Washington's birthday.

Don't miss seeing the huge elk herd which winters right on the edge of the town of Jackson. Beginning in November, as many as 10,000 elk come into the refuge and remain into early May. You can ride horse-drawn feed sleds into the heart of the herd, take pictures of the feeding, and even help distribute the feed to the animals.

From Jackson you may choose to complete this loop tour back to Cheyenne via Rock Springs. If so, take US 187 south and stop off at Pinedale.

This community is really "off beat," and after the crowds in Yellowstone and Grand Teton you'll find a slower tempo. It is the gateway to the Bridger Wilderness and the farthest incorporated town from a railroad. Pinedale is a true western cowtown and is surrounded by working cattle ranches. To the east are Wyoming's highest and most massive mountains, the Wind Rivers. If you like fishing and big-game hunting settle in here for a while and it won't be long before you'll have your limit. There are more than one thousand lakes and streams. Six large lakes are accessible by road. In the quiet retreats of the Bridger National Forest, there are many choice campsites. In Pinedale itself are modern motels, dude ranch accommodations, and restaurants.

If you're in town at noon on the second Sunday in July, don't miss Pinedale's lively celebration of her frontier heritage. The Sublette County Historical Society sponsors the event in which hundreds of local people, horses, mules, wagons, pack strings, and teepees parade as a living memorial to the Mountain Men and the fur trade of yesteryear.

One hundred miles farther south is Rock Springs, a thriving sheep-raising community. Beneath the surface of this town of about 13,000 is a bituminous coal deposit of tremendous proportions. From Rock Springs take I-80 east back to Cheyenne.

Another route from Jackson to Cheyenne lies through Casper. Take US 26 and 89 to Moran Jct., then US 26 and 287 south, with a stopover in Dubois, the Rock Capital of the Nation.

The Dubois area, located on the upper Big Wind River and surrounded on three sides by Shoshone National Forest, is one of the richest places in the nation to prospect and search for rocks. Found in the region are gem quality agatized opalized woods, cast material, pine and fir cone replacements, amethyst lined trees and limb casts, and all types of agate equal or superior to any found elsewhere.

Two Tribes with One Reservation

Bordering the Dubois area is the big Shoshone and Arapahoe Indian Reservation. In July, first the Shoshone and then the Arapahoe Indians hold their sun dances. Dressed in full costume, they dance continuously for three days and nights without taking food or water. US 287 and 26 passes through the reservation, where the Indians tend to their horses and cattle or irrigate their haylands. On your way to Dubois note Crowheart Butte, a State Monument commemorating the scene of the great battle between the Shoshone and Crow Indians.

Continuing on US 26 and 287 from Dubois, the town of Lander, one of Wyoming's oldest communities, is worth a stopover for those of you making a leisurely exploration of the state. Sometimes called the place where the rails end and the trails begin, Lander is a great place to fish, hunt, and mountain climb.

Or follow US 26 into Riverton. Located in the center of the Reservation, the Riverton Museum has Indian displays. There are three Indian Missions in this vicinity: St. Stephens on State 789, St. Michael's Mission at Ethete, and Fort Washakie, the Indian headquarters in Fort Washakie.

Ghost Towns

From Lander a side tour of historic interest and scenic beauty can be made to the ghost mining towns of Atlantic City and South Pass City on State 28. At the latter town the Whitman Monument commemorates the stop on July 7, 1836, of Marcus Whitman's party on their trip to Oregon. Narcissa Whitman and Eliza Hart, members of the party, were the first white women to cross South Pass.

Drive to the Wind River Indian Reservation just outside Lander and bathe in the Reservation Mineral Hot Springs. Also visit Sacajawea's grave in the Indian cemetery at Wind River. She was the guide of the Lewis and Clark expedition from the Missouri River to the Pacific Coast and return during the period of 1805 to 1806. She died here in 1884. And Chief Washakie is buried in the government cemetery.

The Glacier Primitive Area high atop the Wind River Range is an isolated mountain region accessible only by foot or saddle horse. Within an hour astride a horse you become completely cut off from the outside world in a country of mountain grandeur. The region abounds in streams and lakes filled with game fish. These pack trips are under the supervision of competent guides. Rates are kept to a minimum and include everything necessary for the trip except personal items.

If you are in the mood for some meandering off the direct route to

Rawlins, swing on to State 789 on up to Riverton, Shoshoni, Thermopolis, and Worland.

At Riverton you are invited to tour one of the four uranium mills. Tours can be arranged by appointment through the Chamber of Commerce. The world's largest uranium mine is near Riverton.

Shoshoni, home of the Boysen Lake Pike Derby, is a small town with fewer than six hundred people, but with one of the West's finest antique barbed-wire stores.

Thermopolis, on the Big Horn River, is a health resort known for its hot springs. If you're an early riser, wander down at 8 a.m. for a dip in the thermal waters of one of the many swimming pools.

The Thermopolis Indian Pageant, Gift of the Waters, is a colorful festival that takes place on the first Sunday in August. And on Labor Day excitement runs high when cowboys try their luck at riding wild horses at the weekend rodeo.

US 20 from Shoshoni to Thermopolis goes right through the spectacular Wind River canyon. At the entrance to the canyon is Boysen Lake with 220 miles of shore line. It's a state park worth a fishing or sightseeing trip. Marinas are located at both ends of Boysen.

Travel north on State 789 to Worland, and if you've notified the Holly Sugar Corporation of your arrival, they'll reward you with an informative tour through the sugar plant—or visit the National Girl Scout Center West, out of Worland toward Ten Sleep, Close to Rawlins is the Medicine Bow National Forest, with a plentiful supply of coal, placid lakes, rushing, fish-filled streams, and thousands upon thousands of acres of shady forests. Bring a picnic basket and spend some quiet hours—or days, if you prefer—in this lovely region. Skiing is popular at three areas.

Laramie, at the altitude of more than 7,000 feet, offers an invigorating climate and clean, clear air. Nearly a century old, the town has flourished since its inception as a station on the Union Pacific Railroad line. Its name, immortalized in Wild West literature, movies, and television, was taken from one of its first settlers, Jacques La Ramie.

A short jaunt from Laramie proper is historic Old Fort Sanders, a stopping place for Western pioneers and Mormons. Forging west, they used the Overland Trail, now commemorated in the Laramie vicinity with stone markers. Traveling the smooth, well-developed highways of today, it is difficult to appreciate the hardship of crossing this rugged terrain in a prairie schooner.

Touring the University

Visitors are invited to inspect this sprawling, landscaped campus. A brochure entitled "Roaming the University of Wyoming" includes a map and is most helpful in finding your way around. The points of interest include:

Geological Museum. This building contains the skeleton of a huge dinosaur that is more than 100 million years old. One of only five brontosaurus skeletons in the United States, it stands fifteen feet high and is seventy-five feet long. Also on exhibit are fossils, rocks and minerals, diagrams of geological processes, and Indian artifacts.

Library. The spacious Coe Library Building contains more than 500,000 volumes and 5,500 periodicals, and is a depository for more than 700,000 government documents. The Western History Research Center, containing rare volumes , artifacts, and items of general historical interest, is a continuing attraction.

Rocky Mountain Herbarium. Located on the third floor of the Aven Nelson Building, this collection contains more than 270,000 plant specimens. The Herbarium has the largest and most representative collection of plants of the Central Rocky Mountains and is one of the best-known herbaria in the United States.

In addition, the University offers an almost continual selection of cultural events, most of which are open to the general public.

Abraham Lincoln is honored with a Memorial Monument about ten miles east of Laramie on US 30 (also I-80). The bust by Robert Russin commemorates the sesquicentennial of Lincoln's birth and stands approximately 9,000 feet above sea level at the highest point on the Lincoln Highway, US 30. This enormous bronze head weighs almost four tons. Stop at Lusk and ramble around the free museum. Steep yourself in the atmosphere of the "woolly" West. The fascinating memorabilia on display recall the days when Indians roamed and stages rattled through the West.

Two and one-half miles south of Laramie is Monolith Portland Midwest Co., which produces varieties of cement. Tourists are welcome.

From Laramie to Cheyenne, the state capital, I-80 swings past the highest point along the entire Lincoln Highway. A good photo stop nearby is the Ames Monument, located about two miles off US 30 on a marked road. This 65-foot pyramid was erected in honor of the Ames Brothers who helped finance the Union Pacific.

Cheyenne, now a peaceful, prosperous community, was known as "Hell on Wheels" in the days of the Old West. This spirit is revived once a year, usually during the last full week of July, at Cheyenne Frontier Days. At Frontier Park, the nation's top cowboys call on all their skill, strength, and sheer nerve to try to stay astride backs of bucking steers and horses. Parades, too, are a feature of these Frontier Days.

While in Cheyenne, visit the Capitol Building. Guided tours of the Gold Dome are available during June to August, but the panoramic view is worth a visit anytime. The State Museum, located on Central Avenue at 23rd Street, exhibits archeological and historical treasures of Wyoming and the Old West.

From Cheyenne there are three tours recommended by the Wyoming Travel Commission, two of which can be made in a day. These trips take in some fascinating points of interest as well as varied scenery. The tour which takes in "Old Bedlam," Fort Laramie, and the Oregon Trail National Historic Site is 219 miles and is a perfect one-day auto outing. Beginning at Frontier Park, drive north on I-25 from the Randall Avenue Interchange past Warren Air Force Base, then swing northeast on US 85 for eighty-four miles to Torrington in the valley of the North Platte, once a corridor of human migration. Here you'll be following in the footsteps of the Sioux, Cheyenne, and Arapahoe as they hunted the vast herds of buffalo. Torrington was a way station for the Pony Express, as well as a stop on the Oregon and Texas Trails.

A few miles northwest on US 26 (and US 85) is Lingle where, just across the North Platte River, the bloody Grattan Massacre of 1854 took place and started thirty-five years of warfare between the Plains Indians and the U.S. Army.

A little farther along US 26 you'll find Fort Laramie National Historical Site, where eleven of the original buildings still stand. The National Park Service preserved and restored them.

Between the lectures of the park historian and the explanatory signs, you'll learn that the fort was first built privately as a place for traders and trappers to meet. Later it became a military outpost protecting the travelers going on to Utah, Oregon, and California. Kit Carson, Jim Bridger, John C. Fremont, John "Portugee" Philips, and "Buffalo Bill" Cody at one time or another visited the fort. "Old Bedlam," the two-story officers' club known as the gayest spot on the Oregon and California trials, has been restored and refurnished. The fort became a station on the Cheyenne-Deadwood Stage Route after 1876, but was abandoned in 1890.

Oregon Trail ruts can still be seen in Guernsey at the mouth of the Platte River Canyon. If you look closely on Register Cliff you see the names of pioneers carved on rock walls. Because of the Warm Springs here travelers dubbed them the "natural bathtub of the plains." A side road leads six miles north to Sunrise, site of the largest iron mine in the Rockies.

From Guernsey stick to US 26 across the top of the Guernsey Reservoir and start your return trip south on US 87 to Wheatland at the foot of the rocky Laramie Mountains, a part of Medicine Bow National Forest. Twenty-five miles deeper south lies Chugwater, where you begin to follow the route of the old Cheyenne-Black Hills Stage Line. From here State 87 and I-25 take you quickly back to Cheyenne.

Cowboys and Cavalry

If you want to extend this loop, follow US 26 west from the junction with I-25 where, instead of turning south to Wheatland, turn right to Douglas. On your left you'll pass the site of the old Horseshoe Stage Station and a little farther on the site of the Historic Burnt Wagon Train. US 87 and 26 pick up where I-25 leaves off and continue into Douglas, known as Tent Town when it was founded in 1886. Once a town jammed with soldiers, railroaders and cowpokes—rough, tough, and ready to fight at the slightest provocation— Douglas saw its saloons filled nightly. Now only a hint of these rough-and-tumble days survives when, during the last full week in August, Douglas is the site of Wyoming's State Fair, which includes a rodeo, horse show, and exhibits.

While in the Douglas area take some time off to swim in Jackalope Warm Springs, about seven miles away. The natural artesian spring furnishes 163,000 gallons every hour at 84-degree temperature. The water is changed completely four times daily. There is a shady picnic area with tables.

Jackalope is the imaginative name of one of the most implausible animals in North America. Were it not for the strange horns, it might be a large rabbit; where it not for its shape and coloring, it might be a species of antelope.

The first white man to fancy he saw this singular animal was a trapper named Ron Black, in 1851. An odd trait of the jackalope is its ability to imitate the human voice of cowboys singing to their herds at night. Many wranglers have been startled to hear their lonesome melodies repeated faithfully from a nearby hillside. The phantom echo comes from the throat of some jackalope. They sing only on dark nights just before a thunderstorm.

From Douglas take I-25, then US 20 and 26 into Casper, Wyoming's leading industrial city. Casper, a pleasant, scenic community, sits at the foot of Casper Mountain. Oil, uranium, and coal industries contribute a major portion of the city's income, but not far behind are cattle and sheep ranching.

The Old Fort Casper Museum displays Indian and historic Western objects.

If you have time, drive west forty-three miles from Casper on US 20 and 26 to Hell's Half Acre. Here nature has carved some freakish formations in the shapes of towers, spires, and other unusual architectural effects. The locals refer to the area as "Devil's Kitchen."

From Casper you can return to Laramie and Cheyenne by following State 220, then State 487 into Rock River, where US 30 joins I-80.

Another loop tour from Cheyenne covers 274 miles and takes in the scenic forested splendor of the Medicine Bow. This trip can be made easily in a day by getting an early start; take along a picnic lunch, for the area's hills and dells invite eating out in the open.

Take Happy Jack Road (Secondary Route 0107) at the junction with Dey Avenue. Drive west on Happy Jack across I-25, south of Francis Warren Air Force Base, then into the cool of the hills. It is a quick thirty-three miles to Medicine Bow National Forest in the Pole Mountain District, where on either side you'll pass quaking aspen, slender lodgepole pine, douglas fir, and the stately ponderosa pine. A side trip on one of the forest road routes takes you to Blair Campground, site of an old Indian camping spot and a place full of unusual rock formations.

Once back on Happy Jack (Forest Road 1166, which has a good gravel surface) you'll travel along Pole Creek, a stream stocked with trout and occasionally interrupted by beaver dams.

The new Curt Gowdy State Park, named after the famous sports announcer, is just west of Cheyenne not far from the Happy Jack area.

At the junction with US 30 (I-80) you drop down into Laramie, where you pick up State 130 west to Centennial, gateway to the Snowy Range or Medicine Bow. Open late May to early October, the Snowy Range Highway passes through mountain and forest scenery that few regions can match for beauty and variety.

At an elevation of 8,400 feet you'll pass the home base of the University of Wyoming ski team, then descend through the deep scenic canyons of Libby Creek, Silver Run, and North Fork.

If you have time take the side trip north on State 130 to Saratoga, the center of deer and antelope country. There is excellent fishing in the North Platte River, and the medicinal waters in Saratoga Hot Springs State Park are clear, odorless, and piping hot.

This loop tour then turns south to Riverside, through sprawling ranch country. State 230 runs parallel to the Continental Divide and dips briefly into Colorado. Keep on Colorado's State 125 until you reach the junction with Wyoming State 127 above Cowdrey. Turn northeast, and, with the massive Colorado Rockies at your back, continue to Woods Landing, where State 230 runs beside the Laramie River into Laramie. From here, US 30 and I-80 will take you back to Cheyenne.

Looping into Nebraska

A third, and this time 365-mile, tour begins on US 30, at its intersection with US 85, and heads east across the rolling plain. It is about thirty-nine miles to Pine Bluffs on the State line, the highest point in Nebraska (5,424 feet). Continue east to Kimball then turn north on Nebraska State 71 for Wildcat Hills. The Game Refuge here is a good place to photograph wild life.

Viewed from the town of Gering, the landmark of Scotts Bluff rises sharply above the plains. Scotts Bluff National Monument marks the place where thousands of settlers stopped to replenish supplies and refresh themselves for their journey west to Oregon and California. Pony Express riders changed their mounts here for the dash across the country.

From the observation point of the monument (actually in the township of Gering) the landmarks on the trail route are visible for one hundred miles, all the way to Laramie Peak. By picking up Nebraska State 92 east you can visit Chimney Rock National Historic Site, an odd-looking spire of solitary grandeur that served as a beacon to mountain men and emigrants across the plains.

US 26 swings out of Scotts Bluff along the Platte to Torrington and Lingle, Wyoming, whose attractions have already been described. The community of Lusk, north on US 85, hosts the popular Rawhide Pageant in August. Manville, ten miles distant on US 20, is the gateway to the "Spanish diggings," stone quarries of prehistoric man. These represent one of the earliest signs of life in the Platte Valley.

The loop route continues west through Keeline and Shawnee to Orin, where historic "Bridger's Crossing" lies 1½ miles south of the Orin River. Follow US 87 south and as you travel the snowy Laramie Peak can be seen towering above the land in Medicine Bow National Forest.

Ten miles south of Orin is the Glendo Recreation Area, an excellent place to set up camping headquarters. Here you can boat, swim, or water-ski on the broad reservoir. The good fishing in the lake and on the streams promises excellent opportunities to catch your limit.

After Glendo you pick up I-25 to Wheatland, Chugwater, and over US 87 to Cheyenne.

PRACTICAL INFORMATION FOR WYOMING

WYOMING FACTS AND FIGURES. The state gets its name from the Delaware Indian *mecheweami-ing*, which means "at the big plains." Its nicknames are *Cowboy State* and *Equality State*. The Indian paintbrush is the state flower, the cottonwood the state tree, the meadow lark the state bird. "Equal Rights" is the state motto. "Wyoming" is the state song.

Cheyenne is the state capital. State population still remains only 350,000.

Vast plains and rugged mountains are the natural features of this scarcely populated western state. The Great Plains of the east are covered with the hayfields and cattle ranches which, next to oil, are the chief source of income. Wyoming has an abundance of spectacular mountain scenery to counter the rhythm of its plains. In the northwest of the state, the 500 square miles of the Grand Teton National Park and Yellowstone National Park are an outdoorsman's paradise. Dramatic mountain ranges run through the center of the state, marking the Continental Divide. Wyoming's winters are relatively mild. Snowfall is light except in higher mountains. Summer days are warm. Wyoming mountain evenings are cool, though. There is little rainfall.

HOW TO GET THERE. *By air:* Frontier and Western fly into Cheyenne, Casper, and Laramie.

By train: Amtrak passenger service is available to Cheyenne.

By car: I-80 crosses southern Wyoming entering from Nebraska in the east and leaving into Utah in the west. I-25 passes into the state from Colorado in the south. I-90, from Montana in the north and South Dakota in the east, serves the northern part of Wyoming.

By bus: Continental Trailways and Greyhound offer transportation to and within Wyoming.

 HOW TO GET AROUND. *By air:* Frontier Airlines serves Jackson, Cody, Worland, Rock Springs, Riverton-Lander, Casper, Sheridan, Laramie, and Cheyenne.

By car: I-80 crosses the state in the south. I-90 and US 14 and 16 serve the north. I-25, US 26 and 287 run from Cheyenne in the southeast to Yellowstone in the northwest.

By bus: Greyhound, Continental Trailways, Pioneer Transit, and Jackson-Rock Springs Stages provide transportation within the state.

TOURIST INFORMATION. For all Wyoming travel, vacation, resort, and camping information write for brochures from Wyoming Travel Commission, I-25 at Etchepare Circle, Cheyenne, Wyoming 82002.

 SEASONAL EVENTS. *Cheyenne Frontier Days:* this is the world's number one rodeo. During the third week in *July*, over one thousand professional cowboys descend on Cheyenne to compete for $160,000 in prize money. And in addition to the rodeos, there are parades, nationally known entertainment (particularly country and western), carnival, dancing, Indians, band concerts, free chuck wagon breakfasts, and chuck wagon races. With good reason, this has been called the "Daddy of 'em All."

Other famous Wyoming rodeos include *Lander Pioneer Days and Parade* and *Cody Stampede,* the first week in July, the *Fremont County Fair* during the third week of August at Riverton, the *Wyoming State Fair* the last week of August at Douglas, *Central Wyoming Fair and Rodeo* late July to early August in Casper, and Laramie *Jubilee Days,* with world-championship roping, in mid-July.

The *Green River Rendezvous,* on the second Sunday of July at Pinedale, is a pageant that relives the era of Jim Bridger, Marcus Whitman, and Father DeSmet during the days when "mountain men" and the fur trade were king.

All-American Indian Days: in late July and early August at Sheridan. Nearly five thousand Indians from over forty plains tribes arrive for the pageant of the plains. A Miss Indian America is selected each year. The Shoshones and Arapahoes meanwhile have dances outside Dubois.

Almost every Wyoming community holds a pageant, rodeo, or western event during the summer. The *Wyoming Travel Commission* can tell you what events will coincide with your vacation.

In October, Worland celebrates a 2-day *Oktoberfest.*

 NATIONAL PARKS. *Yellowstone National Park.* Two-million acre Yellowstone is the nation's first and largest national park. Located in the northwestern corner of Wyoming, it is a scenic wonderland of spouting geysers, steaming hot springs, magnificent waterfalls, beautiful lakes, towering mountains, big game, wildlife, birds, fishing and, of course, the inevitable bear (don't pet him, he's not tame). Yellowstone is large enough that even with the big crowds you can "get lost" if you wish. Yellowstone is open in the winter, too. Take a "Snow Coach" trip through the south entrance to Old Faithful Lodge. Winter scenery and Old Faithful geyser spouting on a frosty day are sights unsurpassed.

Grand Teton National Park. Just south of Yellowstone lies another great national park, now attracting more visitors than Yellowstone. Huge Jackson Lake reflects the spectacular beauty of the Teton Mountains. Unspoiled wilderness areas start at the roadside. Even the untrained can climb mountains, and gasp at undreamed-of views. Lakes and rivers, fabulous fishing, hiking, boating, square dancing, and real western, mountain pleasures abound. The quaint western town of Jackson is nearby. In winter, ski at Snow King Mountain, Teton Village, or Grand Targhee in the Tetons. Fish through the ice on Jackson Lake. Float the Snake River in summer. Snowmobile into the winter wonderland.

John D. Rockefeller, Jr. Parkway. A new national park dedicated in 1973. It fills the gap between Yellowstone and Teton National parks. Beautiful forested land, camping, hot springs, wilderness horseback riding.

Wyoming has seven National Forests. Among others there are the Black Hills in northeastern Wyoming, Medicine Bow in the southeast, Bridger, Shoshone, and Teton in northwestern Wyoming, and the Big Horn National Forest in north central Wyoming.

Each forest has wilderness and primitive areas, thousands of campsites, all the wonders of the mountain West. Fishing streams abound, snowcapped mountains, wildlife. If you plan to utilize the national forest be sure and obtain a recreation sticker. Write to Shoshone National Forest, Cody, Wyoming; Bridger-Teton National Forest, Jackson, Wyoming; Big Horn National Forest, Sheridan; Medicine Bow National Forest, Laramie.

Fossil Butte National Monument, located near Kemmerer in southwest Wyoming, contains a rich concentration of fossils which illustrates the evolution of freshwater fishes—reminders of the great oceans that once covered this portion of the state. The Butte amounts to a living classroom for studies of ancient life and its evolution.

 STATE PARKS. Wyoming also has eight state parks. *Buffalo Bill State Park* is an hour's drive from the east gate of Yellowstone National Park on the north shore of Buffalo Bill Reservoir. It offers complete picnicking and day-use facilities plus minimum camping facilities. The adjacent reservoir features excellent trout fishing during most of the season, as do the north and south forks of the Shoshone River that feed it. A commercial concession, campground, trailer park, and marina are also available.

Boysen State Park is located in central Wyoming and can be reached by driving either north or west of Shoshoni on US 20 or 26. The park is surrounded by the Wind River Indian Reservation, home grounds for the Shoshone and Arapahoe tribes. Day-use and overnight camping facilities are offered, and the reservoir and the river provide trout and walleye fishing opportunities.

Sinks Canyon State Park. In a spectacular mountain canyon ten miles southwest of Lander, this park is one of the newest additions to the Wyoming park system. Here amid the unspoiled beauty of the Rocky Mountain West are hiking trails, nature walks, scenic overlooks, and countless glacier-fed pools and swirling eddies. Fishing is excellent. As an added attraction the river disappears into a gaping canyon wall cave and reappears in a crystal-clear trout-filled spring pool. Camping facilities are limited.

Seminoe State Park is surrounded by giant dunes of white sand, miles of sagebrush, thousands of pronghorn antelope and sage grouse. Located near Seminoe Reservoir twenty-eight miles from Sinclair, this is primarily a day-use facility, although some overnight camping is permitted. The closeby "Miracle Mile" of the North Platte River got the name for its reputation for trout fishing.

Keyhole State Park is eight miles from I-90 between Sundance and Moorcroft, along the southeastern shore of Keyhole Reservoir and within sight of Devil's Tower. Antelope, deer, and wild turkeys are common in this area, and the reservoir offers excellent fishing for trout, walleye, catfish, and perch. The water is warm, and camping and picnic sites are readily available.

Glendo State Park, four miles out of the town of Glendo, is the best developed area in Wyoming's park system. There are excellent day-use facilities, a complete commercial concession, cabin, trailer court, and marina operation, and some of the finest boating and trout fishing in the state. Arrive early on weekends to be assured of getting picnic and campsites.

Guernsey Lake State Park, a few miles outside of Guernsey on US 26, is located on the shores of one of Wyoming's most attractive reservoirs. High bluffs surround the park and block the wind so the water is always warm for the swimmer and water-skier. Historically, this is the country of the Oregon Trail, and the State Park Museum has full information. Complete day-use facilities are available, but camping space is limited.

Curt Gowdy State Park is located in the foothills of a mountain range separating Cheyenne and Laramie amid massive granite towers, rocky soils, and timbered slopes. Granite Reservoir and Crystal Lake offer fishing opportunities, but no swimming beaches or facilities are provided. The hills around the lakes invite the hiker, rockhound, and, in winter, the snowmobiler. Still under development, this park offers very limited facilities.

HOT SPRINGS. *Hot Springs State Park* is at Thermopolis. This is the world's largest single hot springs and the site of the world-famous Gottsche Rehabilitation Center. Mineral waters and baths, hotel and motel accommodations, and large indoor and outdoor swimming pools are available. *Fort Washakie:* south of Fort Washakie on the road to Ethete, on the Wind River Indian Reservation, is the Washakie Plunge hot springs. This area too has facilities. *Saratoga Hot Springs,* near Saratoga on State 130, is another.

CAMPING OUT. Wyoming has literally hundreds of campgrounds offering everything from minimal to complete facilities. Yellowstone Park and adjacent Teton and Shoshone counties have many campsites available but only on a first-come, first-served basis. Reservations are taken only for large organized group parties such as the Boy Scouts.

Special regulations governing food storage apply at most Wyoming campsites due to the prevalence of bears. All food or similar organic material must be kept completely sealed in a vehicle or camping unit that is constructed of solid, non-pliable material, or it must be suspended at least ten feet above the ground and four feet horizontally from any post or tree trunk. The cleaner a camp is kept the less chance there is of being bothered by bears.

For complete information about the location and facilities of campgrounds in Wyoming, contact the Wyoming Travel Commission, in Cheyenne, Wyoming 82002.

FARM VACATIONS AND GUEST RANCHES. Wyoming is famous for its great variety of guest (dude) ranches. A selection of those available is included here; complete information is available from the Wyoming Travel Commission, Cheyenne, Wyoming 82002 or the Dude Ranchers Assn., Tie Siding, Wyoming 82084.

CM Ranch, six miles from Dubois. Located in the Wind River Mountains amid beautiful scenery and rushing streams where the atmosphere is completely remote.

Separate cabins with private baths. Family groups and teenagers are especially welcome. There are weekly rodeos, riding, fishing, hunting (in season), and pack trips. Open June 15 to Sept. 30 to guests and Oct. 1 to Nov. 15 for hunters. CM Ranch, Dubois, Wyoming 82513.

Rimrock Ranch, 26 miles west of Cody, is famous for its wilderness pack trips.

The same formula—good food, good riding, good clean air—can be had at many more Wyoming dude ranches. Among them: *The Fir Creek Ranch* is located at Moran, 83013. Open the year-round. The *Grizzly Ranch* is half-way between Cody and Yellowstone National Park; the *L & B Ranch* can be found outside Dubois, 82513.

Triangle X Ranch, north of Jackson in Teton National Park, just a mile off US 26. Fall hunting and outfitting. Summer float trips, horseback riding, packing. Winter cross-country skiing, snowmobiling, touring. A family ranch, children are welcome. Triangle X Ranch, Moose, Wyoming 83012.

Outfitters: Big-game hunting for elk, moose, deer, pronghorn antelope, bighorn sheep, and bear abound in Wyoming. Many are found in remote wilderness areas where hiring of an outfitter is a must. Wyoming has more than two hundred outfitters; all must be licensed. It would be impossible to list them all here, but a few from each section of the state are: Pat Self, *Centennial,* Wyoming; James L. Bluejacket, *Shell;* Joe Detimore, *Dubois;* Les Shoemaker, *Dubois*; Jim Dale, *Riverton;* L. D. Fromte, *Afton;* Ted Hale, *Afton;* Stan Siggins, *Cody;* Harold Turner, *Moose;* Bert Turner, *Moran;* William S. Wood, *Ten Sleep;* and Charles B. Nichols, *Dubois.*

MUSEUMS AND GALLERIES. The *Buffalo Bill Historical Center* at Cody features two excellent museums of western lore. They are the *Buffalo Bill Museum* and the *Whitney Gallery of Western Art.* The Buffalo Bill Museum contains the guns, saddles, painting, furniture, letters, personal effects, and a valuable trophy collection of the famed William F. Cody, "Buffalo Bill." The new Whitney Gallery features original art of such figures as Frederic Remington, George Catlin, Alfred Jacob Miller, and Charles M. Russell.

Bradford Brinton Memorial Ranch: This working ranch near Big Horn has a fine collection of pioneer western art, Indian relics, and sculpture. Guided tours begin in the main ranch house and nearby buildings, the horse and carriage barns, and a "trophy" lodge near the main entrance. Western artists Frank Tenney Johnson and Charles M. Russell, among others, are featured.

The *University of Wyoming:* The Geological Museum in Laramie has many exhibits, which include restored dinosaurs made up of the actual fossil bones, fossil fish, prehistoric mammoth. Coe Library contains western lore museum, an oriental art exhibit, many valuable archives. Both are open to the public.

Other Western and pioneer museums can be found at Afton, Buffalo, Casper, Fort Bridger, Fort Laramie, Glendo, Green River, Greybull (rock collection), Kemmerer, Lander, Newcastle, Rawlins, Thermopolis.

The *Wyoming State Museum* in Cheyenne has minerals and gems, Indian and early-day western relics. Famous military button collection.

In Jackson Hole, the centrally located museum pictures guns of the area, and offers a western experience in dioramas.

HISTORIC SITES. Wyoming has many historic sites, some less than a generation removed from the Wild West Frontier.

Fort Laramie: One of Wyoming's most famous historical sites is Fort Laramie on US 26 in southeastern Wyoming, which makes it an interesting "first stop" in the state when entering from the east. Trappers built the original fort in 1834 and named it after Jacques LaRamie, a French fur trapper killed by the Indians in 1820. Later they sold it to the American Fur Company, who then sold it in 1849 to the U.S. Government. For many years it was headquarters for U.S. Cavalry units and protected the pioneer from marauding

Indians. A number of peace treaties with the Indians were signed at Fort Laramie. Abandoned in 1890, it was declared a National Monument by President Roosevelt in 1938. Much of Fort Laramie has been restored, and there are more than twenty historical structures. "Old Bedlam," which served as the bachelor officers quarters, is now completely restored and open to the public.

South Pass City: Gold discoveries were first reported in 1842 in the South Pass area some thirty miles southeast of Lander. Of course, Lander wasn't there at the time. Nobody came to the district, except a few trappers, until 1867 and 1868, mainly because the Indians of that region fought fiercely against encroachment on their lands. For several years mining boomed, but gradually died out after 1870. An authentic western gold ghost town remains, much as it was nearly one hundred years ago. The Carissa and Duncan mines may be seen. There is a museum and restaurant. Neighboring Atlantic City also contains many historical sites, including old Carpenter Hotel.

The Oregon Trail, the Mormon Trail, and the original Pony Express Route pass near South Pass City.

Wind River Indian Reservation: The Shoshone and Arapahoe tribes live on this reservation in one of the garden spots of the West. Chief Washakie made peace with the white man early in order to choose this great hunting and fishing country for the Shoshones. The Shoshone Indian maiden Sacajawea, who guided the Lewis and Clark expedition, is buried near Fort Washakie just off US 287 within easy reach of either Riverton or Lander. Indians in their traditional dress are around the Reservation especially near St. Stephens Jesuit Mission, St. Michael's Mission (Episcopalian), and Fort Washakie.

Forts: Fort Bridger, built in 1842-43 by the trapper and guide Jim Bridger, is located in Fort Bridger State Park in southwestern Wyoming and has been largely restored. Fort Caspar (on the outskirts of the city of Casper) has many pioneer and Indian relics preserved in a museum, and part of the old fort has been restored. Fort Fetterman is near Douglas; Fort Sanders, near Laramie; Jenny's Stockade near Newcastle; Fort Bonneville near Pinedale; Fort Mackenzie near Sheridan; Fort Phil Kearny near Story in the Sheridan area; Fort Stanbaugh near Atlantic City; Fort McKinney near Buffalo; Fort D. A. Russell near Cheyenne; Fort Steele near Sinclair. Travelers should inquire for directions at the chamber of commerce in cities located nearest these famous forts of the West.

Pioneer Sites: St. Mary's Stage Station and the historical marker where ninety Mormons perished in a blizzard and were ravaged by wolves may be reached from South Pass City (inquire there). The first cabin built by a white man in Wyoming is at Bessemer Bend (inquire at Casper Chamber of Commerce). Buffalo Bill Statue (inquire at Cody). Charcoal kilns (inquire at Evanston). Big Sandy Stage Station (inquire at Farson). Register Cliff with names of early pioneers and early graves (inquire at Guernsey). Hole-in-the-wall Gang (inquire at Kaycee). Crowheart Battle, where Chief Washakie cut out the heart of the Crow chief and saved his people (inquire at Riverton). First oil well in Wyoming at Dallas (inquire at Lander). Spanish Diggings, prehistoric quarries (inquire at Lusk). Ghost town Cambria (inquire at Newcastle). Father DeSmet's first Catholic Mass in Wyoming (inquire at Pinedale). Independence Rock (Father DeSmet called it the "Register of the desert"). First Masonic Lodge meeting (1862) at Independence Rock. Site of Sweetwater Stage Station (inquire at Casper). Site of first county church in Wyoming—Methodist (inquire at Sundance). Trapper's Rendezvous point (inquire at Riverton). Early ghost coal mine camps (inquire at Kemmerer and Rock Springs). Tie hacks (inquire at Dubois). Teapot Dome (inquire at Casper). The Big Teepee ranch home (inquire at Shoshoni).

FAMOUS LIBRARIES. *William Robertson Coe Library* in Laramie on the University of Wyoming campus is the state's finest. It is famous for its many rooms of specialized archives. Western lore is featured in one room, another features valuable Chinese and oriental art. The petroleum library is an important one, too. Wyoming library archives preserve many western literary treasures.

 TOURS. Package tours in the park areas can be arranged through the Jackson Lake Lodge at Moran, Wyoming; or Yellowstone Park Company at Mammoth, Wyoming. Frontier Airlines, Stapleton Field, Denver, can be of assistance for tours both summer and winter. Union Pacific Railroad, Omaha, Nebraska, or Cheyenne, Wyoming, are helpful on tours. Or address Wyoming Travel Commission. Travel tours, summer and winter sports can be arranged through the Ramada Snow King Inn in Jackson.

 INDUSTRIAL TOURS. Wyoming is one of America's great natural-resource states. At Riverton, tours of the Gas Hills uranium mines and mills may be arranged. The world's largest open-pit uranium mine is found in the Gas Hills. From Lander you may visit the U. S. Steel taconite iron mine. Located in Atlantic City at an elevation of over 8,300 feet, it is the highest iron mine in Wyoming.

The Green River or Rock Springs chamber of commerce will arrange visits to the trona mines near there. FMC Corporation has the world's largest natural soda-ash mine west of Rock Springs.

The Casper Chamber of Commerce will arrange tours of the Teapot Dome oil field.

Call the Gillette Chamber of Commerce to see oil fields and coal mines.

In Newcastle, visit the Accidental Oil Company, a historic tour of the oil industry, a gift shop in an oil tank.

 SPECIAL INTEREST TOURS. Geological, historical, scenic tours available in both Yellowstone and Grand Teton National Parks. Wyoming's national monuments are worth seeing. They are *Fossil Butte,* off U. S. 30, and *Devil's Tower,* a spectacular volcanic rock near Hulett off US 14.

Wagons West, a program of outdoor vacations with transportation in horse- or mule-drawn replicas of Conestoga wagons, is being operated from spring to fall by L.D. Frome, of Afton, Wyoming. This 5-day tour features chuck-wagon-style meals and accommodations in tents or in the wagons, and travels to the red rock country of Utah and the prairie historic trails and Wyoming Rockies around Escalante, Wyoming.

 GARDENS. The University of Wyoming campus: Beginning about May 15 and extending until about October 1 the campus is a blaze of flowers. Landscaping is spectacular. Many varieties of trees. Botanical gardens. Visitors are welcome. No charge. Laramie, Wyoming.

 MUSIC. From mid-July to mid-August Teton Village in Jackson Hole hosts the *Grand Teton Music Festival.* In past years concerts have included symphonic and chamber pieces. The Watermelon Concerts, so-called because after the performance the audience and musicians sit down to discuss the performance over large slices of watermelon, have been very popular.

The *Concert Hall* in the new Fine Arts Center of the University of Wyoming at Laramie hosts numerous concerts and music festivals throughout the year. Their Walcker pipe organ, designed in Germany especially for the college, is one of the largest tracker organs in the United States.

In Casper, the *Civic Symphony Orchestra* performances are worth a combined symphony-skiing trip during the winter months.

Cheyenne and Lander also have outstanding musical events.

STAGE AND REVUES. Wyoming, once considered culturally deprived, boasts an ever-increasing variety of theatrical entertainment. The University of Wyoming at Laramie has a *Fine Arts Center* whose theatrical section not only provides space where legitimate theater can be performed, but also a teaching center. In Jackson, the *Jackson Hole Opera House,* and *Dirty Jack's* offer theatrical and melodramatic productions throughout the summer. And Cheyenne, Casper, Cody, Sheridan, and Lander all have *Little Theaters.*

NIGHTCLUBS. While Wyoming does have night spots which offer entertainment, many of her bars still retain the decor and atmosphere of the turn-of-the-century Old West. Cheyenne has the Plains Hotel, with its old western "stand-up" bar, as does the Connor Hotel in Laramie. During the annual celebrations, Cheyenne Frontier Days and Laramie Jubilee Days, these two bars are the hub of activity.

Casper has the Reef Lounge, a South Seas nightclub with lively entertainment, and wild music at the Virginian Hotel bar.

Sheridan has the Mint Bar, with a large collection of western cattle brands, and Rosie's Bar in Diamondville near Kemmerer still offers a miner's bucket of beer. The Hole-in-the-Wall in Kaycee finds cowboys, oil patch roughnecks, and traveling men meeting for chatter.

In the New Wonder Bar in Casper millionaires and bums meet and wager on any event, sporting, political—whatever.

Jackson's famous Silver Dollar Bar in the Wort Hotel offers live entertainment year-round.

DRINKING LAWS. Wyoming bars open at 6 a.m. and close at 2 a.m. except Sunday, when it's noon to 10 p.m. Minimum drinking age is nineteen. Liquor may be sold over bars either by the drink or the bottle, in cocktail lounges and in dining rooms by the drink, and in liquor stores by the bottle. No state permit is required.

SUMMER SPORTS. *Boating:* The numerous lakes and reservoirs in Wyoming provide ample opportunity for boating recreation. The Bridger National Forest, Flaming Gorge National Recreation Area, Grand Teton National Park, and all the Wyoming State Parks, offer particularly good boating waters. Raft and canoe trips down the rivers are also possible, but care should be taken to explore the waters thoroughly before heading out. River rafting is also popular in the state.

Fishing: Wyoming's 20,000 miles of streams and over 264,000 acres of lakes provide unlimited fishing possibilities. Trout are particularly abundant, but there are many other species of game fish.

Hunting: There are seasons for pronghorn antelope, moose, elk, black bear, whitetail and mule deer, and bighorn sheep. For complete hunting and fishing information, contact the Wyoming Game and Fish Commission. Box 1589, Cheyenne, Wyoming 82001. Write to the same address about fishing regulations.

Horseback riding and pack trips: Available throughout the state, particularly at dude ranches and in the Bighorn National Forest, Grand Teton and Yellowstone National Parks.

WINTER SPORTS. Skiing is a favorte winter sport, and Wyoming has some great ski areas, including the Teton Village and Snow King at Jackson, Antelope Butte between Sheridan and Greybull on US 14, Medicine Bow west of

Laramie, Happy Jack east of Laramie, Hogadon Basin near Casper, Pinedale, Meadowlark east of Worland between Ten Sleep and Buffalo.

Grand Targhee is a popular ski resort in the Tetons. Snowmobiling and ski touring are popular, especially out of Dubois and Jackson Hole. Or tour Yellowstone National Park in the winter in snow coaches.

SPECTATOR SPORTS. By far the most popular and prevalent spectator sport in Wyoming is the rodeo; nearly every community sponsors at least one. The major events, however, are these: *Cody Night Rodeo,* Jun. to Aug., nightly except Sun; *Cheyenne Frontier Days,* during the third week in July; *Central Wyoming Fair and Rodeo* at Casper, late July to early Aug.; *Lander Pioneer Days* and *Cody Stampede* over the 4th of July weekend; the *Fremont County Fair,* third week in Aug. at Riverton; and the *Wyoming State Fair,* the last week of Aug. at Douglas.

Stock car and motorcycle races are frequent, and the state championships stock car races are held early in Sept. at Gillette.

Registered *quarter-horse racing* takes place at Meadowlark Downs at Riverton.

SHOPPING. Welty's Store at Dubois is a large trading post. You'll find almost everything that you could want from chic styles to buckskin jackets, hunting and camping equipment. Also: Stuart Shop, in Casper, has fine women's wear. Jackson Lake Lodge at Moran and Gift Box at Riverton are outstanding gift shops. Paddy Rhoad's Rocky Mountain Jade Shop in Lander sells fine, authentic jade. Merritt's in Cheyenne supplies western wear. Pink Garter Plaza in Jackson has several specialty shops.

WHAT TO DO WITH THE CHILDREN. Both Yellowstone and Grand Teton National Parks are a paradise for children. At Yellowstone, along with the geysers, hot springs, and bubbling paint pots, there are game preserves where youngsters can see thousands of elk and hundreds of bear, buffalo, moose, deer, mountain sheep, and antelope in a near-natural habitat. Beware the Yellowstone bear who appears cute and cuddly, but is a dangerous wild animal who has lost his fear of man. Under no circumstances should the bears be fed.

On the waters of these parks are swans, wild geese, pelicans, ducks, gulls, and terns.

But mostly the parks afford children the chance to frolic in the waters and along the nature trails and to enjoy the clean, fresh mountain air.

Rodeos, including Little Britches Rodeos where younger cowboys compete, take place in nearly every Wyoming community of any size and offer thrills and excitement to young and old alike.

Indian dances such as those seen at Jackson and Jackson Lake Lodge are performed in full ceremonial dress by the Indians native to Wyoming.

Stagecoaches, pulled by 4-horse teams, leave Roosevelt Lodge in Yellowstone and bounce over forest and sagebrush trails. Or a stagecoach ride is available around the town, leaving Town Square in Jackson.

INDIANS. Arapahoe and Shoshone Indians preserve many of their native customs on one of the nation's largest reservations, the Wind River Agency in Fremont County. Two Indian missions still operate on the reservation—St. Stephens Jesuit Mission near Riverton and St. Michael's Mission near Ethete in the heart of the reservation. Chief Washakie, the famous Shoshone, is buried here and so is Sacajawea, the Shoshone girl Indian scout for the Lewis and Clark Expedition. Many of the old buildings remain from the days when Fort Washakie was an Indian trading post and government fort. It is now the Indian Agency headquarters. Tours of the reservation can be arranged there, or at the Chambers of Commerce in Riverton or Lander. More than 5,000 Indians live on the reservation. A favorite spot to start a tour is at Paul Hines General Store on US 287, fifteen miles northwest of Lander.

During summer many Indian celebrations, traditional Sun Dances and Powwows are held. Inquire for the dates. The Guide Book put out by the Riverton Chamber of Commerce lists the dates and is available by mail or in person.

The Arapahoe, fierce and fearless warriors, were among the last Indians to submit to a reservation. The Shoshone is famed for his horsemanship. Many are cattle ranchers. Both tribes provide sterling bronc busters and race horses for rodeos in Wyoming. A visit to the reservation is a must for Wyoming tourists.

Shoshone and Arapahoe Indian craft may be found at Fort Washakie on the Reservation, at Riverton and Lander, and at the Wind River Native Crafts shop near Crowheart Butte. Museums in Lander and Riverton offer exhibits on Indian history and folk lore. And Indian pictographs and petroglyphs survive on sandstone cliffs.

RECOMMENDED READING. T. A. Larson's *History of Wyoming* is an interesting and informative look at the state's past. *Wyoming: Prelude to Statehood* is an interesting booklet available at no charge from the Wyoming Travel Commission in Cheyenne 82002.

HOTELS AND MOTELS. The larger towns in Wyoming have excellent hotel and motel accommodations; most have parking facilities, restaurants, and bars. Rates are usually higher in summer, though some have special family rates. Cost figures generally are for the minimum or moderate priced rooms, unless a range is indicated. Listings are in order of price category.

The price categories in this section, for double occupancy, will average as follows: *Deluxe* $35, *Expensive* $25, *Moderate* $20, and *Inexpensive* $15. "Expensive" always means that you get plenty of services. For a more complete explanation of these categories see the *Hotels & Motels* part of THE ROCKIES & PLAINS *Facts at Your Fingertips* at the front of this volume.

AFTON

The Corral. *Inexpensive.* Group of rustic cabins in the heart of the Star Valley cheese country. Children's playground. Has AAA listing.

Lazy B Motel. *Inexpensive.* Very nice. Some cooking. On the road from Salt Lake to Jackson Hole. Pets allowed. Open all year.

ALTA

Grand Targhee Resort. *Deluxe.* In the Teton Mountains, out of Driggs, Idaho. One of Wyoming's leading ski resorts. Early and late snow. Open summers. Swimming pool. One-, one-and-a-half- and two-level condominiums.

BUFFALO

Cross Roads Inn. *Expensive.* A 60-unit motel just off the interstate. Dining room, cocktail lounge, swimming pool. Meeting rooms. Pets accepted.

Keahey's Motel. *Inexpensive.* Very nice. Some cooking units. Oldtime hospitality. In the historic downtown.

Mountain View Motel. *Inexpensive.* Sixteen units with Western decor. Picnic area, charcoal broilers and playground.

CASPER

Holiday Inn. *Expensive.* Large motel with restaurant, cocktail lounge and swimming pool.

Imperial "400." *Expensive.* Motel with large, well-appointed rooms and heated pool. Most credit cards.

Ramada Inn. *Expensive.* A 400-room hostelry with colonial lobby. Old West rustic charm. Beauty and barber shops. Pool, cocktails.

Motel Travelier. *Inexpensive.* Small but entirely adequate motel. Pets. Cafe nearby.

CHEYENNE

Hitching Post Inn. *Expensive.* On US 30W. Long a Wyoming landmark near the downtown area. Large attractive rooms, indoor and outdoor pools, sauna, beautiful dining room, coffee shop, cocktail lounge, beauty salon, and gift shop.

Holiday Inn. *Expensive.* Short distance from airport. Large motel. Rollaways and cribs available.

Holding's Little America. *Expensive.* 1½ mi. west at jct. I-80 and I-25. Just west of the city limits, this new installation is a smaller version of the operation at Little America, Wyoming. Heated pool, coffee shop, dining room and cocktail lounge. Antiques and curios.

Buckhorn Motel. *Inexpensive.* Some kitchenettes.

Home Ranch Motel. *Inexpensive.* Medium-sized motel with playground, cafe nearby. Continental breakfast available.

CODY

Holiday Inn. *Expensive.* Buffalo Bill Village. A new motel combined with one of the Cody-country's historic attractions. Dining room, cocktail lounge, swimming pool, meeting rooms. Gift shop. Some cooking.

Sunset Motor Inn. *Expensive.* Medium-sized motel with large, well-furnished rooms, heated pool, and putting green.

Absaroka Mountain Motel. *Moderate.* In the Wapiti Valley, this small, rustic motel is located on a rushing mountain stream. Dining room and large Western lobby with stone fireplace.

Buffalo Bill Village. *Moderate.* Large group of Western cabins, a trailer parking area, playground, heated pool, and western entertainment. Famous for chuckwagon dinners.

Irma Hotel. *Moderate.* US 20, 14 and 16. This Old West landmark, in the heart of downtown Cody, was built by "Buffalo Bill" Cody.

Uptown. *Inexpensive.* Comfortable rooms, TV, playground, pets. Cafe nearby.

DUBOIS

Branding Iron. *Inexpensive.* 1 1/2blks. west on US 26, 287. In the heart of a western town. Nearby cafe and cocktail lounge. Western charm.

Stagecoach Motor Inn. *Inexpensive.* West side on main highway. In the best tourist tradition. Family atmosphere.

EVANSTON

Ramada Inn. *Inexpensive.* 1 mi. west on US 30 at jct. I-80. A sizable 128-unit motel. Pool, restaurant, bar, 9-hole golf course adjacent.

Dunmar Motel. *Moderate.* A small motel with spacious grounds and rooms. Heated pool.

Vagabond. *Moderate.* A well-established hostelry. Playground, pets. Cafe nearby.

New Motel. *Inexpensive.* Comfortable rooms, pets, free coffee. Cafe nearby.

GILLETTE

Sands Motor Lodge. *Expensive.* Spacious, well-appointed rooms with balconies, dining room, cocktail lounge, coffee shop, heated pool.

Ramada. *Expensive.* The newest and biggest in town (120 units).

Western Wheel. *Moderate.* Single motel with heated pool, limited pets, free coffee. Cafe nearby.

GREEN RIVER

Mustang Inn. *Moderate.* Newly remodeled. Dining room, coffee shop, cocktail lounge, meeting room. Open all year.

Tomahawk Hotel. *Inexpensive.* A quiet, well-kept hotel in the heart of town.

JACKSON HOLE

Ramada Snow King Inn. *Deluxe.* A 200-unit resort hotel. Dining room, coffee shop, cocktail lounge, gift shop, boutique, art gallery. Spacious lobby with 50-foot-high window. Tennis courts, sauna, health club. Horseback riding. A complete summer and winter vacation center. At the foot of Snow King ski area on the edge of Jackson.

Teton Village-Jackson Hole. *Deluxe.* 12 mi. northwest on county 2001. This is Wyoming's newest year-round resort area. Among the important establishments are **Alpenhof Lodge,** with continental restaurant, cocktail lounge, bunk rooms, beauty salon, and heated swimming pool; **Sojourner Inn,** featuring exceptional lodging and dining; and the **Hilton Inn,** with room service and some kitchens.

Antler Motel. *Expensive.* Famous for hospitality. Large fireplaces. Coffee shop across the street. Pets allowed. Some kitchenettes.

Executive Inn. *Expensive.* Dining room and coffee shop. Meeting room. Famous for food.

Jackson Hole Lodge and Motel. *Expensive.* A moun ain lodge with well-landscaped grounds and activities for families.

Pony Express Motel. *Expensive.* Small motel with large, well-appointed rooms, children's playground and heated pool.

Virginian Motel. *Expensive.* Dining room, cocktail lounge, gift shop, convention center.

Wort Motor Hotel. *Expensive.* Small Western hotel, long a favorite with skiers, tourists, and the public. The bar is covered with silver dollars. Atmosphere is truly Old West. Dining room, cocktail lounge and art shows. Entertainment.

Alphorn Motor Lodge. *Moderate.* A chalet-type motel. Step out of your room onto Snow King Mountain. Chair lift summer and winter with view of the Grand Tetons. Family bunkbeds.

Woods Motel. *Moderate.* Small motel. Cafe nearby. Closed in winter.

LANDER

Holiday Lodge. *Moderate.* At intersection US 26, 287 on south edge of Lander. Golf privileges.

Maverick Motel. *Moderate.* A small, well-appointed motel with coffee shop and heated pool.

LARAMIE

Holiday Inn. *Expensive.* Large motel with a cocktail lounge in the Gay 90s decor, dining room, coffee shop, heated pool, and spacious rooms.

Ramada Inn. *Expensive.* Eight units. New dining room, cocktail lounge, meeting and banquet room.

Circle S Motel. *Moderate.* On the east edge of town, with attractively landscaped ground and pleasant rooms. Heated pool.

Motel Eight. *Moderate.* A well-run 100-unit motel, open all year.

Wyoming Motel. *Moderate.* Small, friendly motel across the street from the new University dormitories. Well-appointed rooms and heated pool. Some of the units have garages available.

LITTLE AMERICA

Little America Motel. *Expensive.* A large oasis in the middle of the desert with plenty of gasoline pumps. This motel has large, warm rooms, dining room. Coffee shop and cocktail lounge.

LUSK

Pioneer Court. *Moderate.* Small, charming motel with heated pool.

MEDICINE BOW

Virginian Hotel. *Inexpensive.* Wyoming landmark. Dining room, coffee shop and cocktail lounge.

MORAN

(Grand Teton National Park)

Jackson Lake Lodge. *Deluxe.* A large, new hotel with many resort features.

Excellent Old West mural in restaurant, with gourmet menu. Giant picture windows overlook Jackson Lake and the Tetons. Horseback riding and pool, cocktail lounge, shops. Closed in winter.

Jenny Lake Lodge. *Deluxe.* On Teton Park Rd., 11 mi. southwest of Moran. A delightful group of mountain cabins. Informal, with warm, spacious rooms in individual units. Lounge has delightful stone fireplace. Resort atmosphere.

Signal Mountain Lodge. *Moderate.* New lodge on the edge of Jackson Lake in full view of the Grand Teton. Dining room, cooking, cocktail lounge, gift shop, grocery store, filling station, boating. Fishing. Kitchenettes. Float trips.

Togwotee Lodge. *Moderate.* US 26-287. A nicely designed motel with 52 large, well-appointed units. Dining room.

NEWCASTLE

Graham's. *Inexpensive.* Small, well-furnished motel with coffee in the rooms, heated pool.

Fountain Motor Inn. *Moderate.* Heated pool, pets. Free Continental breakfast. Cafe nearby. Most major credit cards.

RAWLINS

Holiday Inn. *Expensive.* New, large, and reliable. All amenities.

Bel Air Inn. *Expensive.* A sleek 100-unit motel. Coffee shop, cocktail lounge, heated pool.

Quality Inn. *Moderate.* Dining and coffee shop, lounge.

RIVERTON

Thunderbird Motel. *Moderate.* A medium-sized motel with well-furnished rooms.

Tomahawk Motel. *Moderate.* Downtown motel on Main St. Closed in winter.

ROCK SPRINGS

Holiday Inn. *Expensive.* Indoor-outdoor heated pool, cafe, bar. Free airport bus.

Nomad Inn. *Expensive.* Well-restored hotel, heated pool, playground, pets limited, free coffee.

Outlaw Inn. *Expensive.* Old West motif, spacious rooms, large interior arcade, indoor heated pool, cocktails, dining.

El Rancho Rodeway Motor Lodge. *Moderate.* A large, modern motel. Heated pools.

Park Hotel. *Inexpensive.* Well-restored hotel, dining room and cocktail lounge.

SARATOGA

Saratoga Inn. *Expensive.* Just across the river in Saratoga. Located on the North Platte River, golf course, tennis. Dining room, cocktail lounge.

SHERIDAN

Sheridan Center Inn. *Expensive.* Large establishment. Dining room, cocktail lounge. Banquet, meeting rooms. Swimming pool.

Trail's End Motel. *Moderate.* Small, attractive motel with an indoor pool.

Wyoming Lodge. *Moderate.* Modern motel with large rooms and heated pool. AAA-member.

THERMOPOLIS

Holiday Inn. *Expensive.* In Hot Springs State Park. Pool, dining room, coffee shop, cocktail lounge, banquets and convention center. Mineral baths.

Moonlighter Motel. *Expensive.* In the heart of town on US 20. Cocktails.

Californian Motel. *Inexpensive.* A small, quiet motel with pleasant, cool lawns and picnic tables.

TORRINGTON

Oregon Trail Lodge. *Inexpensive.* A small motel with large, attractive rooms. Pool.

WORLAND

Townhouse Motor Inn. *Moderate.* Pool, dining room. Most major credit cards.

Sun Valley Motel. *Inexpensive.* A 25-unit motel with attractive, well-planned rooms.

Washakie Hotel. *Inexpensive.* Coffee shop, dining room, and cocktail lounge.

WHEATLAND

Wyoming Motel. *Moderate.* Pool, a family motel.

YELLOWSTONE NATIONAL PARK

Canyon Village Motor Lodge. *Moderate.* A 600-unit hotel. Dining rooms, cocktail lounge, coffee shop, cafeteria, barber and beauty shops. Horses. Closed in winter.

Mammoth Hot Springs Hotel. *Moderate.* At US 89. Offers 240 units, mostly with baths.

Old Faithful Inn. *Moderate.* Large 360-room establishment. Across the road from Old Faithful. Dining rooms, coffee shop, cocktail lounge, beauty and barber shops.

 DINING OUT. Wyoming is not particularly interested in exotic cuisine, and as a result, steak-and-potatoes are often the best fare. Beef is somewhat cheaper here than in some other states, and the cuts are quite good. Native trout is excellent and usually well prepared. For other worthwhile restaurants, check hotel listings. Restaurants are listed in order of price category.

Restaurant price categories are as follows: *Deluxe* $9 and up, *Expensive* $6-$8,

Moderate $4-$5, and *Inexpensive* $2.50-$3. These prices are for *hors d'oeuvre* or soup, *entrée*, and dessert. Not included are drinks, tax, and tips. For a more complete explanation of restaurant categories refer to THE ROCKIES & PLAINS *Facts at Your Fingertips* at the front of this volume.

BUFFALO

American Legion Club. *Moderate.* Open to the general public in the evenings. Smorgasbord served during the summer on Sunday evenings.

Cross Road Inn. *Moderate.* A fine dining room and coffee shop for family and friends.

Idlewild. *Inexpensive.* A pleasant place supported by local service organizations. Specializes in steak and trout.

CASPER

Benham's Supper Club. *Expensive.* Fine businessman's lunches and charcoal-broiled steaks are served in an attractive dinner club atmosphere.

CHEYENNE

Hitching Post. *Expensive.* A good Western restaurant at a large motor hotel. Specialty: prime ribs.

CODY

Bronze Boot. *Expensive.* This Western restaurant offers prime steak and well-prepared accompanying items. Specialty: shrimp boiled in beer.

Irma Grill. *Moderate.* This restaurant, located in the hotel "Buffalo Bill" Cody built, has long been known for good food. Specialties are steak, prime ribs, and trout.

DUBOIS

The Westerner. *Moderate.* In the center of town, the Longhorn Room of this motel offers traditional meals in a relaxed setting.

JACKSON

Open Range. *Expensive.* French and International menu. One of Wyoming's finer restaurants. Good service.

Chateau Family Restaurant. *Moderate.* A restaurant with good family-style food. Specialties are spaghetti, lasagna, frittatas, chicken.

Silver Spur. *Moderate.* Coffee shop and dining room. A favorite local hangout with family appeal.

LANDER

Miner's Delight. *Deluxe.* In Atlantic City (ghost town), out of Lander off US 28. A local tradition. Continental cuisine includes crepes, escargots, coq au vin. A delightful eating experience in the atmosphere of the Old West. By reservation only.

Maverik Restaurant. *Moderate.* A favorite stopping off place for the traveler. Family food. Daily specials.

LARAMIE

Cavalryman. *Expensive.* Steak, prime rib, and lobster served up in an Old West setting.

Diamond Horseshoe. *Moderate.* The menu includes Chinese and American foods, and children's portions are available.

MORAN

Signal Mountain Lodge. *Moderate.* 31 mi. north of Jackson on the shore of Jackson Lake in Teton National Park. A lakeside lodge in full view of the Grand Tetons offers excellent food in the lodge dining room.

RAWLINS

Venice Cafe. *Inexpensive.* A typical small-town restaurant with a good Italian menu. Daily specials.

RIVERTON

Teton Room. *Moderate.* Located in the Teton Hotel, this is a beautifully decorated room. Steaks in the Wyoming tradition and plump Wyoming lamb chops. Smorgasbord on certain evenings.

ROCK SPRINGS

Outlaw Inn. *Moderate.* Hearty food is served in the dining room of this motel. Coffee shop service also available.

WORLAND

Washakie Grill. *Moderate.* A Western hotel from times gone by, but the lounge and dining room are modern. The steak, prime ribs, and lamb chops served here are excellent, and the service is fast.

INDEX

(The letters H and R indicate hotel and restaurant listings.)

General

(See also Practical Information sections for each state.)

IDAHO

Practical Information

F   Fodor, Eugene, 1905-
721
F58   Fodor's Rockies &
           Plains

DATE			
SEP 3 0 1988			
AUG 1 8 1989			